PRAISE FOR UNKNOWN SOLDIER VOL. 1: HAUNTED
EISNER AWARD NOMINEE – BEST NEW SERIES

"A STORY WITH TEETH, UNAFRAID TO CONFRONT SOME HORRIFIC TRUTHS ABOUT THE WORLD WE LIVE IN, JOSHUA DYSART'S UNKNOWN SOLDIER IS A COMIC THAT GENUINELY MATTERS."

— *GARTH ENNIS (PREACHER)*

"THIS IS AN IMMENSELY BRAVE, INTELLIGENT AND RUTHLESS PIECE OF WORK. YOU NEED TO READ IT."

— *WARREN ELLIS (TRANSMETROPOLITAN)*

"DYSART & PONTICELLI ARE CRAFTING THE BEST HORROR BOOK OF THE YEAR."

— *BRIAN AZZARELLO (100 BULLETS)*

"IT REALLY IS ONE OF THE MOST SPECIAL NEW COMIC SERIES I'VE EVER ENCOUNTERED, AND I'M CONVINCED WE'LL BE TALKING ABOUT THIS SERIES FOR YEARS IF NOT DECADES TO COME."

— *IGN*

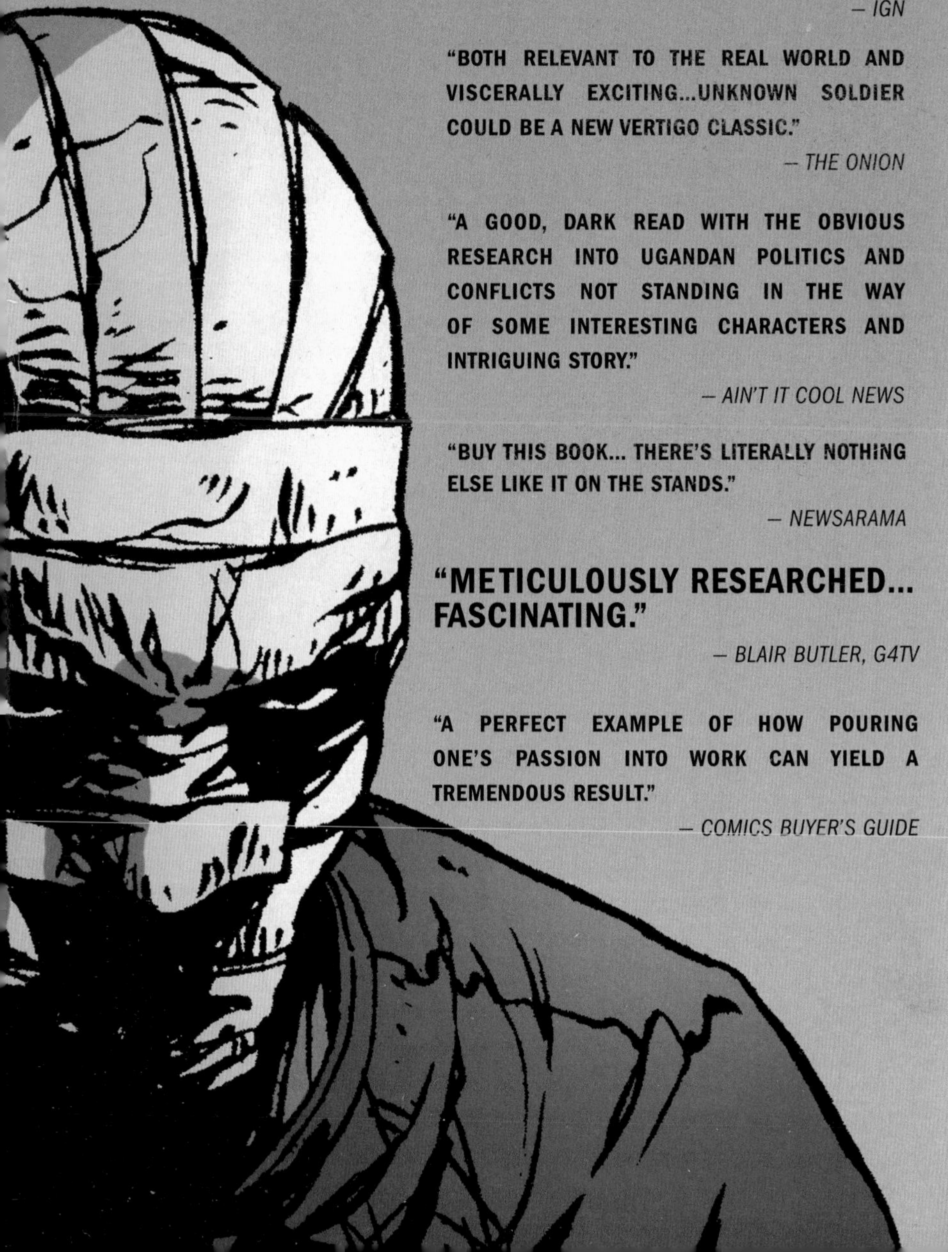

"BOTH RELEVANT TO THE REAL WORLD AND VISCERALLY EXCITING...UNKNOWN SOLDIER COULD BE A NEW VERTIGO CLASSIC."

— *THE ONION*

"A GOOD, DARK READ WITH THE OBVIOUS RESEARCH INTO UGANDAN POLITICS AND CONFLICTS NOT STANDING IN THE WAY OF SOME INTERESTING CHARACTERS AND INTRIGUING STORY."

— *AIN'T IT COOL NEWS*

"BUY THIS BOOK... THERE'S LITERALLY NOTHING ELSE LIKE IT ON THE STANDS."

— *NEWSARAMA*

"METICULOUSLY RESEARCHED... FASCINATING."

— *BLAIR BUTLER, G4TV*

"A PERFECT EXAMPLE OF HOW POURING ONE'S PASSION INTO WORK CAN YIELD A TREMENDOUS RESULT."

— *COMICS BUYER'S GUIDE*

UNKNOWN SOLDIER

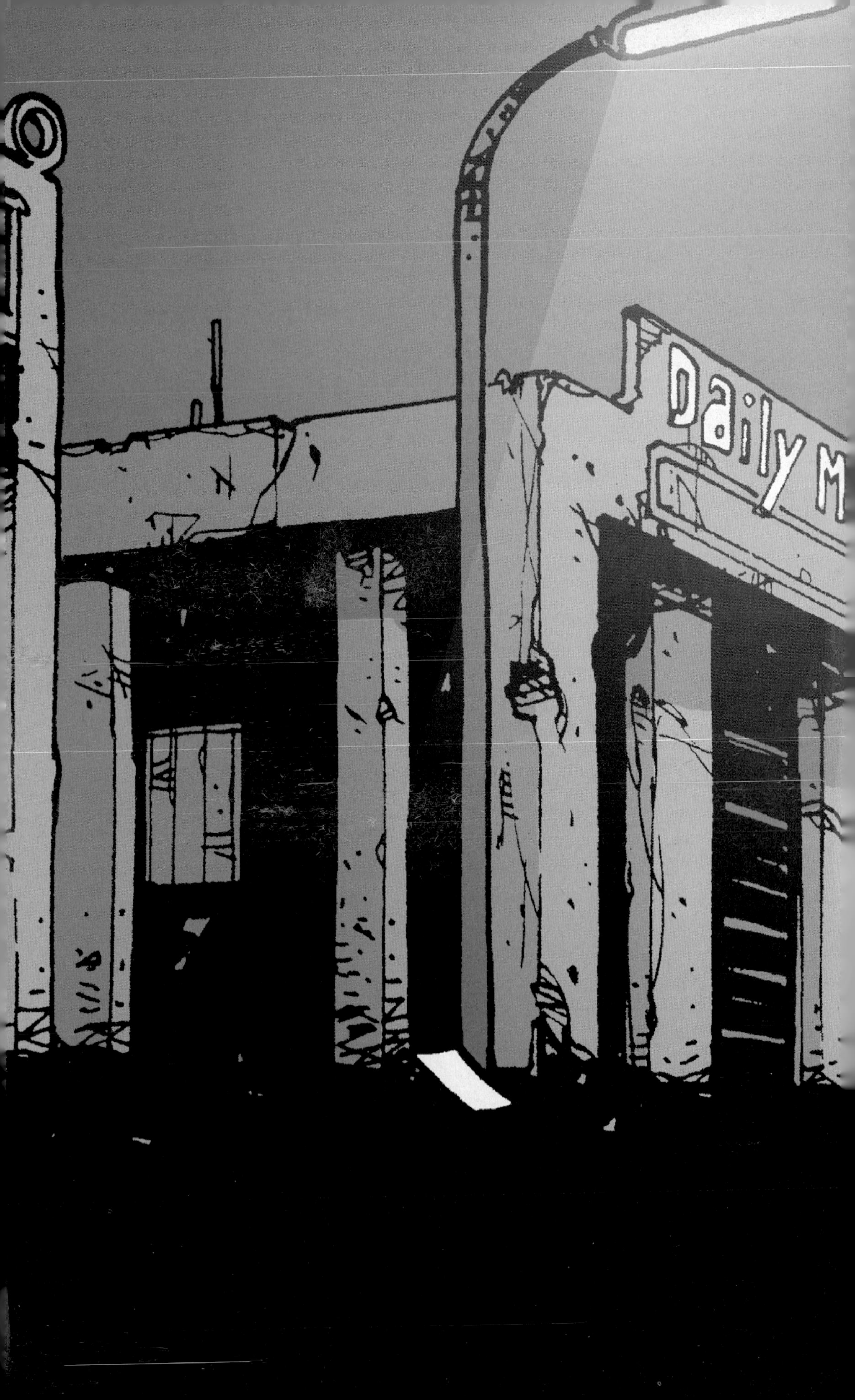
Daily M

UNKNOWN SOLDIER EASY KILL

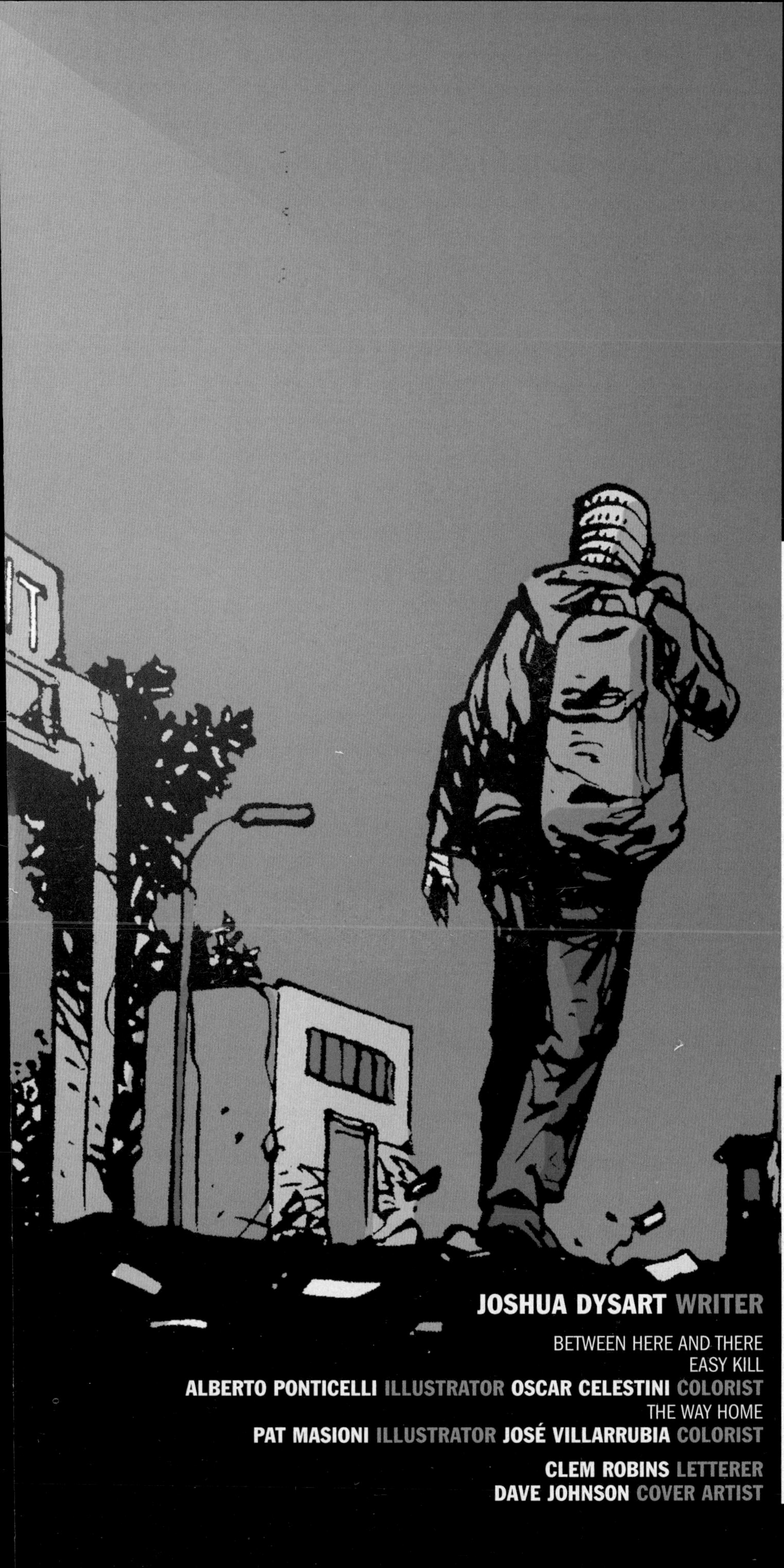

JOSHUA DYSART WRITER

BETWEEN HERE AND THERE
EASY KILL

ALBERTO PONTICELLI ILLUSTRATOR **OSCAR CELESTINI** COLORIST

THE WAY HOME

PAT MASIONI ILLUSTRATOR **JOSÉ VILLARRUBIA** COLORIST

CLEM ROBINS LETTERER
DAVE JOHNSON COVER ARTIST

KAREN BERGER SVP - EXECUTIVE EDITOR
PORNSAK PICHETSHOTE EDITOR — ORIGINAL SERIES
GEORG BREWER VP — DESIGN & DC DIRECT CREATIVE
BOB HARRAS GROUP EDITOR — COLLECTED EDITIONS
SEAN MACKIEWICZ EDITOR
ROBBIN BROSTERMAN DESIGN DIRECTOR - BOOKS

DC COMICS
PAUL LEVITZ PRESIDENT & PUBLISHER
RICHARD BRUNING SVP - CREATIVE DIRECTOR
PATRICK CALDON EVP - FINANCE & OPERATIONS
AMY GENKINS SVP - BUSINESS & LEGAL AFFAIRS
JIM LEE EDITORIAL DIRECTOR - WILDSTORM
GREGORY NOVECK SVP - CREATIVE AFFAIRS
STEVE ROTTERDAM SVP - SALES & MARKETING
CHERYL RUBIN SVP - BRAND MANAGEMENT

Cover by Dave Johnson
Publication design by Robbie Biederman

UNKNOWN SOLDIER: EASY KILL
Published by DC Comics. Cover, text and compilation
Copyright © 2010 DC Comics. All Rights Reserved.

Originally published in single magazine form as UNKNOWN SOLDIER 7-14.
Copyright © 2009, 2010 DC Comics. All Rights Reserved. All characters,
their distinctive likenesses and related elements featured in this publication
are trademarks of DC Comics. VERTIGO is a trademark of DC Comics.
The stories, characters and incidents featured in this publication are
entirely fictional. DC Comics does not read or accept unsolicited
submissions of ideas, stories or artwork.

DC Comics, 1700 Broadway, New York, NY 10019
A Warner Bros. Entertainment Company.
Printed in Canada. First Printing.
ISBN: 978-1-4012-2600-8

SUSTAINABLE
FORESTRY
INITIATIVE

Certified Fiber Sourcing
www.sfiprogram.org

Fiber used in this product line meets the
sourcing requirements of the SFI program.
www.sfiprogram.org PWC-SFICOC-260

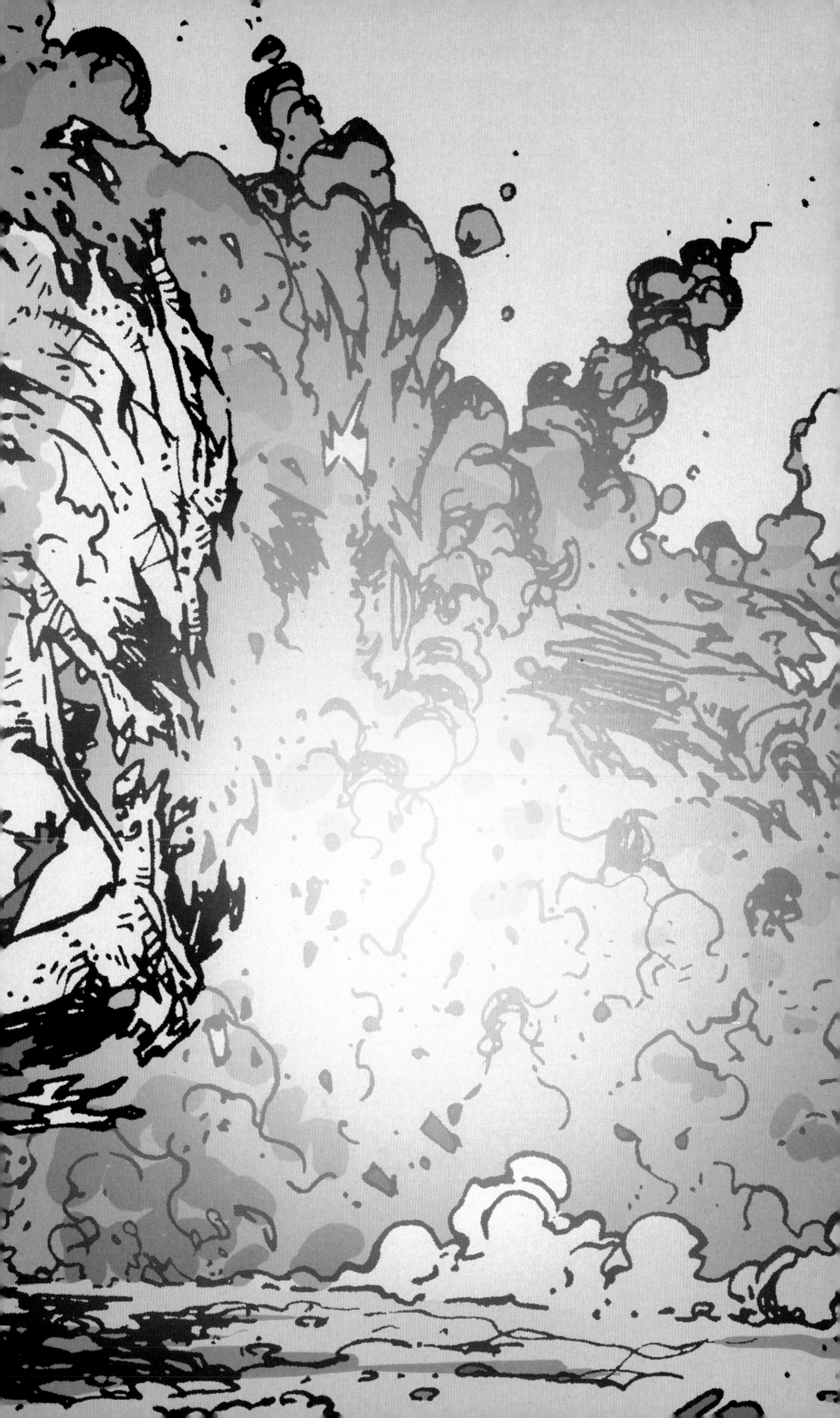

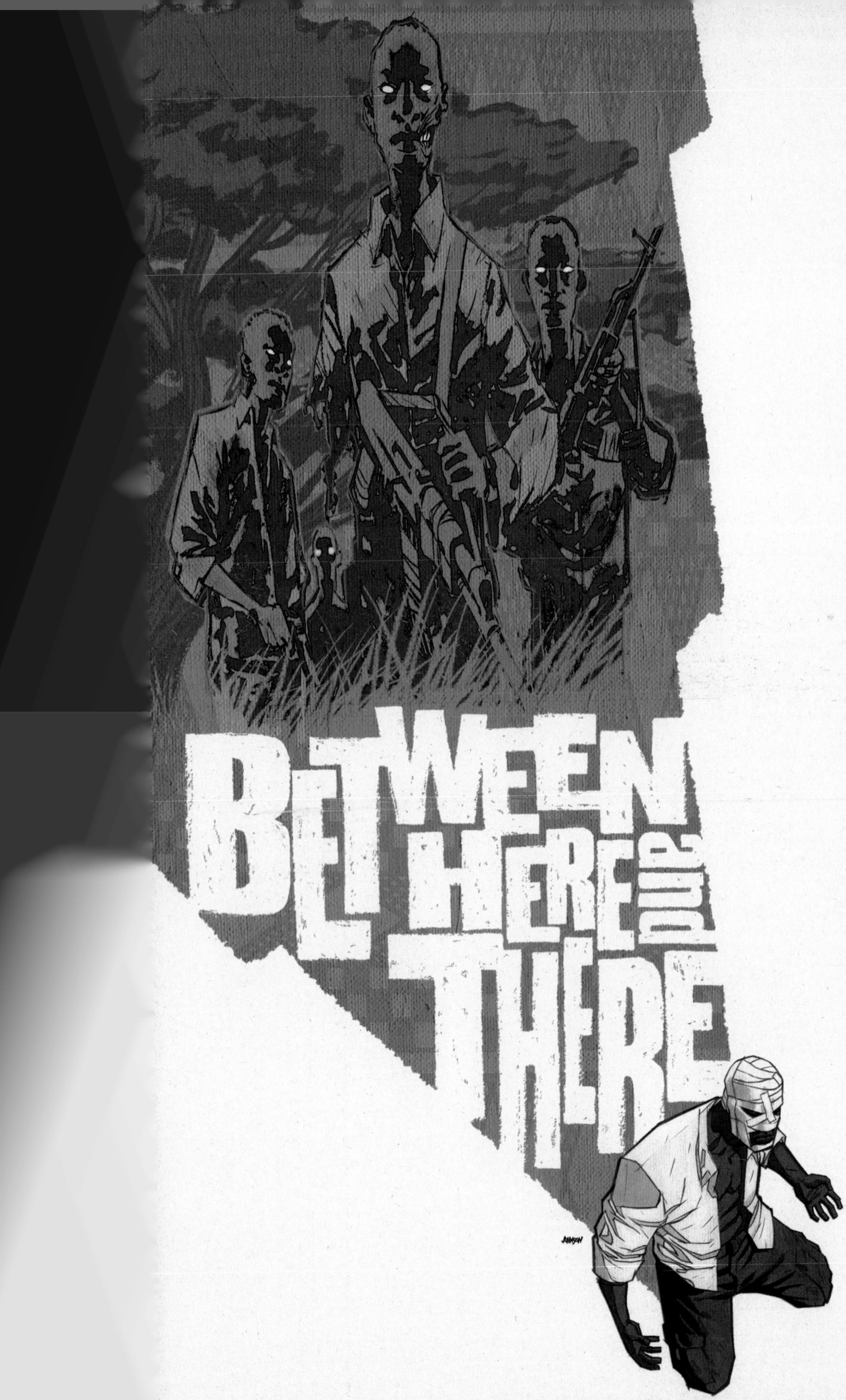
BETWEEN
HERE and
THERE
JOHNSON

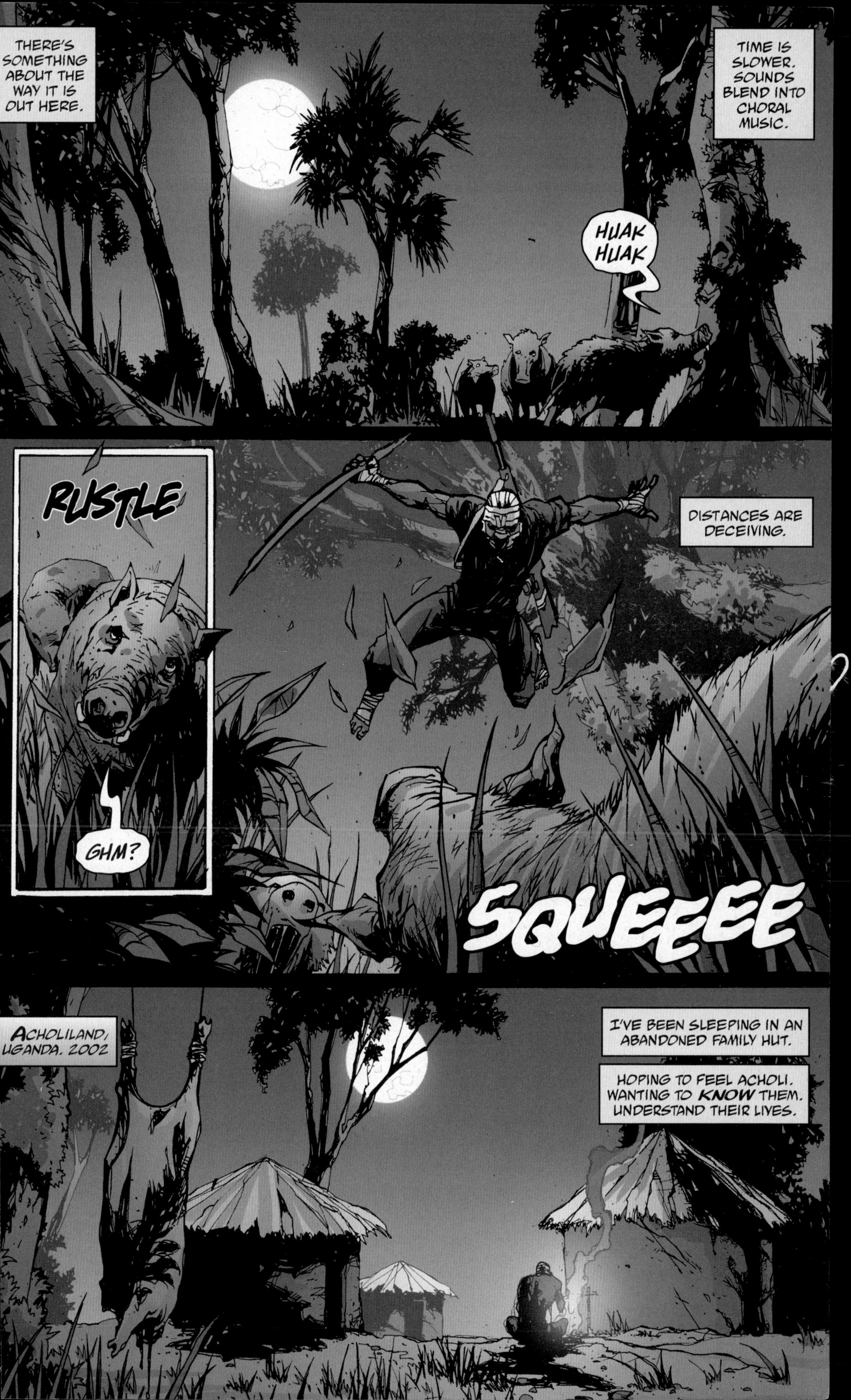
THERE'S SOMETHING ABOUT THE WAY IT IS OUT HERE.
TIME IS SLOWER. SOUNDS BLEND INTO CHORAL MUSIC.
HUAK HUAK
RUSTLE
GHM?
DISTANCES ARE DECEIVING.
SQUEEEE
ACHOLILAND, UGANDA. 2002
I'VE BEEN SLEEPING IN AN ABANDONED FAMILY HUT.
HOPING TO FEEL ACHOLI. WANTING TO KNOW THEM. UNDERSTAND THEIR LIVES.

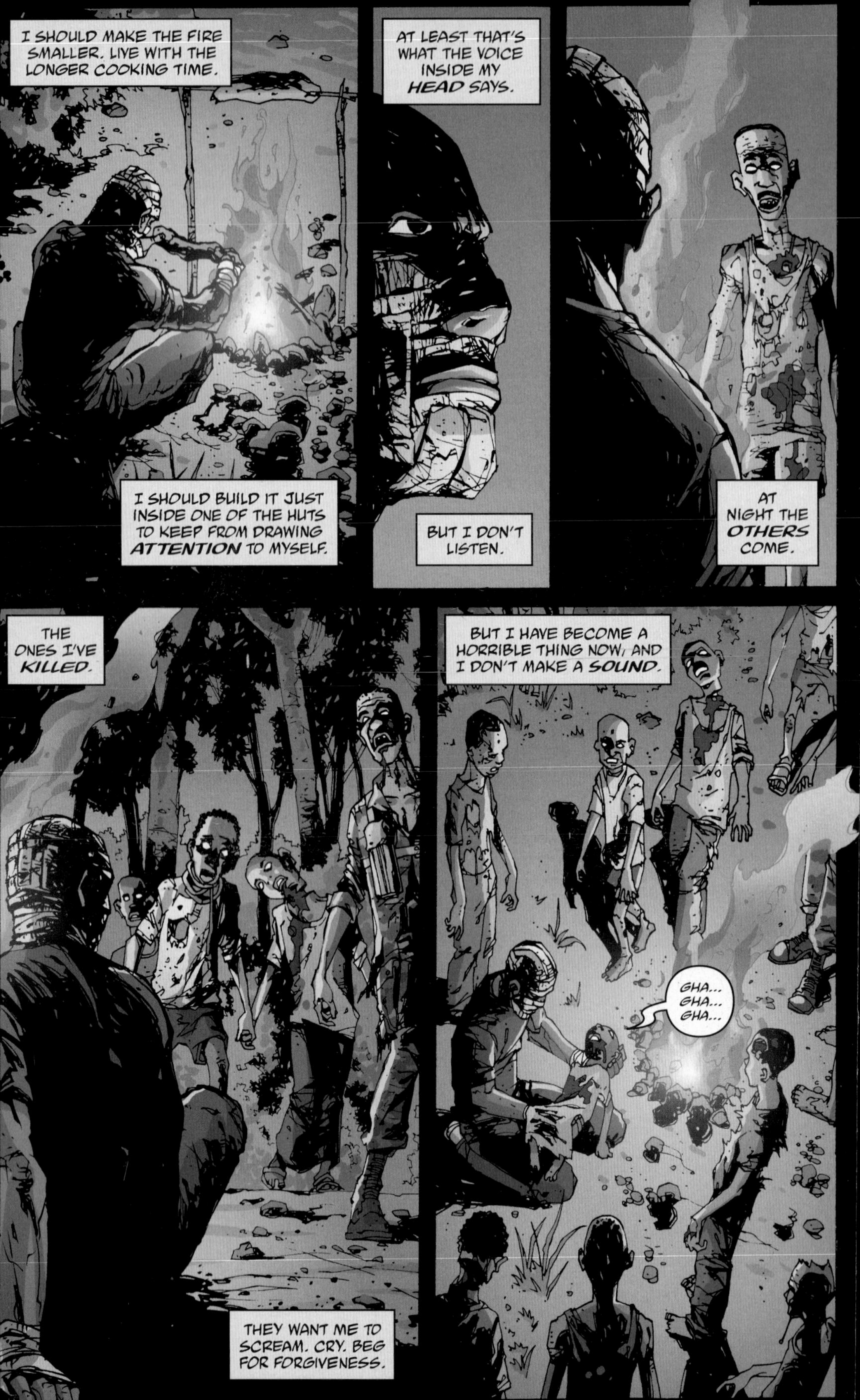
I SHOULD MAKE THE FIRE SMALLER. LIVE WITH THE LONGER COOKING TIME.
I SHOULD BUILD IT JUST INSIDE ONE OF THE HUTS TO KEEP FROM DRAWING ATTENTION TO MYSELF.
AT LEAST THAT'S WHAT THE VOICE INSIDE MY HEAD SAYS.
BUT I DON'T LISTEN.
AT NIGHT THE OTHERS COME.
THE ONES I'VE KILLED.
THEY WANT ME TO SCREAM. CRY. BEG FOR FORGIVENESS.
BUT I HAVE BECOME A HORRIBLE THING NOW, AND I DON'T MAKE A SOUND.
GHA... GHA... GHA...

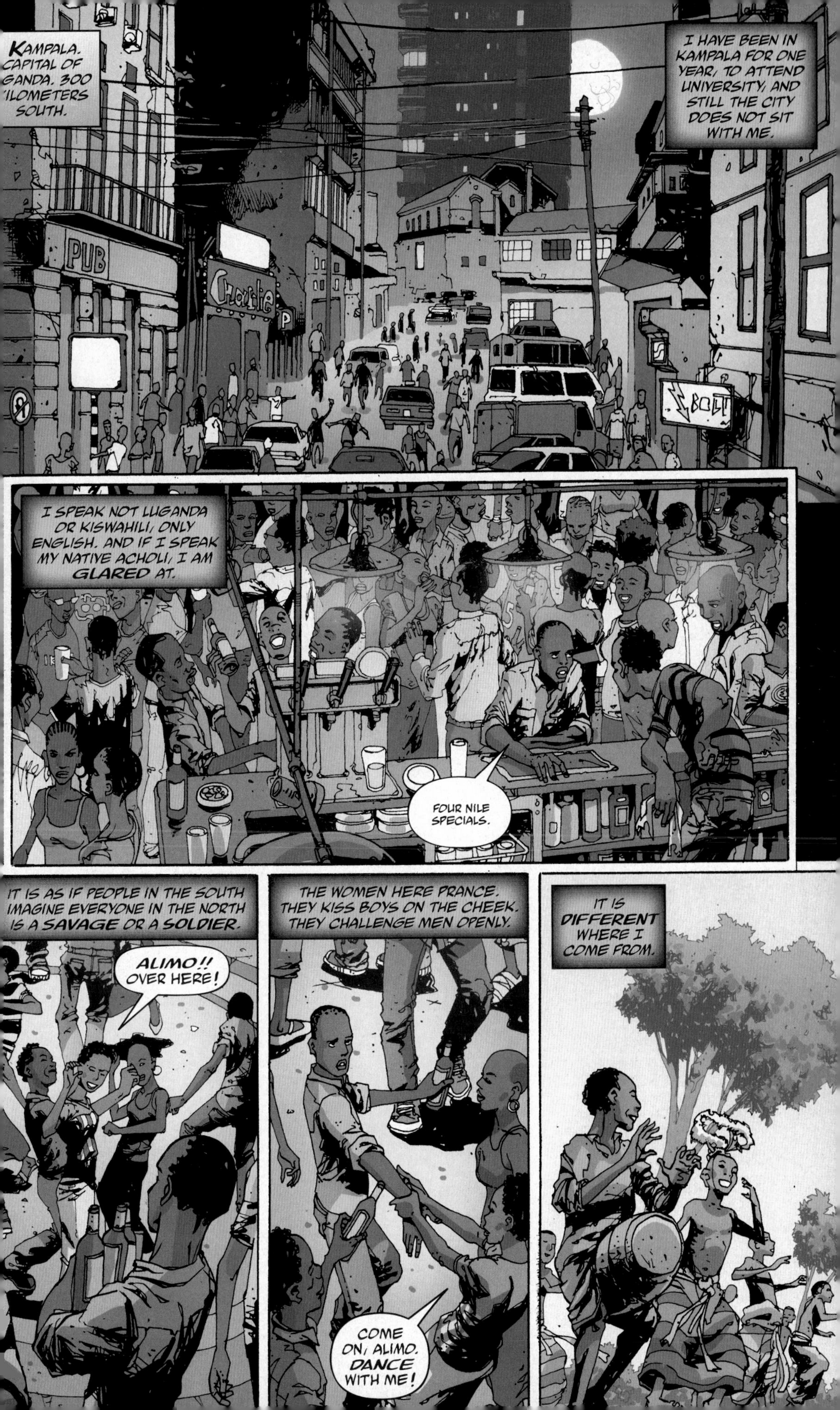
KAMPALA. CAPITAL OF UGANDA. 300 KILOMETERS SOUTH.
I HAVE BEEN IN KAMPALA FOR ONE YEAR, TO ATTEND UNIVERSITY, AND STILL THE CITY DOES NOT SIT WITH ME.
PUB
BOLT
I SPEAK NOT LUGANDA OR KISWAHILI, ONLY ENGLISH. AND IF I SPEAK MY NATIVE ACHOLI, I AM GLARED AT.
FOUR NILE SPECIALS.
IT IS AS IF PEOPLE IN THE SOUTH IMAGINE EVERYONE IN THE NORTH IS A SAVAGE OR A SOLDIER.
ALIMO!! OVER HERE!
THE WOMEN HERE PRANCE. THEY KISS BOYS ON THE CHEEK. THEY CHALLENGE MEN OPENLY.
COME ON, ALIMO. DANCE WITH ME!
IT IS DIFFERENT WHERE I COME FROM.

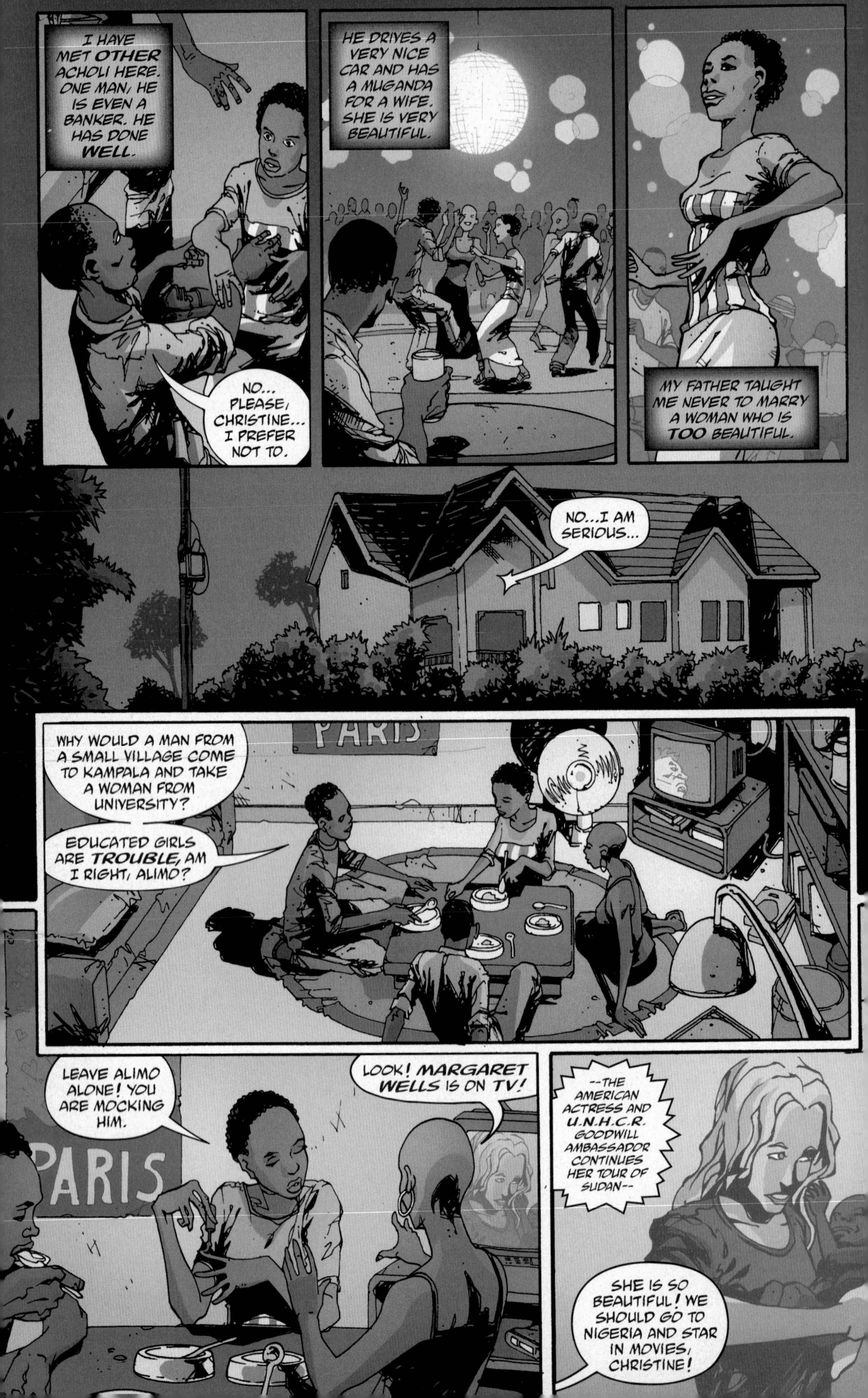
I HAVE MET OTHER ACHOLI HERE. ONE MAN, HE IS EVEN A BANKER. HE HAS DONE WELL.
NO... PLEASE, CHRISTINE... I PREFER NOT TO.
HE DRIVES A VERY NICE CAR AND HAS A MUGANDA FOR A WIFE. SHE IS VERY BEAUTIFUL.
MY FATHER TAUGHT ME NEVER TO MARRY A WOMAN WHO IS TOO BEAUTIFUL.
NO...I AM SERIOUS...
PARIS
WHY WOULD A MAN FROM A SMALL VILLAGE COME TO KAMPALA AND TAKE A WOMAN FROM UNIVERSITY?
EDUCATED GIRLS ARE TROUBLE, AM I RIGHT, ALIMO?
LEAVE ALIMO ALONE! YOU ARE MOCKING HIM.
LOOK! MARGARET WELLS IS ON TV!
PARIS
--THE AMERICAN ACTRESS AND U.N.H.C.R. GOODWILL AMBASSADOR CONTINUES HER TOUR OF SUDAN--
SHE IS SO BEAUTIFUL! WE SHOULD GO TO NIGERIA AND STAR IN MOVIES, CHRISTINE!

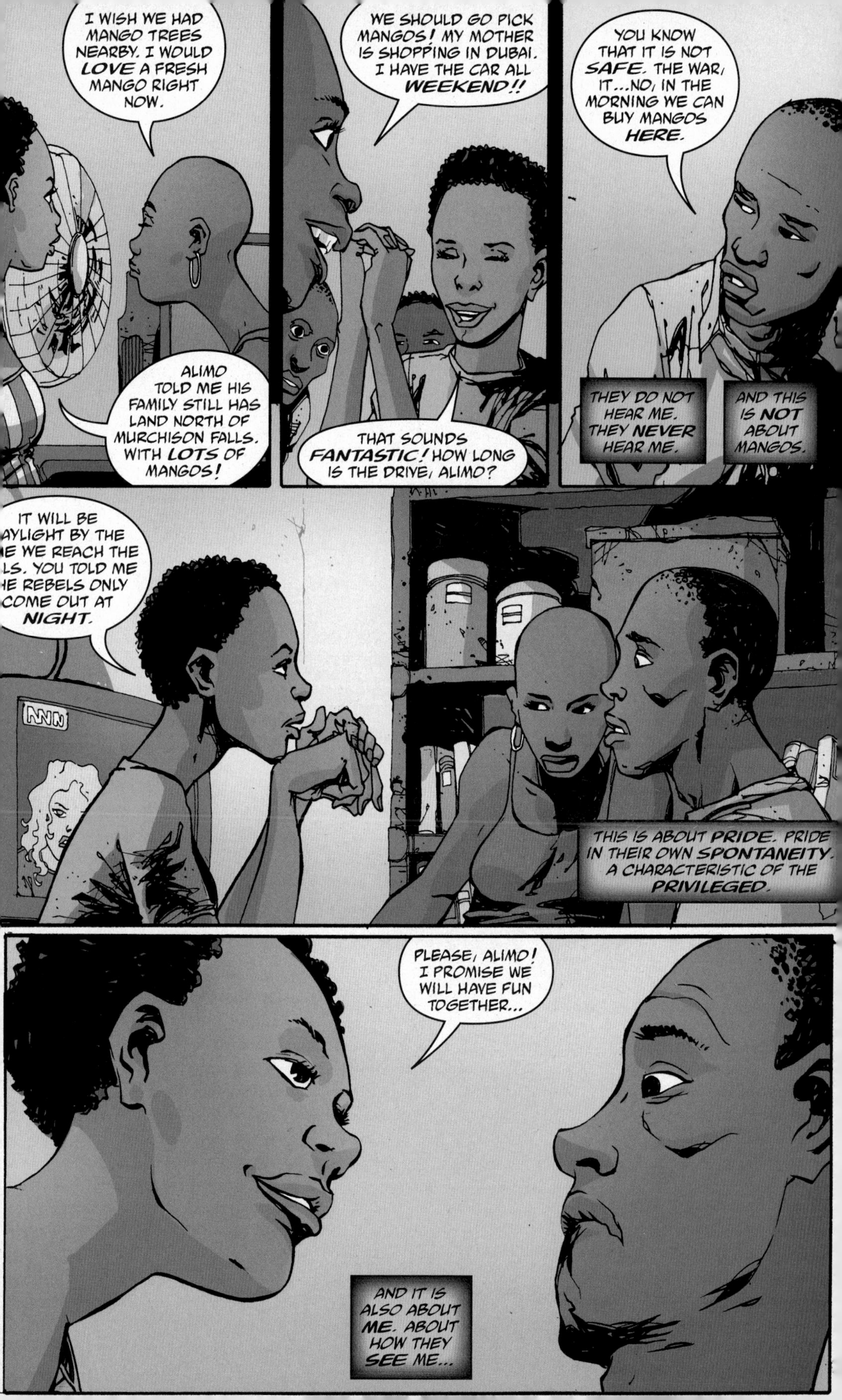
I WISH WE HAD MANGO TREES NEARBY. I WOULD LOVE A FRESH MANGO RIGHT NOW.
ALIMO TOLD ME HIS FAMILY STILL HAS LAND NORTH OF MURCHISON FALLS. WITH LOTS OF MANGOS!
WE SHOULD GO PICK MANGOS! MY MOTHER IS SHOPPING IN DUBAI. I HAVE THE CAR ALL WEEKEND!!
THAT SOUNDS FANTASTIC! HOW LONG IS THE DRIVE, ALIMO?
YOU KNOW THAT IT IS NOT SAFE. THE WAR, IT...NO, IN THE MORNING WE CAN BUY MANGOS HERE.
THEY DO NOT HEAR ME. THEY NEVER HEAR ME.
AND THIS IS NOT ABOUT MANGOS.
IT WILL BE AYLIGHT BY THE E WE REACH THE LS. YOU TOLD ME E REBELS ONLY COME OUT AT NIGHT.
THIS IS ABOUT PRIDE. PRIDE IN THEIR OWN SPONTANEITY. A CHARACTERISTIC OF THE PRIVILEGED.
PLEASE, ALIMO! I PROMISE WE WILL HAVE FUN TOGETHER...
AND IT IS ALSO ABOUT ME. ABOUT HOW THEY SEE ME...

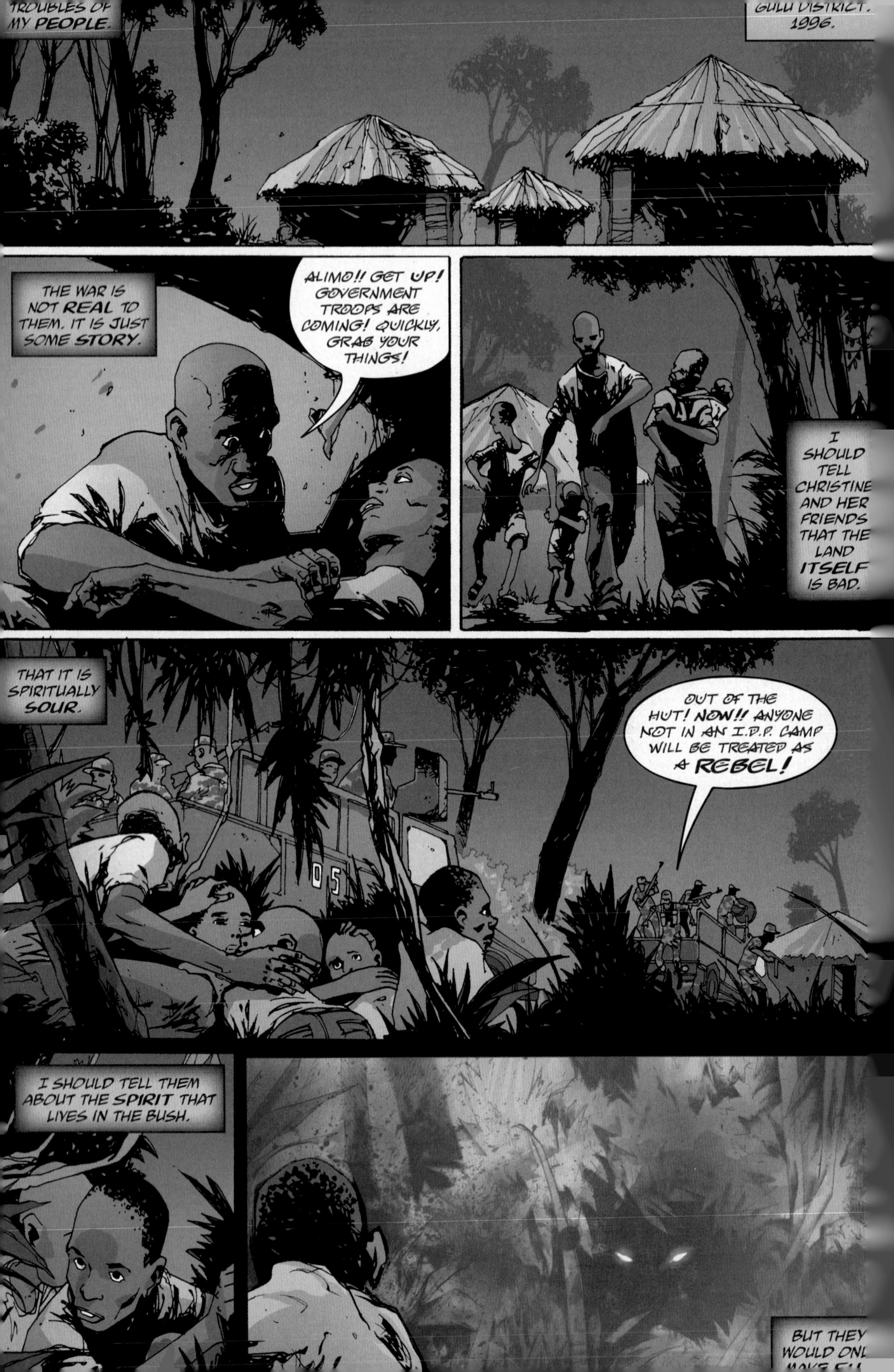
TROUBLES OF MY PEOPLE.
GULU DISTRICT. 1996.
THE WAR IS NOT REAL TO THEM. IT IS JUST SOME STORY.
ALIMO!! GET UP! GOVERNMENT TROOPS ARE COMING! QUICKLY, GRAB YOUR THINGS!
I SHOULD TELL CHRISTINE AND HER FRIENDS THAT THE LAND ITSELF IS BAD.
THAT IT IS SPIRITUALLY SOUR.
OUT OF THE HUT! NOW!! ANYONE NOT IN AN I.D.P. CAMP WILL BE TREATED AS A REBEL!
05
I SHOULD TELL THEM ABOUT THE SPIRIT THAT LIVES IN THE BUSH.
BUT THEY WOULD ONL

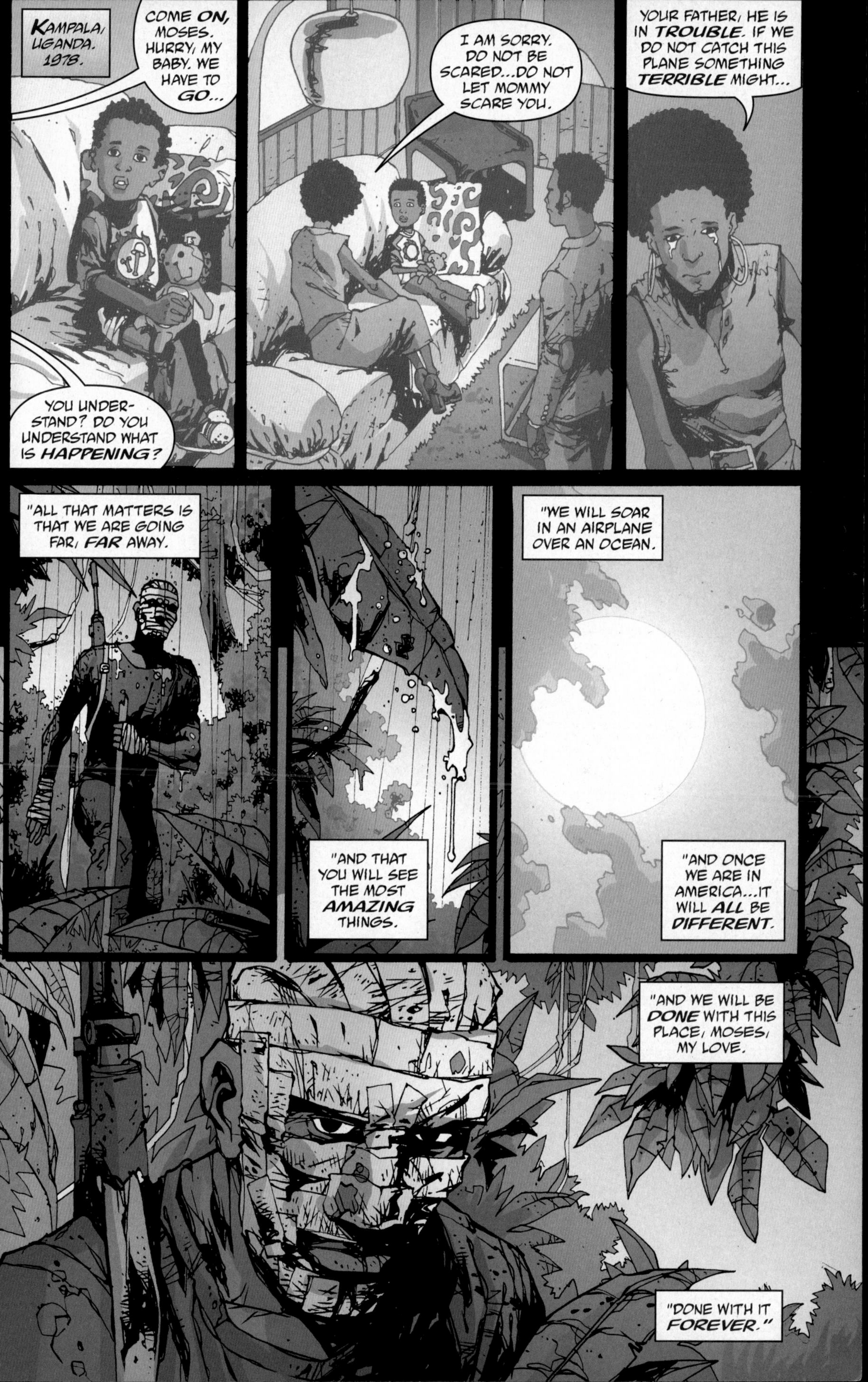
KAMPALA, UGANDA. 1978.
COME ON, MOSES. HURRY, MY BABY. WE HAVE TO GO...
YOU UNDERSTAND? DO YOU UNDERSTAND WHAT IS HAPPENING?
I AM SORRY. DO NOT BE SCARED...DO NOT LET MOMMY SCARE YOU.
YOUR FATHER, HE IS IN TROUBLE. IF WE DO NOT CATCH THIS PLANE SOMETHING TERRIBLE MIGHT...
"ALL THAT MATTERS IS THAT WE ARE GOING FAR, FAR AWAY.
"AND THAT YOU WILL SEE THE MOST AMAZING THINGS.
"WE WILL SOAR IN AN AIRPLANE OVER AN OCEAN.
"AND ONCE WE ARE IN AMERICA...IT WILL ALL BE DIFFERENT.
"AND WE WILL BE DONE WITH THIS PLACE, MOSES, MY LOVE.
"DONE WITH IT FOREVER."

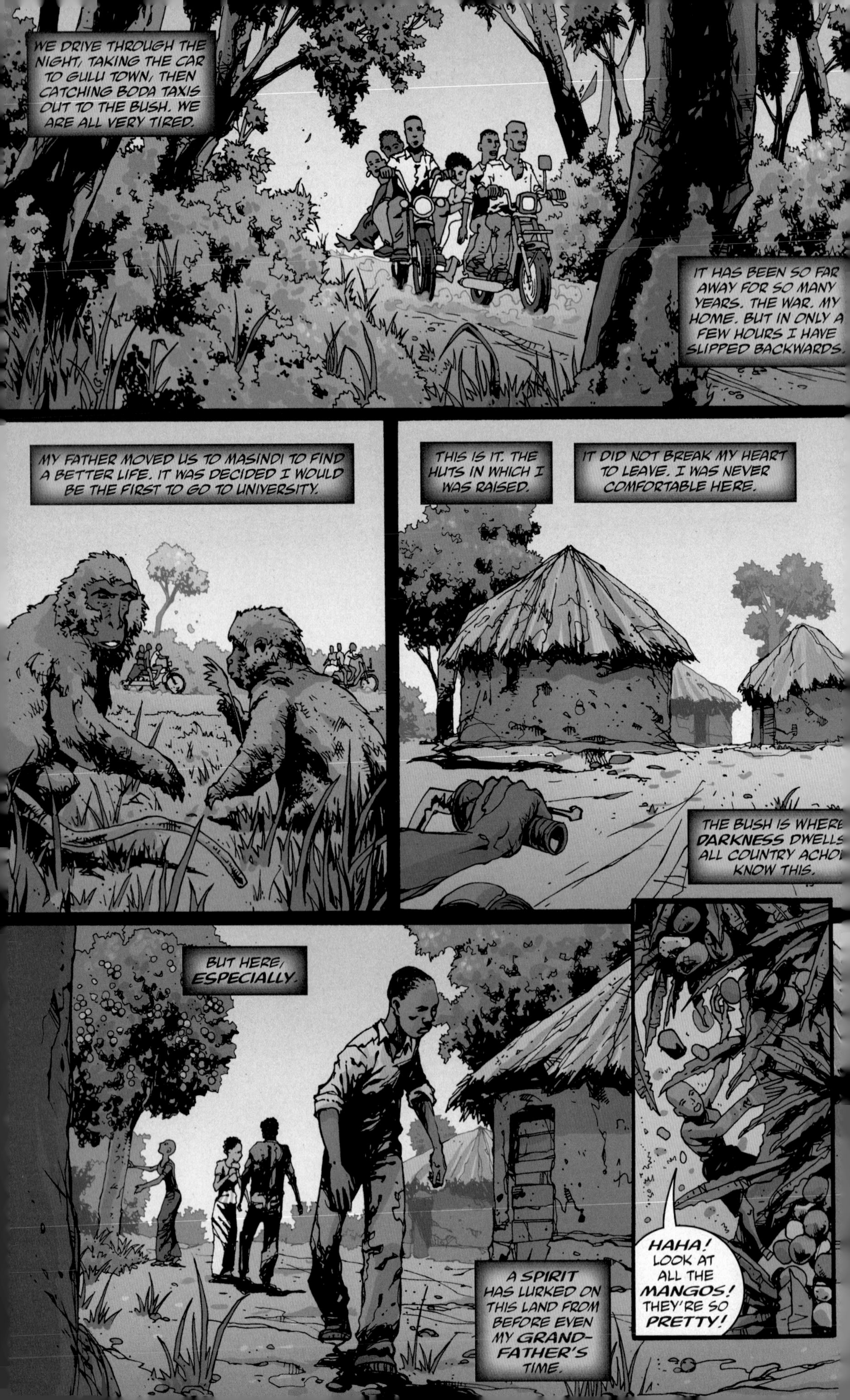

WE DRIVE THROUGH THE NIGHT, TAKING THE CAR TO GULU TOWN, THEN CATCHING BODA TAXIS OUT TO THE BUSH. WE ARE ALL VERY TIRED.
IT HAS BEEN SO FAR AWAY FOR SO MANY YEARS. THE WAR. MY HOME. BUT IN ONLY A FEW HOURS I HAVE SLIPPED BACKWARDS.
MY FATHER MOVED US TO MASINDI TO FIND A BETTER LIFE. IT WAS DECIDED I WOULD BE THE FIRST TO GO TO UNIVERSITY.
THIS IS IT. THE HUTS IN WHICH I WAS RAISED.
IT DID NOT BREAK MY HEART TO LEAVE. I WAS NEVER COMFORTABLE HERE.
THE BUSH IS WHERE DARKNESS DWELLS. ALL COUNTRY ACHO KNOW THIS.
BUT HERE, ESPECIALLY.
A SPIRIT HAS LURKED ON THIS LAND FROM BEFORE EVEN MY GRAND-FATHER'S TIME.
HAHA! LOOK AT ALL THE MANGOS! THEY'RE SO PRETTY!

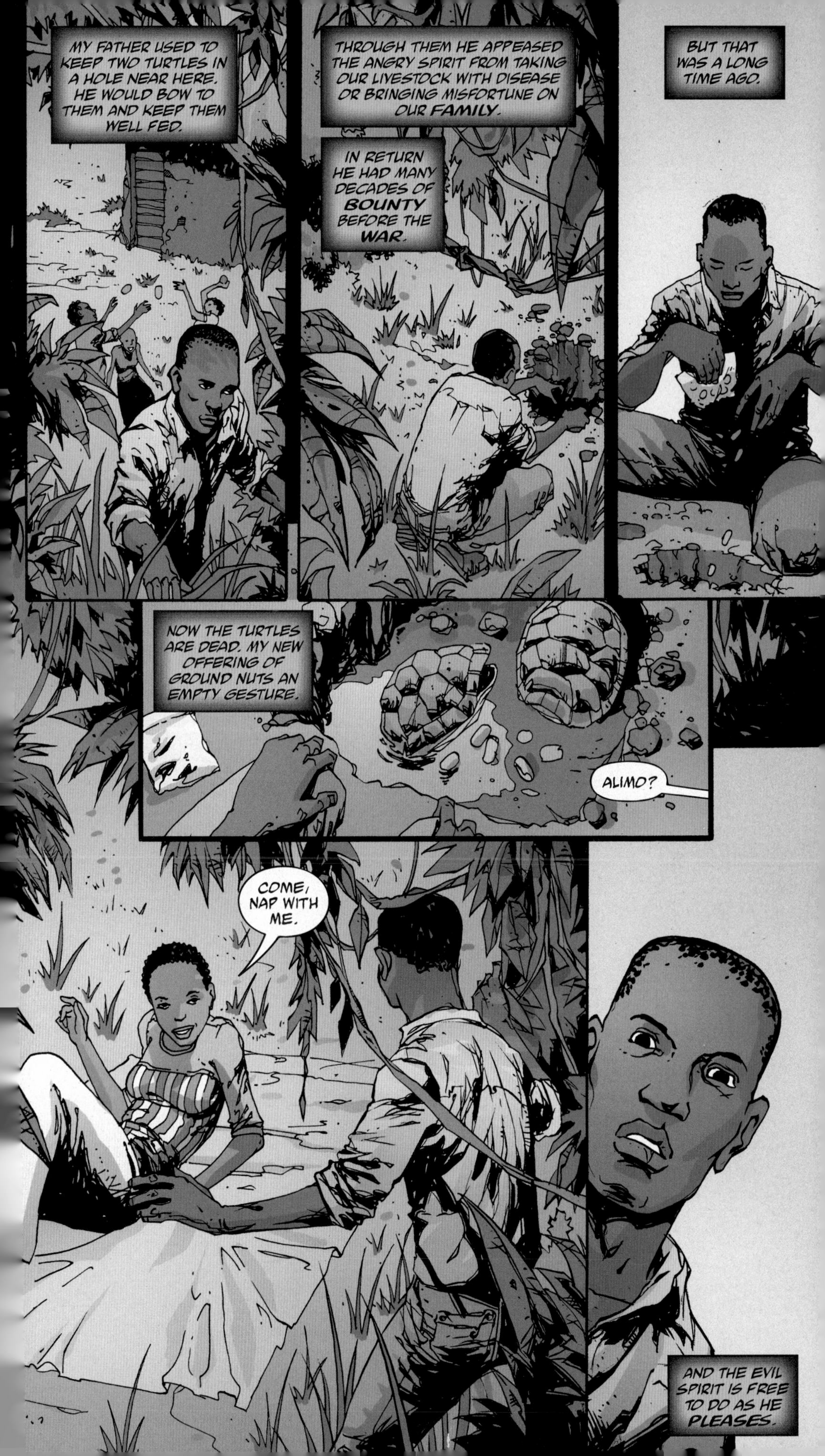
MY FATHER USED TO KEEP TWO TURTLES IN A HOLE NEAR HERE. HE WOULD BOW TO THEM AND KEEP THEM WELL FED.
THROUGH THEM HE APPEASED THE ANGRY SPIRIT FROM TAKING OUR LIVESTOCK WITH DISEASE OR BRINGING MISFORTUNE ON OUR FAMILY.
IN RETURN HE HAD MANY DECADES OF BOUNTY BEFORE THE WAR.
BUT THAT WAS A LONG TIME AGO.
NOW THE TURTLES ARE DEAD. MY NEW OFFERING OF GROUND NUTS AN EMPTY GESTURE.
ALIMO?
COME, NAP WITH ME.
AND THE EVIL SPIRIT IS FREE TO DO AS HE PLEASES.

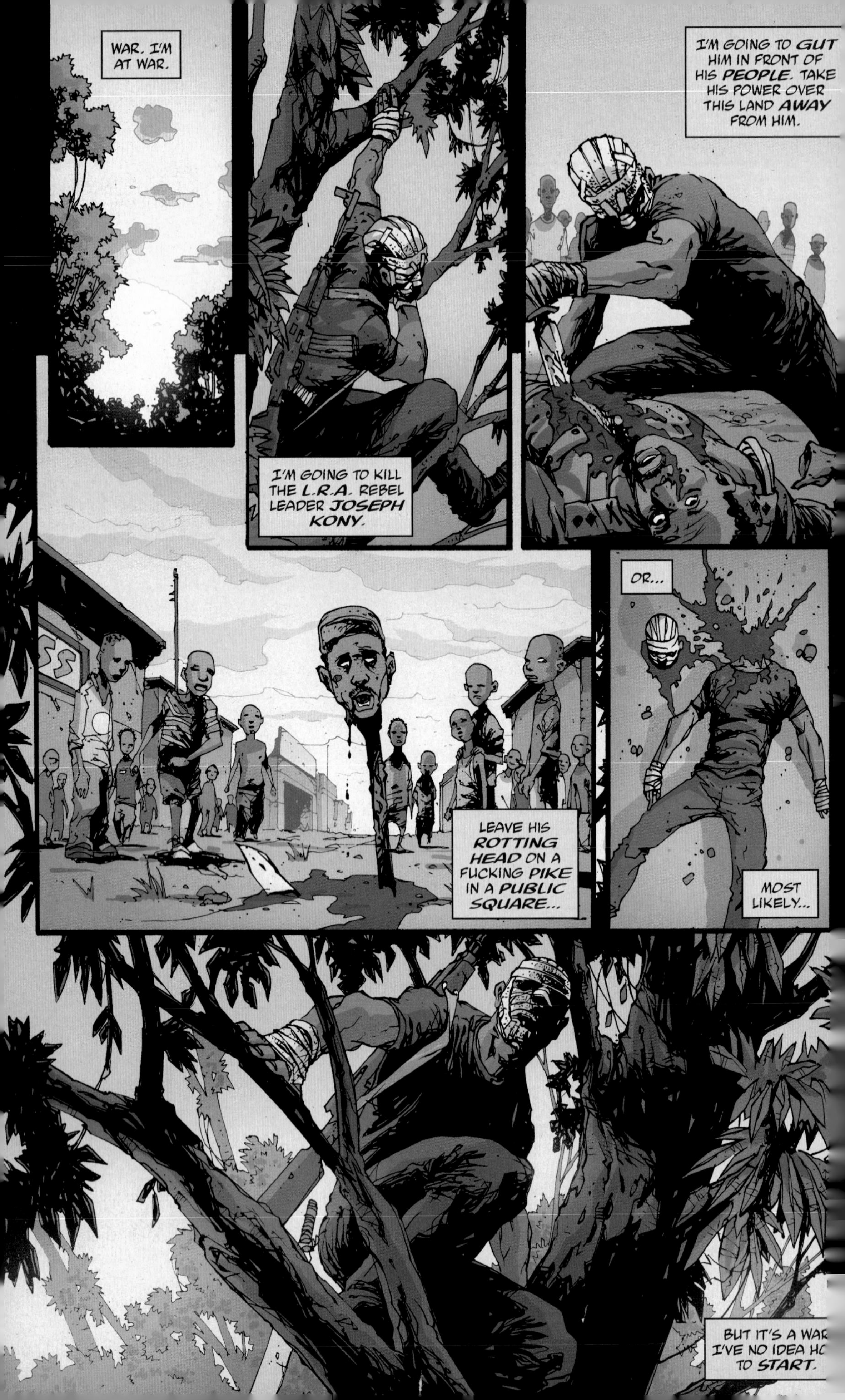
WAR. I'M AT WAR.
I'M GOING TO KILL THE L.R.A. REBEL LEADER JOSEPH KONY.
I'M GOING TO GUT HIM IN FRONT OF HIS PEOPLE. TAKE HIS POWER OVER THIS LAND AWAY FROM HIM.
LEAVE HIS ROTTING HEAD ON A FUCKING PIKE IN A PUBLIC SQUARE...
OR...
MOST LIKELY...
BUT IT'S A WAR I'VE NO IDEA HO TO START.

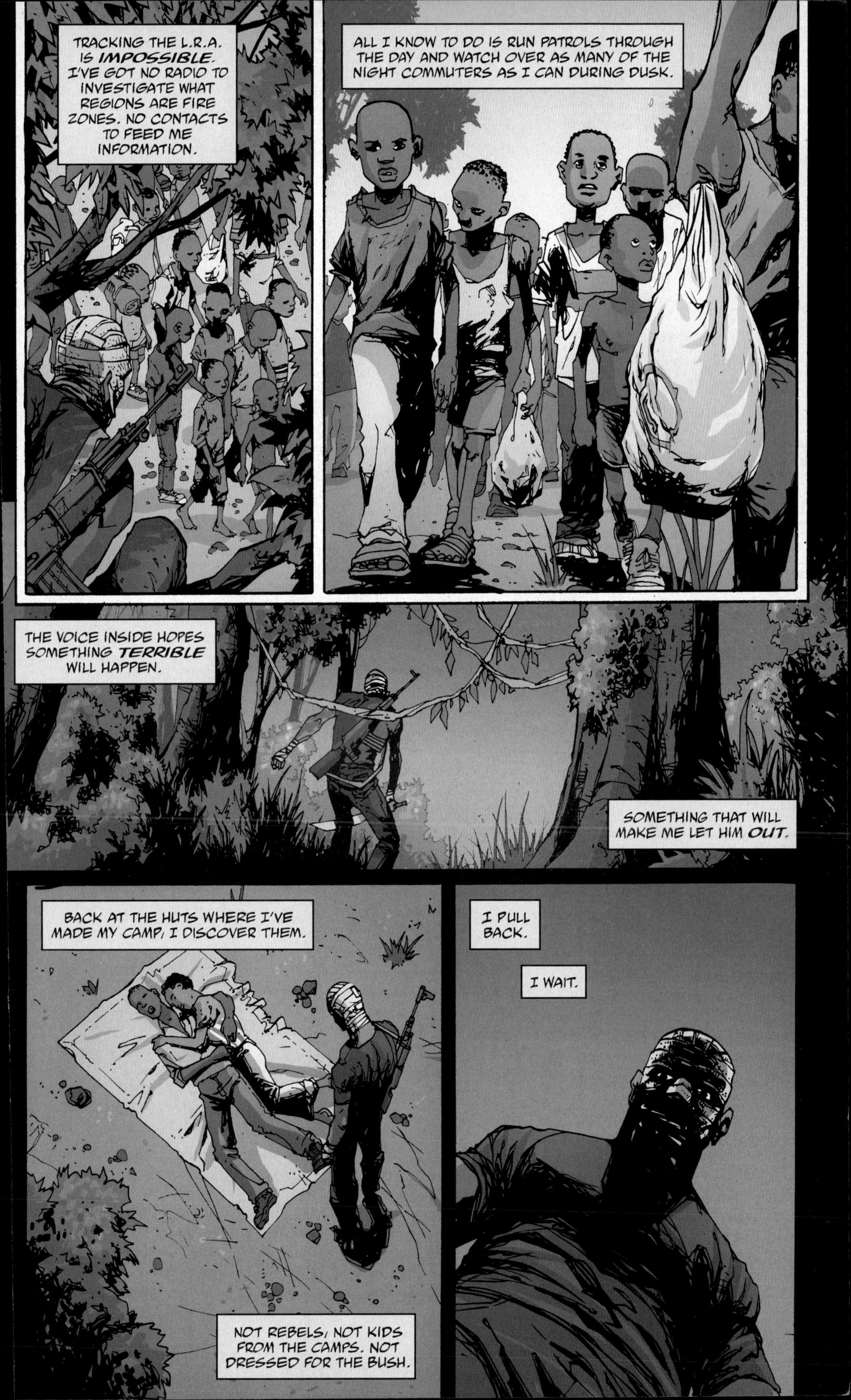
TRACKING THE L.R.A. IS IMPOSSIBLE. I'VE GOT NO RADIO TO INVESTIGATE WHAT REGIONS ARE FIRE ZONES. NO CONTACTS TO FEED ME INFORMATION.
ALL I KNOW TO DO IS RUN PATROLS THROUGH THE DAY AND WATCH OVER AS MANY OF THE NIGHT COMMUTERS AS I CAN DURING DUSK.
THE VOICE INSIDE HOPES SOMETHING TERRIBLE WILL HAPPEN.
SOMETHING THAT WILL MAKE ME LET HIM OUT.
BACK AT THE HUTS WHERE I'VE MADE MY CAMP, I DISCOVER THEM.
NOT REBELS, NOT KIDS FROM THE CAMPS. NOT DRESSED FOR THE BUSH.
I PULL BACK.
I WAIT.

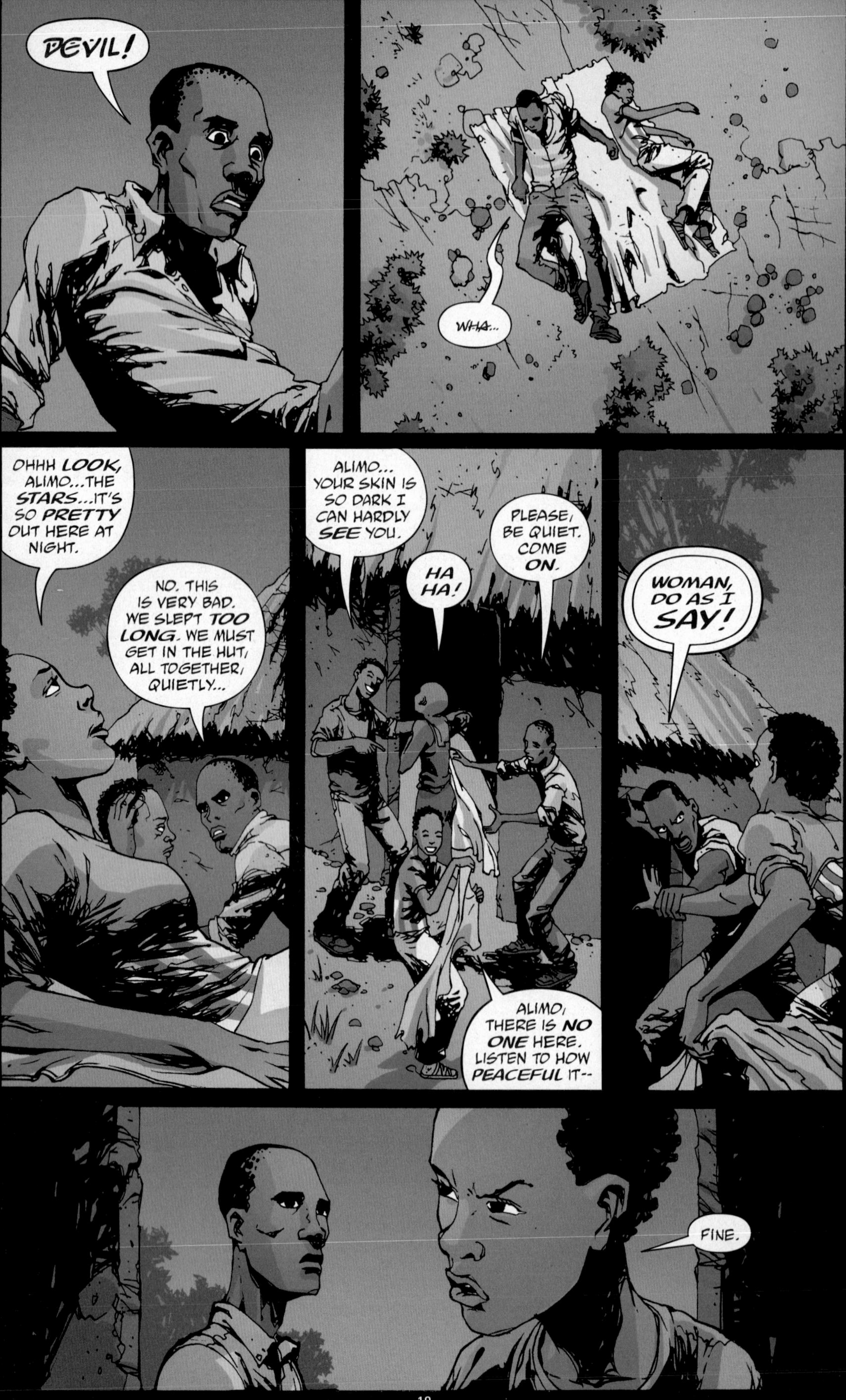
DEVIL!
WHA...
OHHH LOOK, ALIMO...THE STARS...IT'S SO PRETTY OUT HERE AT NIGHT.
NO. THIS IS VERY BAD. WE SLEPT TOO LONG. WE MUST GET IN THE HUT, ALL TOGETHER, QUIETLY...
ALIMO... YOUR SKIN IS SO DARK I CAN HARDLY SEE YOU.
HA HA!
PLEASE, BE QUIET. COME ON.
ALIMO, THERE IS NO ONE HERE. LISTEN TO HOW PEACEFUL IT--
WOMAN, DO AS I SAY!
FINE.

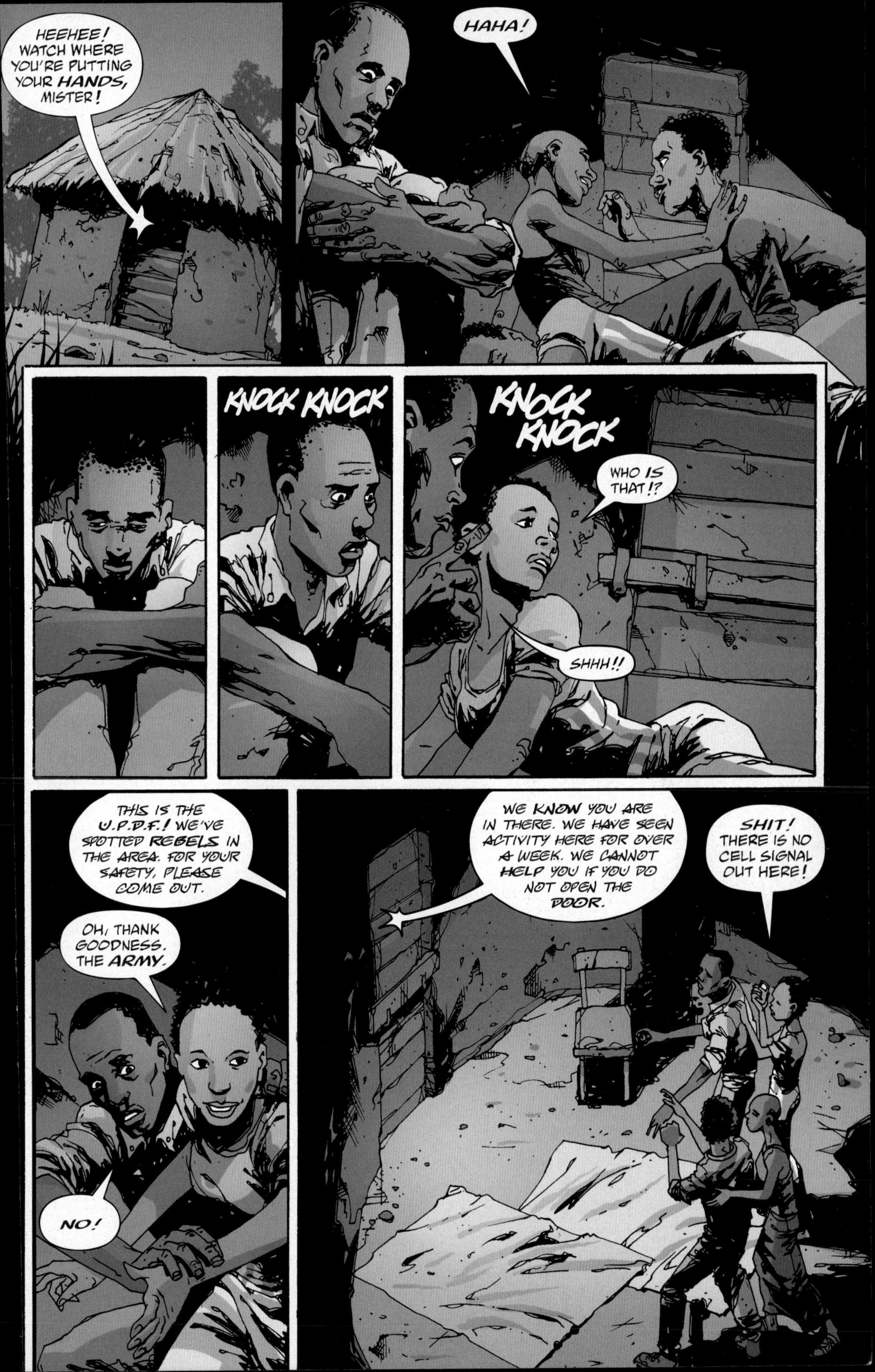
HEEHEE! WATCH WHERE YOU'RE PUTTING YOUR HANDS, MISTER!
HAHA!
KNOCK KNOCK
KNOCK KNOCK
WHO IS THAT!?
SHHH!!
THIS IS THE U.P.D.F.! WE'VE SPOTTED REBELS IN THE AREA. FOR YOUR SAFETY, PLEASE COME OUT.
OH, THANK GOODNESS. THE ARMY.
NO!
WE KNOW YOU ARE IN THERE. WE HAVE SEEN ACTIVITY HERE FOR OVER A WEEK. WE CANNOT HELP YOU IF YOU DO NOT OPEN THE DOOR.
SHIT! THERE IS NO CELL SIGNAL OUT HERE!

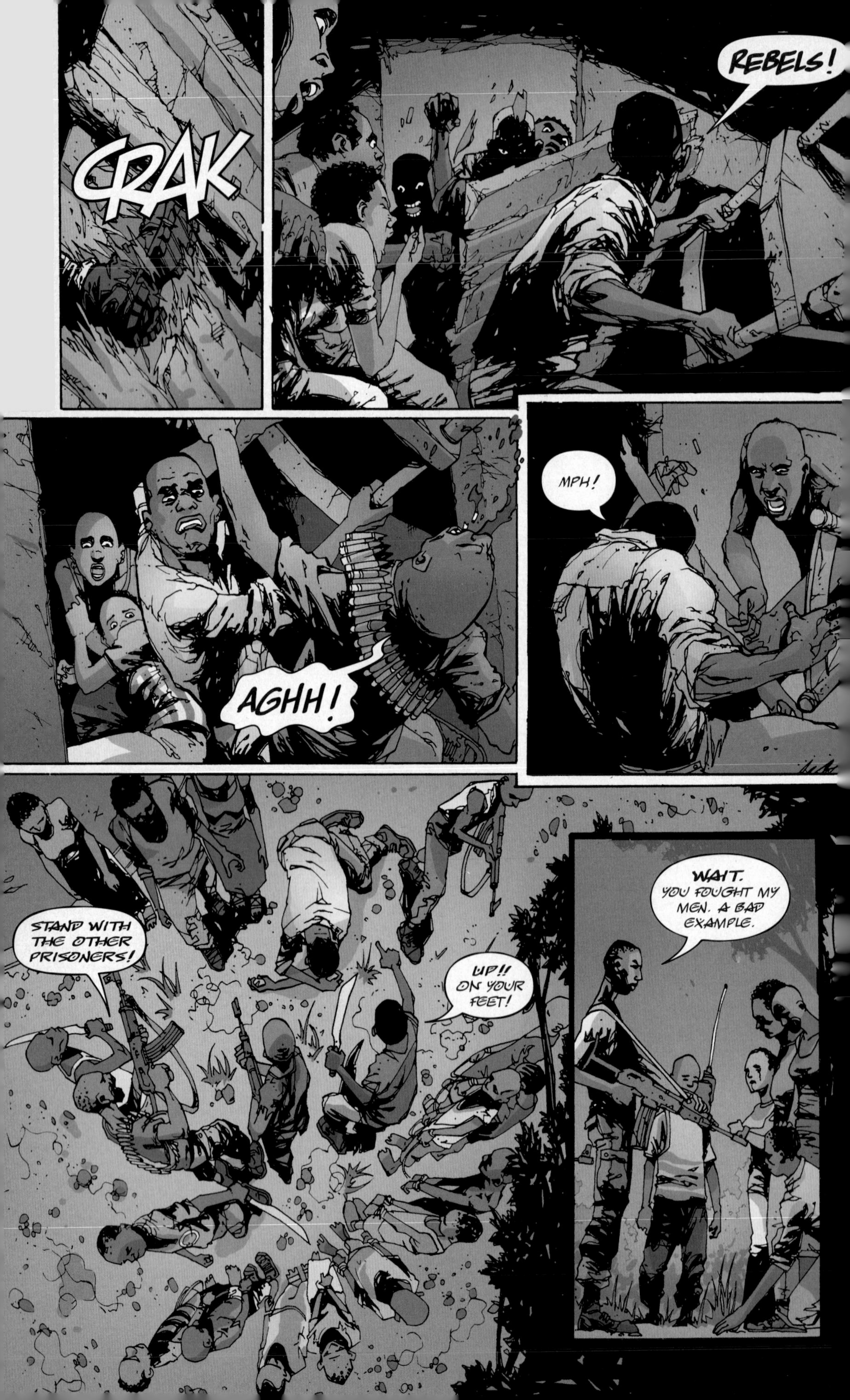
CRAK
REBELS!
AGHH!
MPH!
STAND WITH THE OTHER PRISONERS!
UP!! ON YOUR FEET!
WAIT. YOU FOUGHT MY MEN. A BAD EXAMPLE.

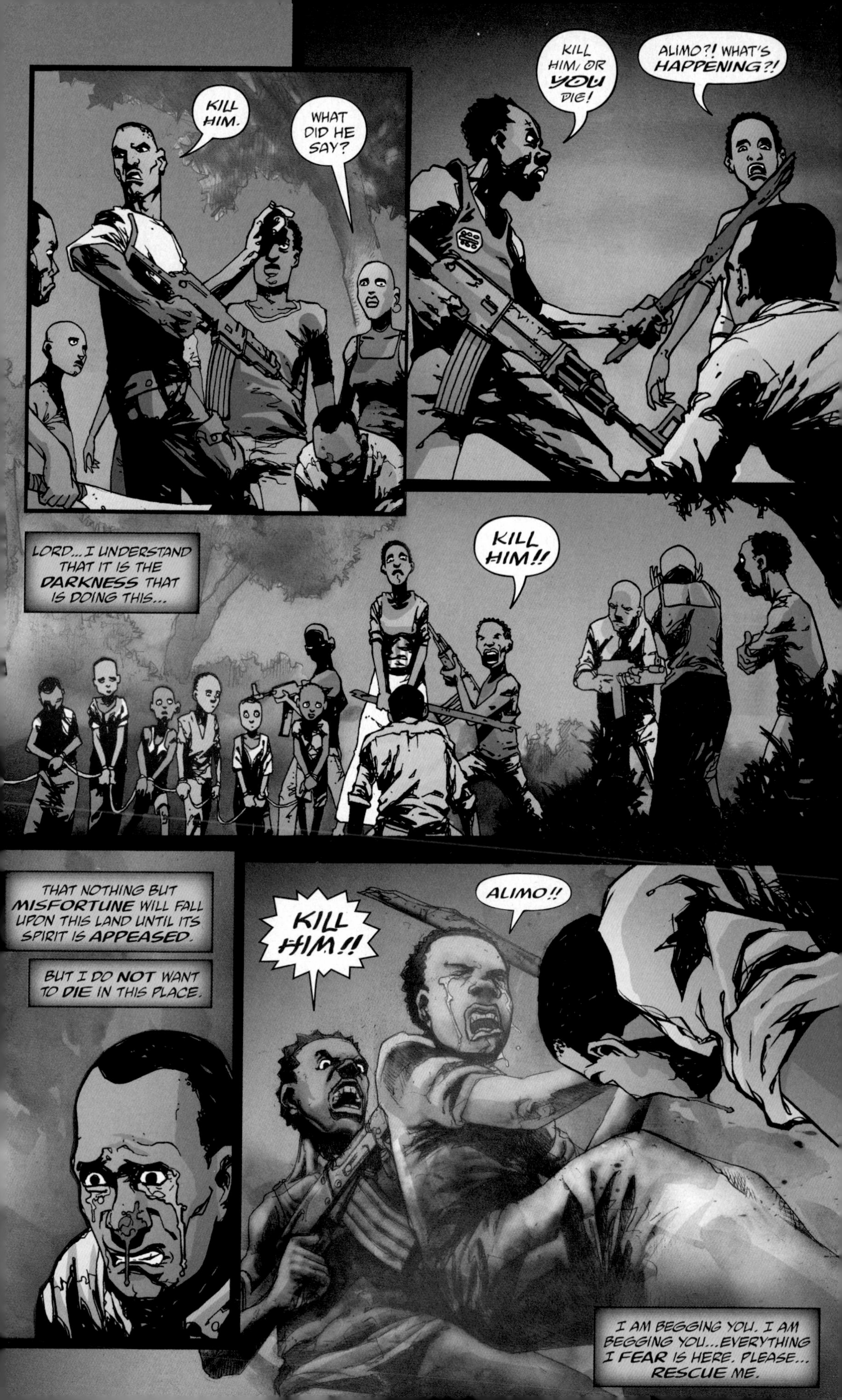
KILL HIM.
WHAT DID HE SAY?
KILL HIM, OR YOU DIE!
ALIMO?! WHAT'S HAPPENING?!
LORD... I UNDERSTAND THAT IT IS THE DARKNESS THAT IS DOING THIS...
KILL HIM!!
THAT NOTHING BUT MISFORTUNE WILL FALL UPON THIS LAND UNTIL ITS SPIRIT IS APPEASED.
BUT I DO NOT WANT TO DIE IN THIS PLACE.
KILL HIM!!
ALIMO!!
I AM BEGGING YOU. I AM BEGGING YOU... EVERYTHING I FEAR IS HERE. PLEASE... RESCUE ME.

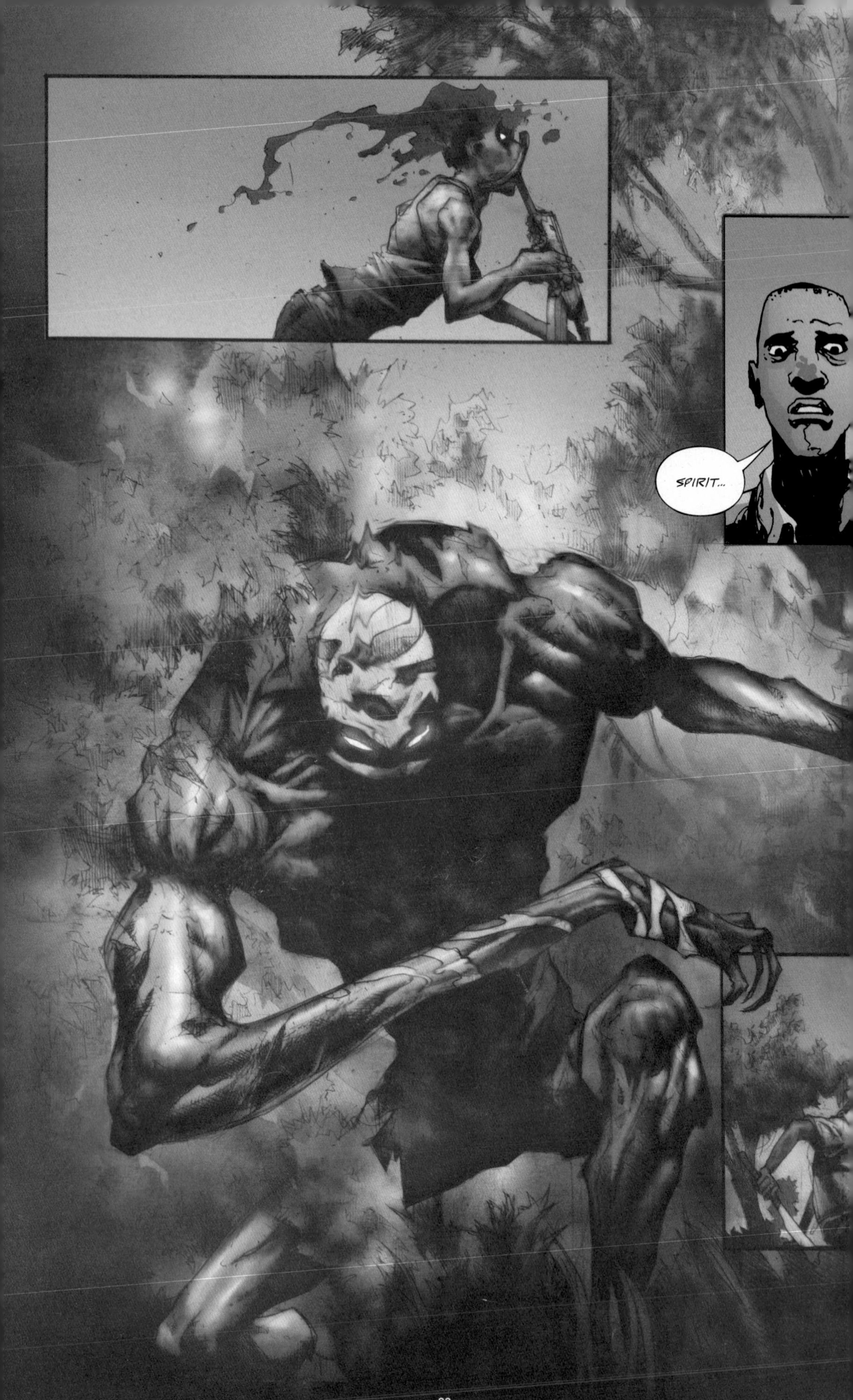
SPIRIT...

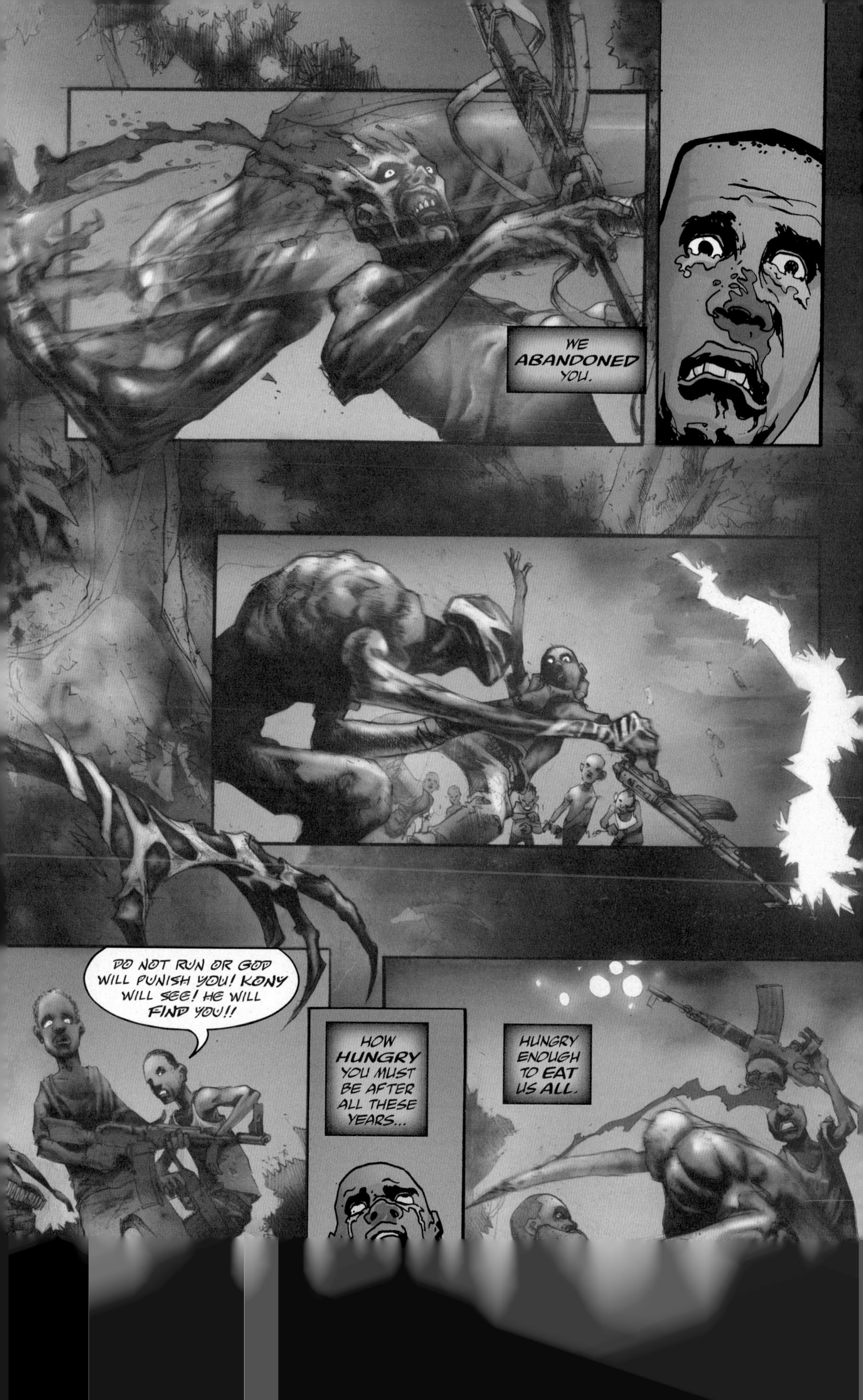
WE ABANDONED YOU.
DO NOT RUN OR GOD WILL PUNISH YOU! KONY WILL SEE! HE WILL FIND YOU!!
HOW HUNGRY YOU MUST BE AFTER ALL THESE YEARS...
HUNGRY ENOUGH TO EAT US ALL.

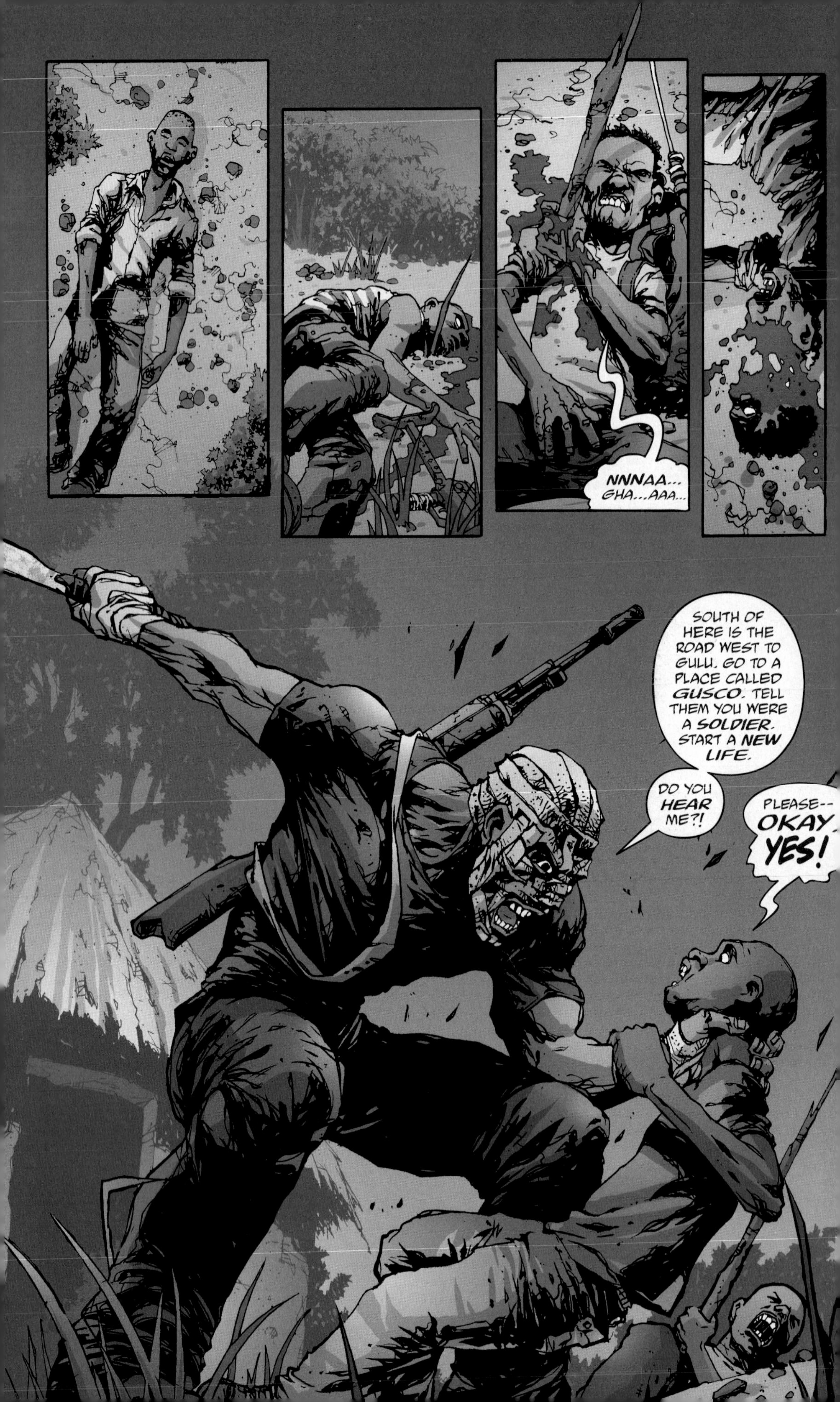
NNNAA...
GHA...AAA...
SOUTH OF HERE IS THE ROAD WEST TO GULU. GO TO A PLACE CALLED GUSCO. TELL THEM YOU WERE A SOLDIER. START A NEW LIFE.
DO YOU HEAR ME?!
PLEASE-- OKAY YES!

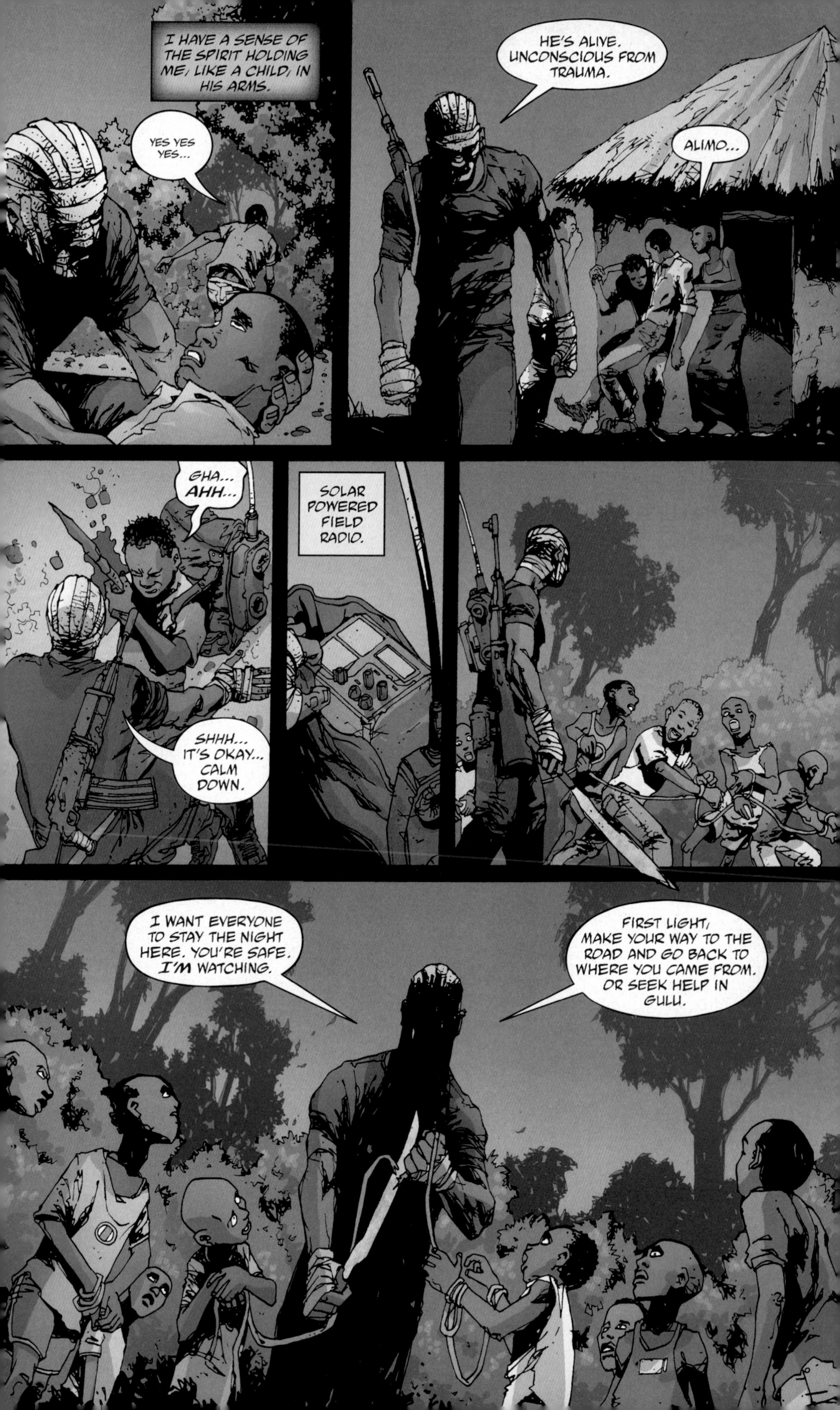
I HAVE A SENSE OF THE SPIRIT HOLDING ME, LIKE A CHILD, IN HIS ARMS.
YES YES YES...
HE'S ALIVE. UNCONSCIOUS FROM TRAUMA.
ALIMO...
GHA... AHH...
SHHH... IT'S OKAY... CALM DOWN.
SOLAR POWERED FIELD RADIO.
I WANT EVERYONE TO STAY THE NIGHT HERE. YOU'RE SAFE. I'M WATCHING.
FIRST LIGHT, MAKE YOUR WAY TO THE ROAD AND GO BACK TO WHERE YOU CAME FROM. OR SEEK HELP IN GULU.

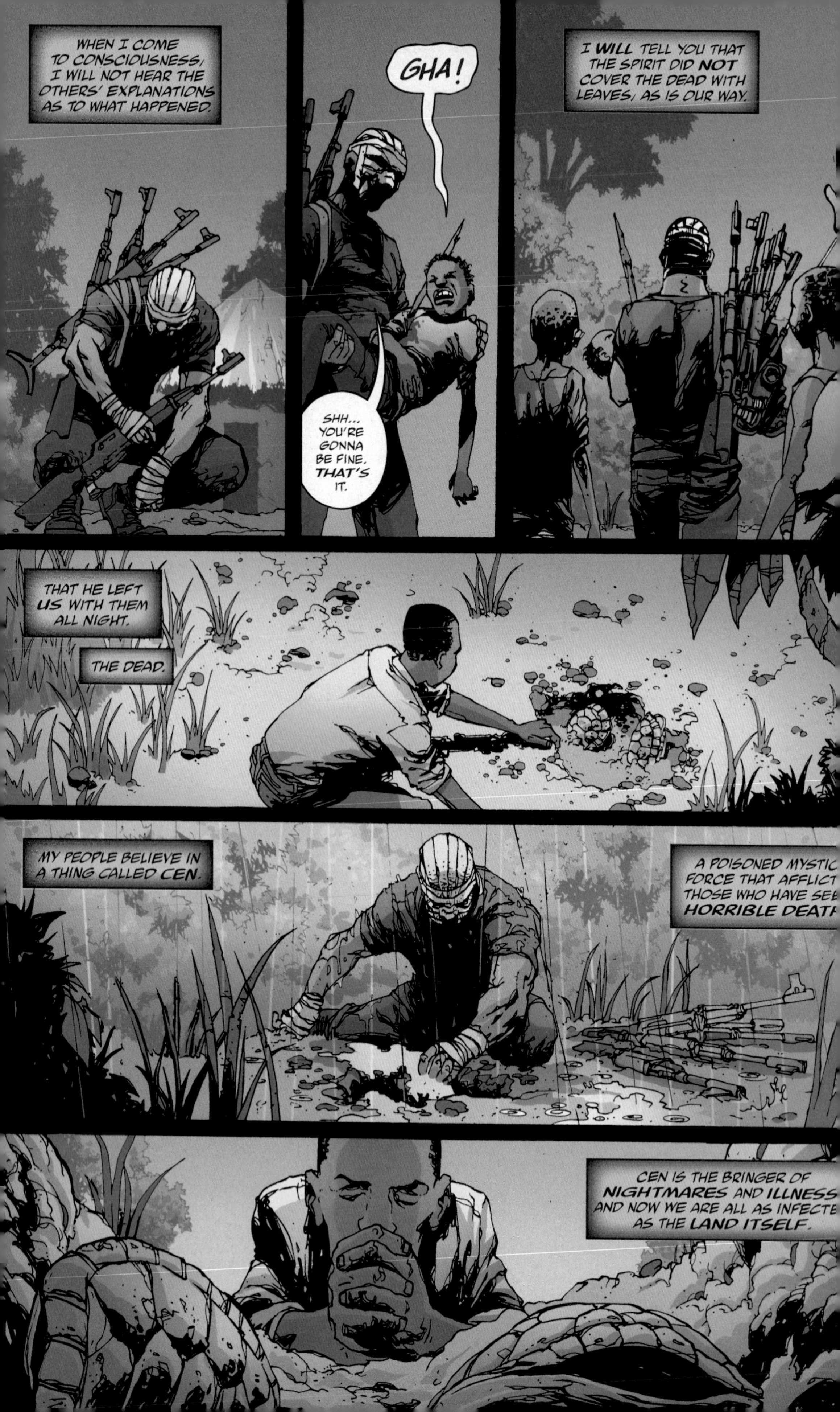
WHEN I COME TO CONSCIOUSNESS, I WILL NOT HEAR THE OTHERS' EXPLANATIONS AS TO WHAT HAPPENED.
GHA!
SHH... YOU'RE GONNA BE FINE. THAT'S IT.
I WILL TELL YOU THAT THE SPIRIT DID NOT COVER THE DEAD WITH LEAVES, AS IS OUR WAY.
THAT HE LEFT US WITH THEM ALL NIGHT.
THE DEAD.
MY PEOPLE BELIEVE IN A THING CALLED CEN.
A POISONED MYSTIC FORCE THAT AFFLICT THOSE WHO HAVE SE HORRIBLE DEAT
CEN IS THE BRINGER OF NIGHTMARES AND ILLNESS AND NOW WE ARE ALL AS INFECTE AS THE LAND ITSELF.

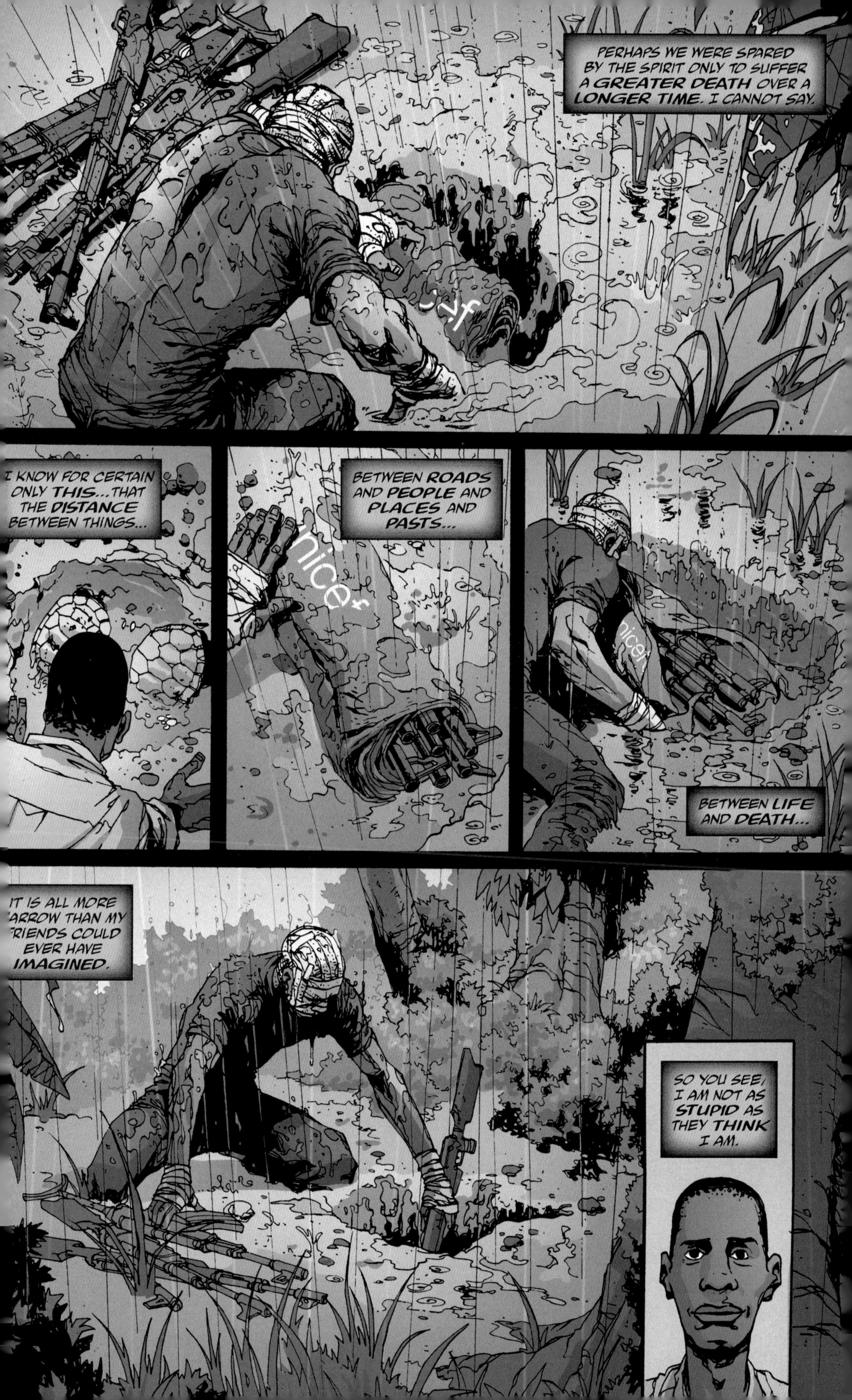

PERHAPS WE WERE SPARED BY THE SPIRIT ONLY TO SUFFER A GREATER DEATH OVER A LONGER TIME. I CANNOT SAY.
I KNOW FOR CERTAIN ONLY THIS...THAT THE DISTANCE BETWEEN THINGS...
BETWEEN ROADS AND PEOPLE AND PLACES AND PASTS...
BETWEEN LIFE AND DEATH...
IT IS ALL MORE NARROW THAN MY FRIENDS COULD EVER HAVE IMAGINED.
SO YOU SEE, I AM NOT AS STUPID AS THEY THINK I AM.

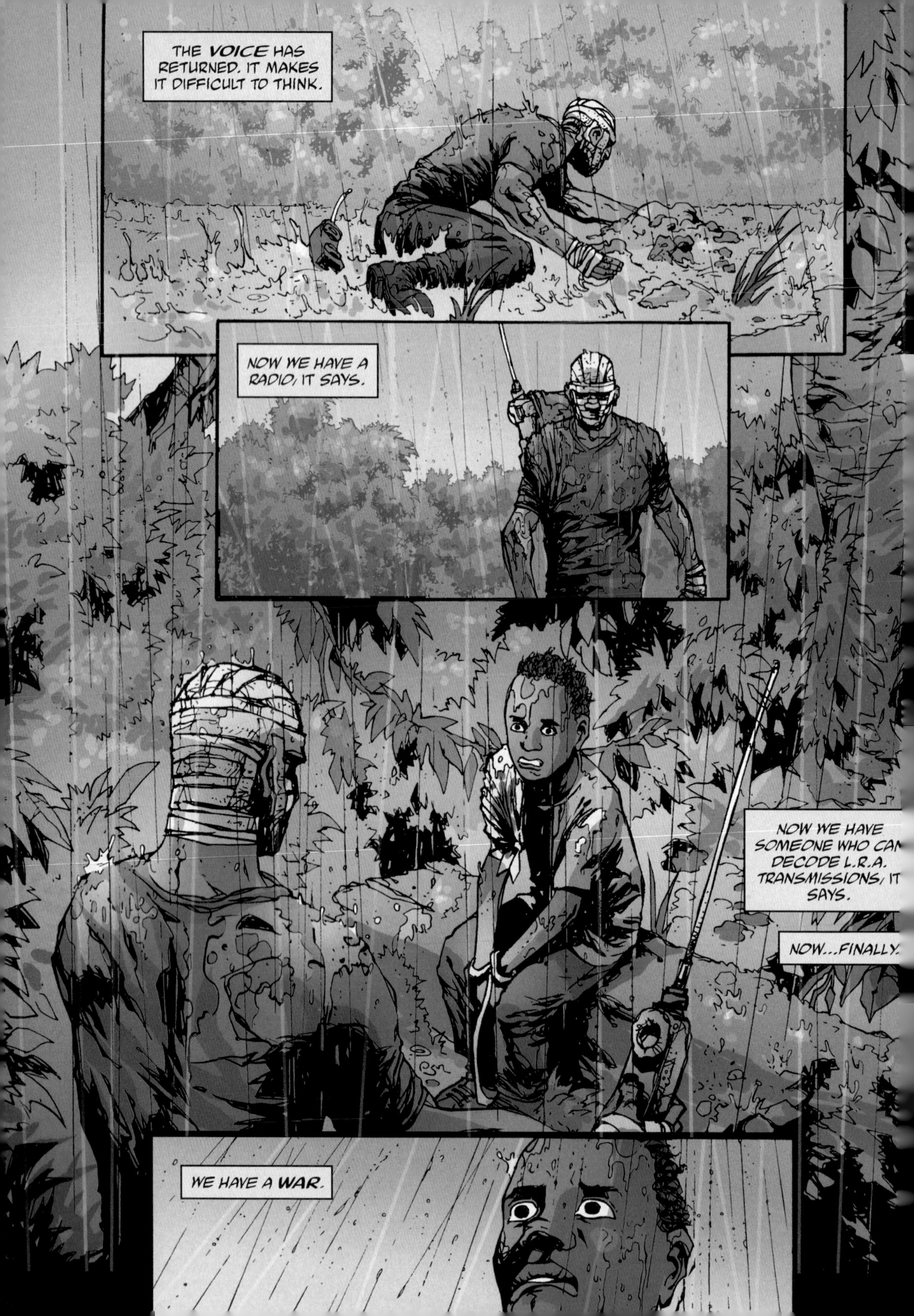
THE VOICE HAS RETURNED. IT MAKES IT DIFFICULT TO THINK.
NOW WE HAVE A RADIO, IT SAYS.
NOW WE HAVE SOMEONE WHO CAN DECODE L.R.A. TRANSMISSIONS, IT SAYS.
NOW...FINALLY.
WE HAVE A WAR.

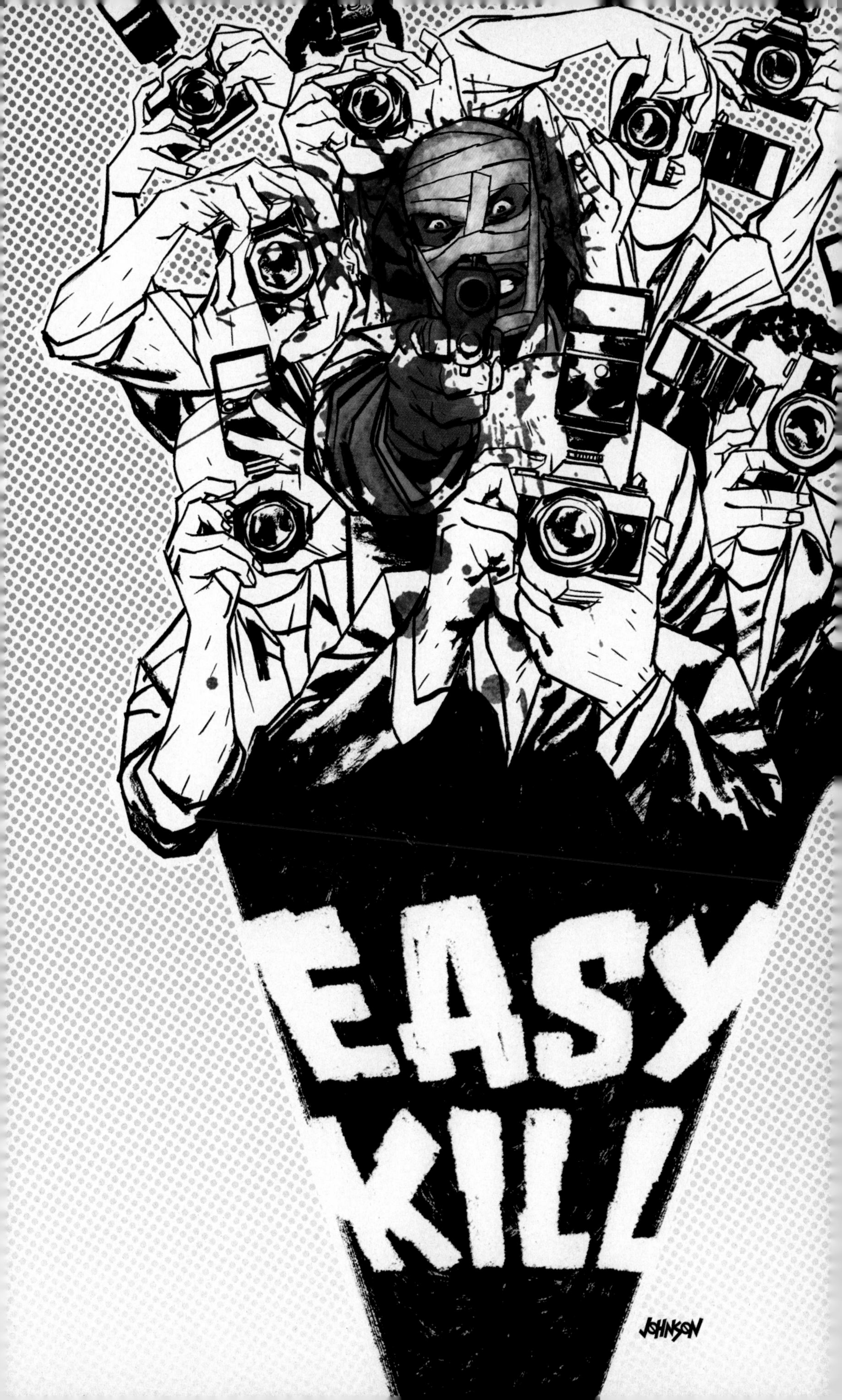
EASY
KILL
JOHNSON

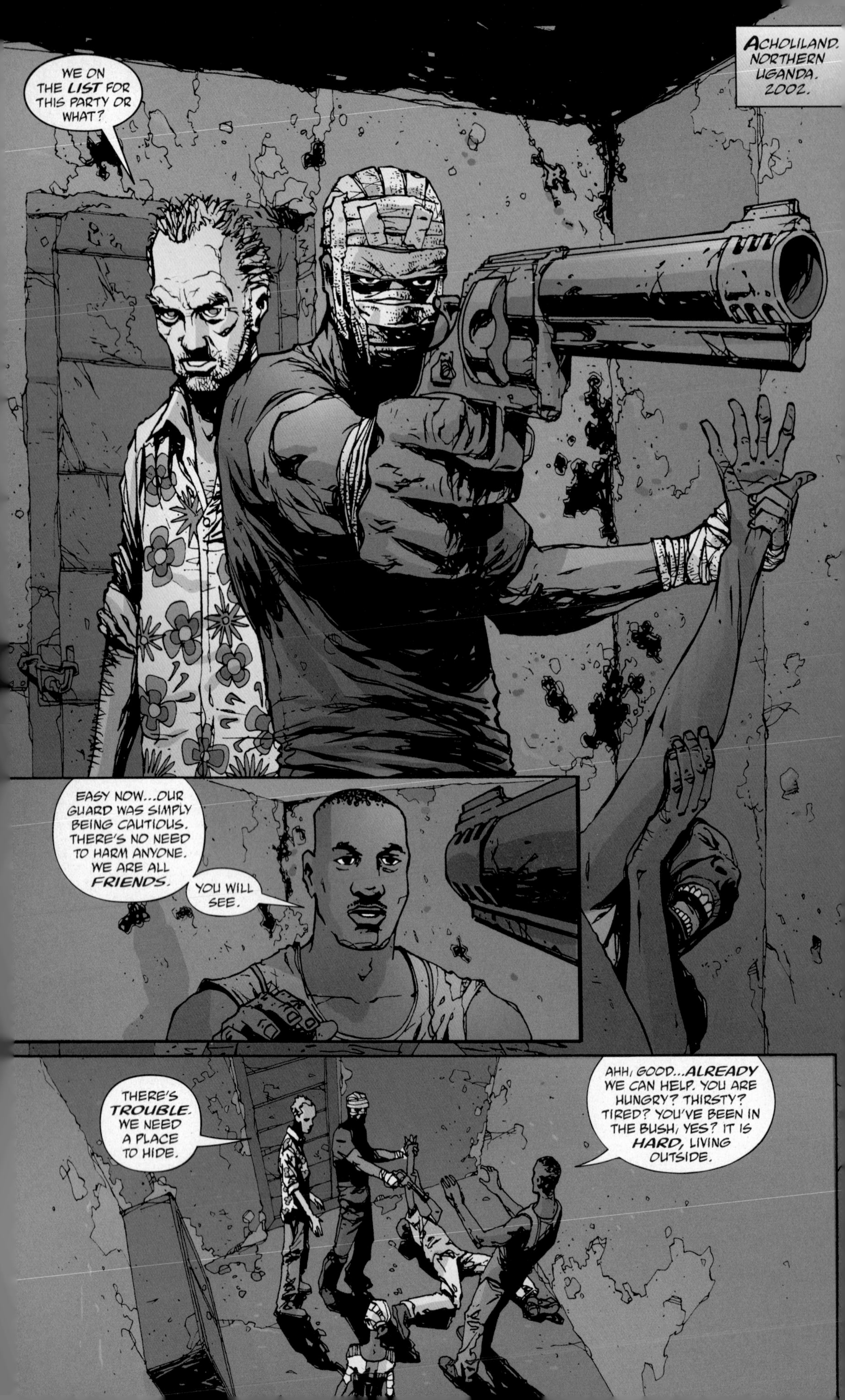
ACHOLILAND. NORTHERN UGANDA. 2002.
WE ON THE LIST FOR THIS PARTY OR WHAT?
EASY NOW...OUR GUARD WAS SIMPLY BEING CAUTIOUS. THERE'S NO NEED TO HARM ANYONE. WE ARE ALL FRIENDS.
YOU WILL SEE.
THERE'S TROUBLE. WE NEED A PLACE TO HIDE.
AHH, GOOD...ALREADY WE CAN HELP. YOU ARE HUNGRY? THIRSTY? TIRED? YOU'VE BEEN IN THE BUSH, YES? IT IS HARD, LIVING OUTSIDE.

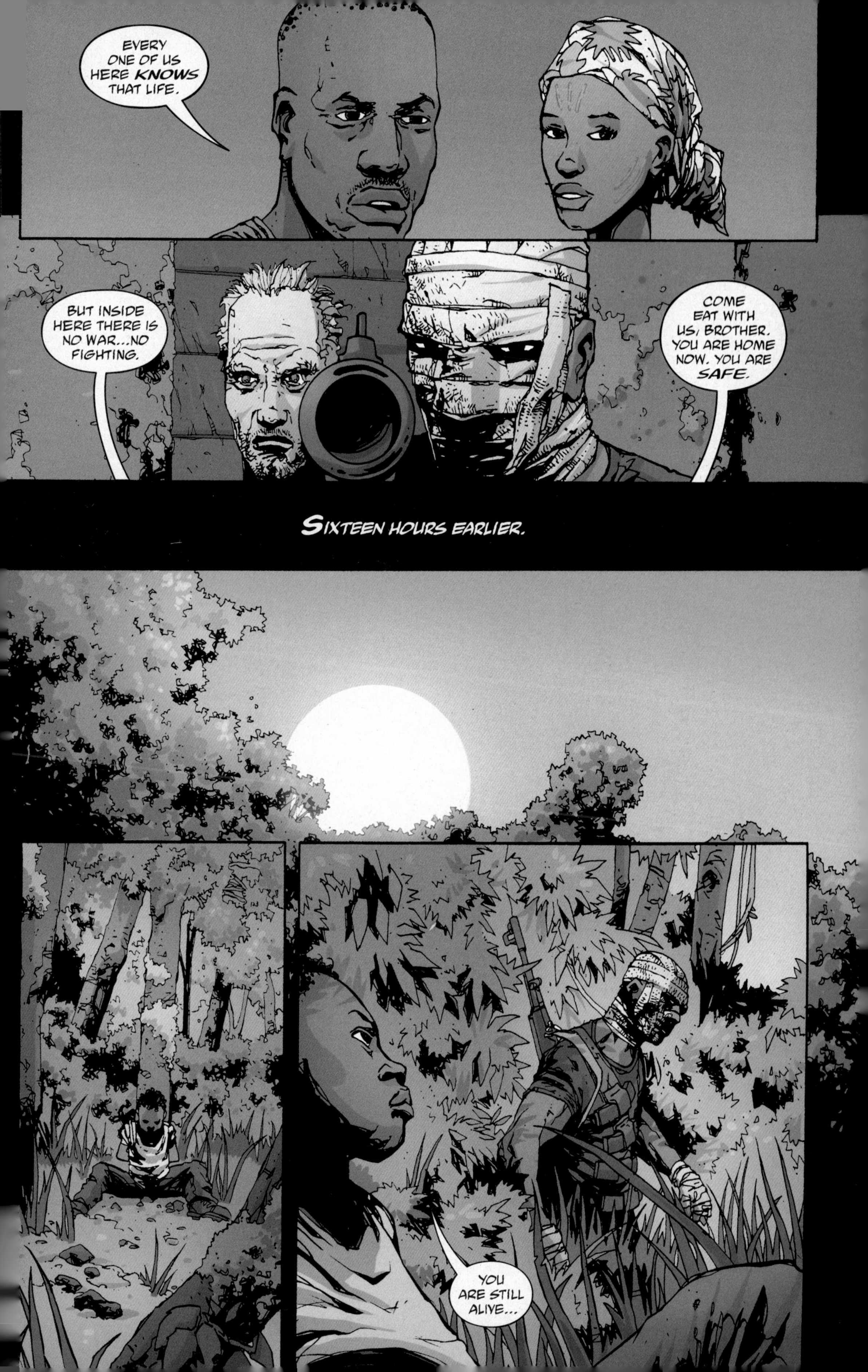
EVERY ONE OF US HERE KNOWS THAT LIFE.
BUT INSIDE HERE THERE IS NO WAR...NO FIGHTING.
COME EAT WITH US, BROTHER. YOU ARE HOME NOW. YOU ARE SAFE.
SIXTEEN HOURS EARLIER.
YOU ARE STILL ALIVE...

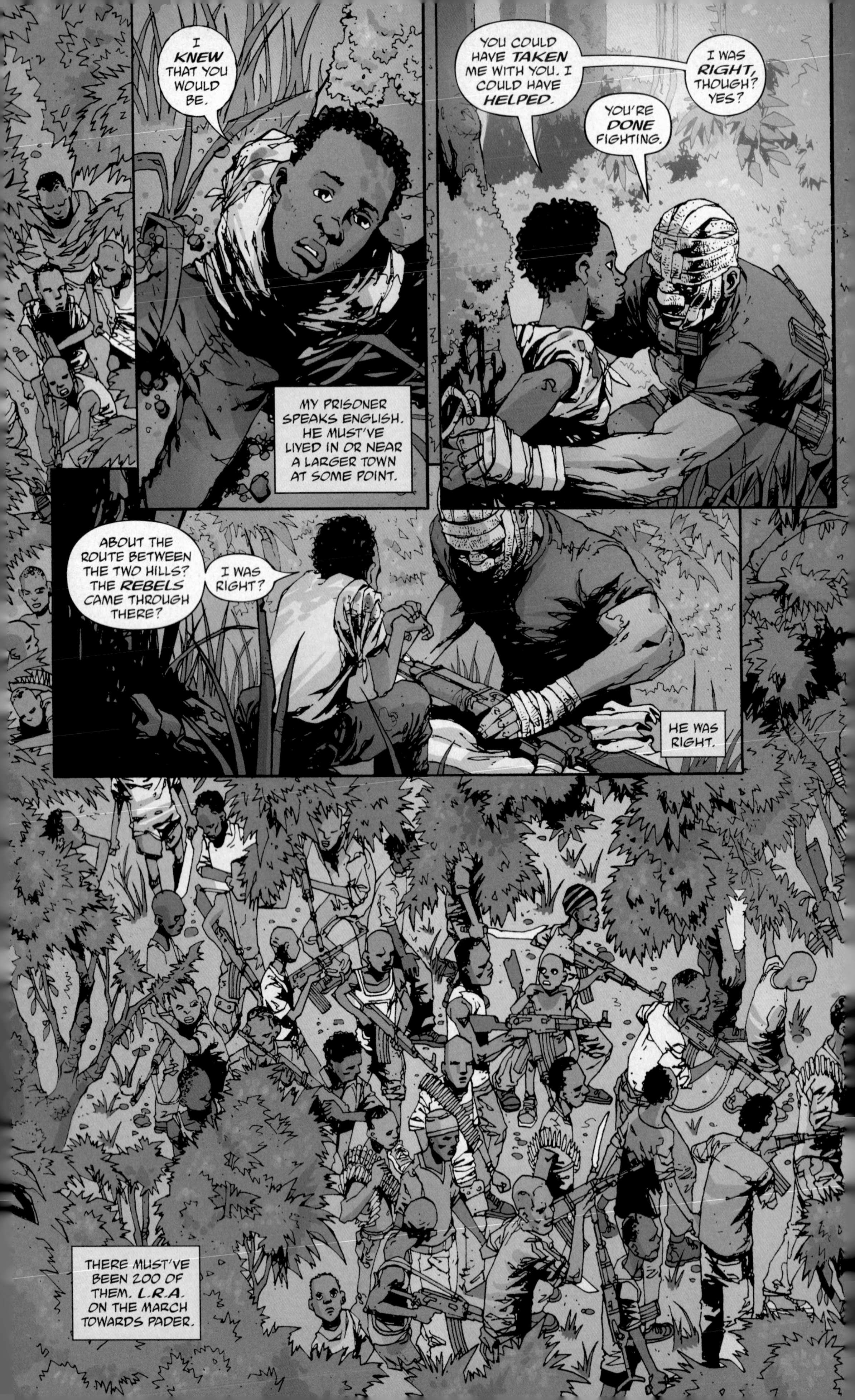
I KNEW THAT YOU WOULD BE.
MY PRISONER SPEAKS ENGLISH. HE MUST'VE LIVED IN OR NEAR A LARGER TOWN AT SOME POINT.
YOU COULD HAVE TAKEN ME WITH YOU. I COULD HAVE HELPED.
I WAS RIGHT, THOUGH? YES?
YOU'RE DONE FIGHTING.
ABOUT THE ROUTE BETWEEN THE TWO HILLS? THE REBELS CAME THROUGH THERE?
I WAS RIGHT?
HE WAS RIGHT.
THERE MUST'VE BEEN 200 OF THEM. L.R.A. ON THE MARCH TOWARDS PADER.

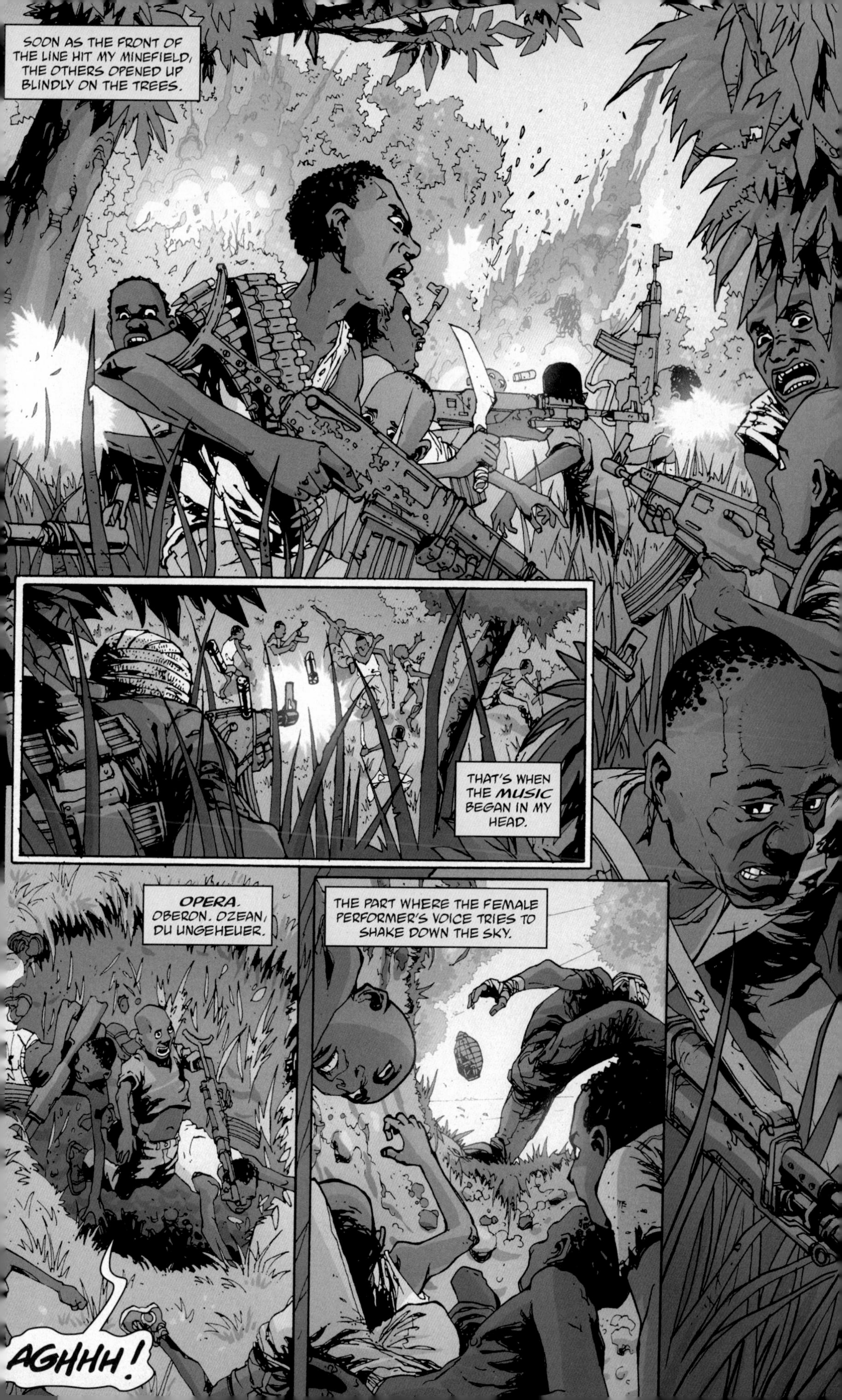
SOON AS THE FRONT OF THE LINE HIT MY MINEFIELD, THE OTHERS OPENED UP BLINDLY ON THE TREES.
THAT'S WHEN THE MUSIC BEGAN IN MY HEAD.
OPERA. OBERON. OZEAN, DU UNGEHEUER.
AGHHH!
THE PART WHERE THE FEMALE PERFORMER'S VOICE TRIES TO SHAKE DOWN THE SKY.

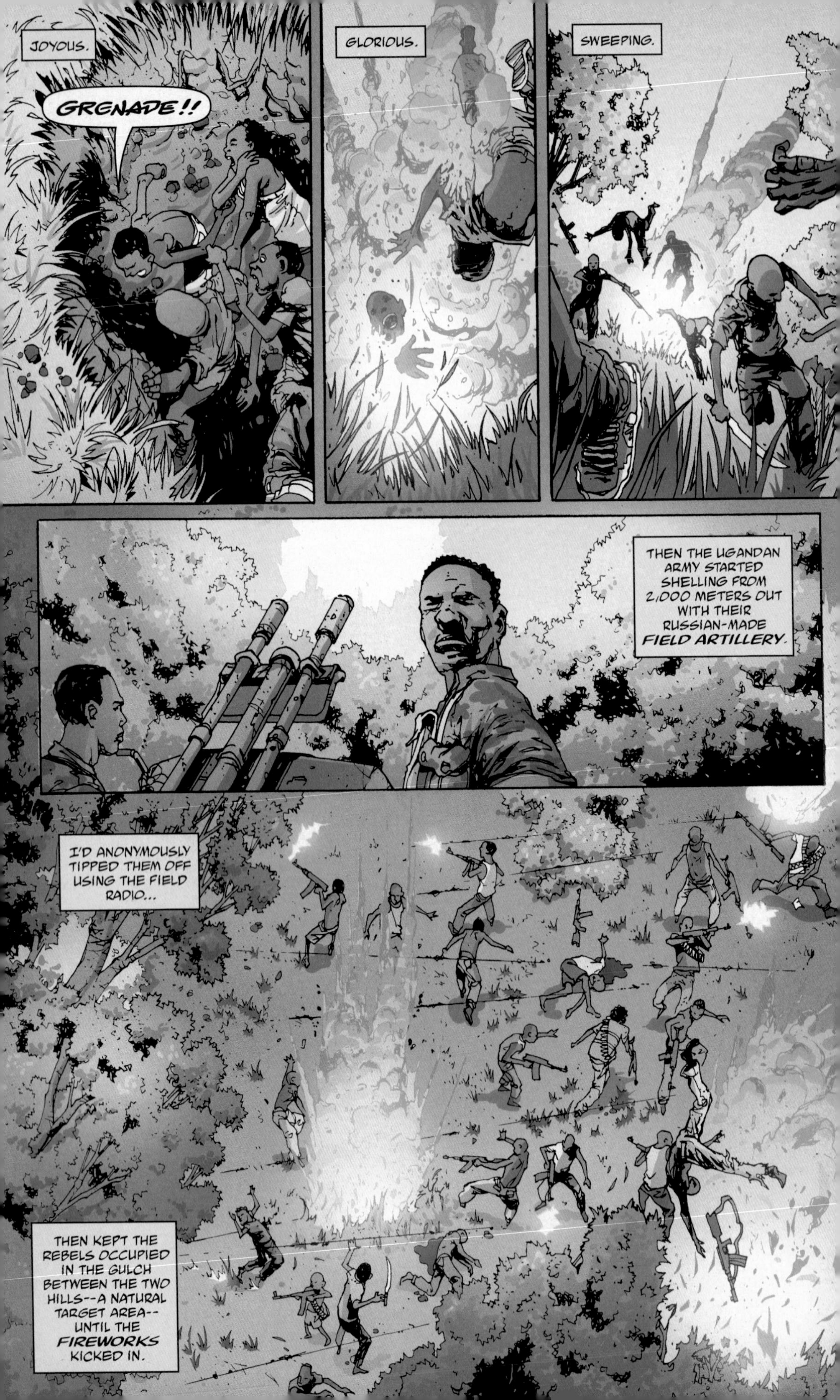
JOYOUS.
GRENADE!!
GLORIOUS.
SWEEPING.
THEN THE UGANDAN ARMY STARTED SHELLING FROM 2,000 METERS OUT WITH THEIR RUSSIAN-MADE FIELD ARTILLERY.
I'D ANONYMOUSLY TIPPED THEM OFF USING THE FIELD RADIO...
THEN KEPT THE REBELS OCCUPIED IN THE GULCH BETWEEN THE TWO HILLS--A NATURAL TARGET AREA--UNTIL THE FIREWORKS KICKED IN.

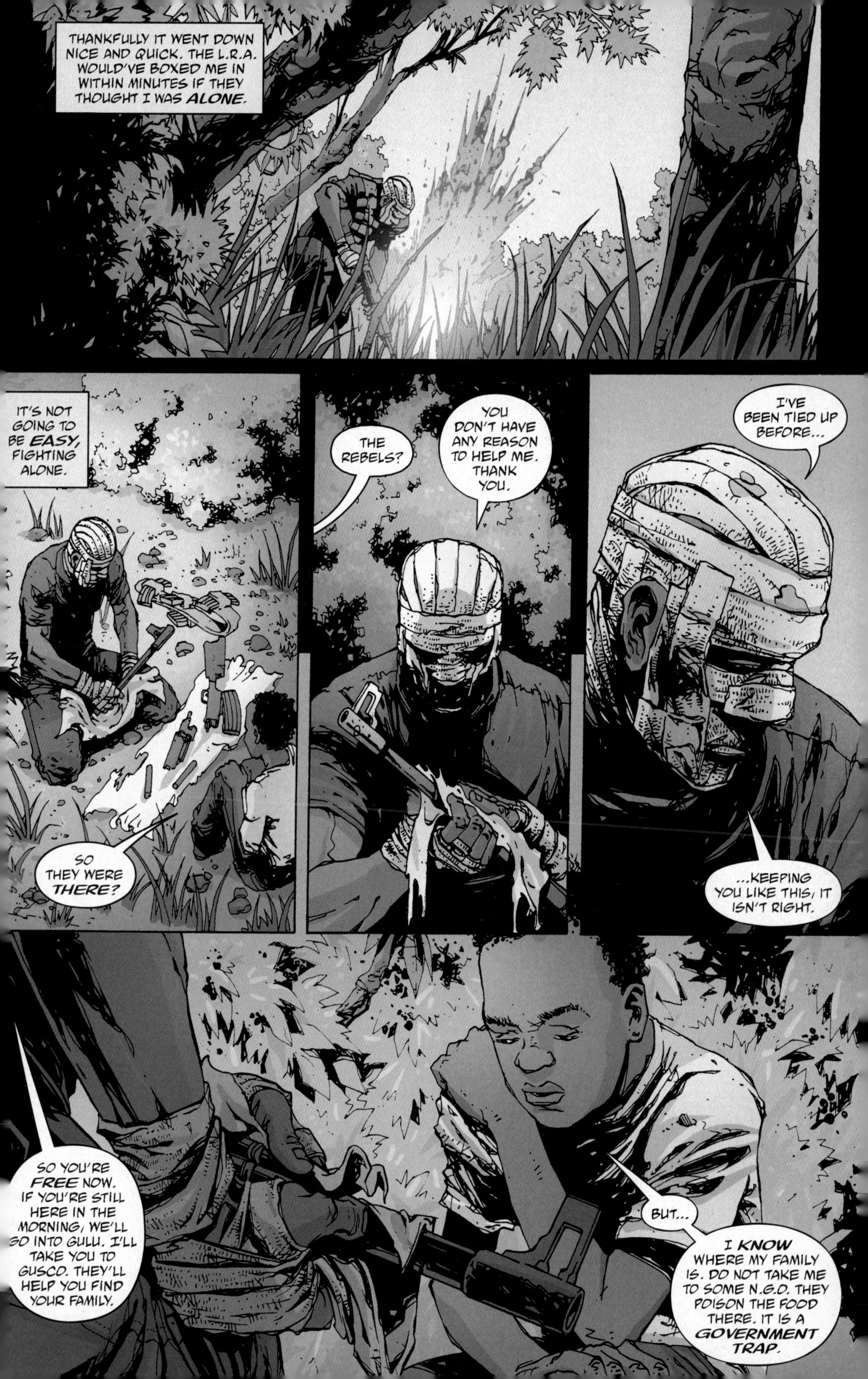
THANKFULLY IT WENT DOWN NICE AND QUICK. THE L.R.A. WOULD'VE BOXED ME IN WITHIN MINUTES IF THEY THOUGHT I WAS ALONE.
IT'S NOT GOING TO BE EASY, FIGHTING ALONE.
SO THEY WERE THERE?
THE REBELS?
YOU DON'T HAVE ANY REASON TO HELP ME. THANK YOU.
I'VE BEEN TIED UP BEFORE...
...KEEPING YOU LIKE THIS, IT ISN'T RIGHT.
SO YOU'RE FREE NOW. IF YOU'RE STILL HERE IN THE MORNING, WE'LL GO INTO GULU. I'LL TAKE YOU TO GUSCO. THEY'LL HELP YOU FIND YOUR FAMILY.
BUT...
I KNOW WHERE MY FAMILY IS. DO NOT TAKE ME TO SOME N.G.O. THEY POISON THE FOOD THERE. IT IS A GOVERNMENT TRAP.

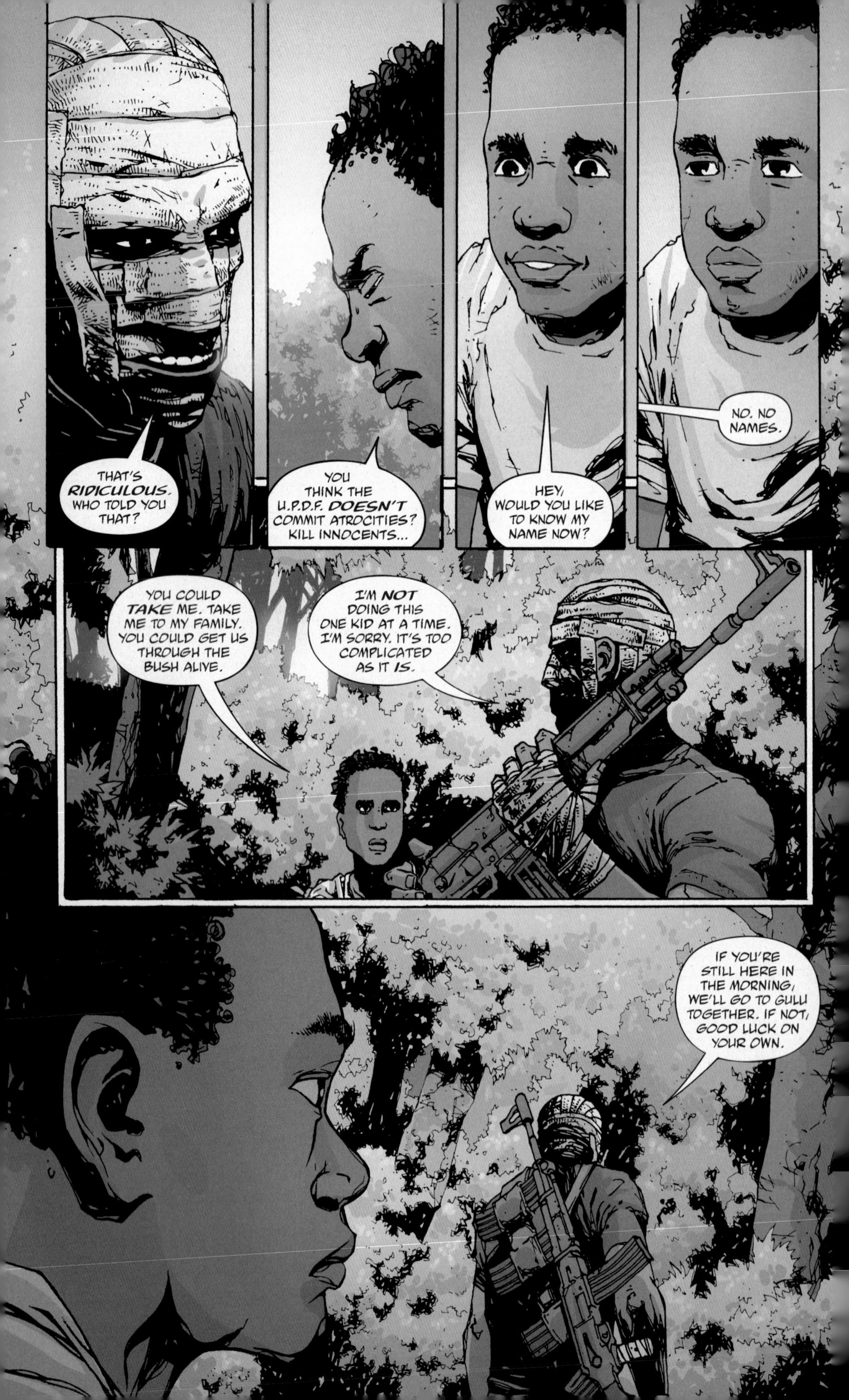
THAT'S RIDICULOUS. WHO TOLD YOU THAT?
YOU THINK THE U.P.D.F. DOESN'T COMMIT ATROCITIES? KILL INNOCENTS...
HEY, WOULD YOU LIKE TO KNOW MY NAME NOW?
NO. NO NAMES.
YOU COULD TAKE ME. TAKE ME TO MY FAMILY. YOU COULD GET US THROUGH THE BUSH ALIVE.
I'M NOT DOING THIS ONE KID AT A TIME. I'M SORRY. IT'S TOO COMPLICATED AS IT IS.
IF YOU'RE STILL HERE IN THE MORNING, WE'LL GO TO GULU TOGETHER. IF NOT, GOOD LUCK ON YOUR OWN.

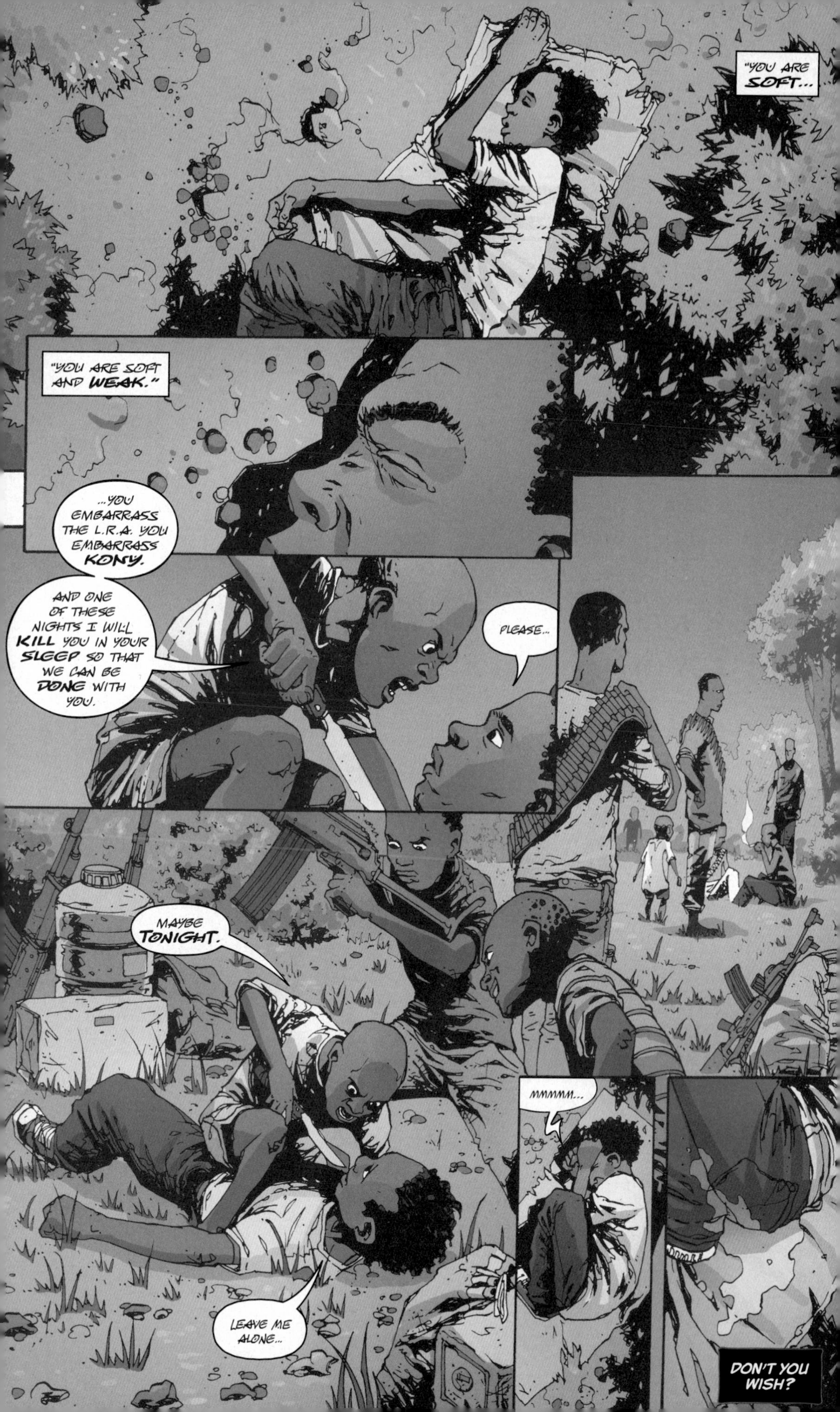
"YOU ARE SOFT...
"YOU ARE SOFT AND WEAK."
...YOU EMBARRASS THE L.R.A. YOU EMBARRASS KONY.
AND ONE OF THESE NIGHTS I WILL KILL YOU IN YOUR SLEEP SO THAT WE CAN BE DONE WITH YOU.
PLEASE...
MAYBE TONIGHT.
LEAVE ME ALONE...
MMMMM...
DON'T YOU WISH?

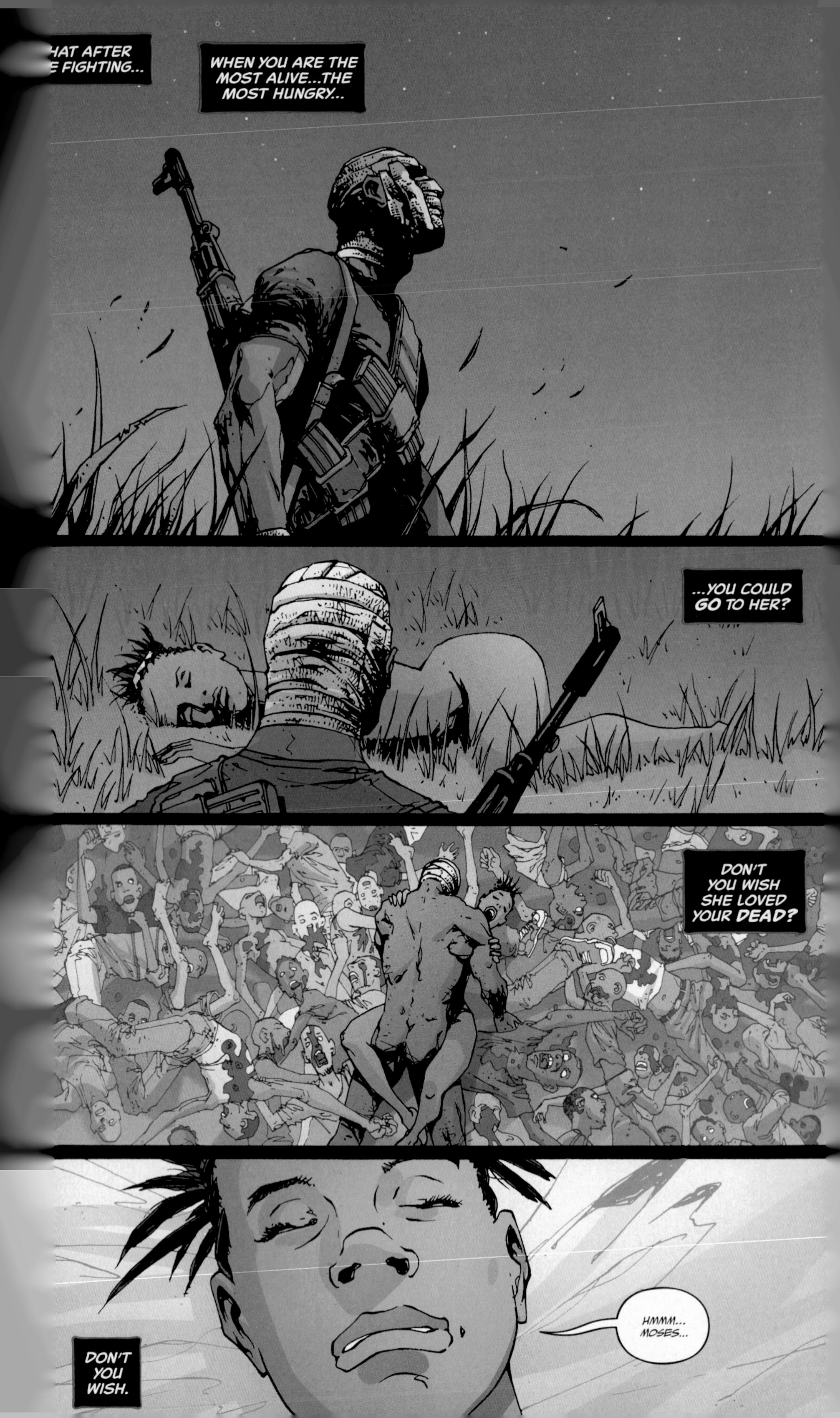
HAT AFTER
E FIGHTING...
WHEN YOU ARE THE MOST ALIVE...THE MOST HUNGRY...
...YOU COULD GO TO HER?
DON'T YOU WISH SHE LOVED YOUR DEAD?
HMMM... MOSES...
DON'T YOU WISH.

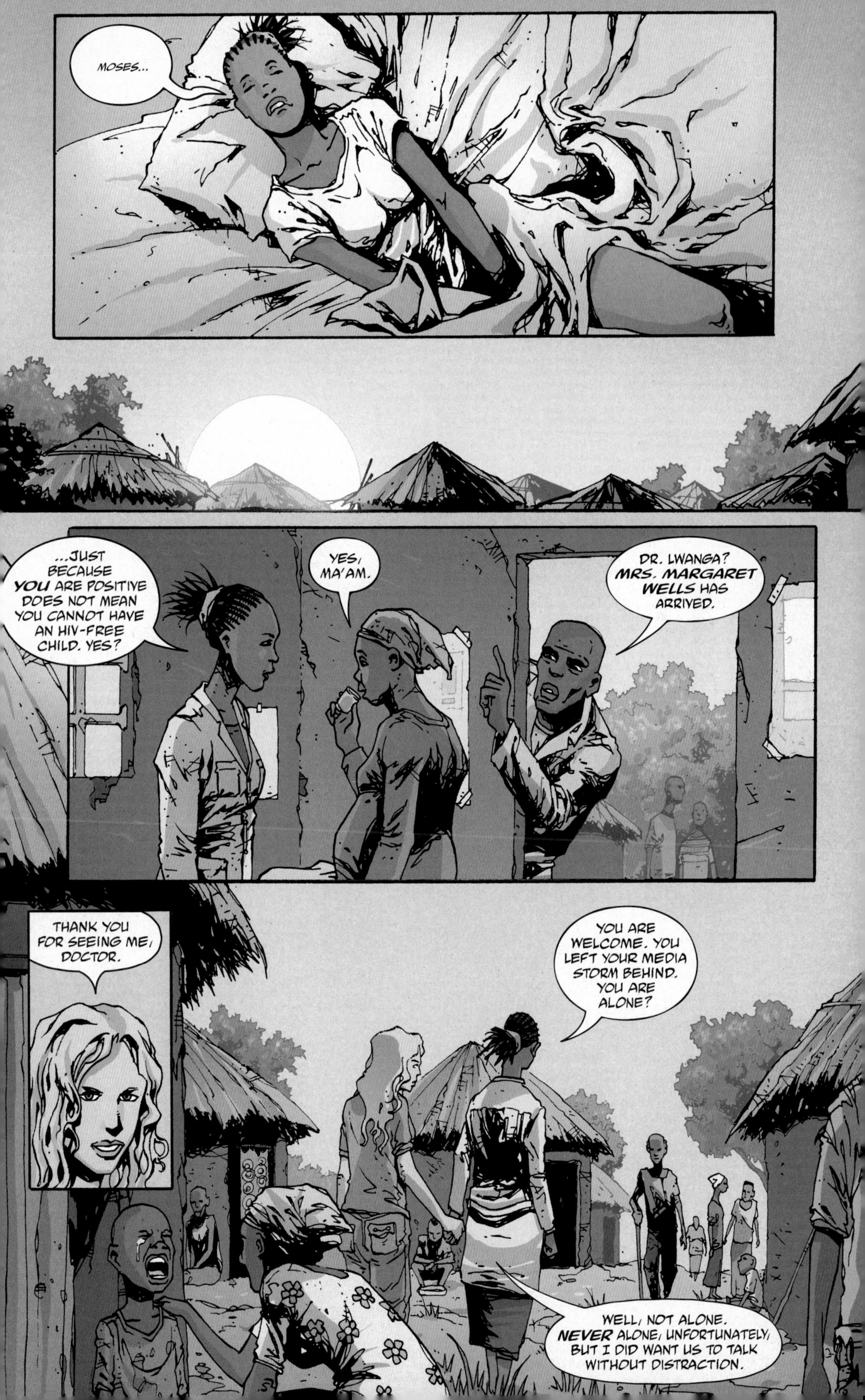

MOSES...
...JUST BECAUSE **YOU** ARE POSITIVE DOES NOT MEAN YOU CANNOT HAVE AN HIV-FREE CHILD. YES?
YES, MA'AM.
DR. LWANGA? **MRS. MARGARET WELLS** HAS ARRIVED.
THANK YOU FOR SEEING ME, DOCTOR.
YOU ARE WELCOME. YOU LEFT YOUR MEDIA STORM BEHIND. YOU ARE ALONE?
WELL, NOT ALONE. **NEVER** ALONE, UNFORTUNATELY, BUT I DID WANT US TO TALK WITHOUT DISTRACTION.

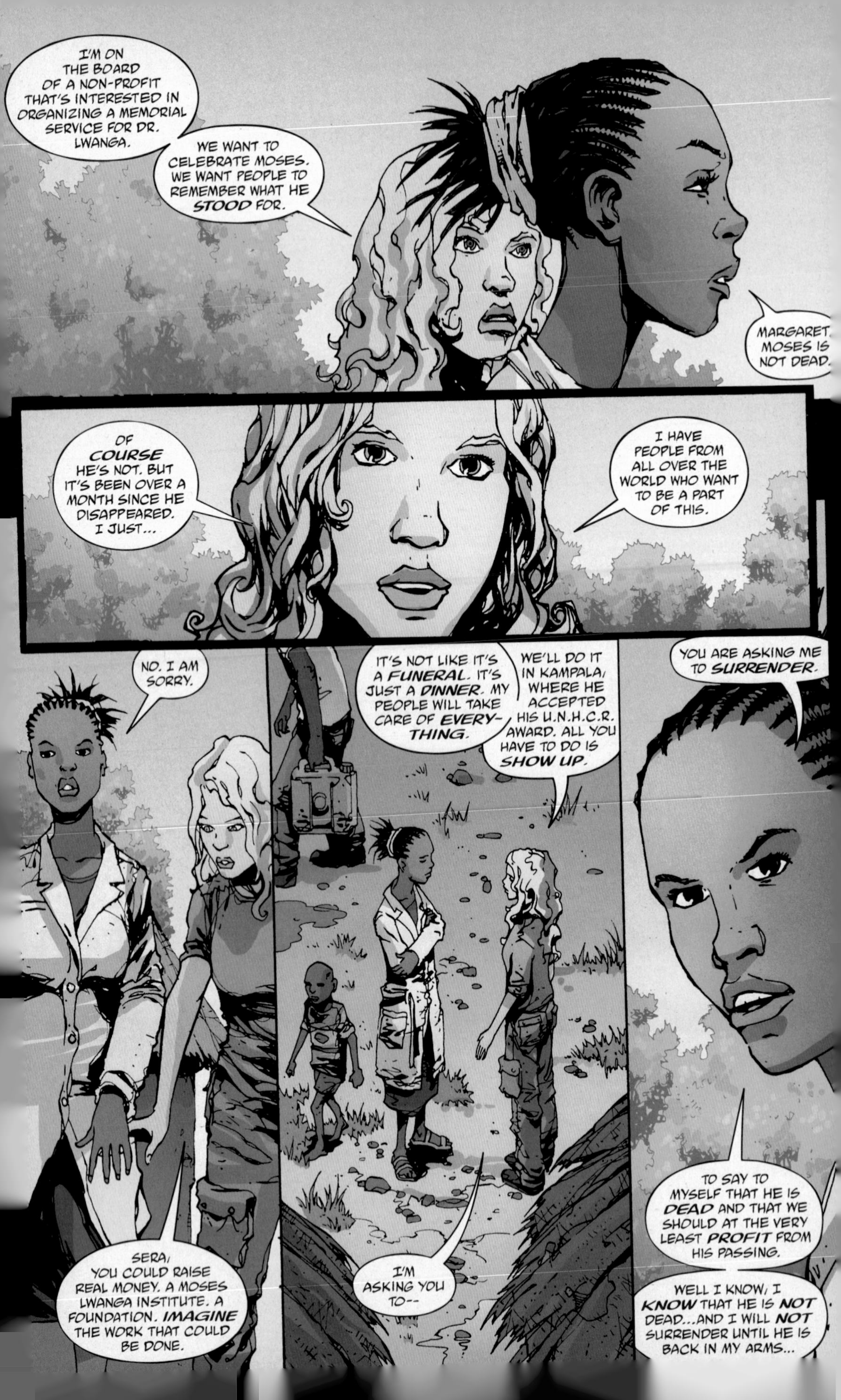

I'M ON THE BOARD OF A NON-PROFIT THAT'S INTERESTED IN ORGANIZING A MEMORIAL SERVICE FOR DR. LWANGA.
WE WANT TO CELEBRATE MOSES. WE WANT PEOPLE TO REMEMBER WHAT HE STOOD FOR.
MARGARET. MOSES IS NOT DEAD.
OF COURSE HE'S NOT. BUT IT'S BEEN OVER A MONTH SINCE HE DISAPPEARED. I JUST...
I HAVE PEOPLE FROM ALL OVER THE WORLD WHO WANT TO BE A PART OF THIS.
NO. I AM SORRY.
SERA, YOU COULD RAISE REAL MONEY. A MOSES LWANGA INSTITUTE. A FOUNDATION. IMAGINE THE WORK THAT COULD BE DONE.
IT'S NOT LIKE IT'S A FUNERAL. IT'S JUST A DINNER. MY PEOPLE WILL TAKE CARE OF EVERY-THING.
WE'LL DO IT IN KAMPALA, WHERE HE ACCEPTED HIS U.N.H.C.R. AWARD. ALL YOU HAVE TO DO IS SHOW UP.
I'M ASKING YOU TO--
YOU ARE ASKING ME TO SURRENDER.
TO SAY TO MYSELF THAT HE IS DEAD AND THAT WE SHOULD AT THE VERY LEAST PROFIT FROM HIS PASSING.
WELL I KNOW, I KNOW THAT HE IS NOT DEAD...AND I WILL NOT SURRENDER UNTIL HE IS BACK IN MY ARMS...

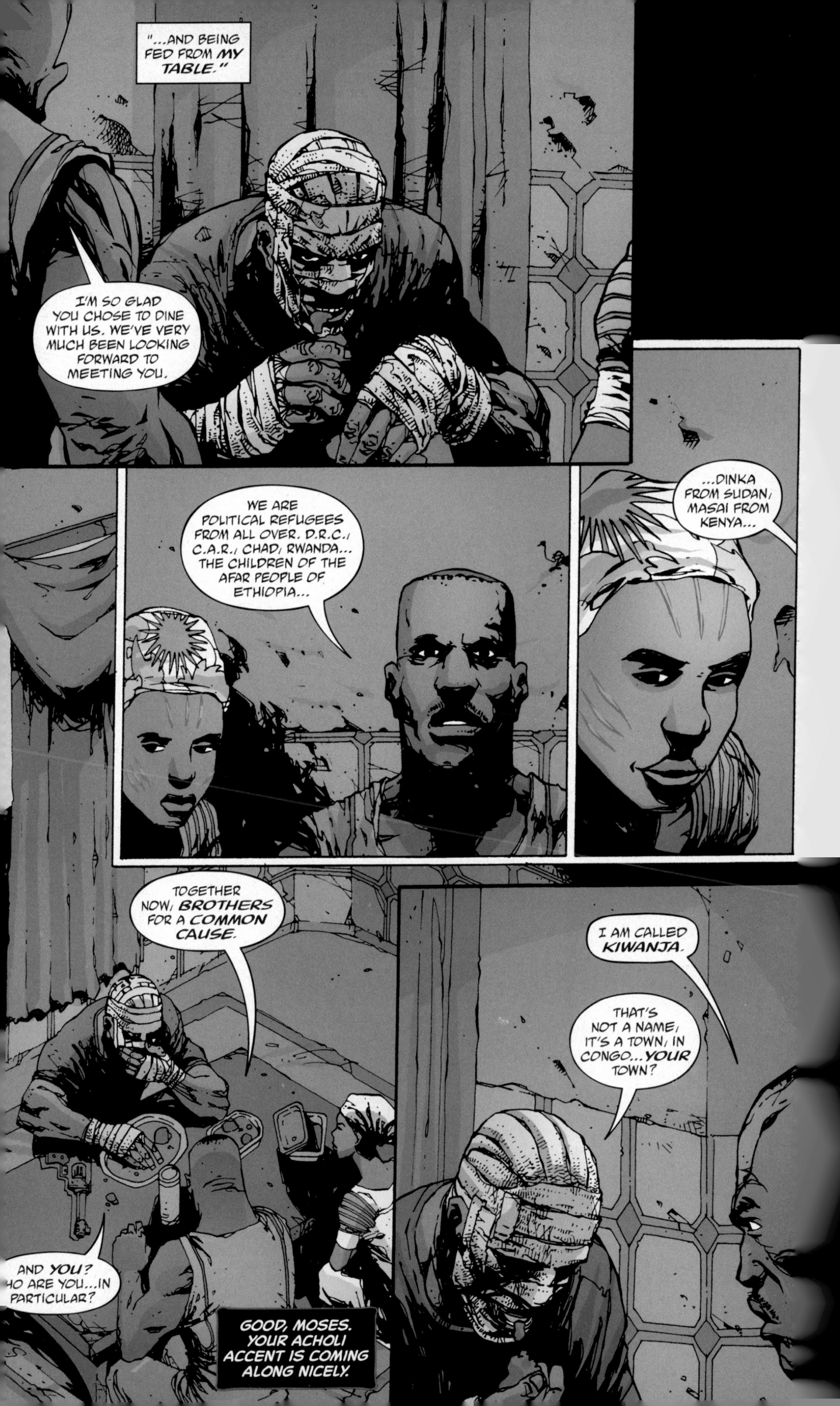
"...AND BEING FED FROM MY TABLE."
I'M SO GLAD YOU CHOSE TO DINE WITH US. WE'VE VERY MUCH BEEN LOOKING FORWARD TO MEETING YOU.
WE ARE POLITICAL REFUGEES FROM ALL OVER. D.R.C., C.A.R., CHAD, RWANDA... THE CHILDREN OF THE AFAR PEOPLE OF ETHIOPIA...
...DINKA FROM SUDAN, MASAI FROM KENYA...
TOGETHER NOW, BROTHERS FOR A COMMON CAUSE.
AND YOU? HO ARE YOU...IN PARTICULAR?
I AM CALLED KIWANJA.
THAT'S NOT A NAME, IT'S A TOWN, IN CONGO...YOUR TOWN?
GOOD, MOSES. YOUR ACHOLI ACCENT IS COMING ALONG NICELY.

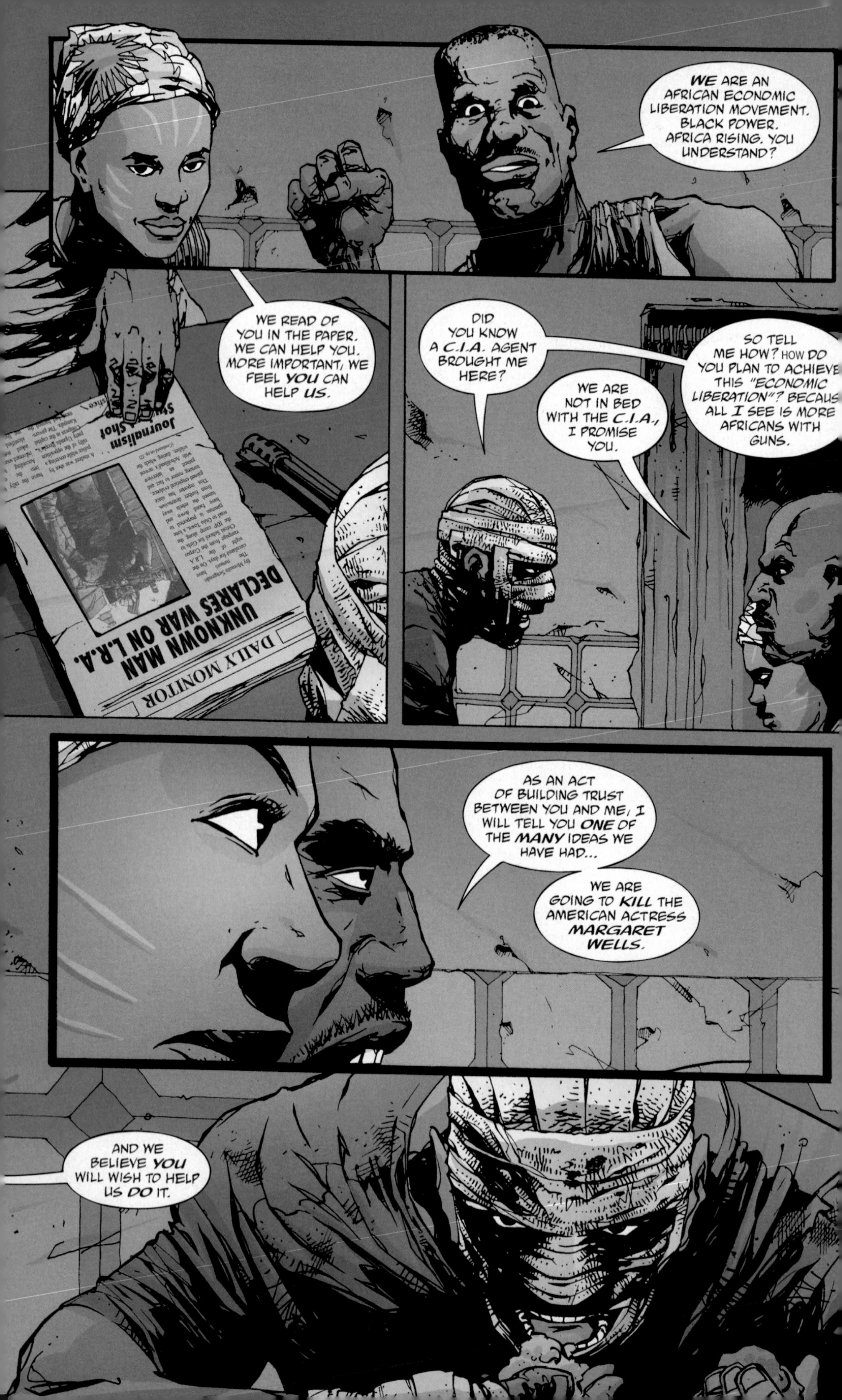
WE ARE AN AFRICAN ECONOMIC LIBERATION MOVEMENT. BLACK POWER. AFRICA RISING. YOU UNDERSTAND?
WE READ OF YOU IN THE PAPER. WE CAN HELP YOU. MORE IMPORTANT, WE FEEL YOU CAN HELP US.
DAILY MONITOR
UNKNOWN MAN DECLARES WAR ON L.R.A.
Journalism Shot
DID YOU KNOW A C.I.A. AGENT BROUGHT ME HERE?
WE ARE NOT IN BED WITH THE C.I.A., I PROMISE YOU.
SO TELL ME HOW? HOW DO YOU PLAN TO ACHIEVE THIS "ECONOMIC LIBERATION"? BECAUS ALL I SEE IS MORE AFRICANS WITH GUNS.
AS AN ACT OF BUILDING TRUST BETWEEN YOU AND ME, I WILL TELL YOU ONE OF THE MANY IDEAS WE HAVE HAD...
WE ARE GOING TO KILL THE AMERICAN ACTRESS MARGARET WELLS.
AND WE BELIEVE YOU WILL WISH TO HELP US DO IT.

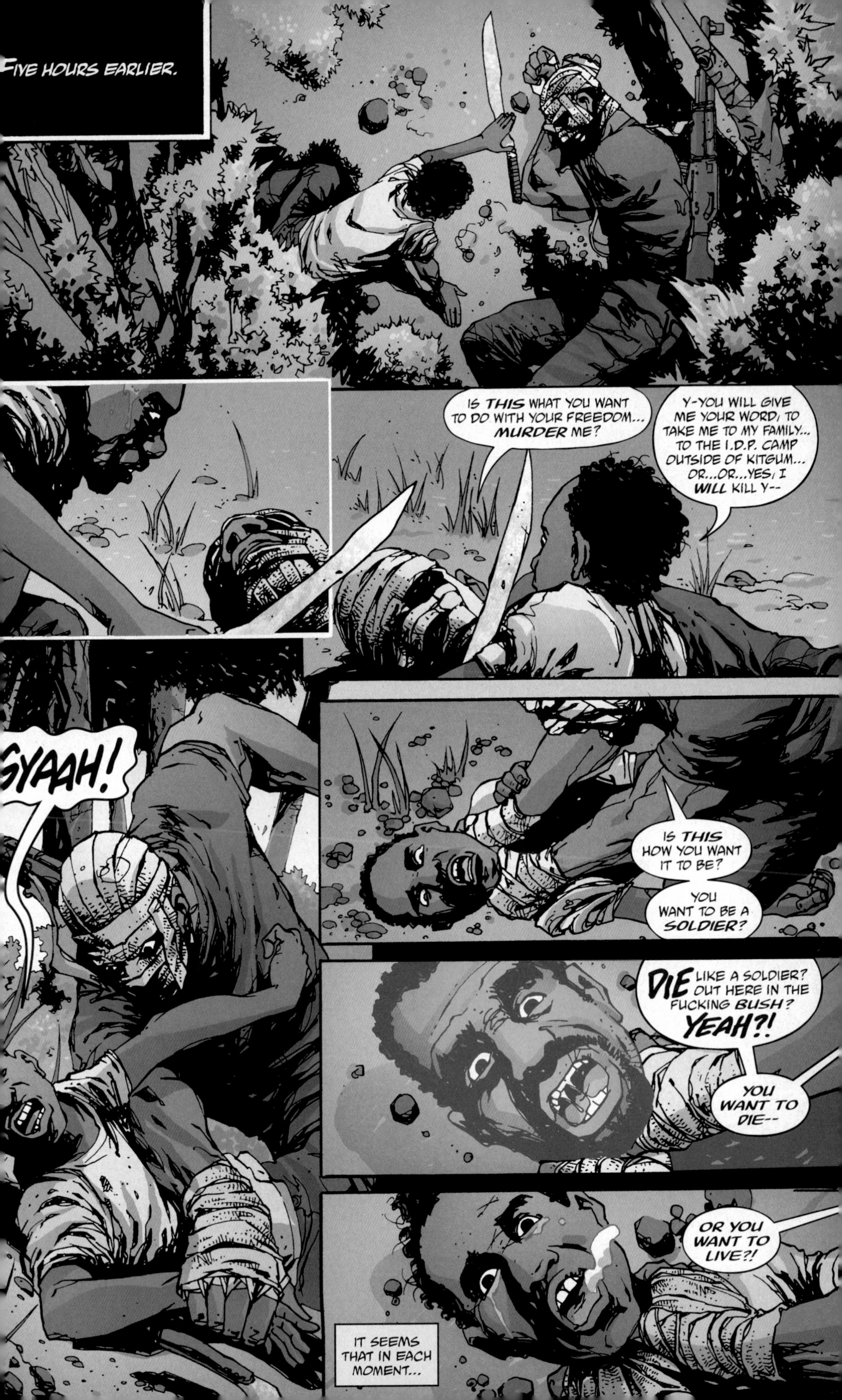
FIVE HOURS EARLIER.
IS THIS WHAT YOU WANT TO DO WITH YOUR FREEDOM... MURDER ME?
Y-YOU WILL GIVE ME YOUR WORD, TO TAKE ME TO MY FAMILY... TO THE I.D.P. CAMP OUTSIDE OF KITGUM... OR...OR...YES, I WILL KILL Y--
GYAAH!
IS THIS HOW YOU WANT IT TO BE?
YOU WANT TO BE A SOLDIER?
DIE LIKE A SOLDIER? OUT HERE IN THE FUCKING BUSH? YEAH?!
YOU WANT TO DIE--
OR YOU WANT TO LIVE?!
IT SEEMS THAT IN EACH MOMENT...

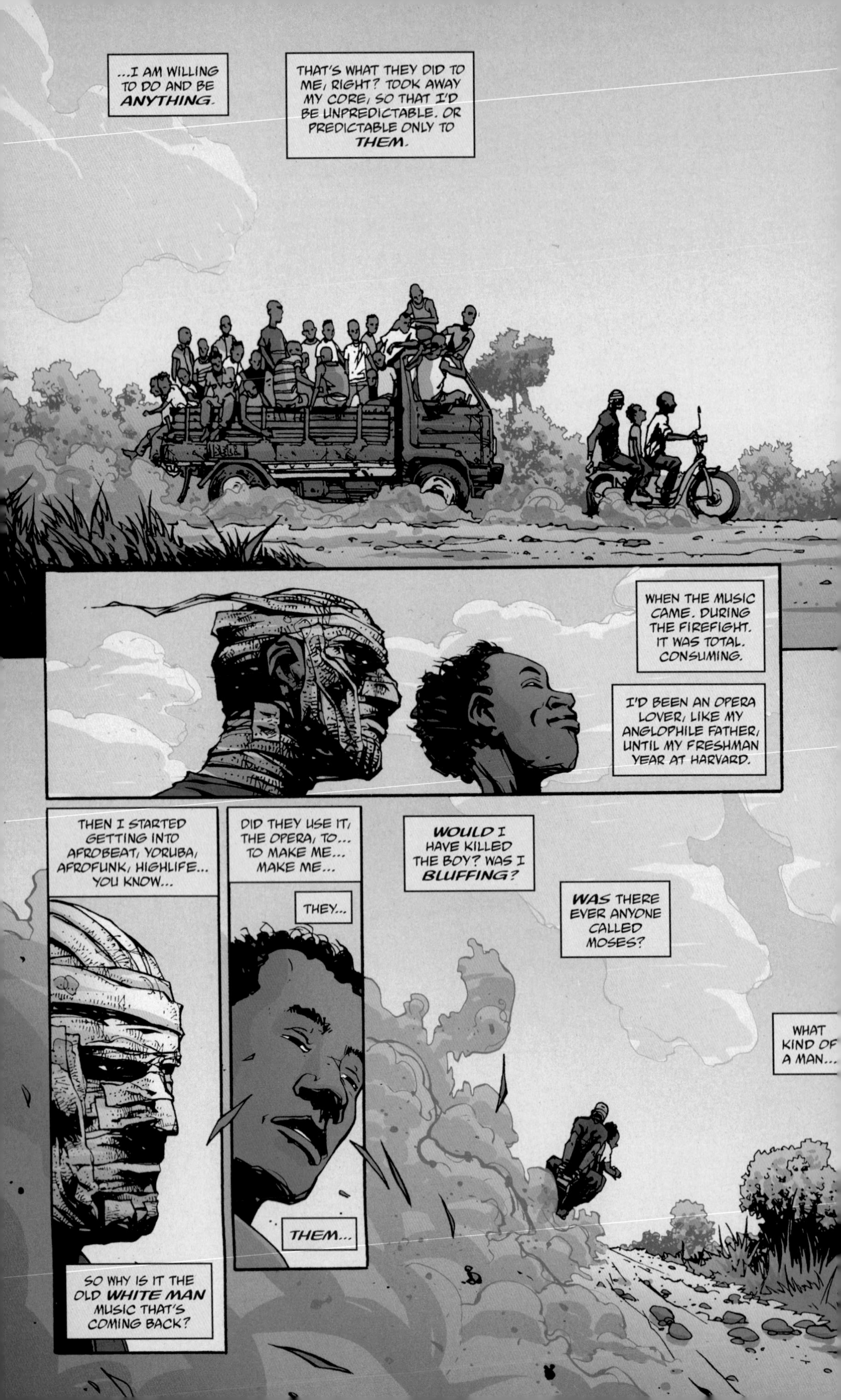

...I AM WILLING TO DO AND BE ANYTHING.
THAT'S WHAT THEY DID TO ME, RIGHT? TOOK AWAY MY CORE, SO THAT I'D BE UNPREDICTABLE. OR PREDICTABLE ONLY TO THEM.
WHEN THE MUSIC CAME. DURING THE FIREFIGHT. IT WAS TOTAL. CONSUMING.
I'D BEEN AN OPERA LOVER, LIKE MY ANGLOPHILE FATHER, UNTIL MY FRESHMAN YEAR AT HARVARD.
THEN I STARTED GETTING INTO AFROBEAT, YORUBA, AFROFUNK, HIGHLIFE... YOU KNOW...
SO WHY IS IT THE OLD WHITE MAN MUSIC THAT'S COMING BACK?
DID THEY USE IT, THE OPERA, TO... TO MAKE ME... MAKE ME...
THEY...
THEM...
WOULD I HAVE KILLED THE BOY? WAS I BLUFFING?
WAS THERE EVER ANYONE CALLED MOSES?
WHAT KIND OF A MAN...

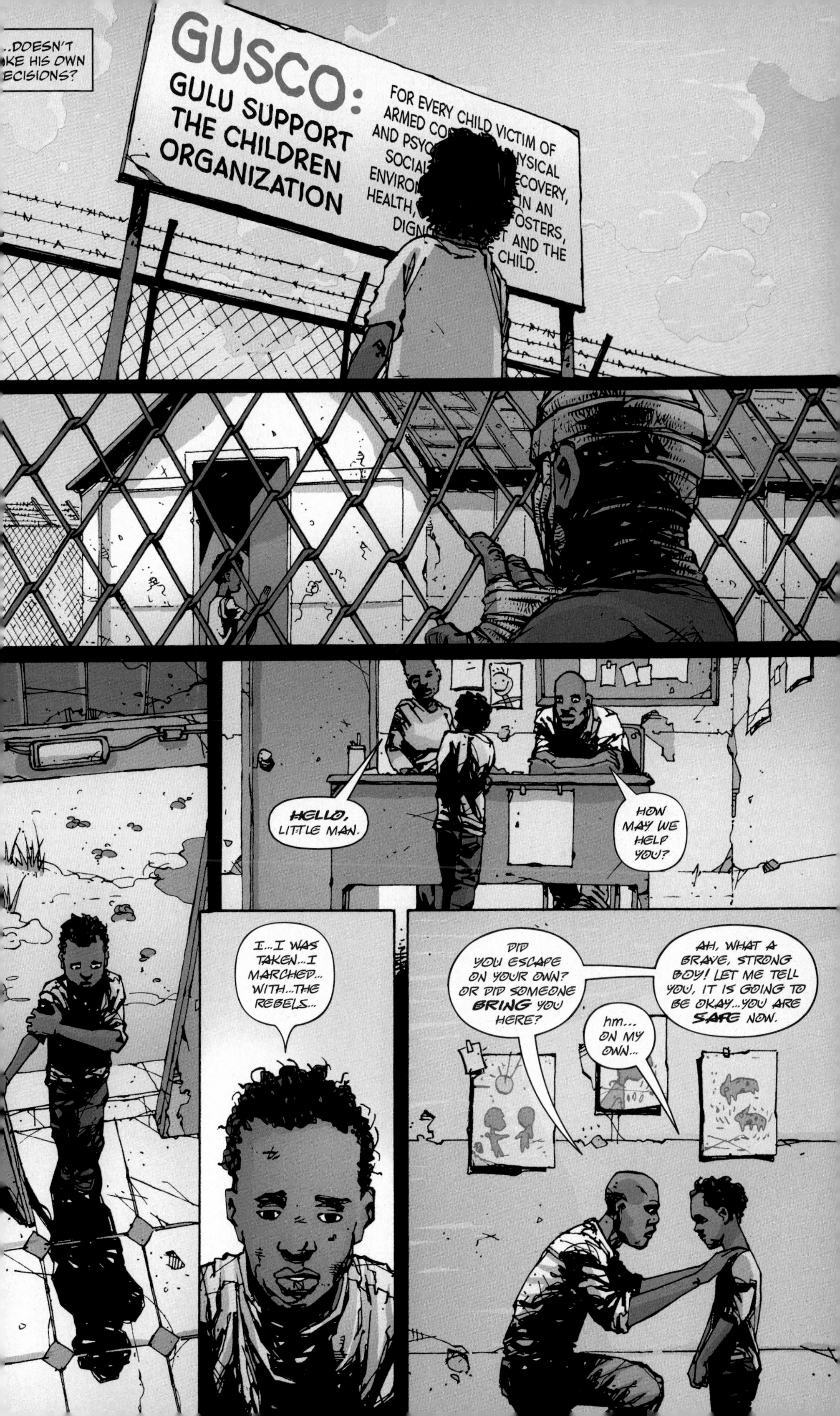

..DOESN'T KE HIS OWN ECISIONS?
GUSCO:
GULU SUPPORT THE CHILDREN ORGANIZATION
FOR EVERY CHILD VICTIM OF ARMED CO AND PSYC SOCIAL ENVIRON HEALTH, DIGNI HYSICAL ECOVERY, IN AN OSTERS, T AND THE CHILD.
HELLO, LITTLE MAN.
HOW MAY WE HELP YOU?
I...I WAS TAKEN...I MARCHED... WITH...THE REBELS...
AH, WHAT A BRAVE, STRONG BOY! LET ME TELL YOU, IT IS GOING TO BE OKAY...YOU ARE SAFE NOW.
DID YOU ESCAPE ON YOUR OWN? OR DID SOMEONE BRING YOU HERE?
hm... ON MY OWN...

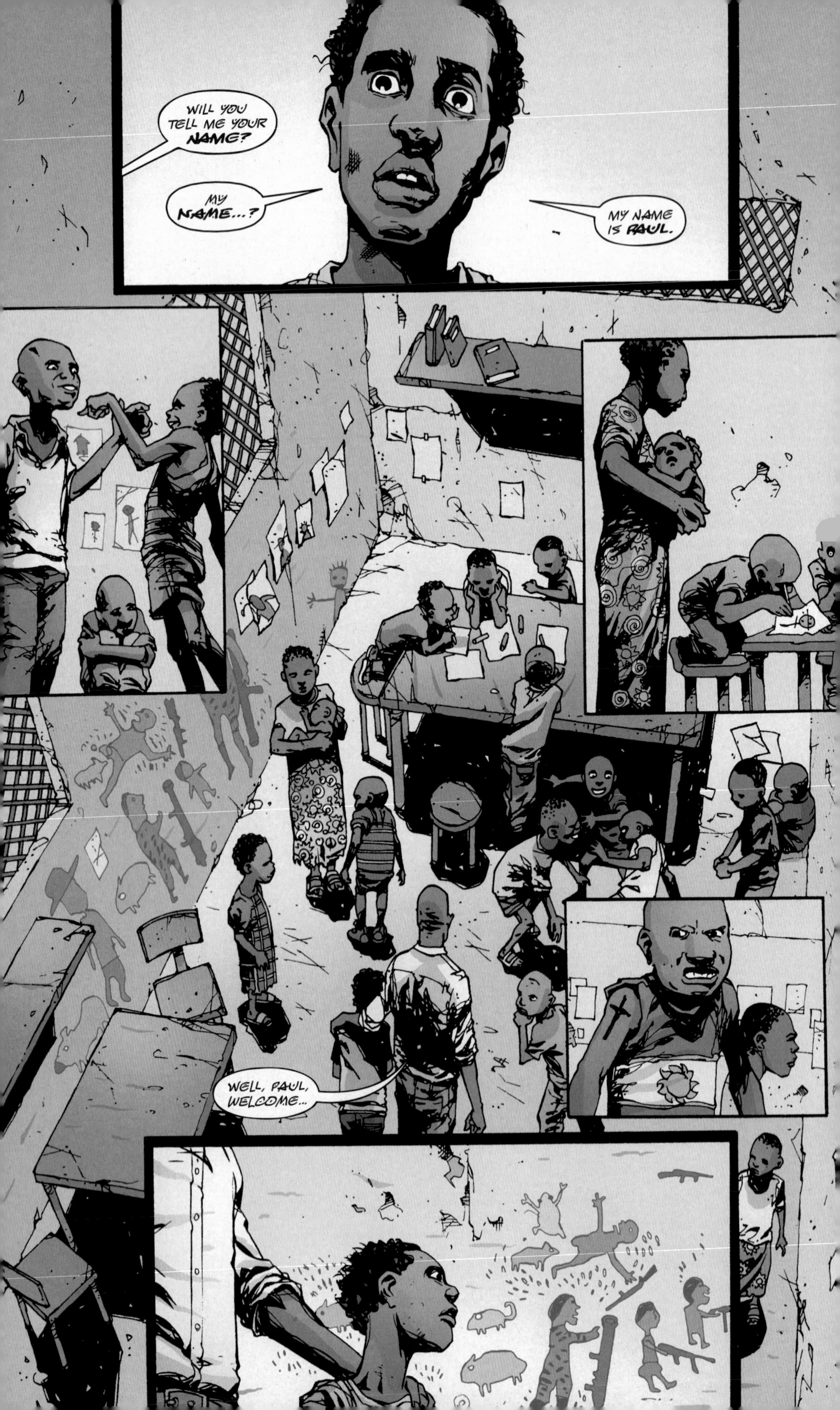
WILL YOU TELL ME YOUR NAME?
MY NAME...?
MY NAME IS PAUL.
WELL, PAUL, WELCOME...

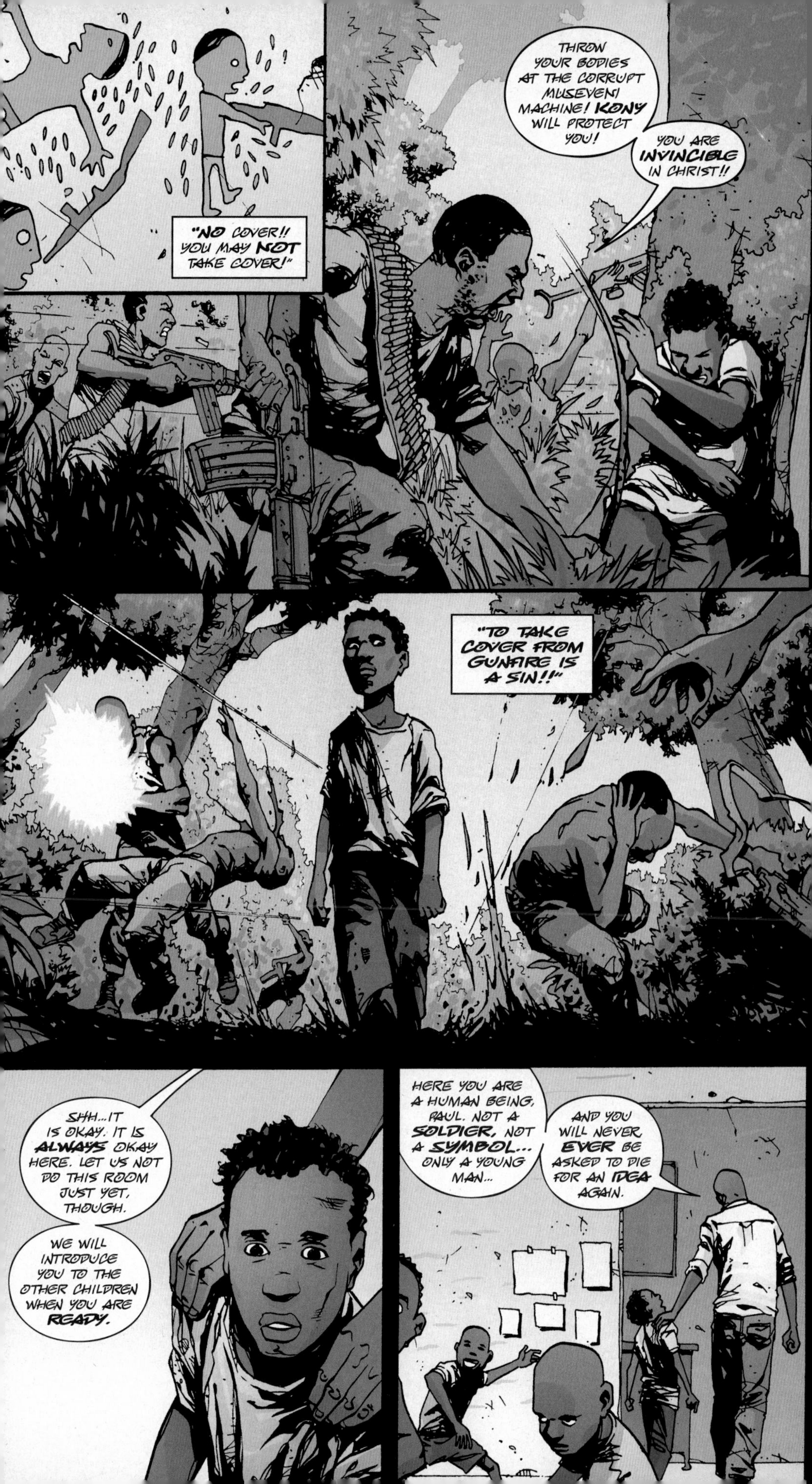
"NO COVER!! YOU MAY NOT TAKE COVER!"
THROW YOUR BODIES AT THE CORRUPT MUSEVENI MACHINE! KONY WILL PROTECT YOU!
YOU ARE INVINCIBLE IN CHRIST!!
"TO TAKE COVER FROM GUNFIRE IS A SIN!!"
SHH...IT IS OKAY. IT IS ALWAYS OKAY HERE. LET US NOT DO THIS ROOM JUST YET, THOUGH.
WE WILL INTRODUCE YOU TO THE OTHER CHILDREN WHEN YOU ARE READY.
HERE YOU ARE A HUMAN BEING, PAUL. NOT A SOLDIER. NOT A SYMBOL... ONLY A YOUNG MAN...
AND YOU WILL NEVER EVER BE ASKED TO DIE FOR AN IDEA AGAIN.

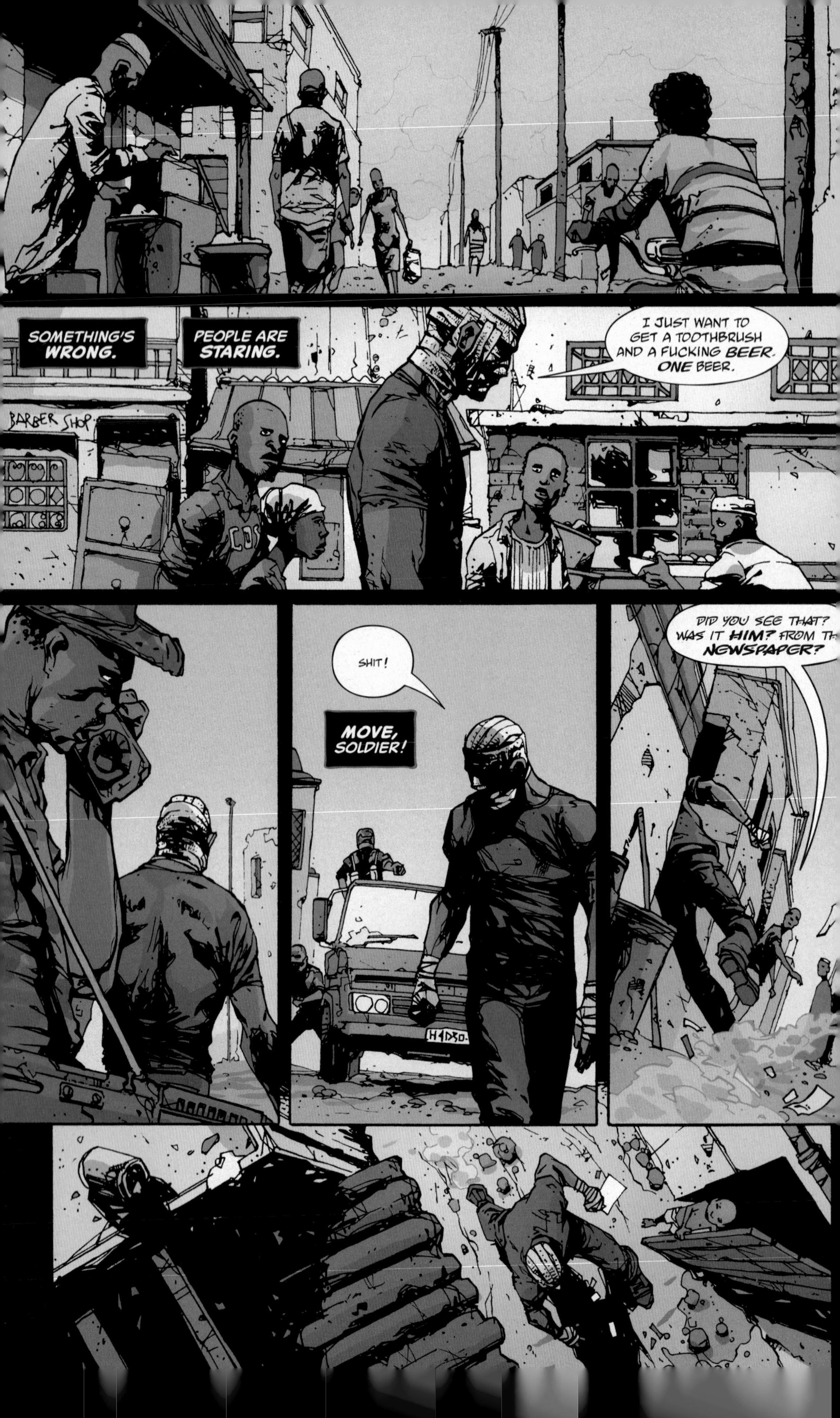
SOMETHING'S WRONG.
PEOPLE ARE STARING.
I JUST WANT TO GET A TOOTHBRUSH AND A FUCKING BEER. ONE BEER.
BARBER SHOP
SHIT!
MOVE, SOLDIER!
DID YOU SEE THAT? WAS IT HIM? FROM TH NEWSPAPER?

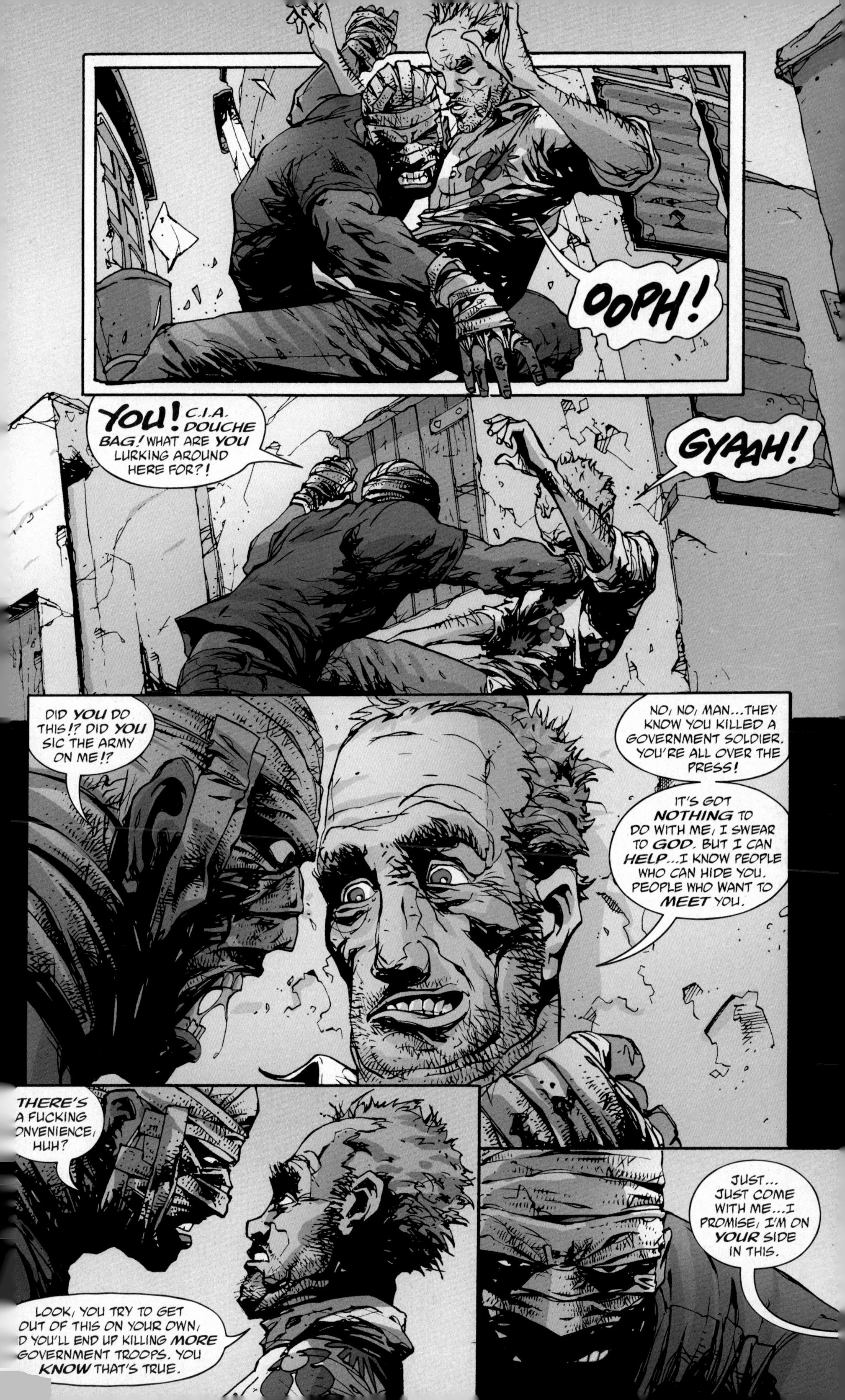
OOPH!
YOU! C.I.A. DOUCHE BAG! WHAT ARE YOU LURKING AROUND HERE FOR?!
GYAAH!
DID YOU DO THIS!? DID YOU SIC THE ARMY ON ME!?
NO, NO, MAN...THEY KNOW YOU KILLED A GOVERNMENT SOLDIER. YOU'RE ALL OVER THE PRESS!
IT'S GOT NOTHING TO DO WITH ME, I SWEAR TO GOD. BUT I CAN HELP...I KNOW PEOPLE WHO CAN HIDE YOU. PEOPLE WHO WANT TO MEET YOU.
THERE'S A FUCKING ONVENIENCE, HUH?
LOOK, YOU TRY TO GET OUT OF THIS ON YOUR OWN, D YOU'LL END UP KILLING MORE GOVERNMENT TROOPS. YOU KNOW THAT'S TRUE.
JUST... JUST COME WITH ME...I PROMISE, I'M ON YOUR SIDE IN THIS.

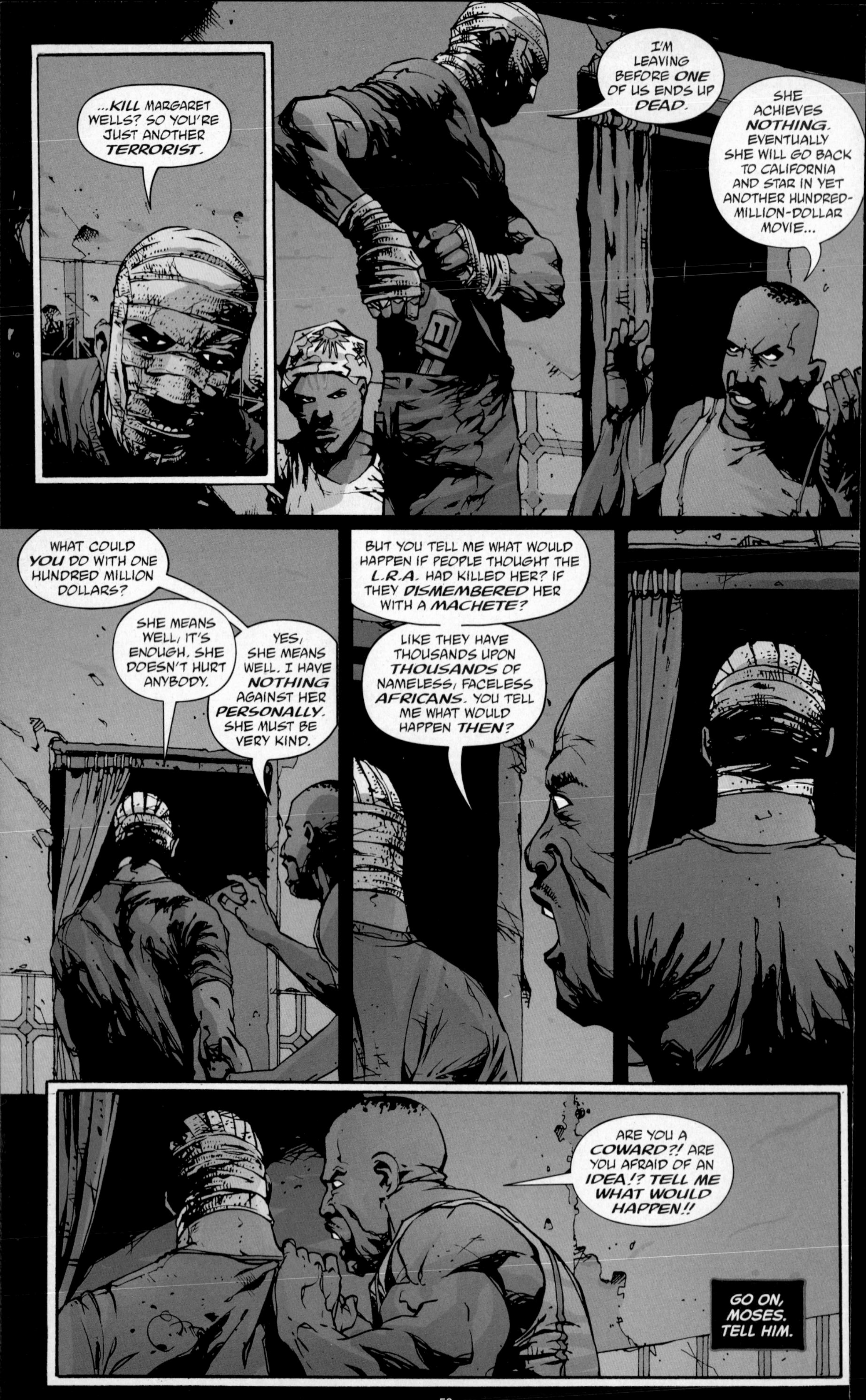
...KILL MARGARET WELLS? SO YOU'RE JUST ANOTHER TERRORIST.
I'M LEAVING BEFORE ONE OF US ENDS UP DEAD.
SHE ACHIEVES NOTHING. EVENTUALLY SHE WILL GO BACK TO CALIFORNIA AND STAR IN YET ANOTHER HUNDRED-MILLION-DOLLAR MOVIE...
WHAT COULD YOU DO WITH ONE HUNDRED MILLION DOLLARS?
SHE MEANS WELL, IT'S ENOUGH. SHE DOESN'T HURT ANYBODY.
YES, SHE MEANS WELL. I HAVE NOTHING AGAINST HER PERSONALLY. SHE MUST BE VERY KIND.
BUT YOU TELL ME WHAT WOULD HAPPEN IF PEOPLE THOUGHT THE L.R.A. HAD KILLED HER? IF THEY DISMEMBERED HER WITH A MACHETE?
LIKE THEY HAVE THOUSANDS UPON THOUSANDS OF NAMELESS, FACELESS AFRICANS. YOU TELL ME WHAT WOULD HAPPEN THEN?
ARE YOU A COWARD?! ARE YOU AFRAID OF AN IDEA!? TELL ME WHAT WOULD HAPPEN!!
GO ON, MOSES. TELL HIM.

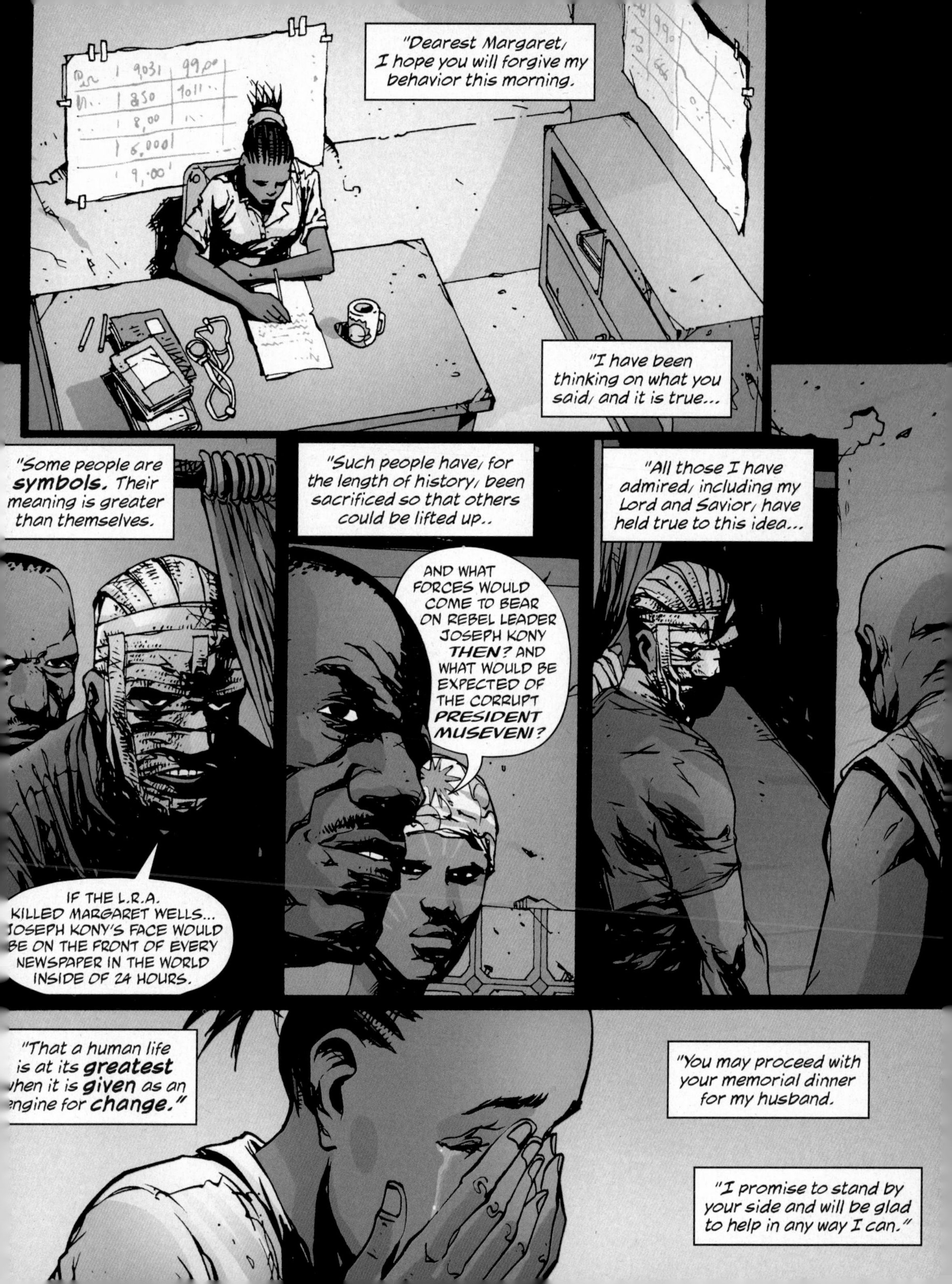
"Dearest Margaret, I hope you will forgive my behavior this morning.
"I have been thinking on what you said, and it is true...
"Some people are **symbols.** Their meaning is greater than themselves.
IF THE L.R.A. KILLED MARGARET WELLS... JOSEPH KONY'S FACE WOULD BE ON THE FRONT OF EVERY NEWSPAPER IN THE WORLD INSIDE OF 24 HOURS.
"Such people have, for the length of history, been sacrificed so that others could be lifted up..
AND WHAT FORCES WOULD COME TO BEAR ON REBEL LEADER JOSEPH KONY ***THEN?*** AND WHAT WOULD BE EXPECTED OF THE CORRUPT ***PRESIDENT MUSEVENI?***
"All those I have admired, including my Lord and Savior, have held true to this idea...
"That a human life is at its **greatest** when it is **given** as an engine for **change.**"
"You may proceed with your memorial dinner for my husband.
"I promise to stand by your side and will be glad to help in any way I can."

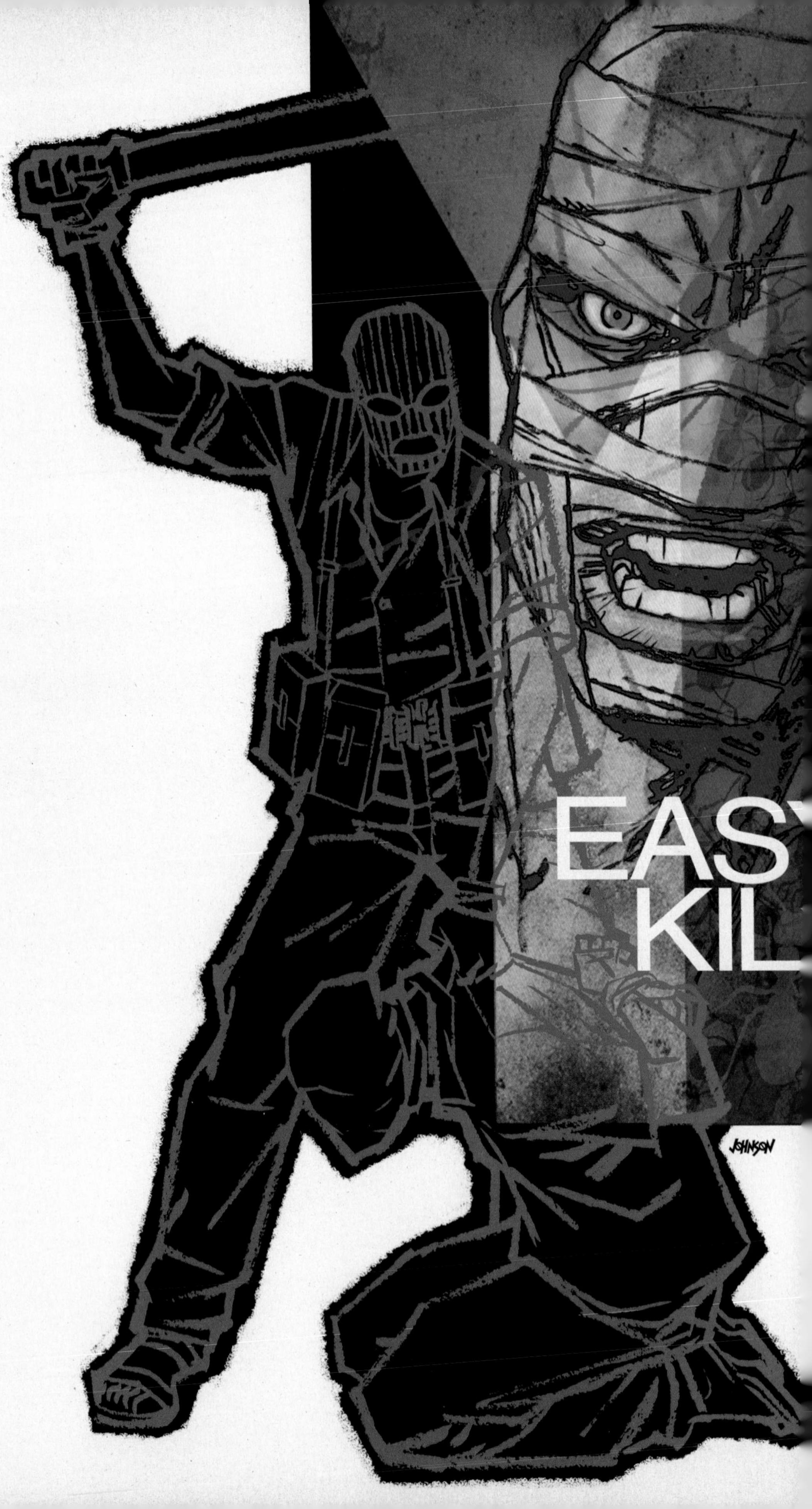
EAS
KIL
JOHNSON

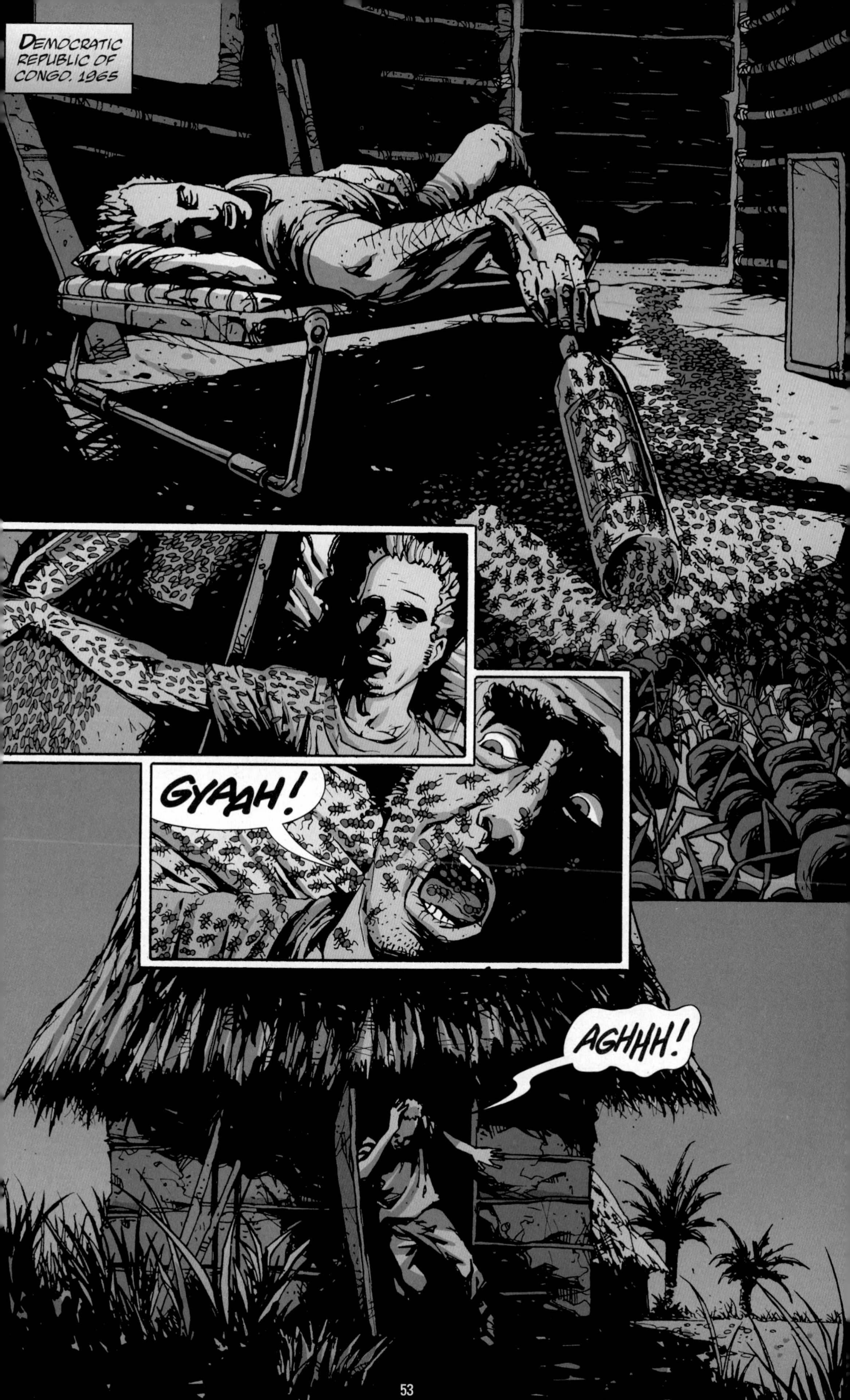

DEMOCRATIC REPUBLIC OF CONGO, 1965
GYAAH!
AGHHH!

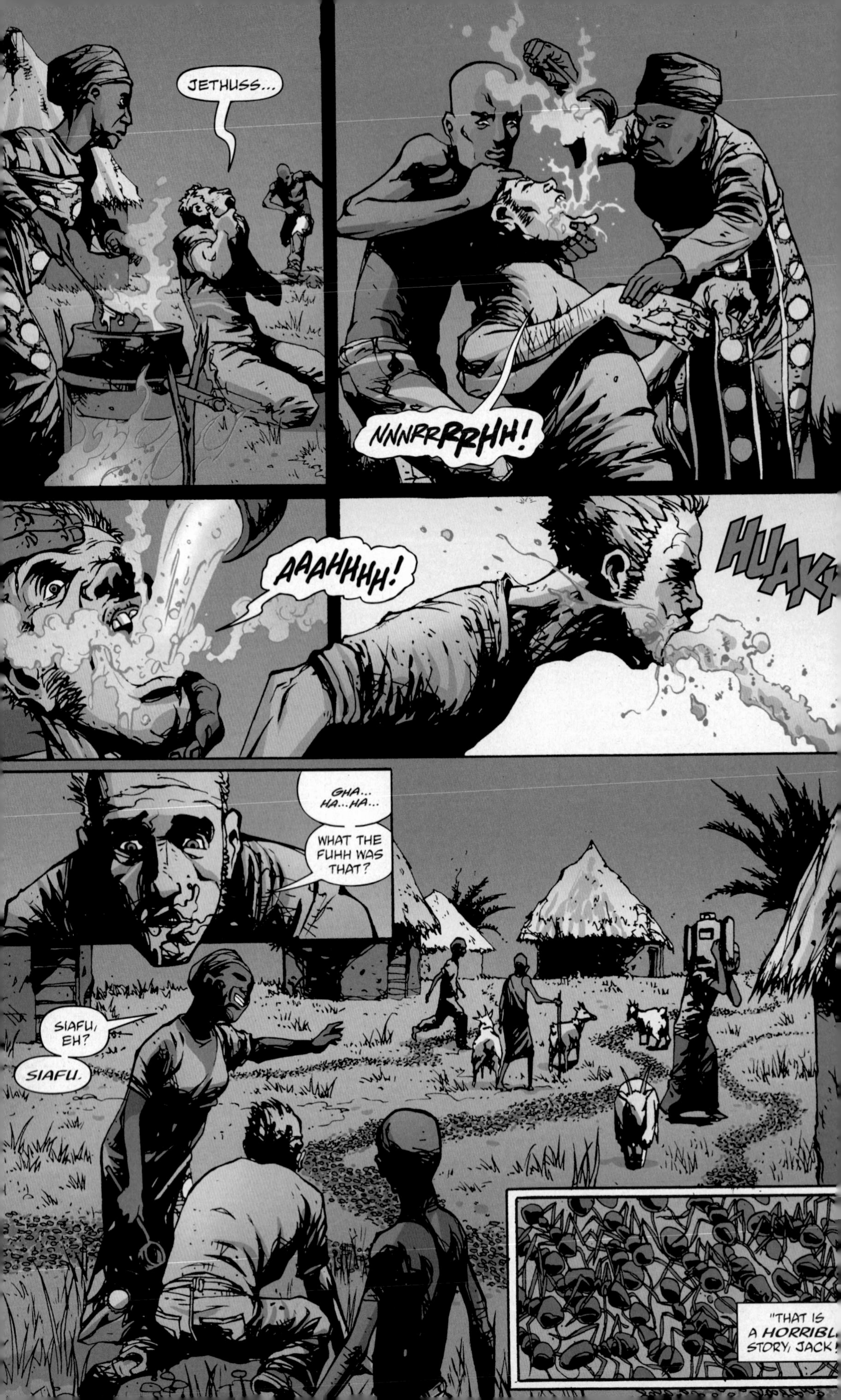
JETHUSS...
NNNRRRRHH!
AAAHHHH!
HUAK
GHA... HA...HA...
WHAT THE FUHH WAS THAT?
SIAFU, EH?
SIAFU.
"THAT IS A HORRIBL STORY, JACK!

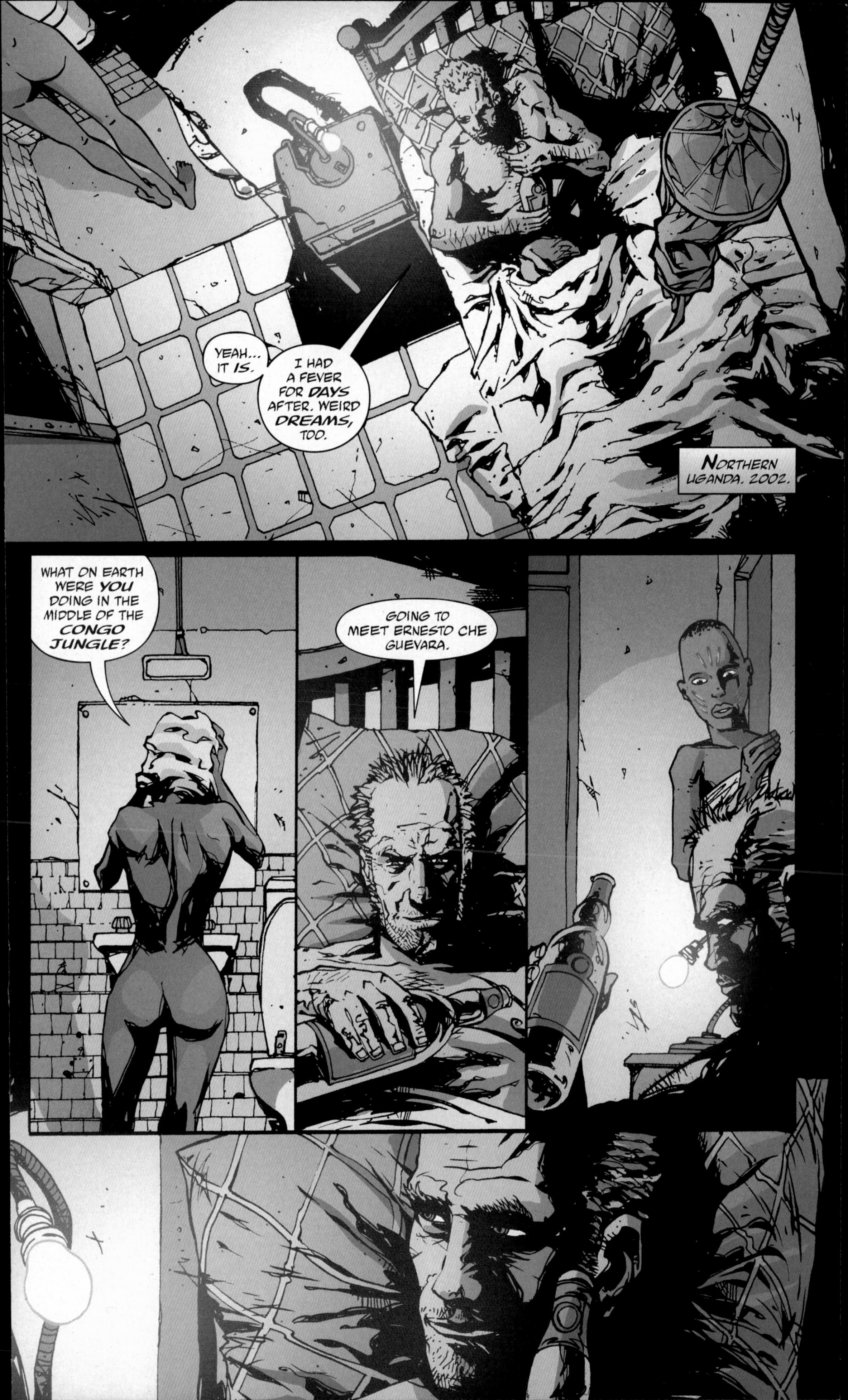
YEAH... IT IS.
I HAD A FEVER FOR DAYS AFTER. WEIRD DREAMS, TOO.
NORTHERN UGANDA. 2002.
WHAT ON EARTH WERE YOU DOING IN THE MIDDLE OF THE CONGO JUNGLE?
GOING TO MEET ERNESTO CHE GUEVARA.

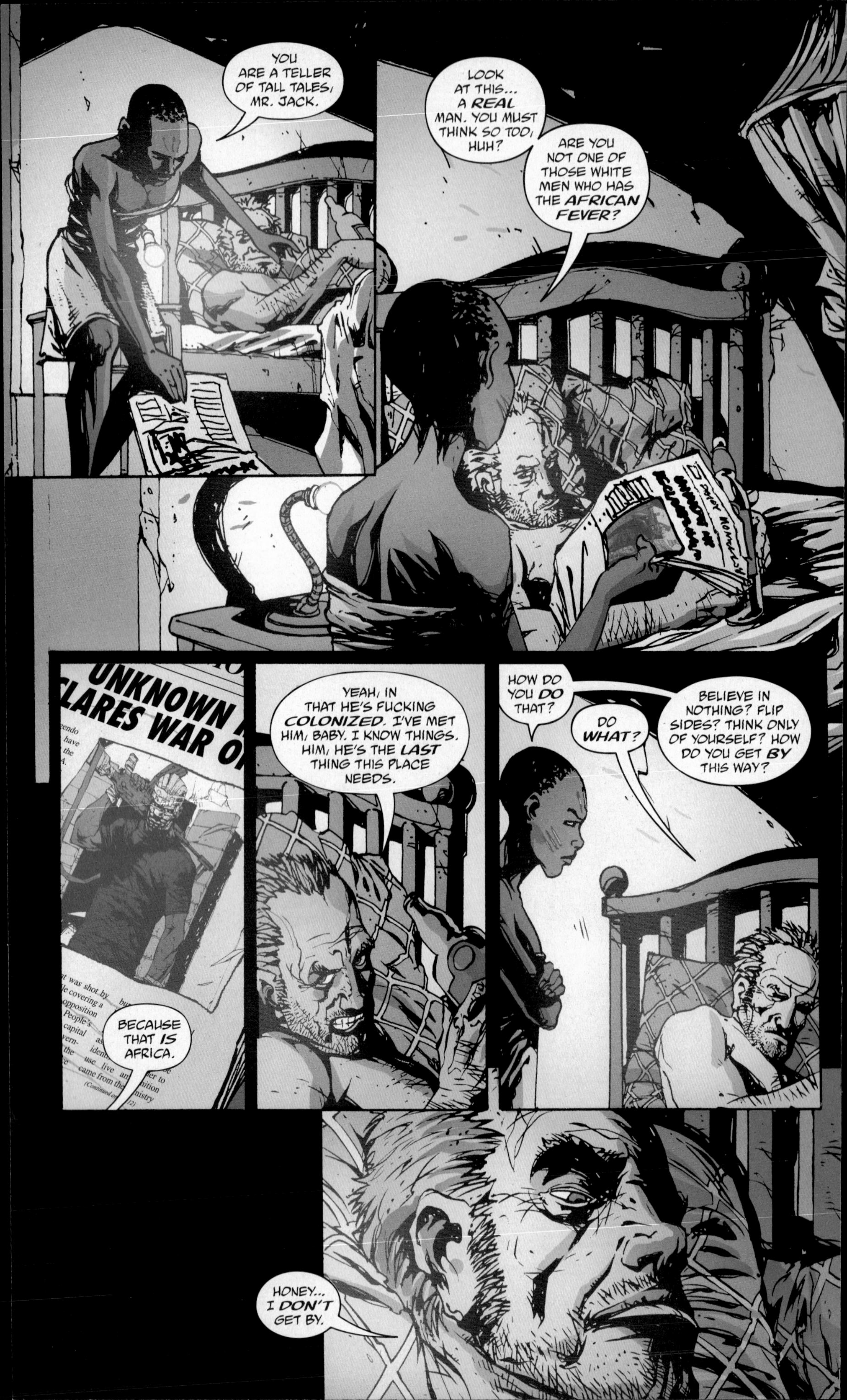
YOU ARE A TELLER OF TALL TALES, MR. JACK.
LOOK AT THIS... A REAL MAN. YOU MUST THINK SO TOO, HUH?
ARE YOU NOT ONE OF THOSE WHITE MEN WHO HAS THE AFRICAN FEVER?
BECAUSE THAT IS AFRICA.
YEAH, IN THAT HE'S FUCKING COLONIZED. I'VE MET HIM, BABY. I KNOW THINGS. HIM, HE'S THE LAST THING THIS PLACE NEEDS.
HOW DO YOU DO THAT?
DO WHAT?
BELIEVE IN NOTHING? FLIP SIDES? THINK ONLY OF YOURSELF? HOW DO YOU GET BY THIS WAY?
HONEY... I DON'T GET BY.

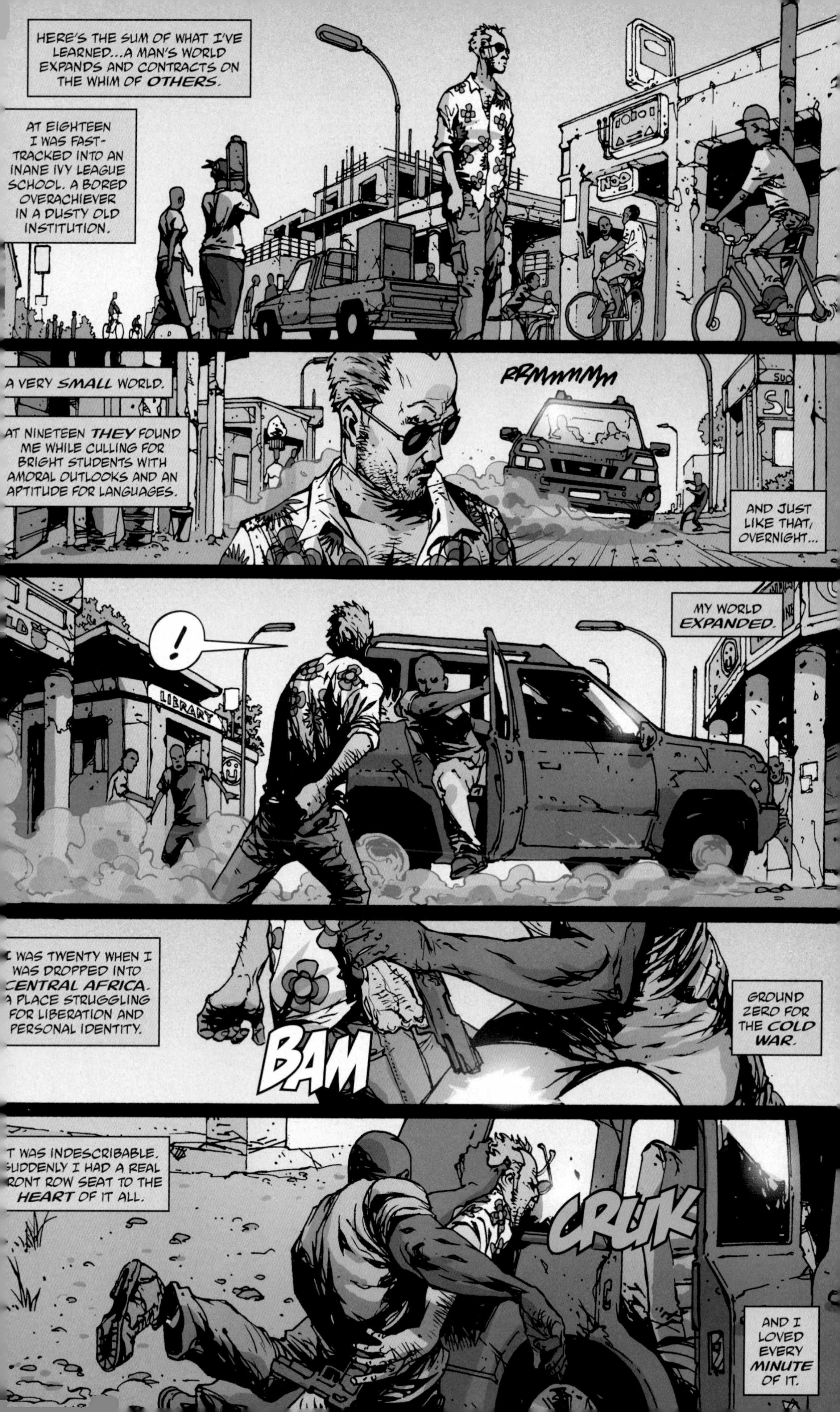
HERE'S THE SUM OF WHAT I'VE LEARNED...A MAN'S WORLD EXPANDS AND CONTRACTS ON THE WHIM OF OTHERS.
AT EIGHTEEN I WAS FAST-TRACKED INTO AN INANE IVY LEAGUE SCHOOL. A BORED OVERACHIEVER IN A DUSTY OLD INSTITUTION.
A VERY SMALL WORLD.
RRMMMMM
AT NINETEEN THEY FOUND ME WHILE CULLING FOR BRIGHT STUDENTS WITH AMORAL OUTLOOKS AND AN APTITUDE FOR LANGUAGES.
AND JUST LIKE THAT, OVERNIGHT...
MY WORLD EXPANDED.
!
LIBRARY
I WAS TWENTY WHEN I WAS DROPPED INTO CENTRAL AFRICA. A PLACE STRUGGLING FOR LIBERATION AND PERSONAL IDENTITY.
GROUND ZERO FOR THE COLD WAR.
BAM
IT WAS INDESCRIBABLE. SUDDENLY I HAD A REAL FRONT ROW SEAT TO THE HEART OF IT ALL.
CRUK
AND I LOVED EVERY MINUTE OF IT.

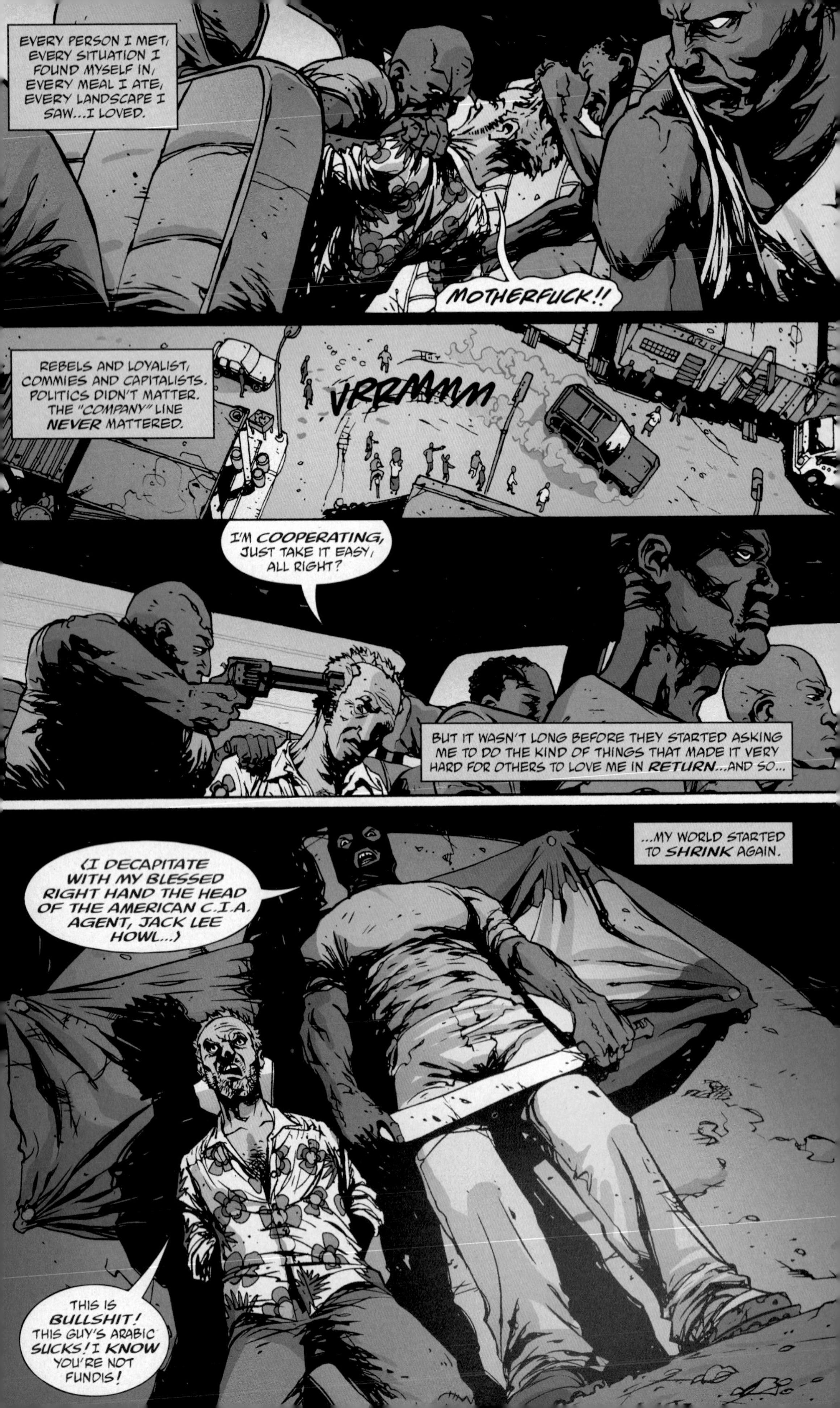
EVERY PERSON I MET, EVERY SITUATION I FOUND MYSELF IN, EVERY MEAL I ATE, EVERY LANDSCAPE I SAW...I LOVED.
MOTHERFUCK!!
REBELS AND LOYALIST, COMMIES AND CAPITALISTS. POLITICS DIDN'T MATTER. THE "COMPANY" LINE NEVER MATTERED.
VRRMMM
I'M COOPERATING, JUST TAKE IT EASY, ALL RIGHT?
BUT IT WASN'T LONG BEFORE THEY STARTED ASKING ME TO DO THE KIND OF THINGS THAT MADE IT VERY HARD FOR OTHERS TO LOVE ME IN RETURN...AND SO...
...MY WORLD STARTED TO SHRINK AGAIN.
‹I DECAPITATE WITH MY BLESSED RIGHT HAND THE HEAD OF THE AMERICAN C.I.A. AGENT, JACK LEE HOWL...›
THIS IS BULLSHIT! THIS GUY'S ARABIC SUCKS! I KNOW YOU'RE NOT FUNDIS!

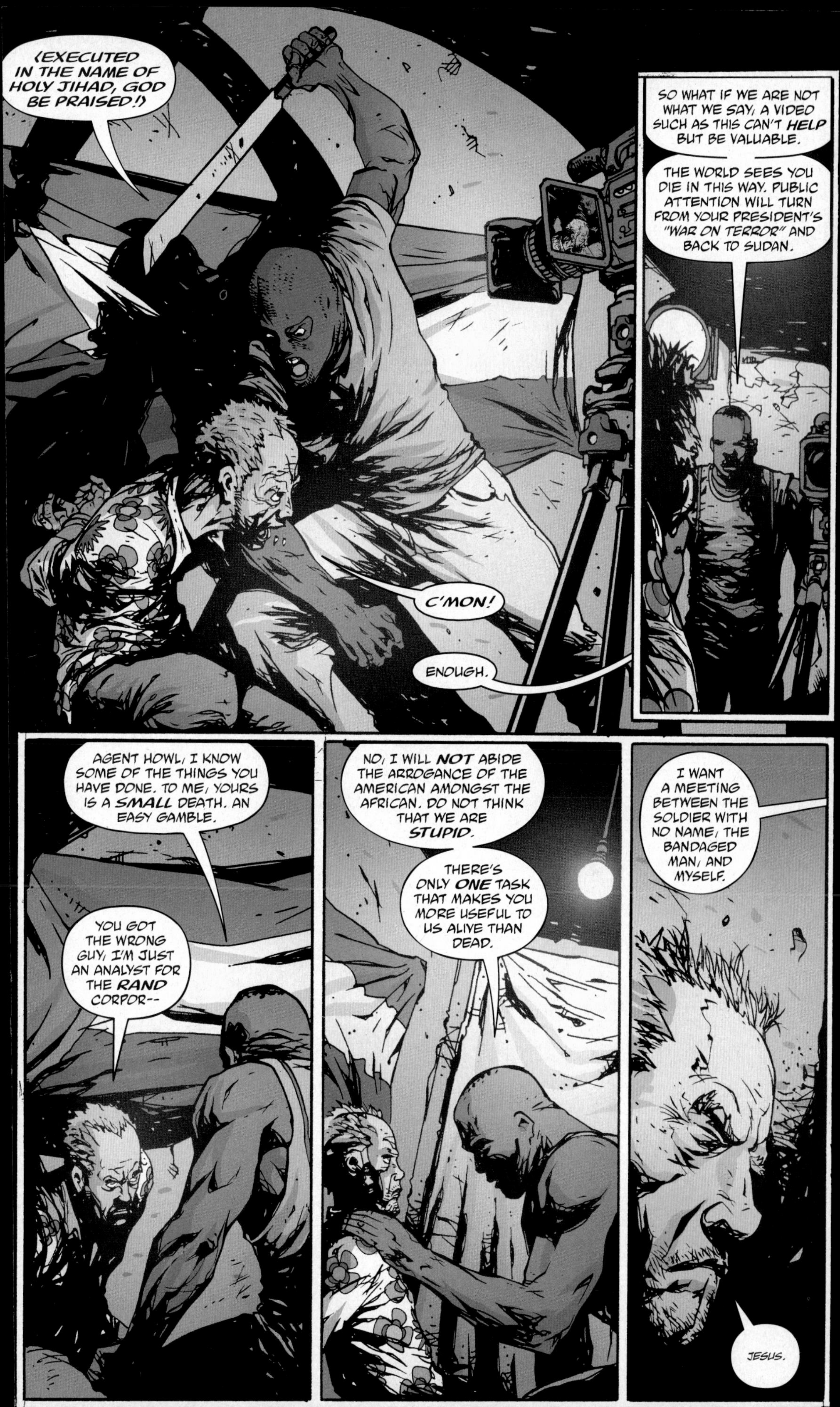

‹EXECUTED IN THE NAME OF HOLY JIHAD, GOD BE PRAISED!›
SO WHAT IF WE ARE NOT WHAT WE SAY, A VIDEO SUCH AS THIS CAN'T HELP BUT BE VALUABLE.
THE WORLD SEES YOU DIE IN THIS WAY. PUBLIC ATTENTION WILL TURN FROM YOUR PRESIDENT'S "WAR ON TERROR" AND BACK TO SUDAN.
C'MON!
ENOUGH.
AGENT HOWL, I KNOW SOME OF THE THINGS YOU HAVE DONE. TO ME, YOURS IS A SMALL DEATH. AN EASY GAMBLE.
YOU GOT THE WRONG GUY, I'M JUST AN ANALYST FOR THE RAND CORPOR--
NO, I WILL NOT ABIDE THE ARROGANCE OF THE AMERICAN AMONGST THE AFRICAN. DO NOT THINK THAT WE ARE STUPID.
THERE'S ONLY ONE TASK THAT MAKES YOU MORE USEFUL TO US ALIVE THAN DEAD.
I WANT A MEETING BETWEEN THE SOLDIER WITH NO NAME, THE BANDAGED MAN, AND MYSELF.
JESUS.

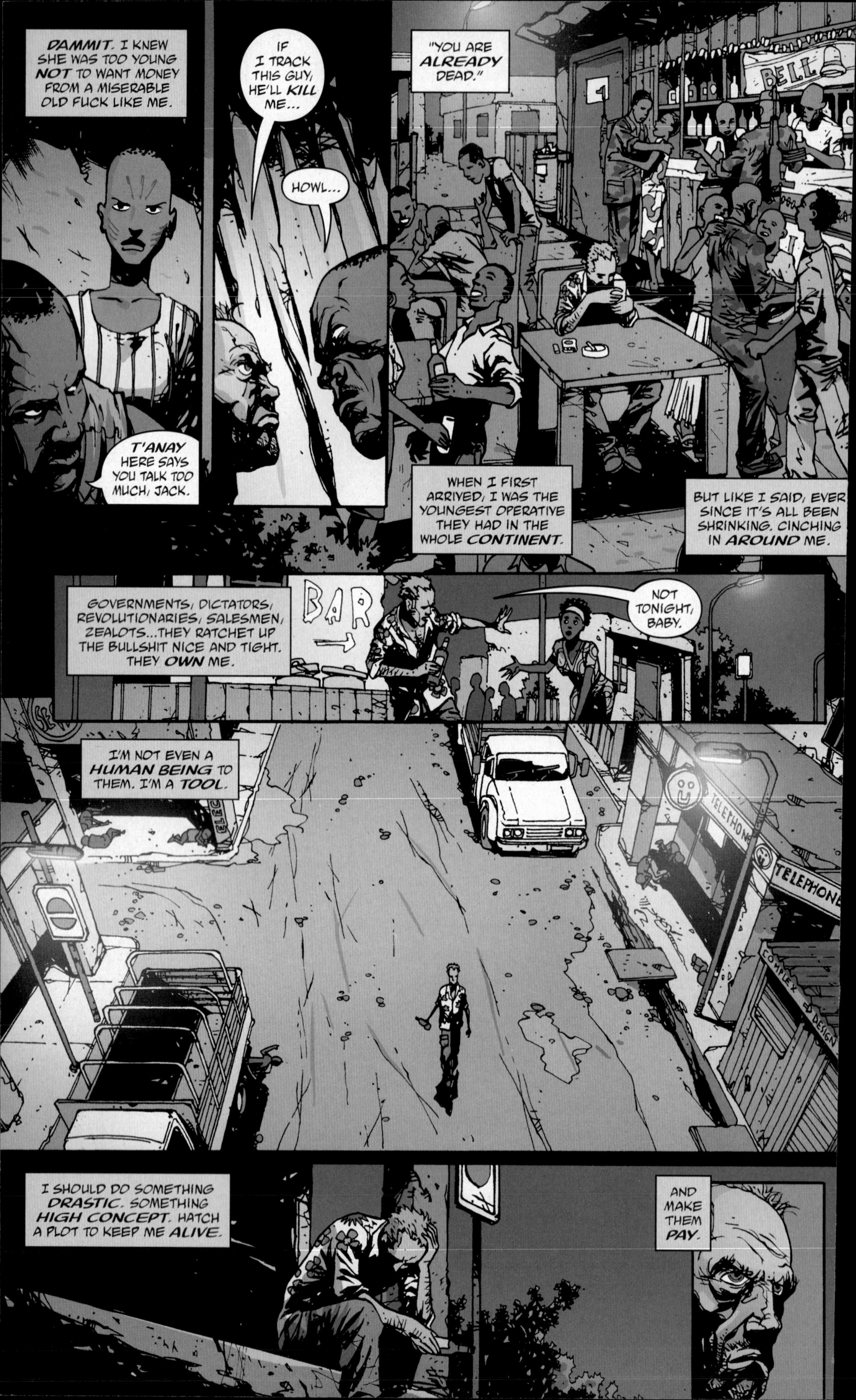
DAMMIT. I KNEW SHE WAS TOO YOUNG NOT TO WANT MONEY FROM A MISERABLE OLD FUCK LIKE ME.
T'ANAY HERE SAYS YOU TALK TOO MUCH, JACK.
IF I TRACK THIS GUY, HE'LL KILL ME...
HOWL...
"YOU ARE ALREADY DEAD."
BELL
WHEN I FIRST ARRIVED, I WAS THE YOUNGEST OPERATIVE THEY HAD IN THE WHOLE CONTINENT.
BUT LIKE I SAID, EVER SINCE IT'S ALL BEEN SHRINKING. CINCHING IN AROUND ME.
GOVERNMENTS, DICTATORS, REVOLUTIONARIES, SALESMEN, ZEALOTS...THEY RATCHET UP THE BULLSHIT NICE AND TIGHT. THEY OWN ME.
BAR
NOT TONIGHT, BABY.
I'M NOT EVEN A HUMAN BEING TO THEM. I'M A TOOL.
TELEPHONE
COMPLEX
DESIGN
I SHOULD DO SOMETHING DRASTIC. SOMETHING HIGH CONCEPT. HATCH A PLOT TO KEEP ME ALIVE.
AND MAKE THEM PAY.

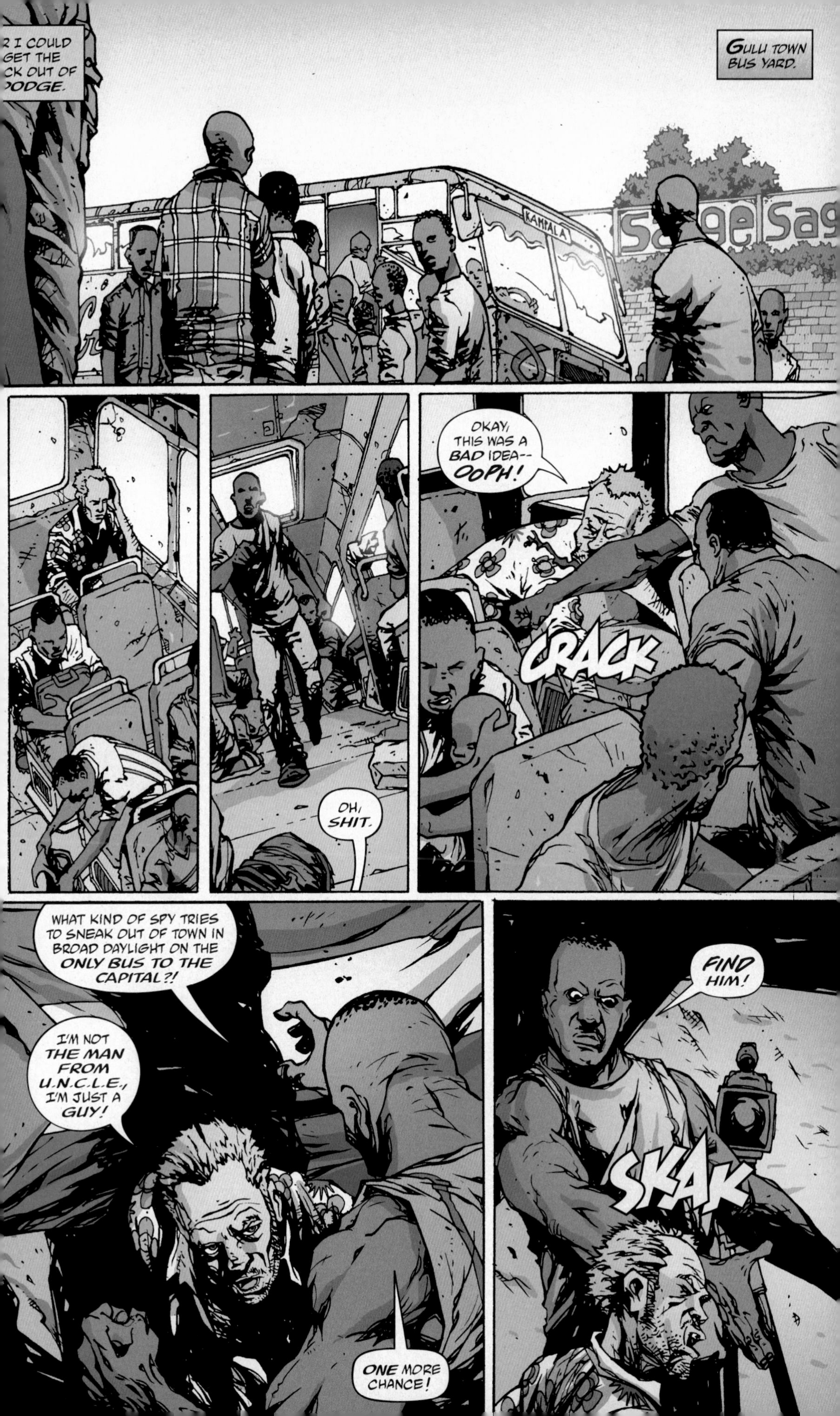
R I COULD GET THE CK OUT OF DODGE.
GULU TOWN BUS YARD.
KAMPALA
OH, SHIT.
OKAY, THIS WAS A BAD IDEA-- OOPH!
CRACK
WHAT KIND OF SPY TRIES TO SNEAK OUT OF TOWN IN BROAD DAYLIGHT ON THE ONLY BUS TO THE CAPITAL?!
I'M NOT THE MAN FROM U.N.C.L.E., I'M JUST A GUY!
ONE MORE CHANCE!
FIND HIM!
SKAK

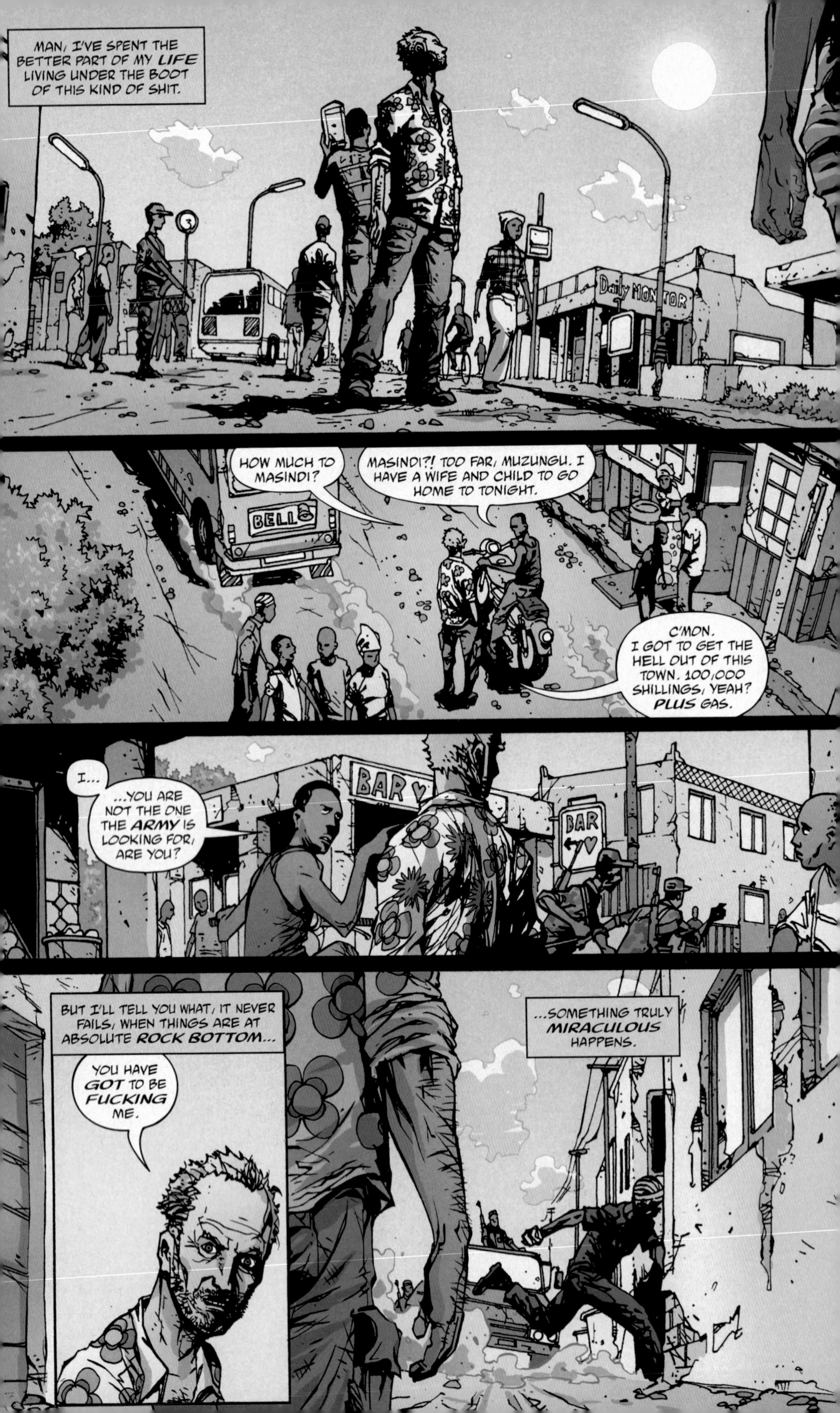
MAN, I'VE SPENT THE BETTER PART OF MY LIFE LIVING UNDER THE BOOT OF THIS KIND OF SHIT.
Daily MONITOR
HOW MUCH TO MASINDI?
MASINDI?! TOO FAR, MUZUNGU. I HAVE A WIFE AND CHILD TO GO HOME TO TONIGHT.
BELL
C'MON. I GOT TO GET THE HELL OUT OF THIS TOWN. 100,000 SHILLINGS, YEAH? PLUS GAS.
BAR
BAR
I...
...YOU ARE NOT THE ONE THE ARMY IS LOOKING FOR, ARE YOU?
BUT I'LL TELL YOU WHAT, IT NEVER FAILS, WHEN THINGS ARE AT ABSOLUTE ROCK BOTTOM...
YOU HAVE GOT TO BE FUCKING ME.
...SOMETHING TRULY MIRACULOUS HAPPENS.

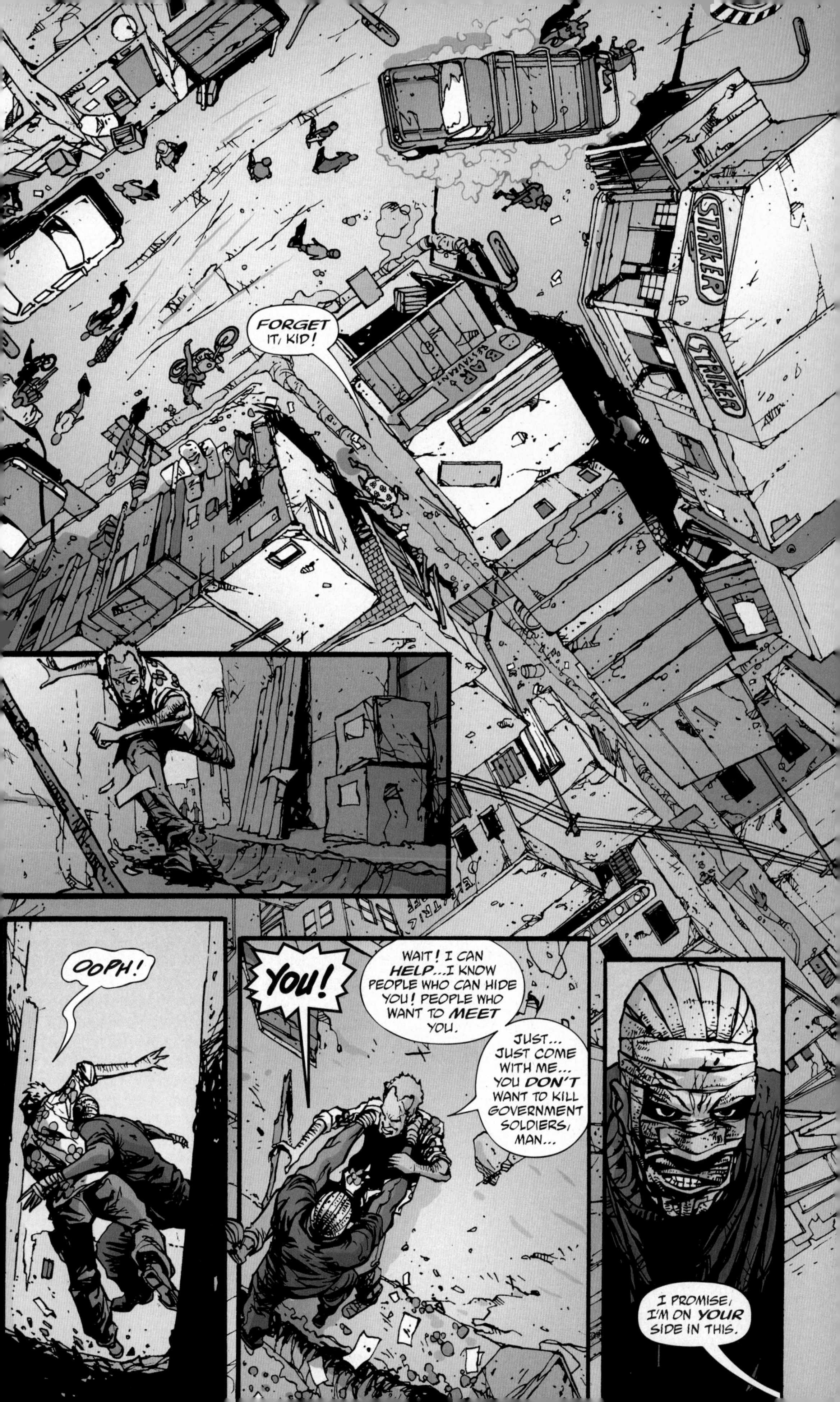
STRIKER
STRIKER
FORGET IT, KID!
OOPH!
YOU!
WAIT! I CAN HELP...I KNOW PEOPLE WHO CAN HIDE YOU! PEOPLE WHO WANT TO MEET YOU.
JUST... JUST COME WITH ME... YOU DON'T WANT TO KILL GOVERNMENT SOLDIERS, MAN...
I PROMISE, I'M ON YOUR SIDE IN THIS.

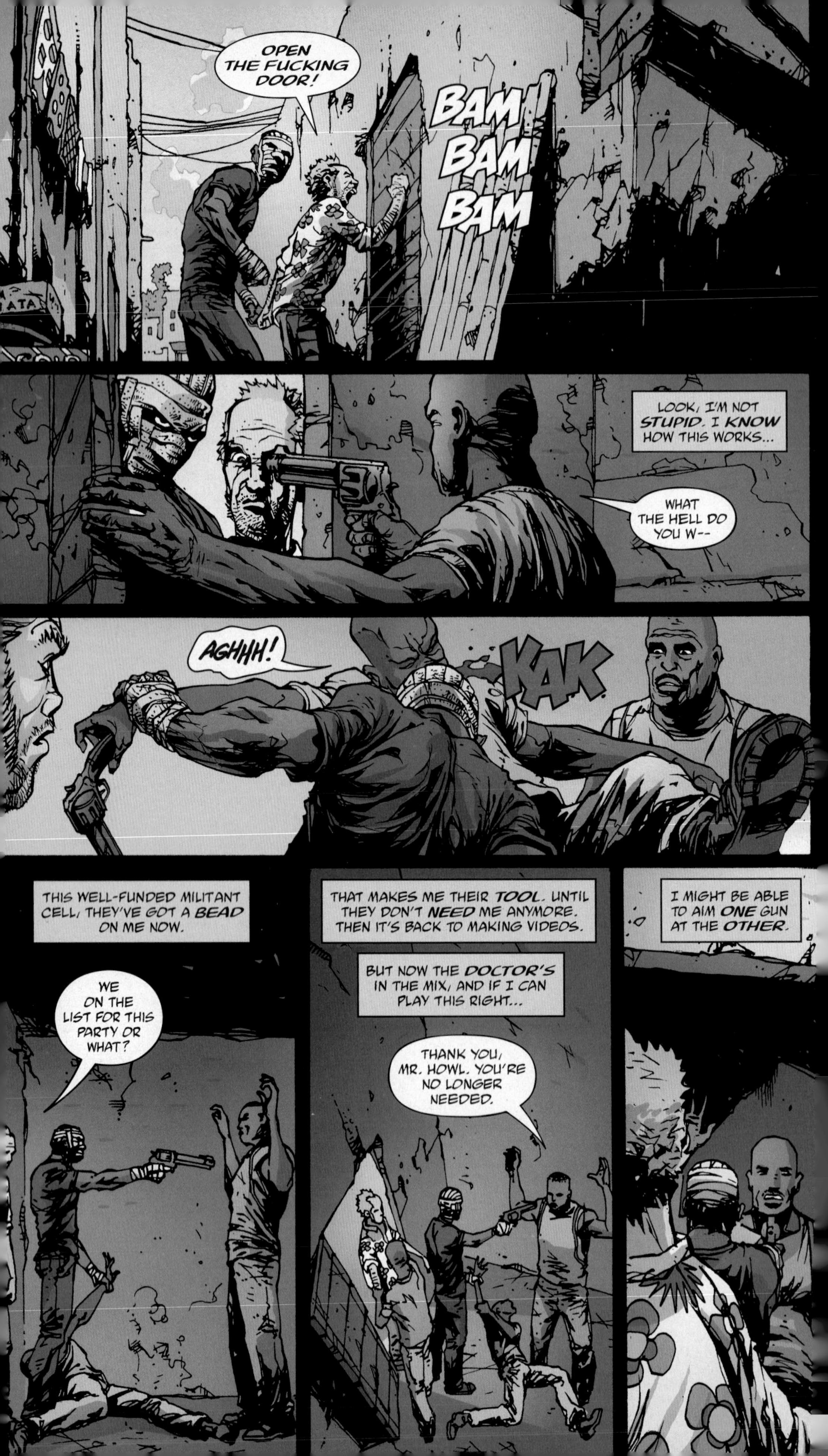
OPEN THE FUCKING DOOR!
BAM BAM BAM
LOOK, I'M NOT STUPID. I KNOW HOW THIS WORKS...
WHAT THE HELL DO YOU W--
AGHHH!
KAK
THIS WELL-FUNDED MILITANT CELL, THEY'VE GOT A BEAD ON ME NOW.
WE ON THE LIST FOR THIS PARTY OR WHAT?
THAT MAKES ME THEIR TOOL. UNTIL THEY DON'T NEED ME ANYMORE. THEN IT'S BACK TO MAKING VIDEOS.
BUT NOW THE DOCTOR'S IN THE MIX, AND IF I CAN PLAY THIS RIGHT...
THANK YOU, MR. HOWL. YOU'RE NO LONGER NEEDED.
I MIGHT BE ABLE TO AIM ONE GUN AT THE OTHER.

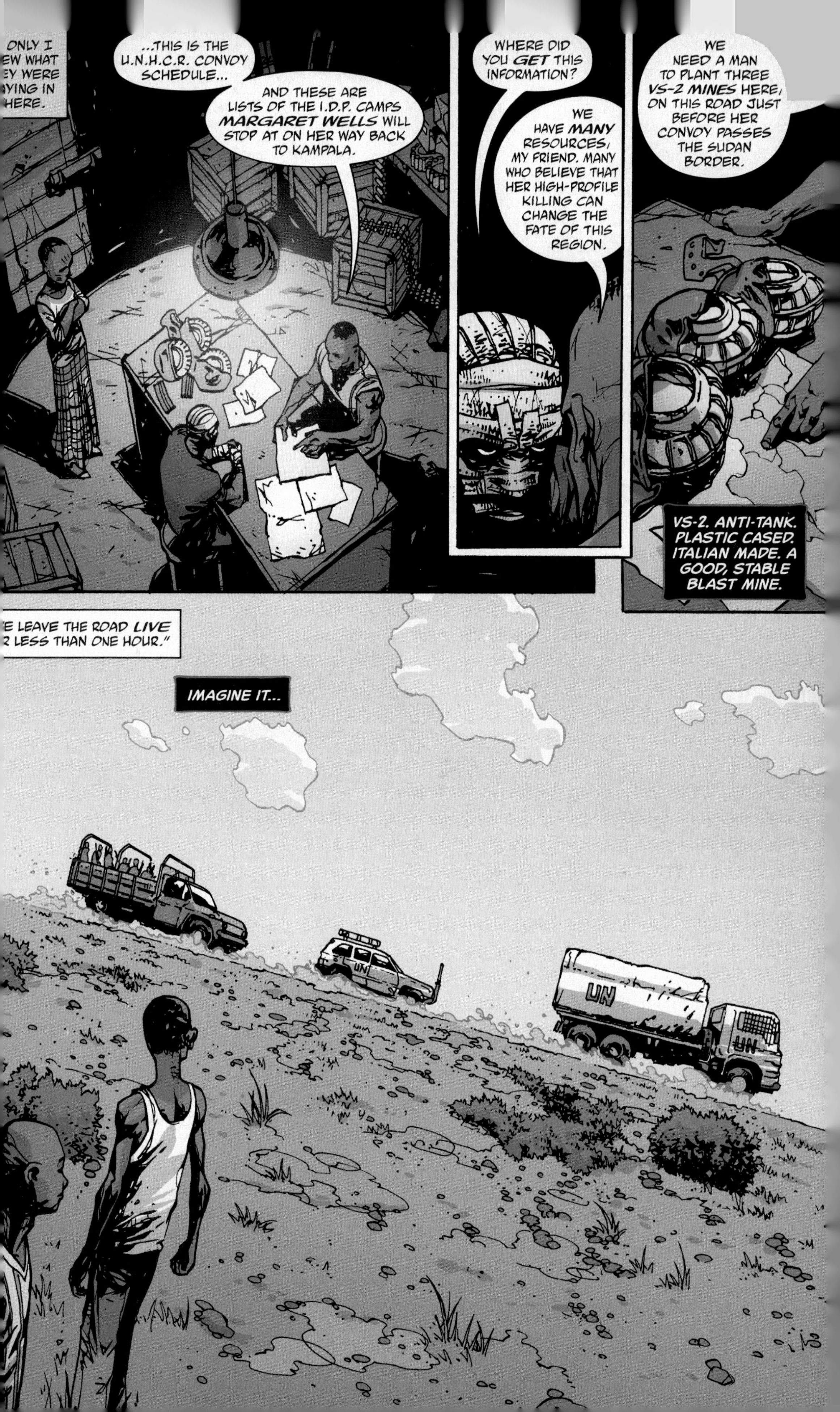
ONLY I
EW WHAT
EY WERE
YING IN
HERE.
...THIS IS THE U.N.H.C.R. CONVOY SCHEDULE...
AND THESE ARE LISTS OF THE I.D.P. CAMPS MARGARET WELLS WILL STOP AT ON HER WAY BACK TO KAMPALA.
WHERE DID YOU GET THIS INFORMATION?
WE HAVE MANY RESOURCES, MY FRIEND. MANY WHO BELIEVE THAT HER HIGH-PROFILE KILLING CAN CHANGE THE FATE OF THIS REGION.
WE NEED A MAN TO PLANT THREE VS-2 MINES HERE, ON THIS ROAD JUST BEFORE HER CONVOY PASSES THE SUDAN BORDER.
VS-2. ANTI-TANK. PLASTIC CASED. ITALIAN MADE. A GOOD, STABLE BLAST MINE.
E LEAVE THE ROAD LIVE
R LESS THAN ONE HOUR."
IMAGINE IT...
UN
UN
UN

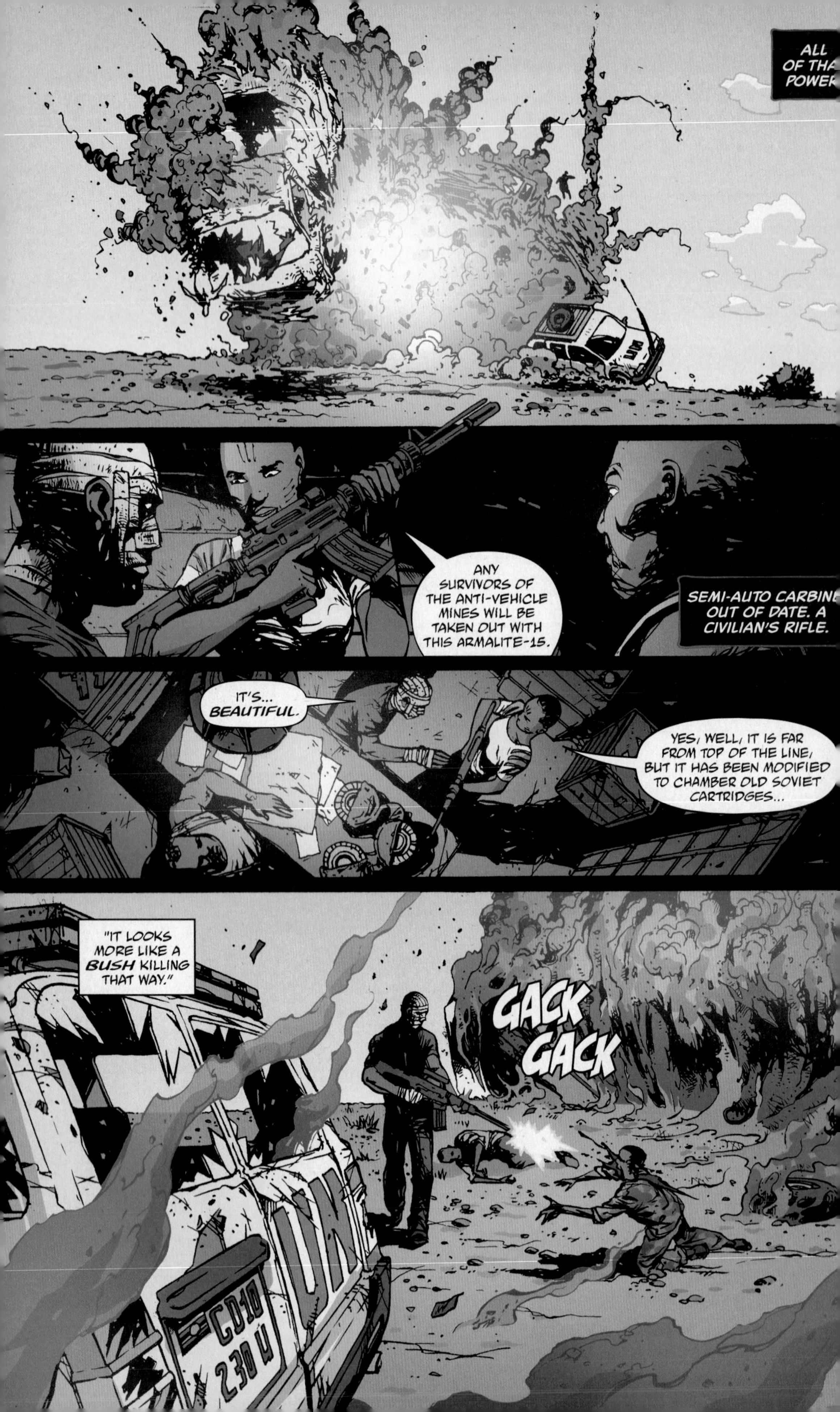
ALL OF THA
POWER
ANY SURVIVORS OF THE ANTI-VEHICLE MINES WILL BE TAKEN OUT WITH THIS ARMALITE-15.
SEMI-AUTO CARBINE OUT OF DATE. A CIVILIAN'S RIFLE.
IT'S... BEAUTIFUL.
YES, WELL, IT IS FAR FROM TOP OF THE LINE, BUT IT HAS BEEN MODIFIED TO CHAMBER OLD SOVIET CARTRIDGES...
"IT LOOKS MORE LIKE A BUSH KILLING THAT WAY."
GACK GACK
CD10 230 U

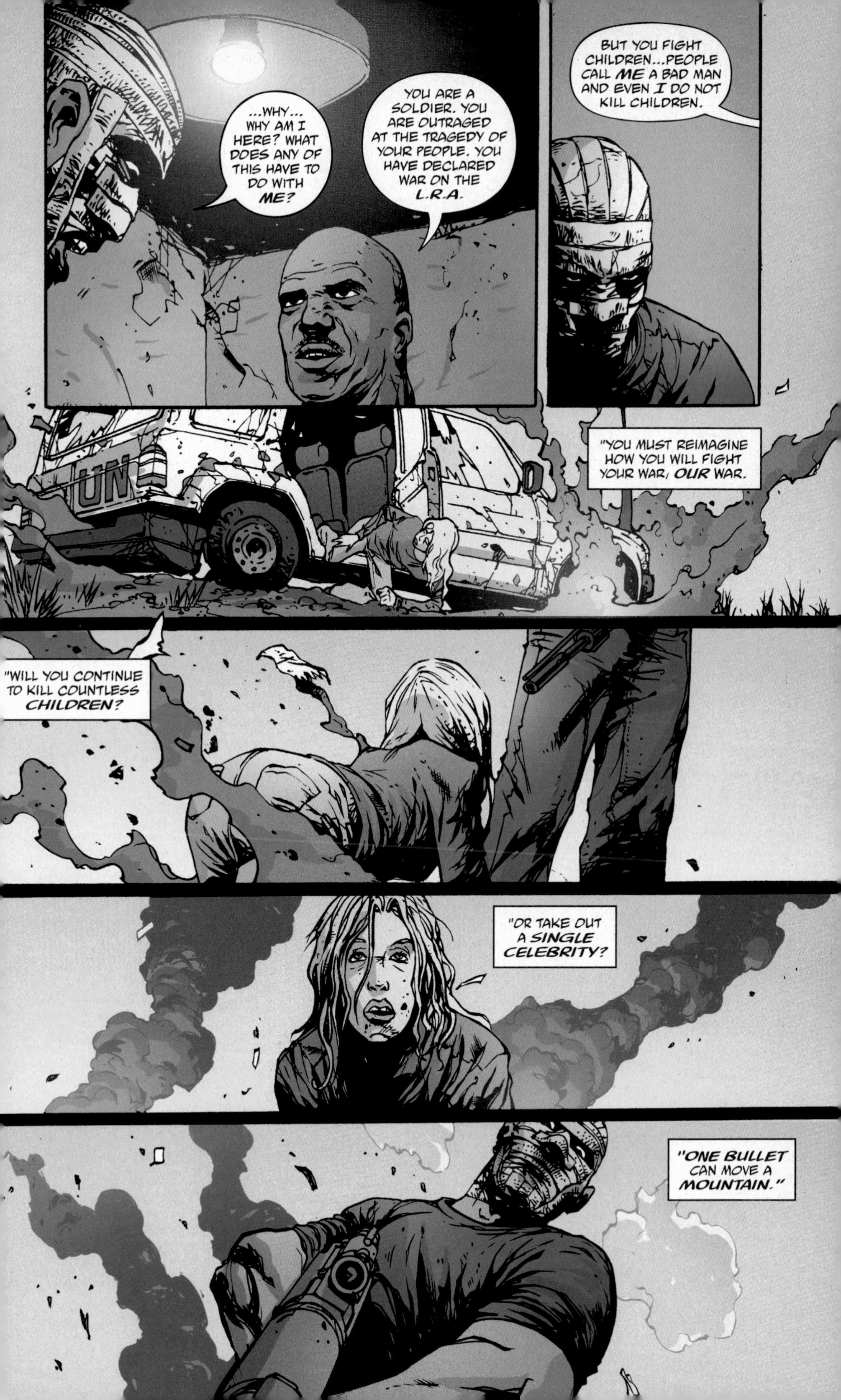
...WHY... WHY AM I HERE? WHAT DOES ANY OF THIS HAVE TO DO WITH ME?
YOU ARE A SOLDIER. YOU ARE OUTRAGED AT THE TRAGEDY OF YOUR PEOPLE. YOU HAVE DECLARED WAR ON THE L.R.A.
BUT YOU FIGHT CHILDREN...PEOPLE CALL ME A BAD MAN AND EVEN I DO NOT KILL CHILDREN.
"YOU MUST REIMAGINE HOW YOU WILL FIGHT YOUR WAR, OUR WAR.
UN
"WILL YOU CONTINUE TO KILL COUNTLESS CHILDREN?
"OR TAKE OUT A SINGLE CELEBRITY?
"ONE BULLET CAN MOVE A MOUNTAIN."

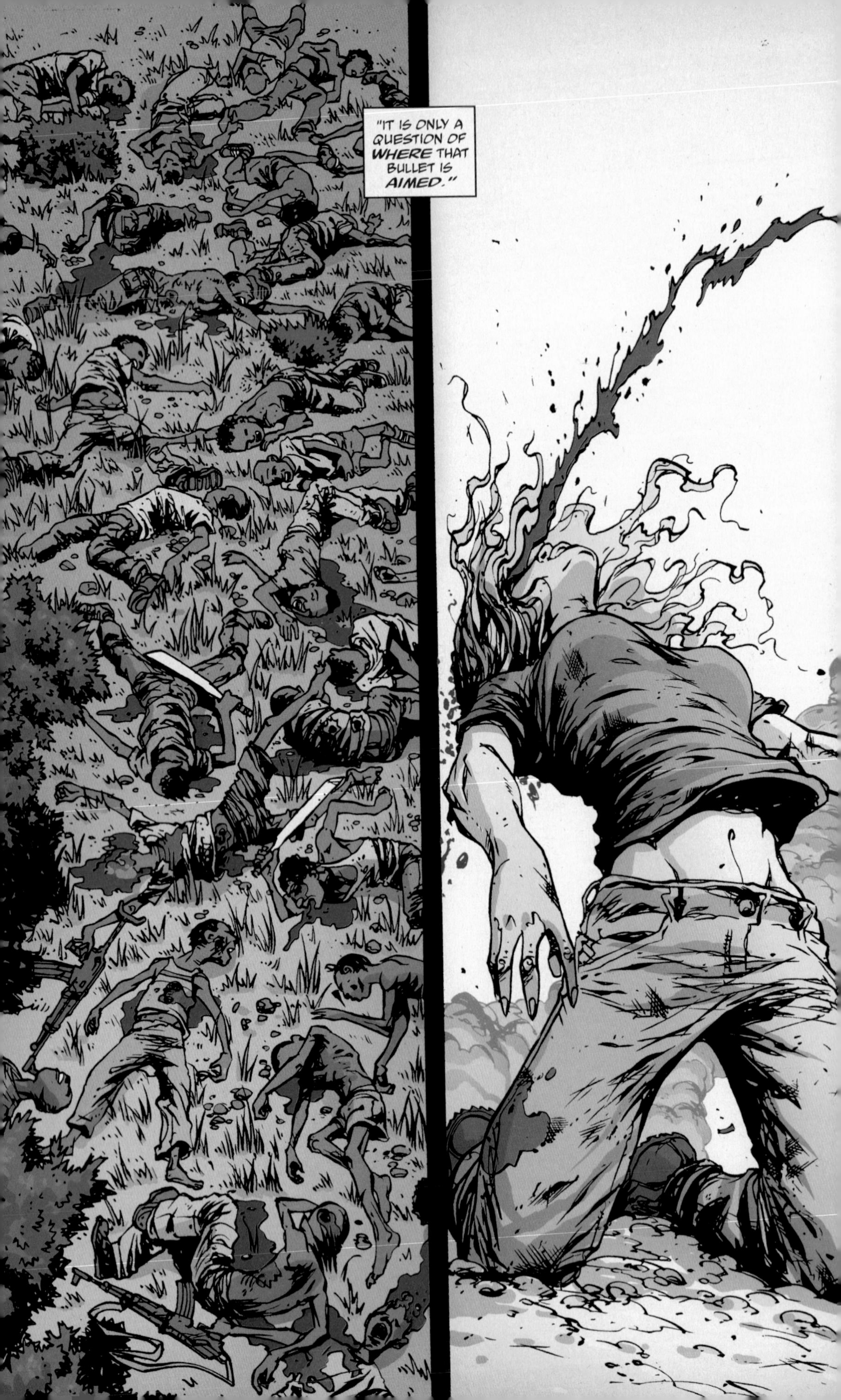
"IT IS ONLY A QUESTION OF WHERE THAT BULLET IS AIMED."

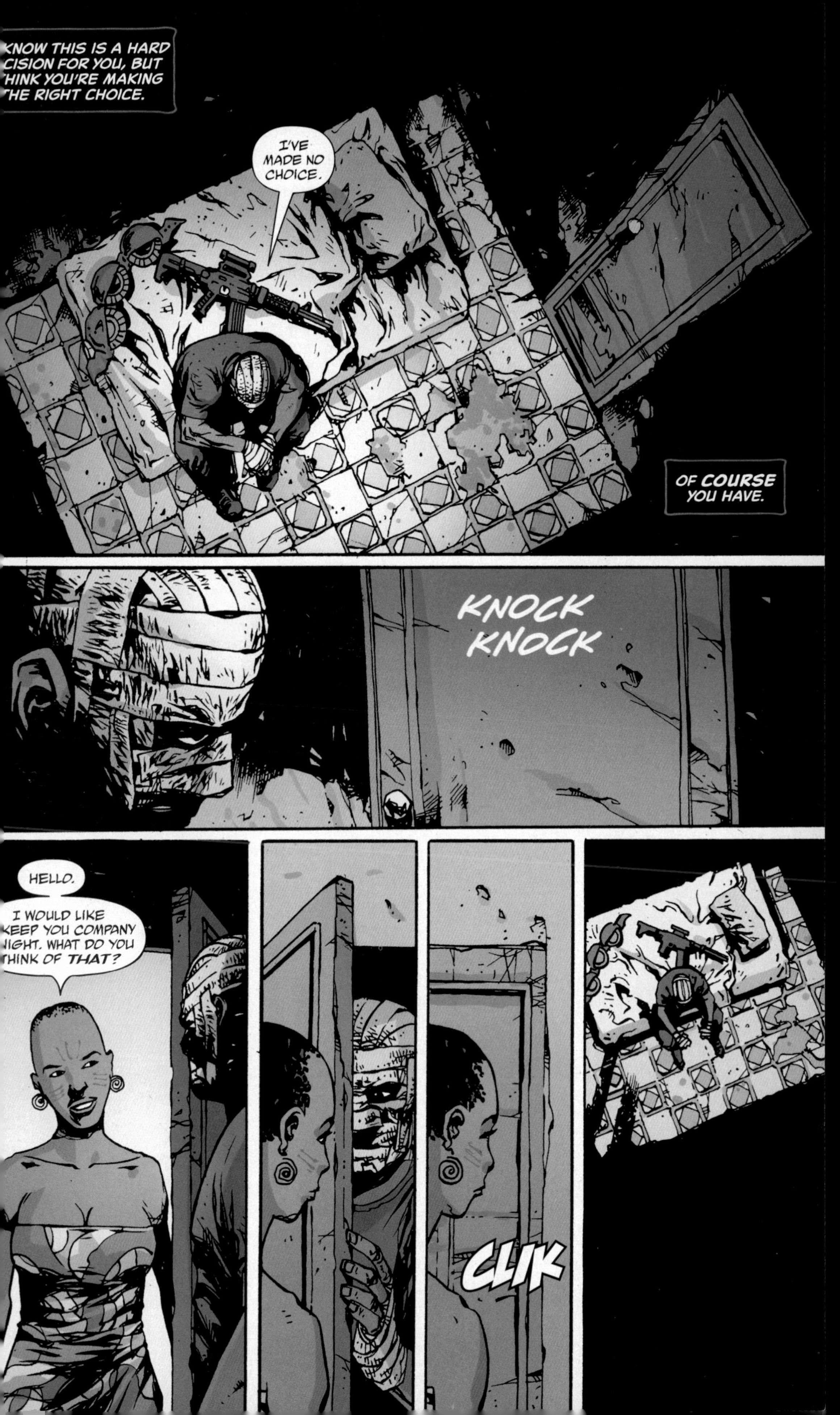
KNOW THIS IS A HARD CISION FOR YOU, BUT THINK YOU'RE MAKING THE RIGHT CHOICE.
I'VE MADE NO CHOICE.
OF COURSE YOU HAVE.
KNOCK KNOCK
HELLO.
I WOULD LIKE KEEP YOU COMPANY NIGHT. WHAT DO YOU THINK OF THAT?
CLIK

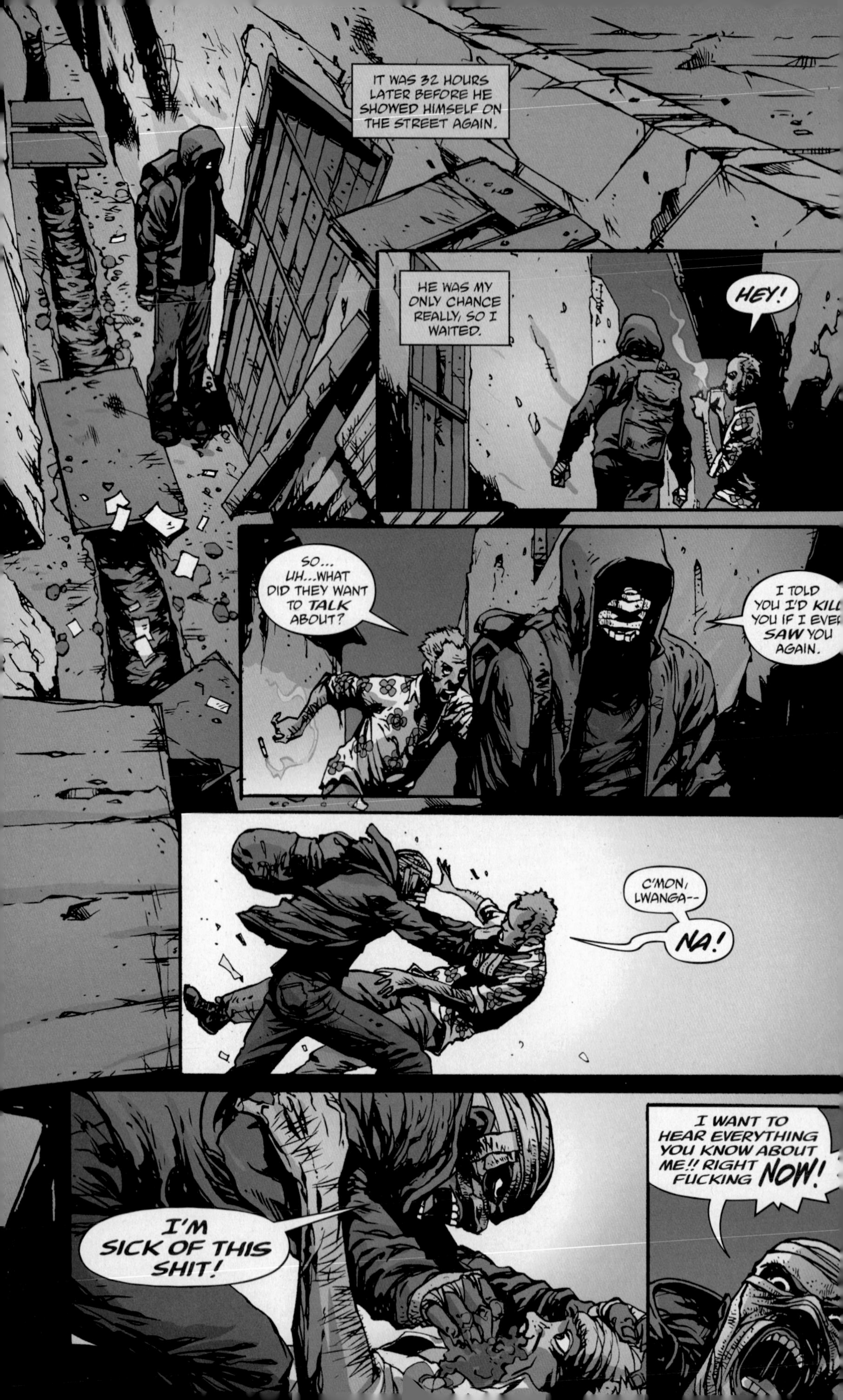

IT WAS 32 HOURS LATER BEFORE HE SHOWED HIMSELF ON THE STREET AGAIN.
HE WAS MY ONLY CHANCE REALLY, SO I WAITED.
HEY!
SO... UH...WHAT DID THEY WANT TO TALK ABOUT?
I TOLD YOU I'D KILL YOU IF I EVER SAW YOU AGAIN.
C'MON, LWANGA--
NA!
I'M SICK OF THIS SHIT!
I WANT TO HEAR EVERYTHING YOU KNOW ABOUT ME!! RIGHT FUCKING NOW!

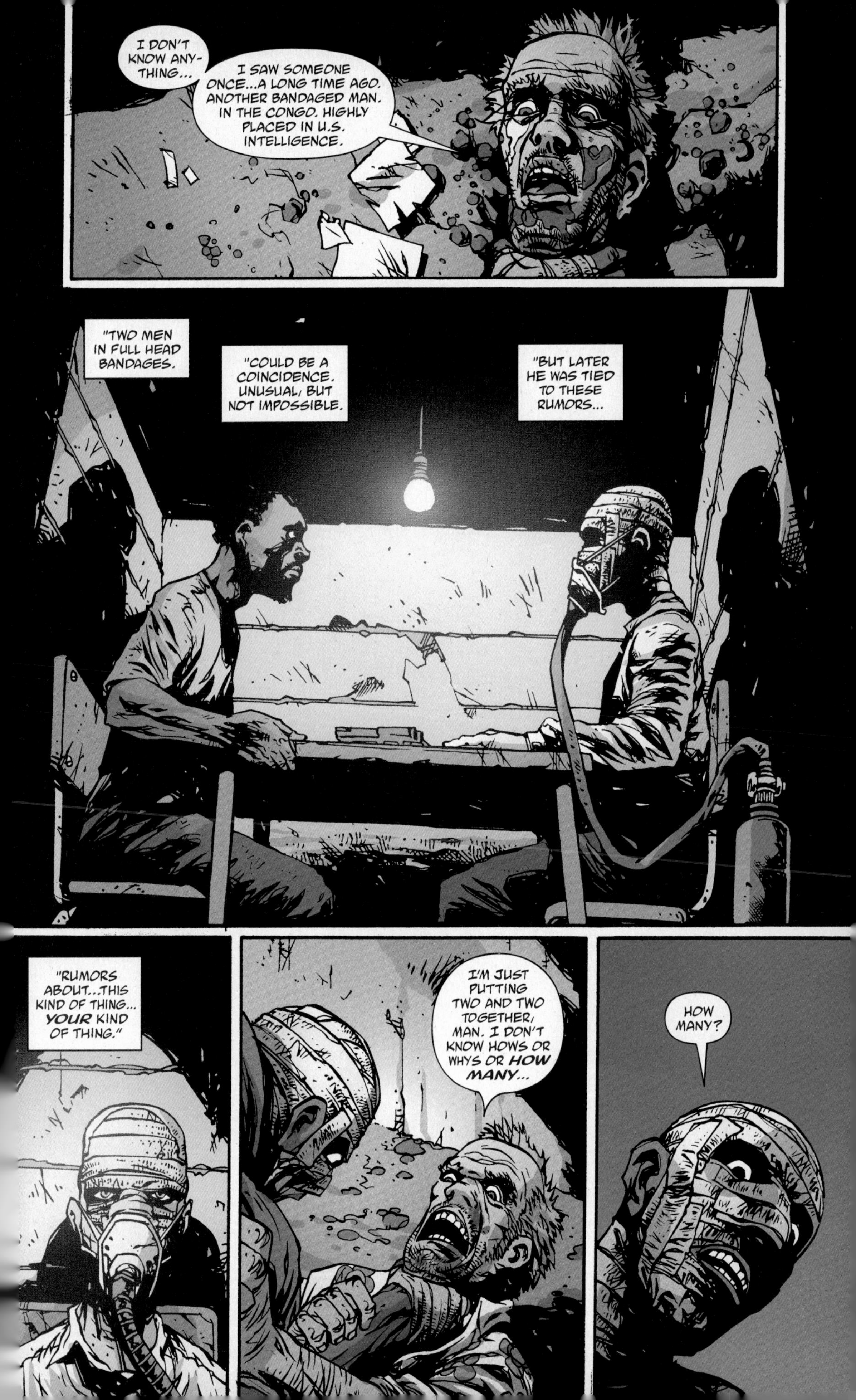
I DON'T KNOW ANY-THING...
I SAW SOMEONE ONCE...A LONG TIME AGO. ANOTHER BANDAGED MAN. IN THE CONGO. HIGHLY PLACED IN U.S. INTELLIGENCE.
"TWO MEN IN FULL HEAD BANDAGES.
"COULD BE A COINCIDENCE. UNUSUAL, BUT NOT IMPOSSIBLE.
"BUT LATER HE WAS TIED TO THESE RUMORS...
"RUMORS ABOUT...THIS KIND OF THING... YOUR KIND OF THING."
I'M JUST PUTTING TWO AND TWO TOGETHER, MAN. I DON'T KNOW HOWS OR WHYS OR HOW MANY...
HOW MANY?

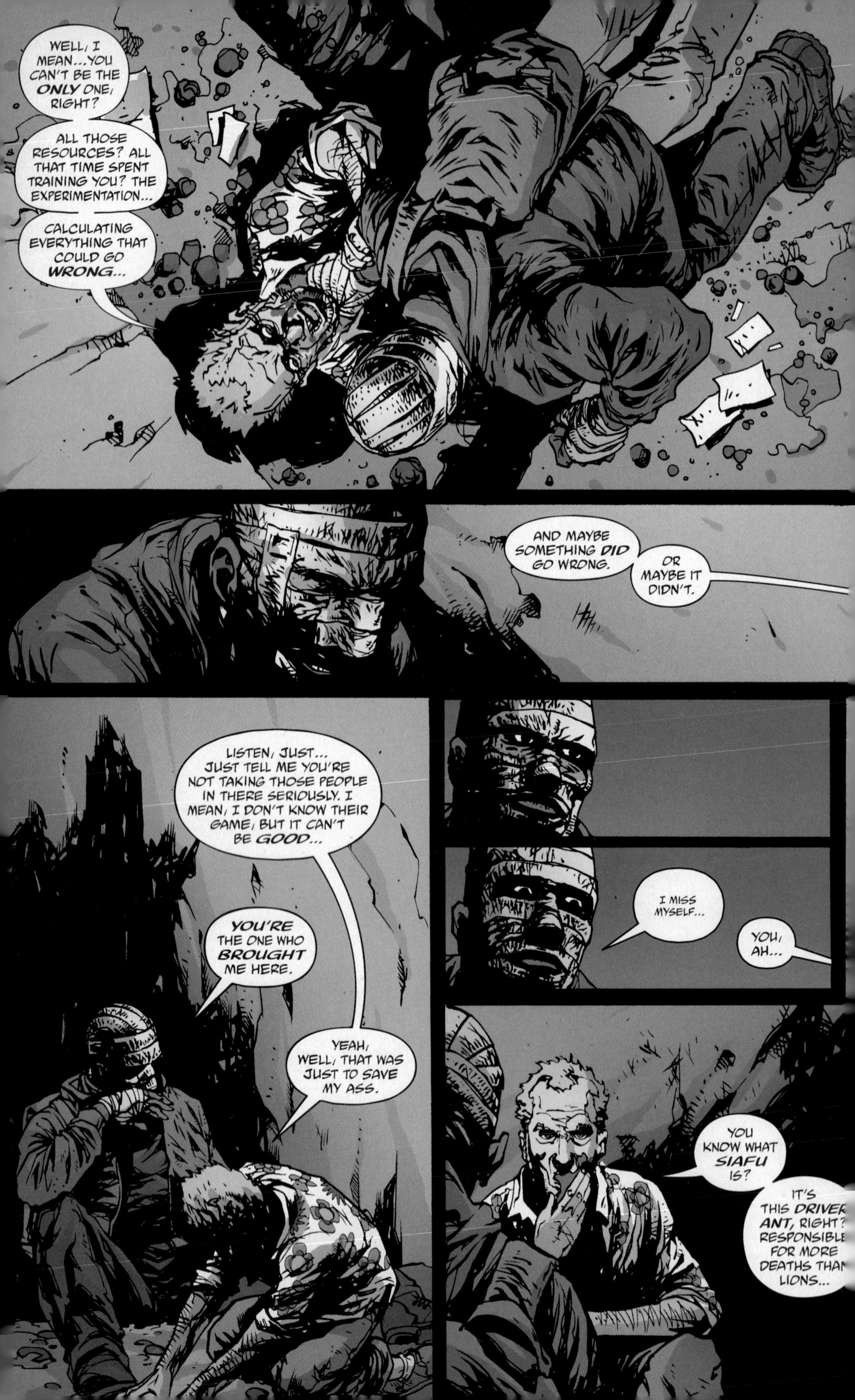
WELL, I MEAN...YOU CAN'T BE THE ONLY ONE, RIGHT?
ALL THOSE RESOURCES? ALL THAT TIME SPENT TRAINING YOU? THE EXPERIMENTATION...
CALCULATING EVERYTHING THAT COULD GO WRONG...
AND MAYBE SOMETHING DID GO WRONG.
OR MAYBE IT DIDN'T.
LISTEN, JUST... JUST TELL ME YOU'RE NOT TAKING THOSE PEOPLE IN THERE SERIOUSLY. I MEAN, I DON'T KNOW THEIR GAME, BUT IT CAN'T BE GOOD...
YOU'RE THE ONE WHO BROUGHT ME HERE.
YEAH, WELL, THAT WAS JUST TO SAVE MY ASS.
I MISS MYSELF...
YOU, AH...
YOU KNOW WHAT SIAFU IS?
IT'S THIS DRIVER ANT, RIGHT? RESPONSIBLE FOR MORE DEATHS THAN LIONS...

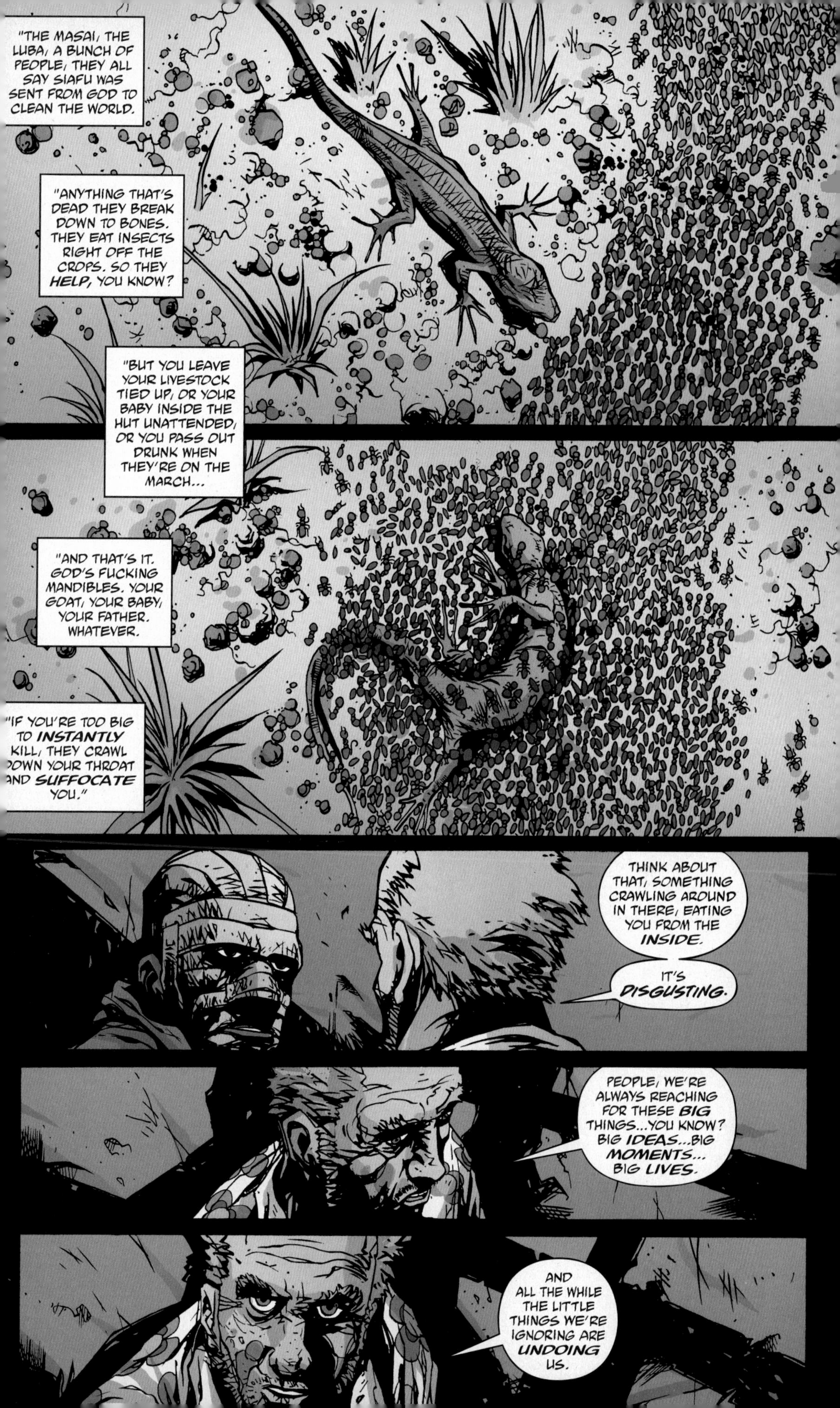
"THE MASAI, THE LUBA, A BUNCH OF PEOPLE, THEY ALL SAY SIAFU WAS SENT FROM GOD TO CLEAN THE WORLD.
"ANYTHING THAT'S DEAD THEY BREAK DOWN TO BONES. THEY EAT INSECTS RIGHT OFF THE CROPS. SO THEY HELP, YOU KNOW?
"BUT YOU LEAVE YOUR LIVESTOCK TIED UP, OR YOUR BABY INSIDE THE HUT UNATTENDED, OR YOU PASS OUT DRUNK WHEN THEY'RE ON THE MARCH...
"AND THAT'S IT. GOD'S FUCKING MANDIBLES. YOUR GOAT, YOUR BABY, YOUR FATHER. WHATEVER.
"IF YOU'RE TOO BIG TO INSTANTLY KILL, THEY CRAWL DOWN YOUR THROAT AND SUFFOCATE YOU."
THINK ABOUT THAT, SOMETHING CRAWLING AROUND IN THERE, EATING YOU FROM THE INSIDE.
IT'S DISGUSTING.
PEOPLE, WE'RE ALWAYS REACHING FOR THESE BIG THINGS...YOU KNOW? BIG IDEAS...BIG MOMENTS... BIG LIVES.
AND ALL THE WHILE THE LITTLE THINGS WE'RE IGNORING ARE UNDOING US.

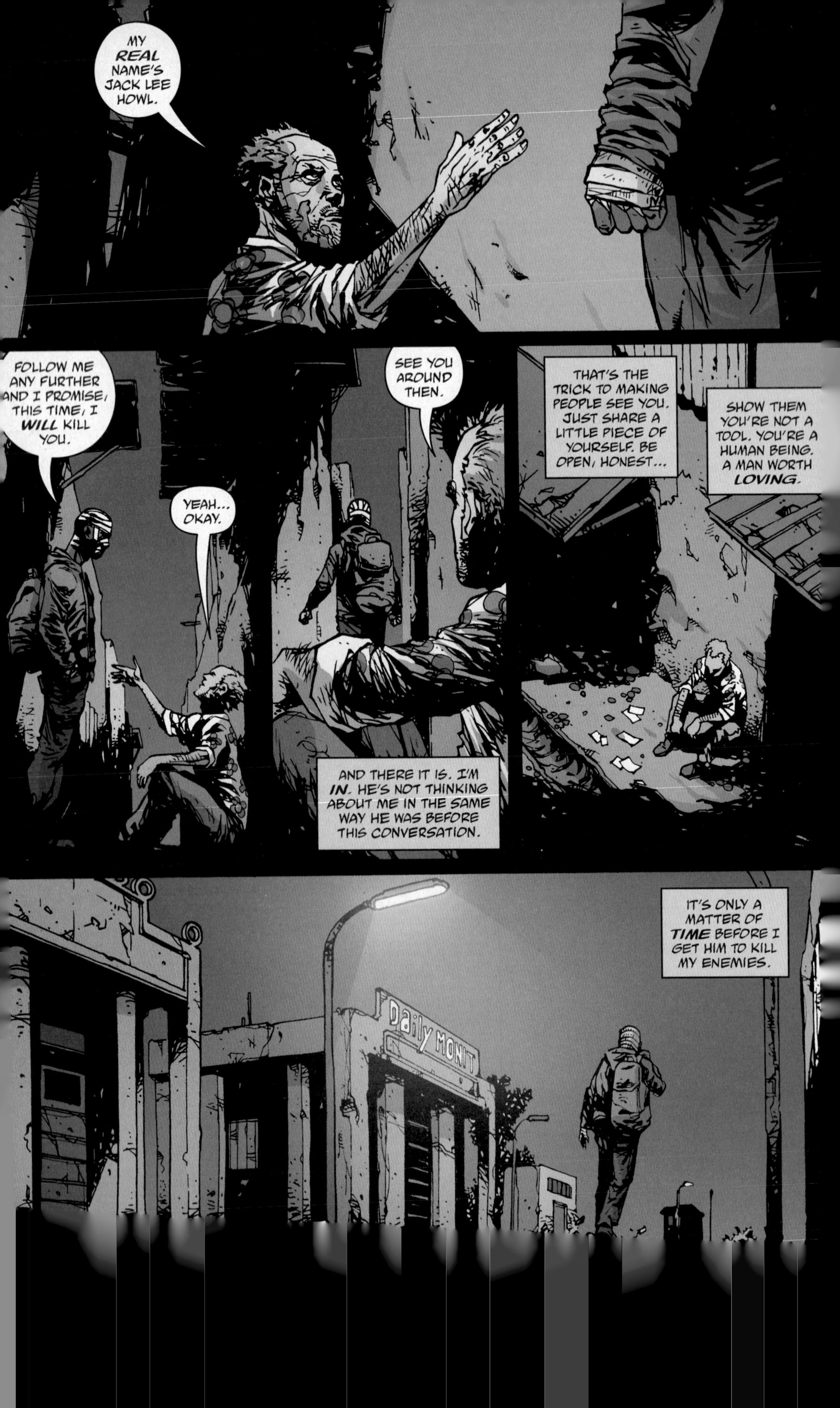

MY REAL NAME'S JACK LEE HOWL.
FOLLOW ME ANY FURTHER AND I PROMISE, THIS TIME, I WILL KILL YOU.
YEAH... OKAY.
SEE YOU AROUND THEN.
AND THERE IT IS. I'M IN. HE'S NOT THINKING ABOUT ME IN THE SAME WAY HE WAS BEFORE THIS CONVERSATION.
THAT'S THE TRICK TO MAKING PEOPLE SEE YOU. JUST SHARE A LITTLE PIECE OF YOURSELF. BE OPEN, HONEST...
SHOW THEM YOU'RE NOT A TOOL. YOU'RE A HUMAN BEING. A MAN WORTH LOVING.
Daily MONIT
IT'S ONLY A MATTER OF TIME BEFORE I GET HIM TO KILL MY ENEMIES.

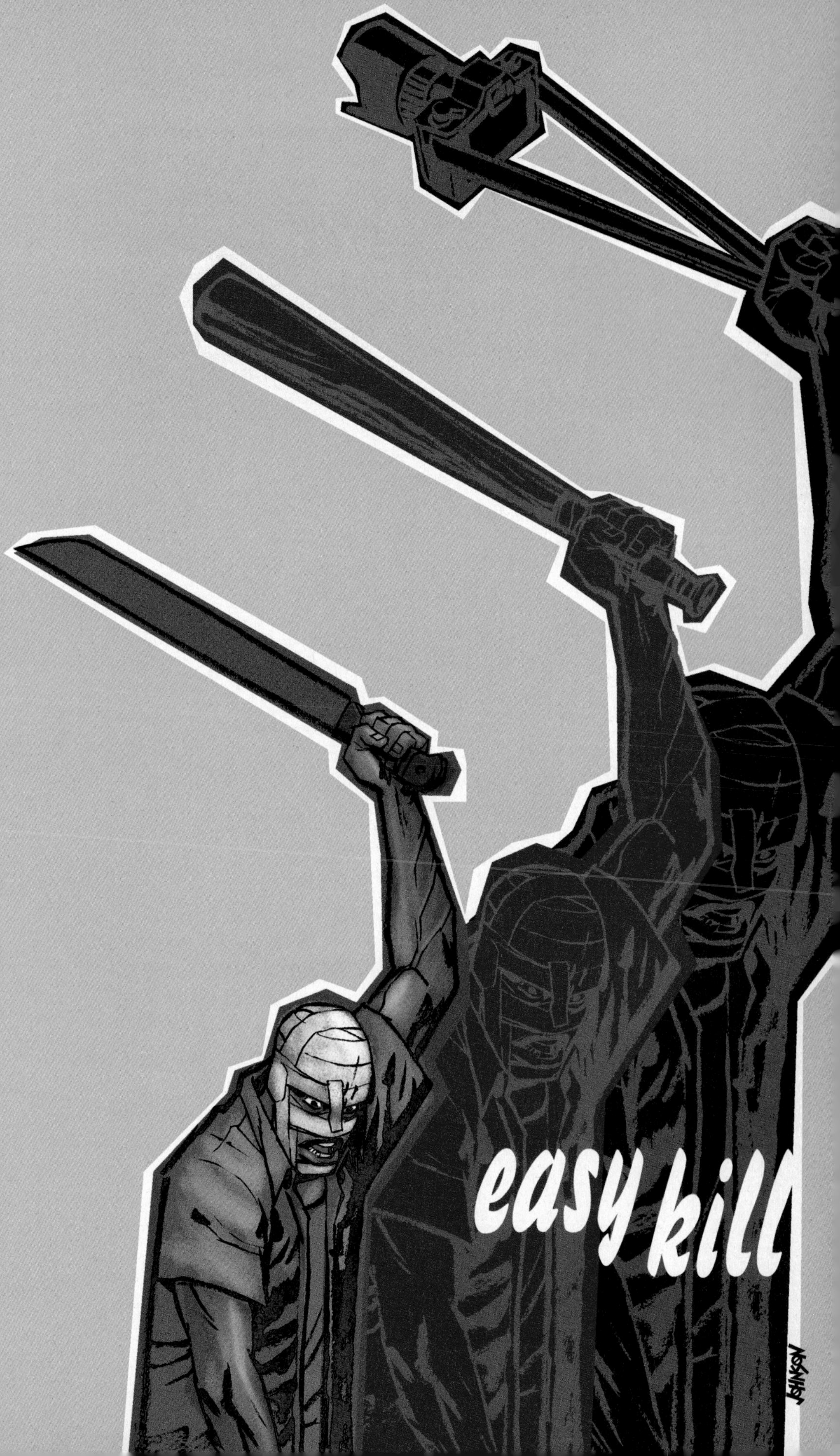
easy kill

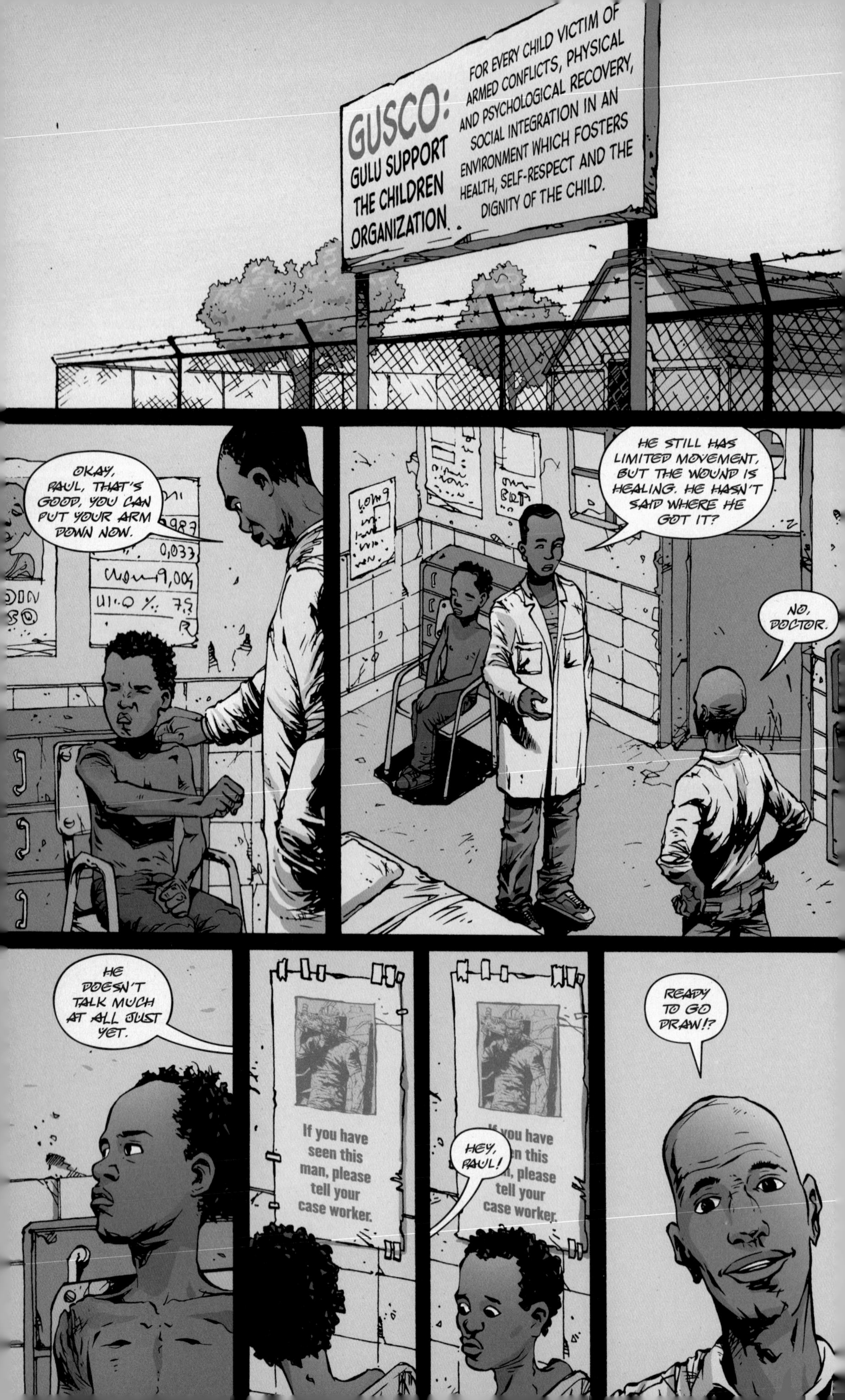
GUSCO:
GULU SUPPORT THE CHILDREN ORGANIZATION
FOR EVERY CHILD VICTIM OF ARMED CONFLICTS, PHYSICAL AND PSYCHOLOGICAL RECOVERY, SOCIAL INTEGRATION IN AN ENVIRONMENT WHICH FOSTERS HEALTH, SELF-RESPECT AND THE DIGNITY OF THE CHILD.
OKAY, PAUL, THAT'S GOOD, YOU CAN PUT YOUR ARM DOWN NOW.
HE STILL HAS LIMITED MOVEMENT, BUT THE WOUND IS HEALING. HE HASN'T SAID WHERE HE GOT IT?
NO, DOCTOR.
HE DOESN'T TALK MUCH AT ALL JUST YET.
If you have seen this man, please tell your case worker.
HEY, PAUL!
READY TO GO DRAW!?

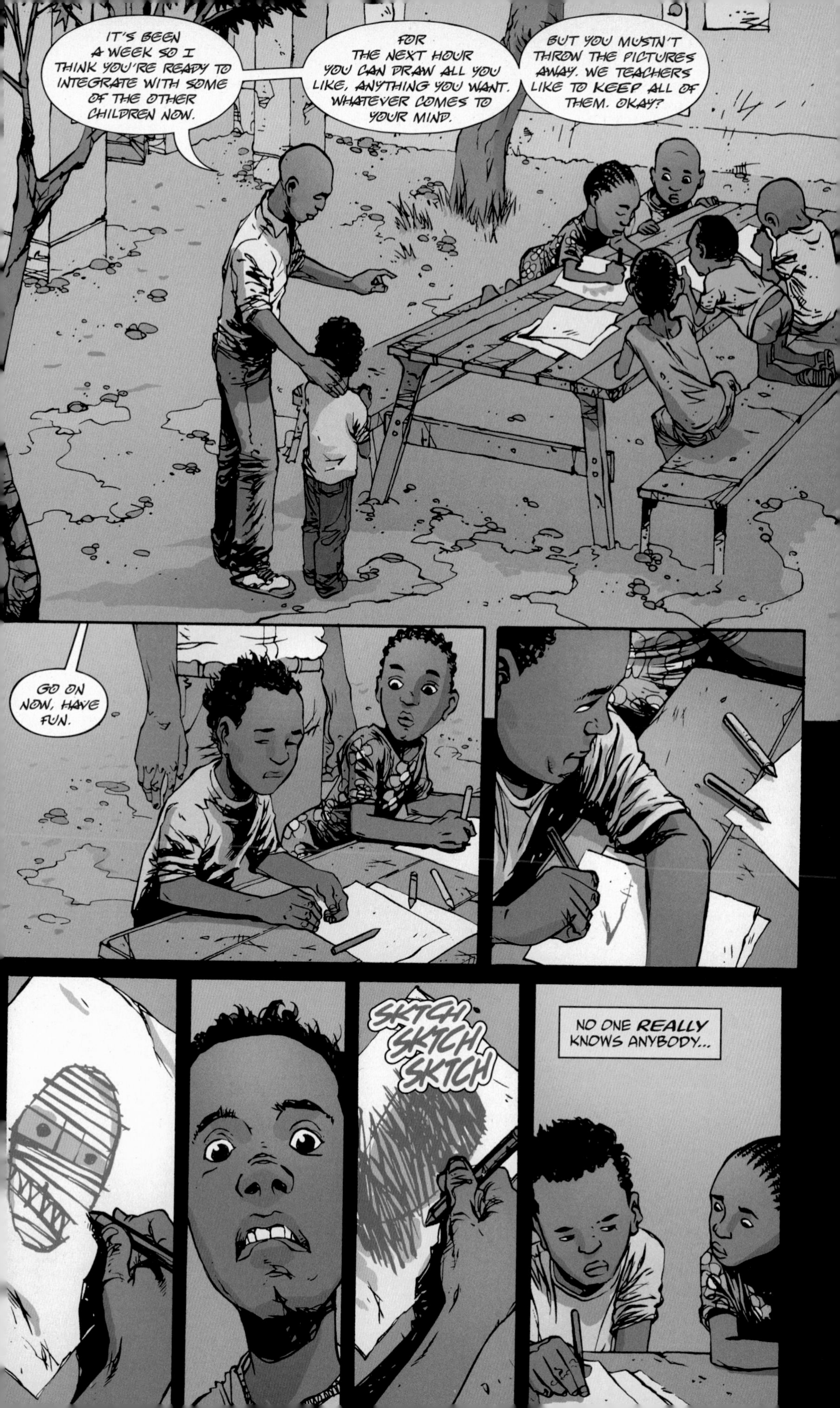
IT'S BEEN A WEEK SO I THINK YOU'RE READY TO INTEGRATE WITH SOME OF THE OTHER CHILDREN NOW.
FOR THE NEXT HOUR YOU CAN DRAW ALL YOU LIKE, ANYTHING YOU WANT. WHATEVER COMES TO YOUR MIND.
BUT YOU MUSTN'T THROW THE PICTURES AWAY. WE TEACHERS LIKE TO KEEP ALL OF THEM. OKAY?
GO ON NOW, HAVE FUN.
SKTCH SKTCH SKTCH
NO ONE REALLY KNOWS ANYBODY...

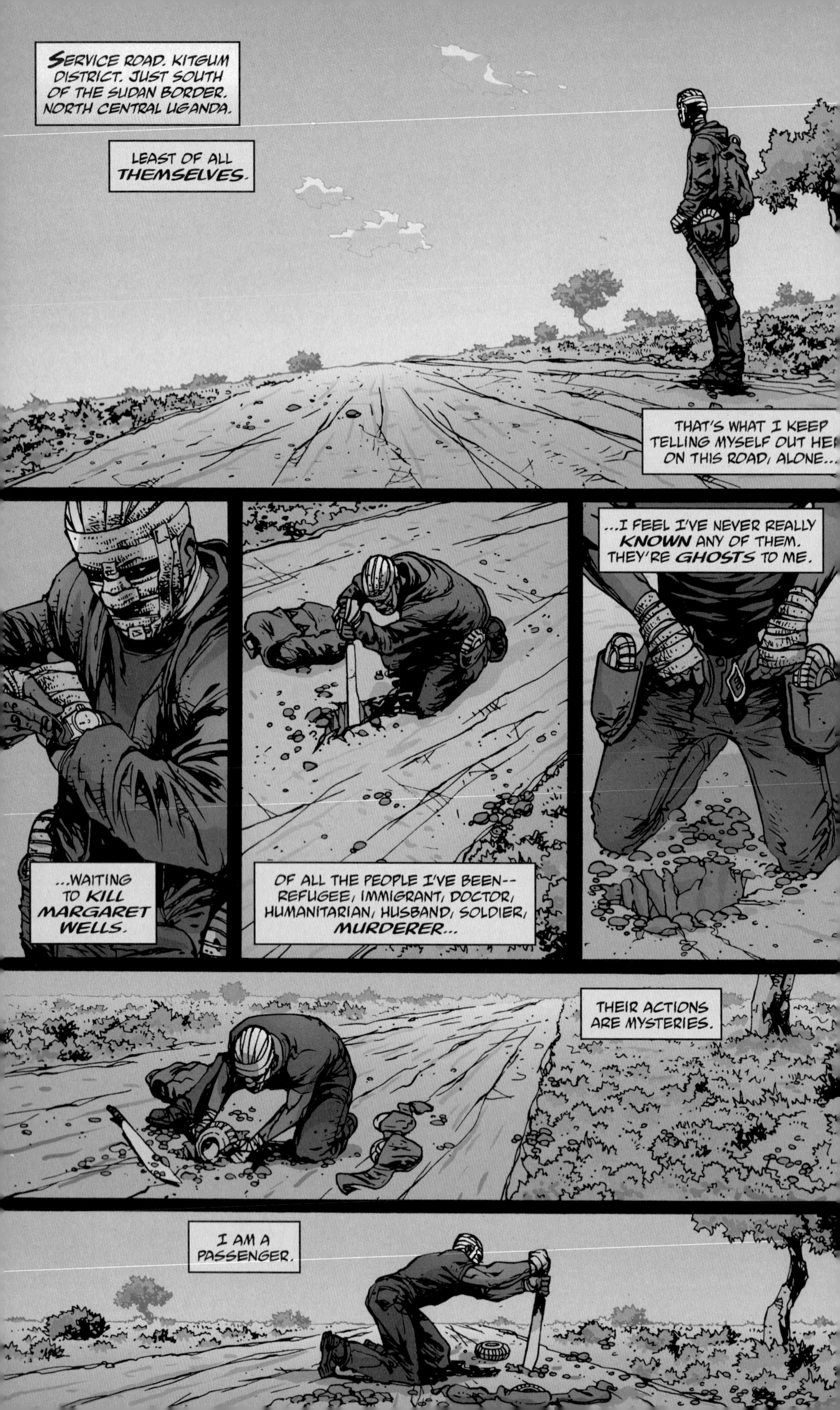
SERVICE ROAD. KITGUM DISTRICT. JUST SOUTH OF THE SUDAN BORDER. NORTH CENTRAL UGANDA.
LEAST OF ALL THEMSELVES.
THAT'S WHAT I KEEP TELLING MYSELF OUT HE[RE] ON THIS ROAD, ALONE...
...WAITING TO KILL MARGARET WELLS.
OF ALL THE PEOPLE I'VE BEEN-- REFUGEE, IMMIGRANT, DOCTOR, HUMANITARIAN, HUSBAND, SOLDIER, MURDERER...
...I FEEL I'VE NEVER REALLY KNOWN ANY OF THEM. THEY'RE GHOSTS TO ME.
THEIR ACTIONS ARE MYSTERIES.
I AM A PASSENGER.

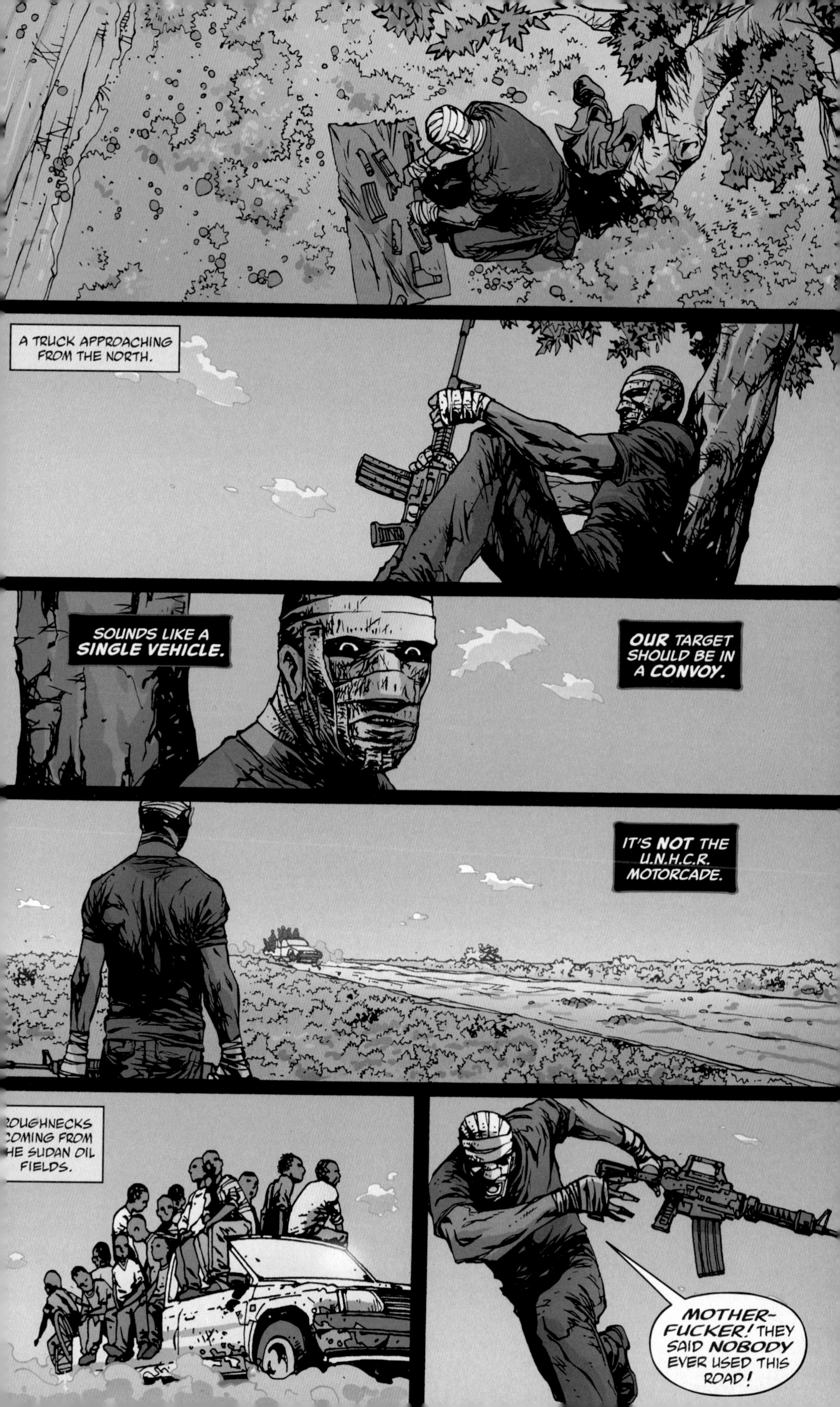
A TRUCK APPROACHING FROM THE NORTH.
SOUNDS LIKE A SINGLE VEHICLE.
OUR TARGET SHOULD BE IN A CONVOY.
IT'S NOT THE U.N.H.C.R. MOTORCADE.
ROUGHNECKS COMING FROM THE SUDAN OIL FIELDS.
MOTHER-FUCKER! THEY SAID NOBODY EVER USED THIS ROAD!

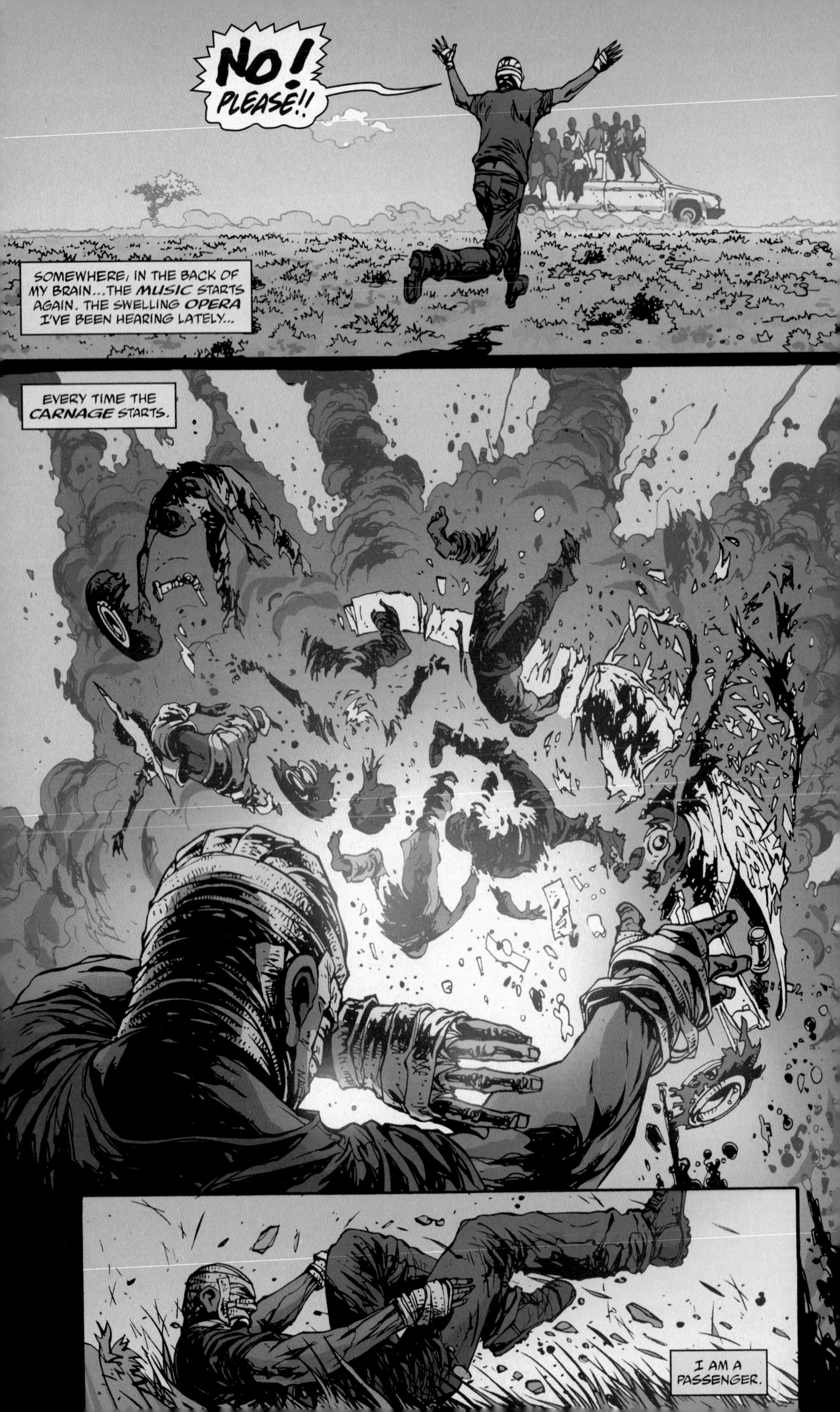
NO! PLEASE!!
SOMEWHERE, IN THE BACK OF MY BRAIN...THE MUSIC STARTS AGAIN. THE SWELLING OPERA I'VE BEEN HEARING LATELY...
EVERY TIME THE CARNAGE STARTS.
I AM A PASSENGER.

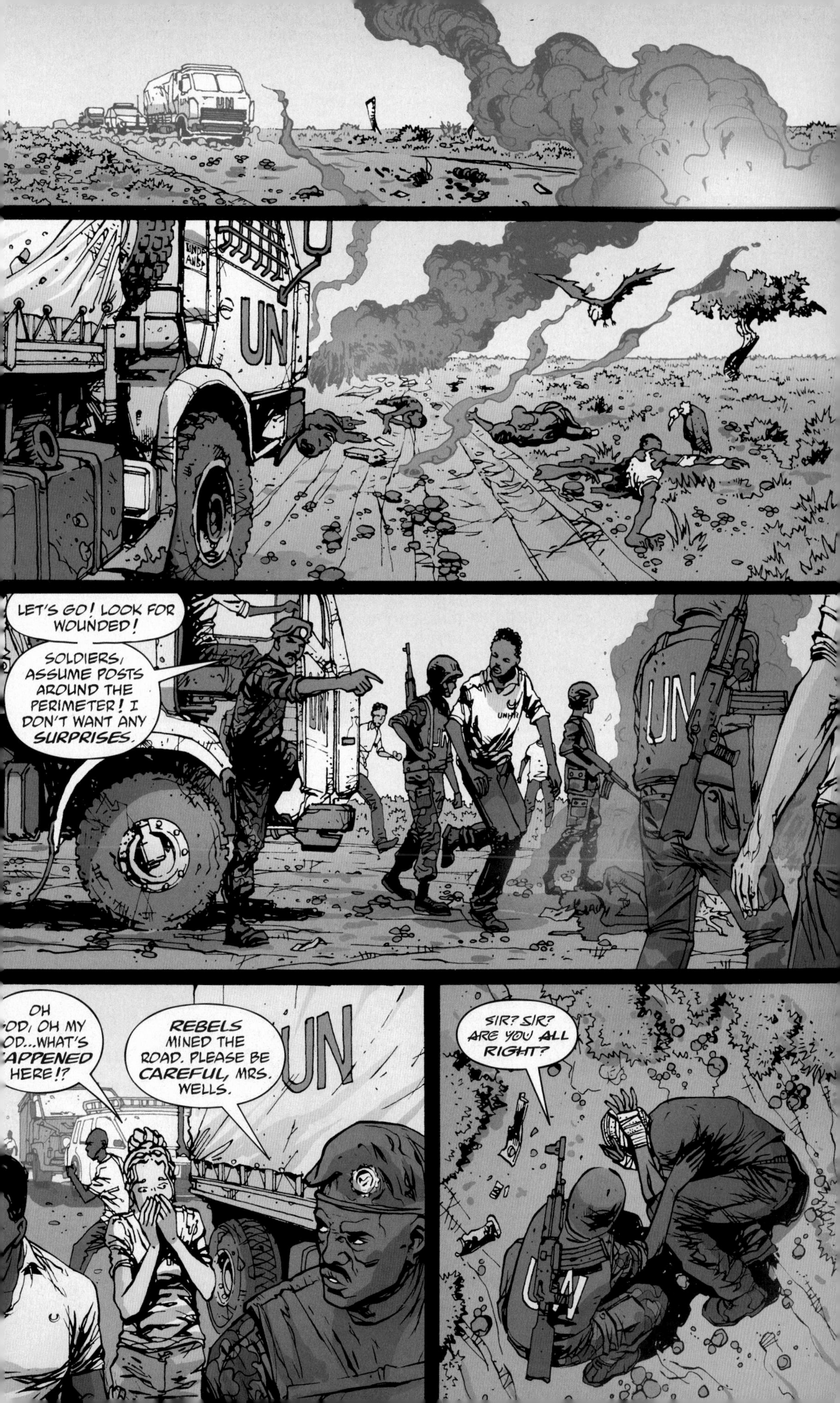
LET'S GO! LOOK FOR WOUNDED!
SOLDIERS, ASSUME POSTS AROUND THE PERIMETER! I DON'T WANT ANY SURPRISES.
OH ...OD, OH MY ...OD...WHAT'S ...APPENED HERE!?
REBELS MINED THE ROAD. PLEASE BE CAREFUL, MRS. WELLS.
SIR? SIR? ARE YOU ALL RIGHT?

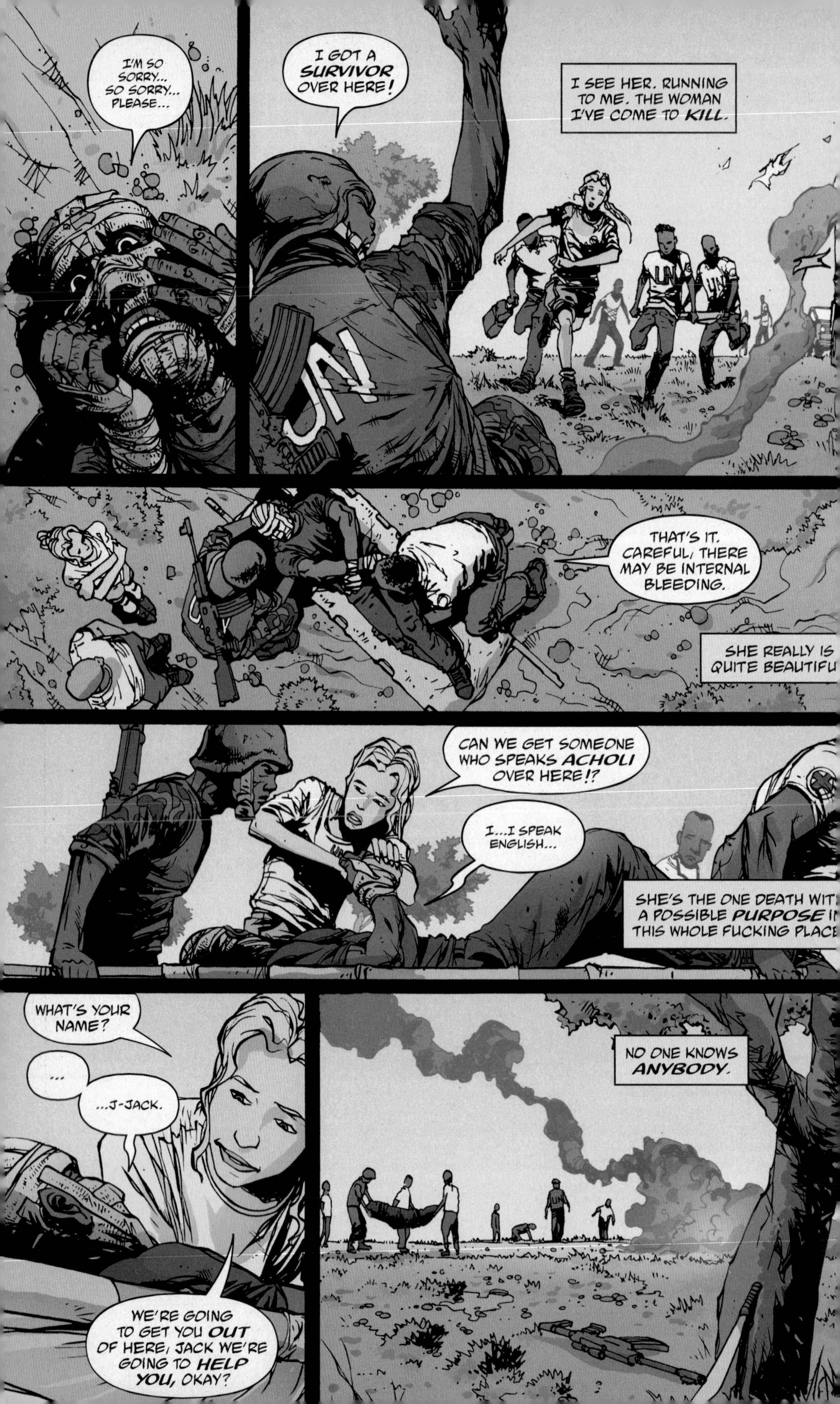

I'M SO SORRY... SO SORRY... PLEASE...
I GOT A SURVIVOR OVER HERE!
I SEE HER. RUNNING TO ME. THE WOMAN I'VE COME TO KILL.
THAT'S IT. CAREFUL, THERE MAY BE INTERNAL BLEEDING.
SHE REALLY IS QUITE BEAUTIFU
CAN WE GET SOMEONE WHO SPEAKS ACHOLI OVER HERE!?
I...I SPEAK ENGLISH...
SHE'S THE ONE DEATH WIT A POSSIBLE PURPOSE I THIS WHOLE FUCKING PLACE
WHAT'S YOUR NAME?
...
...J-JACK.
WE'RE GOING TO GET YOU OUT OF HERE, JACK WE'RE GOING TO HELP YOU, OKAY?
NO ONE KNOWS ANYBODY.

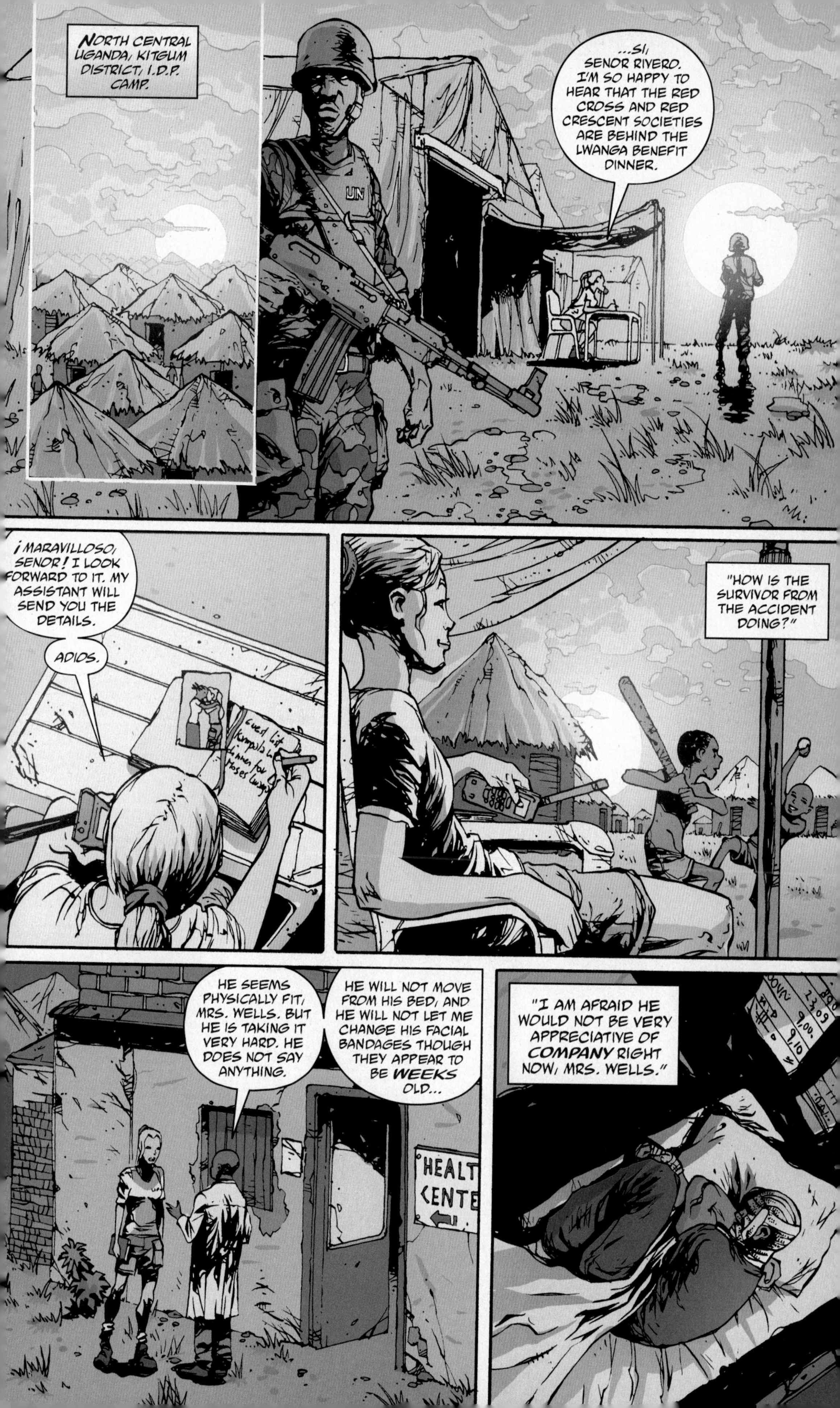
NORTH CENTRAL UGANDA, KITGUM DISTRICT, I.D.P. CAMP.
...SI, SENOR RIVERO. I'M SO HAPPY TO HEAR THAT THE RED CROSS AND RED CRESCENT SOCIETIES ARE BEHIND THE LWANGA BENEFIT DINNER.
¡MARAVILLOSO, SENOR! I LOOK FORWARD TO IT. MY ASSISTANT WILL SEND YOU THE DETAILS.
ADIOS.
"HOW IS THE SURVIVOR FROM THE ACCIDENT DOING?"
HE SEEMS PHYSICALLY FIT, MRS. WELLS. BUT HE IS TAKING IT VERY HARD. HE DOES NOT SAY ANYTHING.
HE WILL NOT MOVE FROM HIS BED, AND HE WILL NOT LET ME CHANGE HIS FACIAL BANDAGES THOUGH THEY APPEAR TO BE WEEKS OLD...
HEALT CENTE
"I AM AFRAID HE WOULD NOT BE VERY APPRECIATIVE OF COMPANY RIGHT NOW, MRS. WELLS."

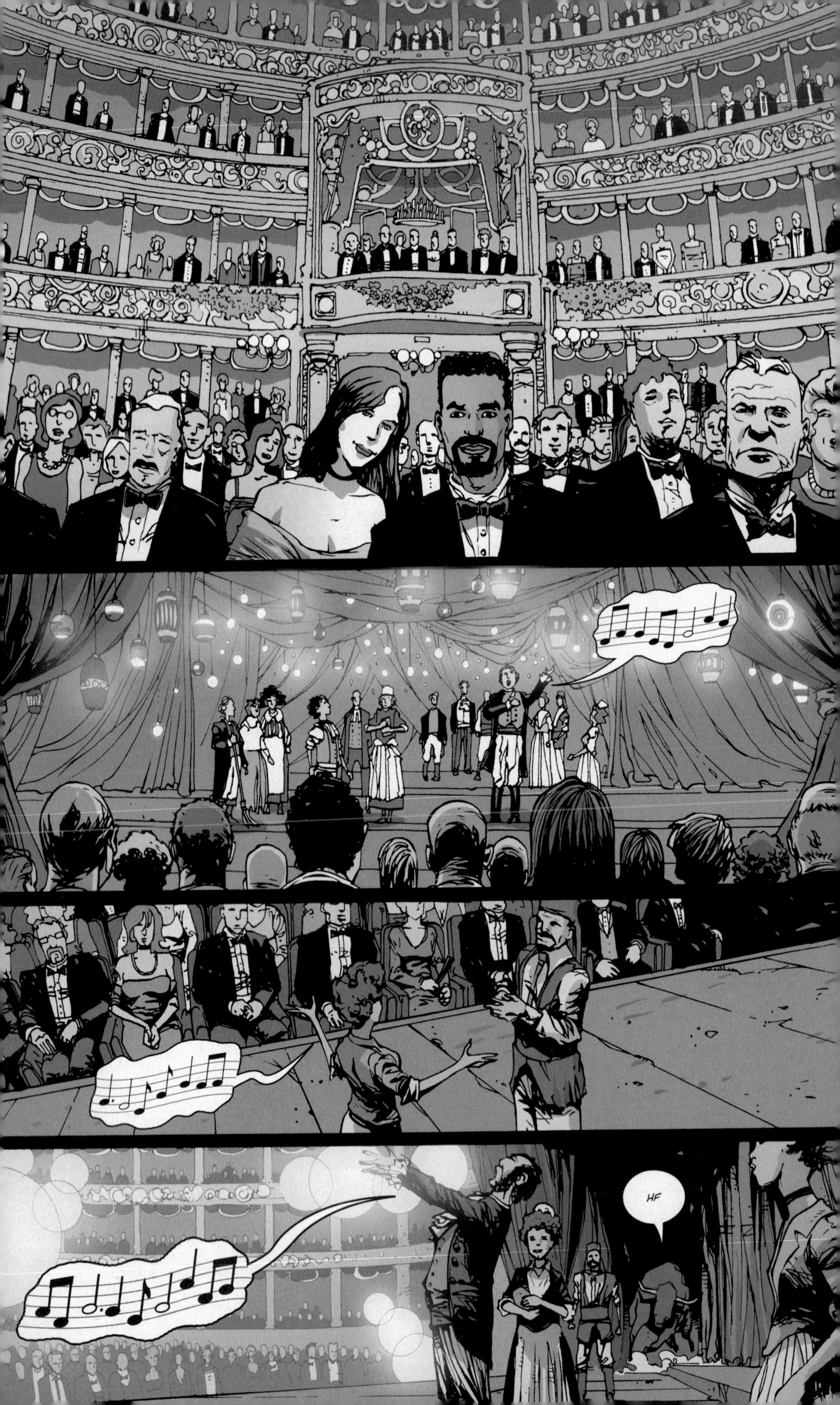
HF

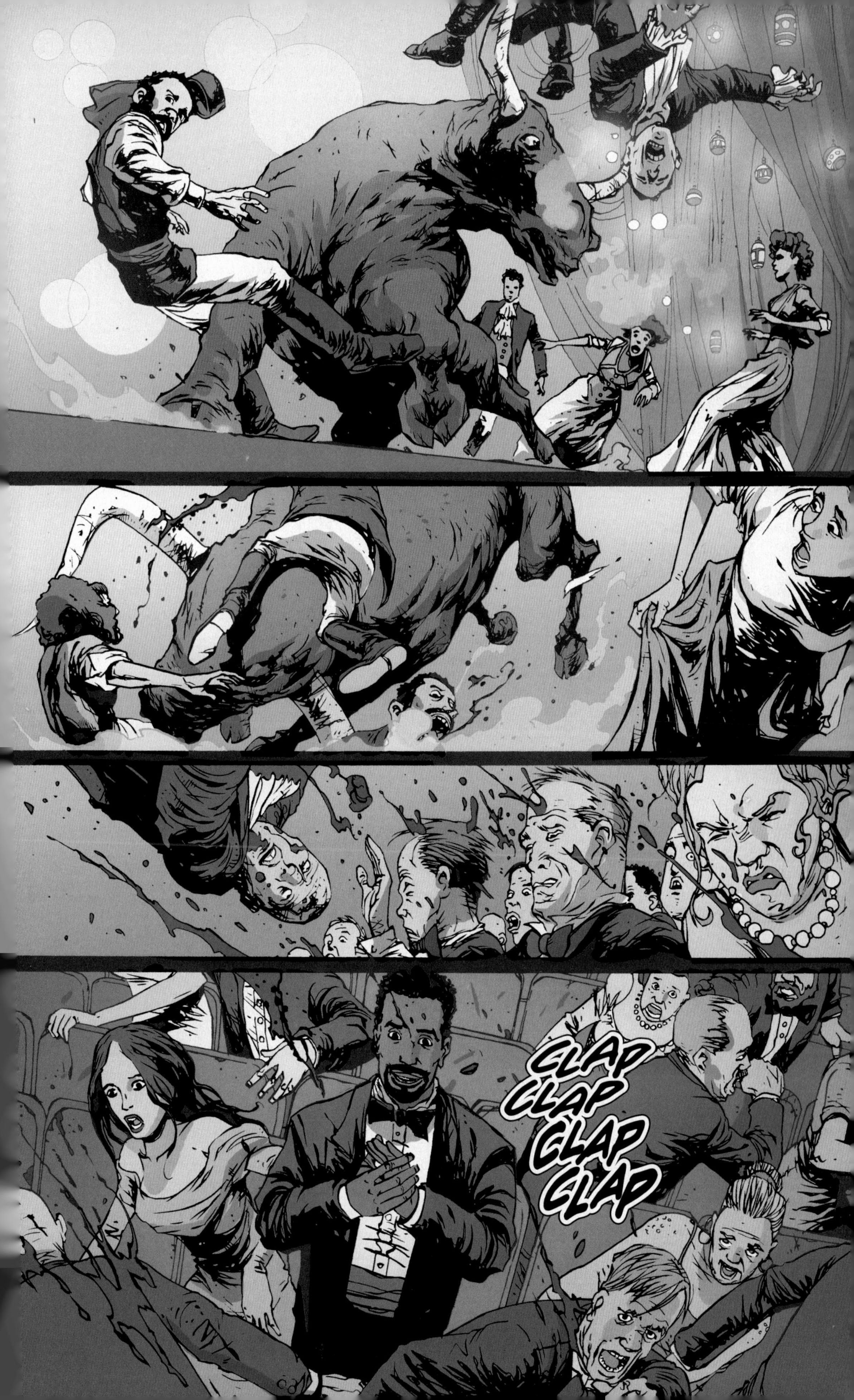
CLAP
CLAP
CLAP
CLAP

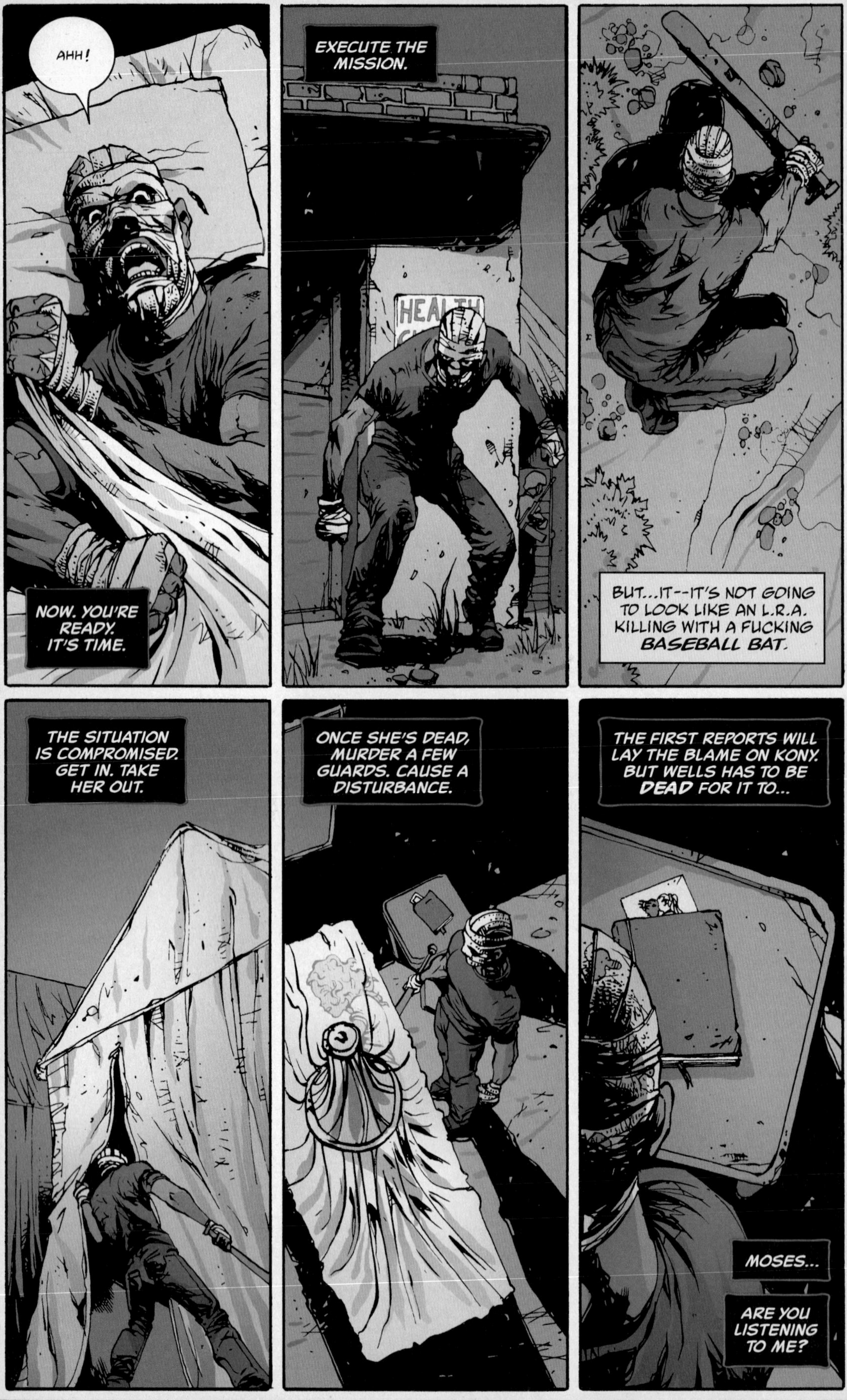
AHH!
NOW. YOU'RE READY. IT'S TIME.
EXECUTE THE MISSION.
HEALTH
BUT...IT--IT'S NOT GOING TO LOOK LIKE AN L.R.A. KILLING WITH A FUCKING BASEBALL BAT.
THE SITUATION IS COMPROMISED. GET IN. TAKE HER OUT.
ONCE SHE'S DEAD, MURDER A FEW GUARDS. CAUSE A DISTURBANCE.
THE FIRST REPORTS WILL LAY THE BLAME ON KONY. BUT WELLS HAS TO BE DEAD FOR IT TO...
MOSES...
ARE YOU LISTENING TO ME?

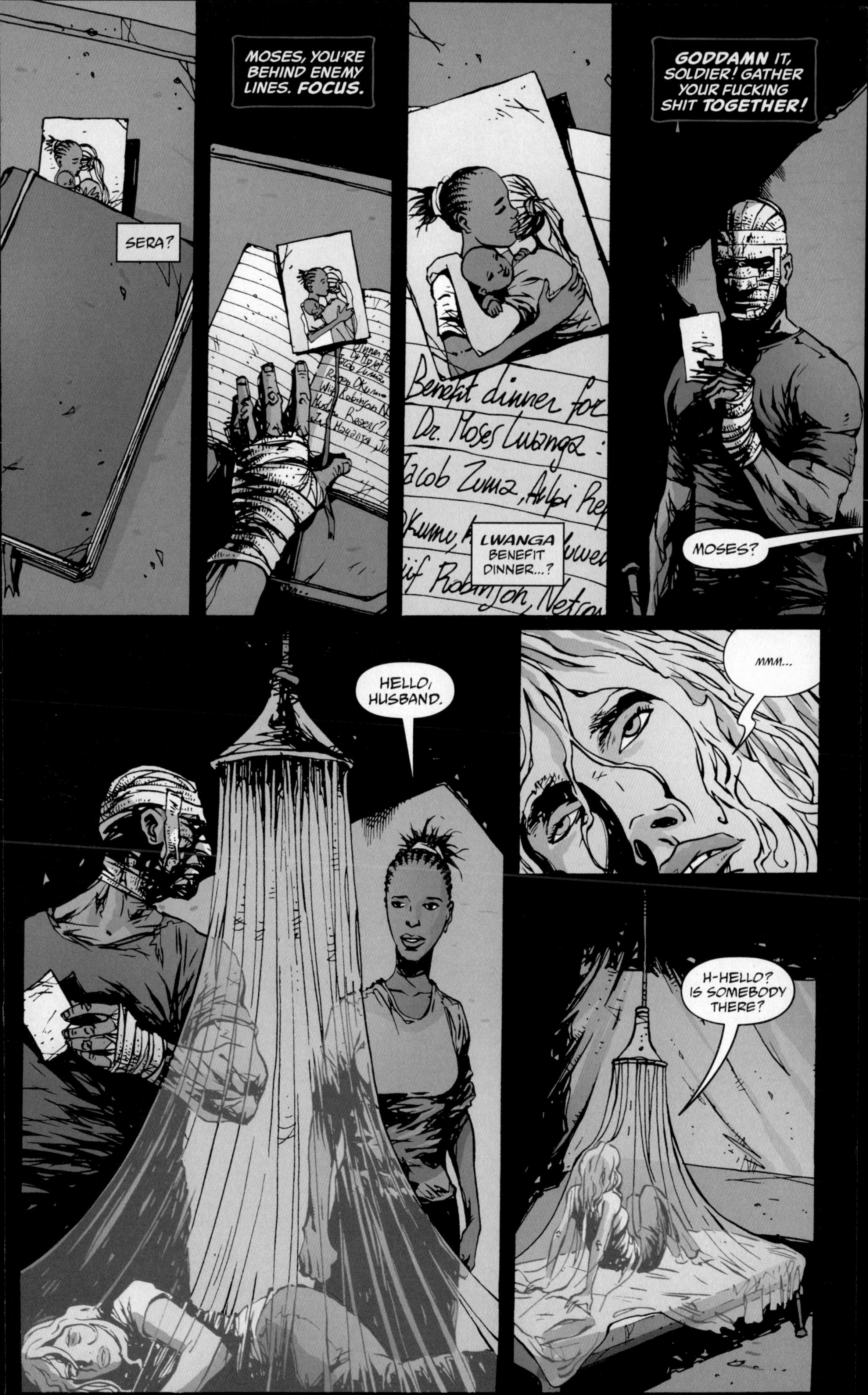
SERA?
MOSES, YOU'RE BEHIND ENEMY LINES. FOCUS.
Benefit dinner for
Dr. Moses Lwanga :
LWANGA BENEFIT DINNER...?
GODDAMN IT, SOLDIER! GATHER YOUR FUCKING SHIT TOGETHER!
MOSES?
HELLO, HUSBAND.
MMM...
H-HELLO? IS SOMEBODY THERE?

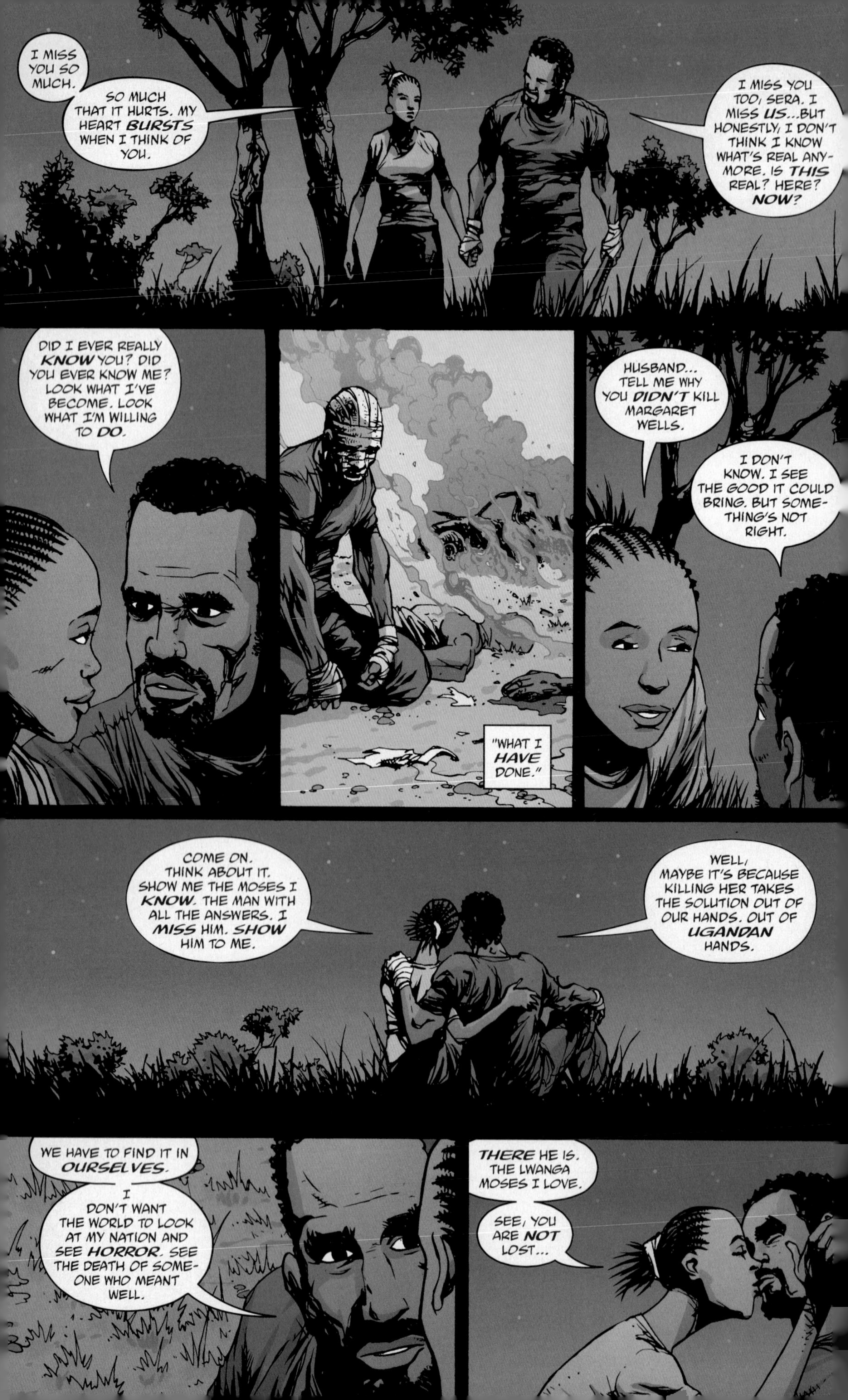
I MISS YOU SO MUCH.
SO MUCH THAT IT HURTS. MY HEART BURSTS WHEN I THINK OF YOU.
I MISS YOU TOO, SERA. I MISS US...BUT HONESTLY, I DON'T THINK I KNOW WHAT'S REAL ANYMORE. IS THIS REAL? HERE? NOW?
DID I EVER REALLY KNOW YOU? DID YOU EVER KNOW ME? LOOK WHAT I'VE BECOME. LOOK WHAT I'M WILLING TO DO.
"WHAT I HAVE DONE."
HUSBAND... TELL ME WHY YOU DIDN'T KILL MARGARET WELLS.
I DON'T KNOW. I SEE THE GOOD IT COULD BRING. BUT SOMETHING'S NOT RIGHT.
COME ON. THINK ABOUT IT. SHOW ME THE MOSES I KNOW. THE MAN WITH ALL THE ANSWERS. I MISS HIM. SHOW HIM TO ME.
WELL, MAYBE IT'S BECAUSE KILLING HER TAKES THE SOLUTION OUT OF OUR HANDS. OUT OF UGANDAN HANDS.
WE HAVE TO FIND IT IN OURSELVES.
I DON'T WANT THE WORLD TO LOOK AT MY NATION AND SEE HORROR. SEE THE DEATH OF SOMEONE WHO MEANT WELL.
THERE HE IS. THE LWANGA MOSES I LOVE.
SEE, YOU ARE NOT LOST...

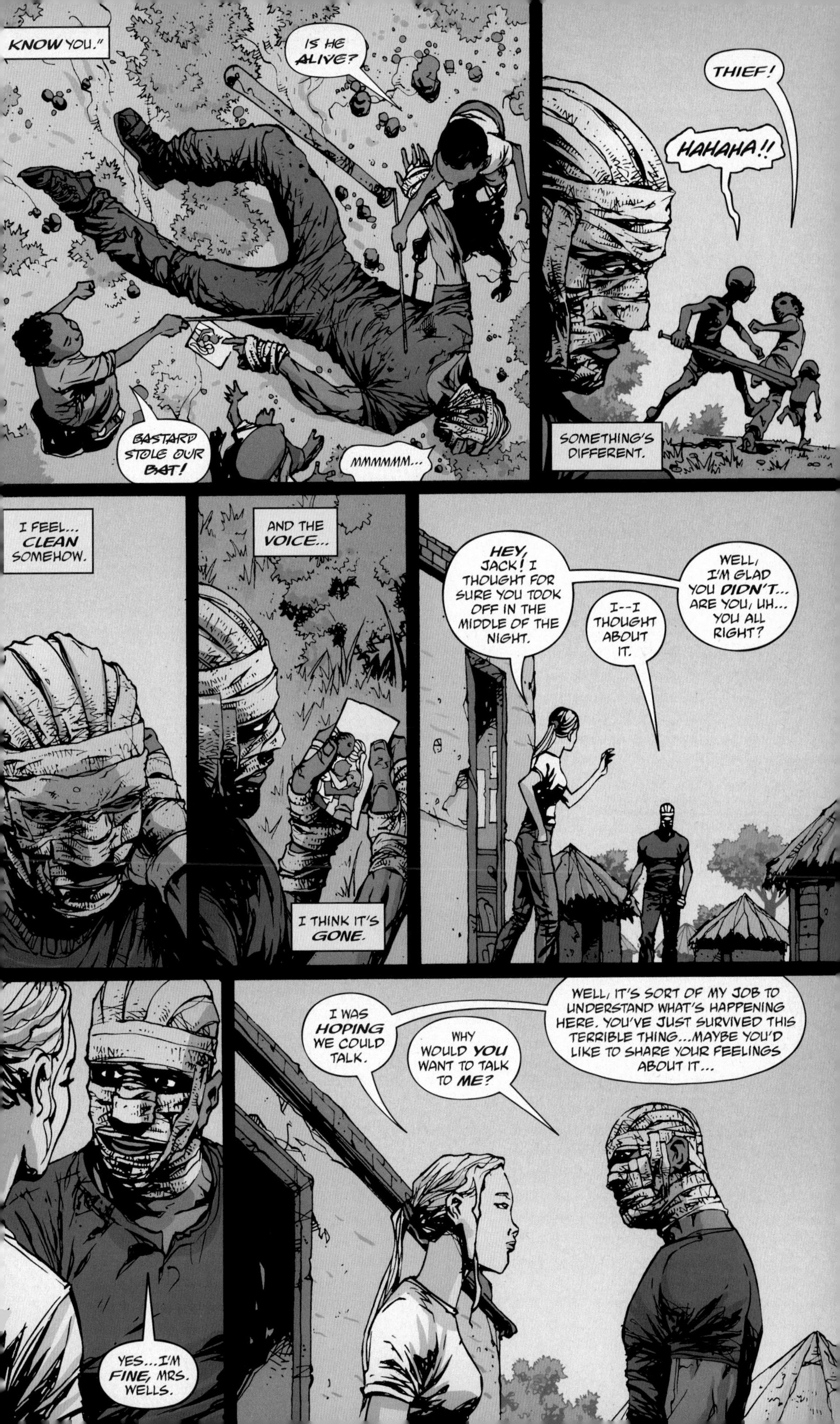
KNOW YOU."
IS HE ALIVE?
BASTARD STOLE OUR BAT!
MMMMMM...
THIEF!
HAHAHA!!
SOMETHING'S DIFFERENT.
I FEEL... CLEAN SOMEHOW.
AND THE VOICE...
I THINK IT'S GONE.
HEY, JACK! I THOUGHT FOR SURE YOU TOOK OFF IN THE MIDDLE OF THE NIGHT.
I--I THOUGHT ABOUT IT.
WELL, I'M GLAD YOU DIDN'T... ARE YOU, UH... YOU ALL RIGHT?
YES... I'M FINE, MRS. WELLS.
I WAS HOPING WE COULD TALK.
WHY WOULD YOU WANT TO TALK TO ME?
WELL, IT'S SORT OF MY JOB TO UNDERSTAND WHAT'S HAPPENING HERE. YOU'VE JUST SURVIVED THIS TERRIBLE THING... MAYBE YOU'D LIKE TO SHARE YOUR FEELINGS ABOUT IT...

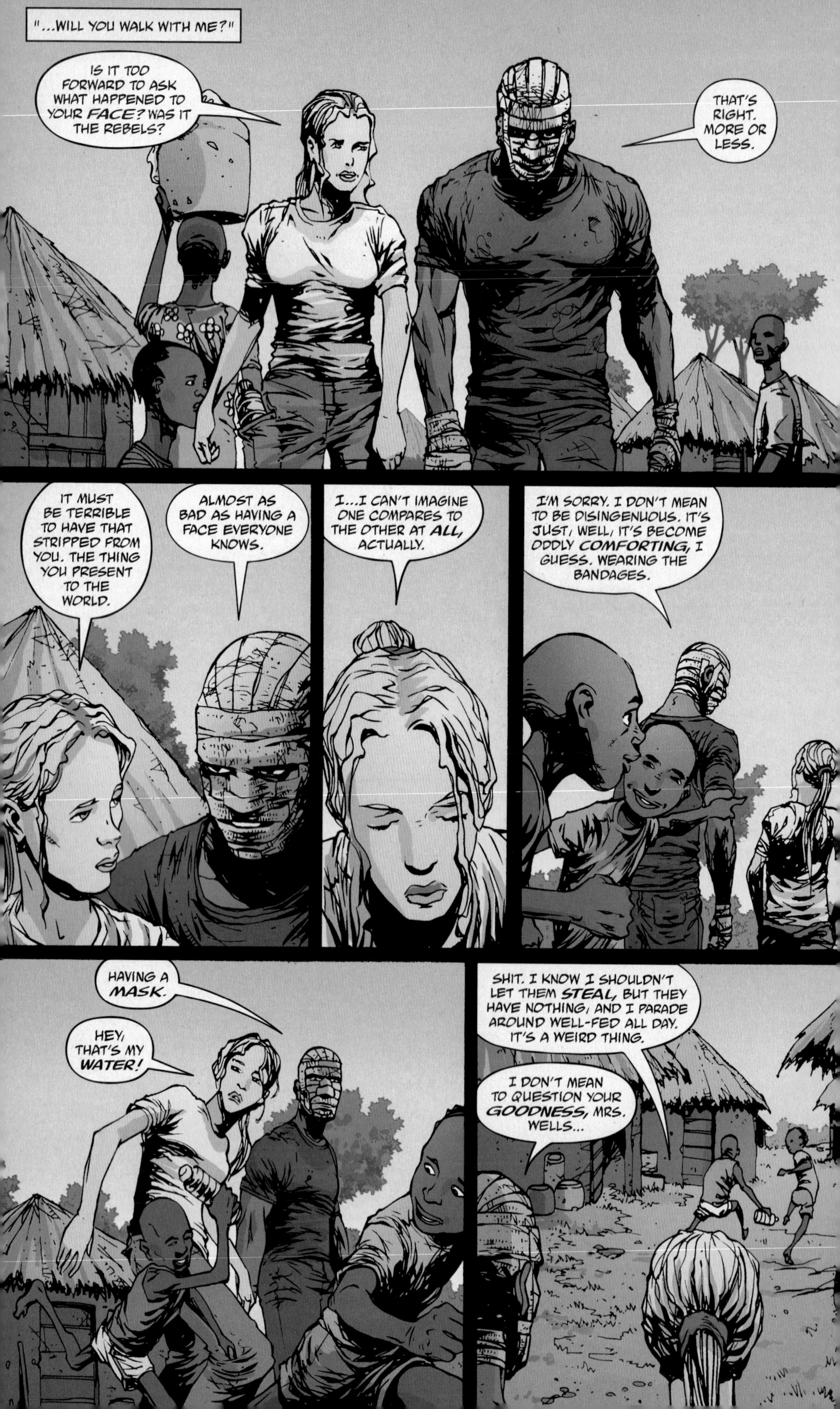
"...WILL YOU WALK WITH ME?"
IS IT TOO FORWARD TO ASK WHAT HAPPENED TO YOUR *FACE?* WAS IT THE REBELS?
THAT'S RIGHT. MORE OR LESS.
IT MUST BE TERRIBLE TO HAVE THAT STRIPPED FROM YOU. THE THING YOU PRESENT TO THE WORLD.
ALMOST AS BAD AS HAVING A FACE EVERYONE KNOWS.
I...I CAN'T IMAGINE ONE COMPARES TO THE OTHER AT *ALL,* ACTUALLY.
I'M SORRY. I DON'T MEAN TO BE DISINGENUOUS. IT'S JUST, WELL, IT'S BECOME ODDLY *COMFORTING,* I GUESS. WEARING THE BANDAGES.
HAVING A *MASK.*
HEY, THAT'S MY *WATER!*
SHIT. I KNOW I SHOULDN'T LET THEM *STEAL,* BUT THEY HAVE NOTHING, AND I PARADE AROUND WELL-FED ALL DAY. IT'S A WEIRD THING.
I DON'T MEAN TO QUESTION YOUR *GOODNESS,* MRS. WELLS...

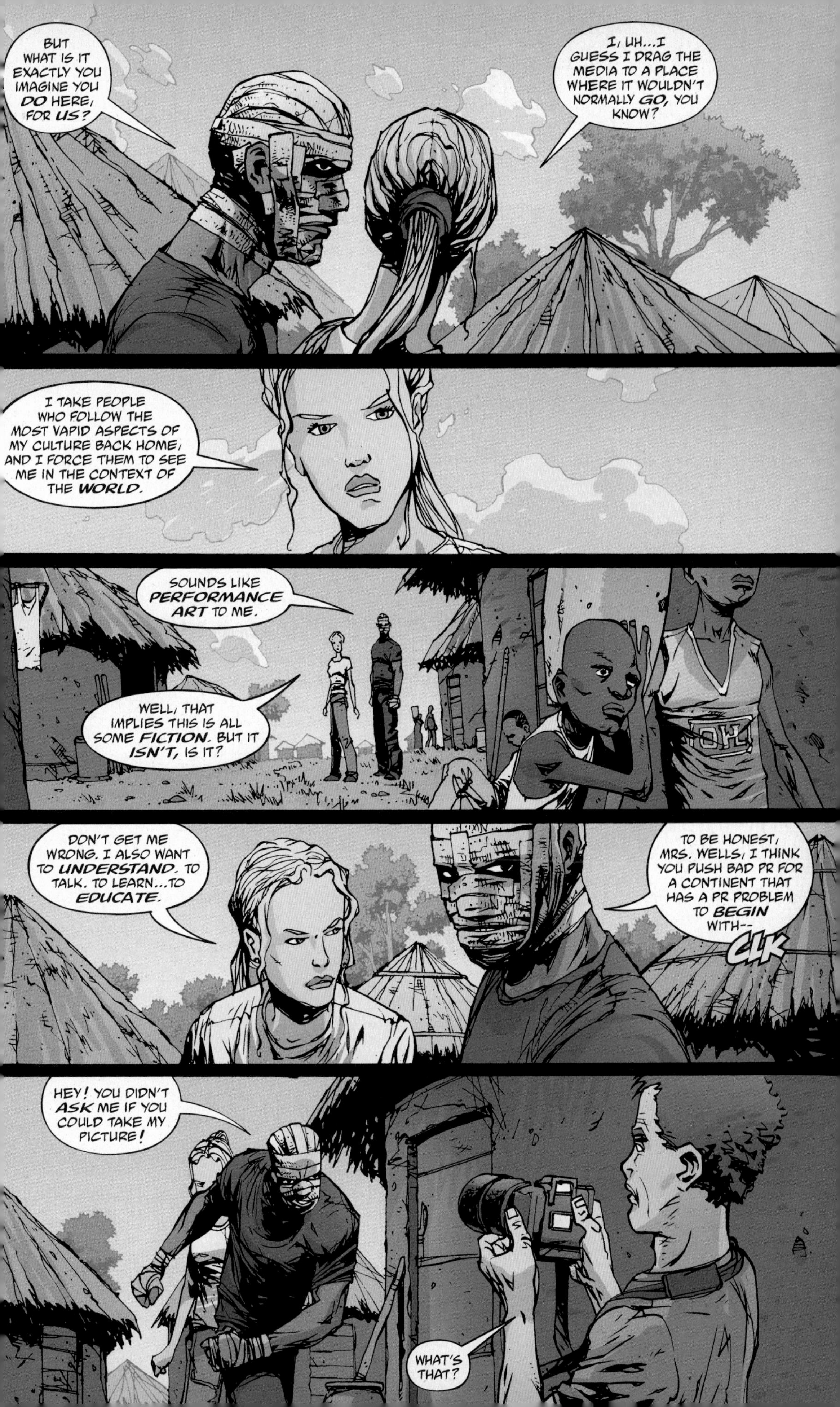
BUT WHAT IS IT EXACTLY YOU IMAGINE YOU DO HERE, FOR US?
I, UH...I GUESS I DRAG THE MEDIA TO A PLACE WHERE IT WOULDN'T NORMALLY GO, YOU KNOW?
I TAKE PEOPLE WHO FOLLOW THE MOST VAPID ASPECTS OF MY CULTURE BACK HOME, AND I FORCE THEM TO SEE ME IN THE CONTEXT OF THE WORLD.
SOUNDS LIKE PERFORMANCE ART TO ME.
WELL, THAT IMPLIES THIS IS ALL SOME FICTION. BUT IT ISN'T, IS IT?
DON'T GET ME WRONG. I ALSO WANT TO UNDERSTAND. TO TALK. TO LEARN...TO EDUCATE.
TO BE HONEST, MRS. WELLS, I THINK YOU PUSH BAD PR FOR A CONTINENT THAT HAS A PR PROBLEM TO BEGIN WITH--
CLK
HEY! YOU DIDN'T ASK ME IF YOU COULD TAKE MY PICTURE!
WHAT'S THAT?

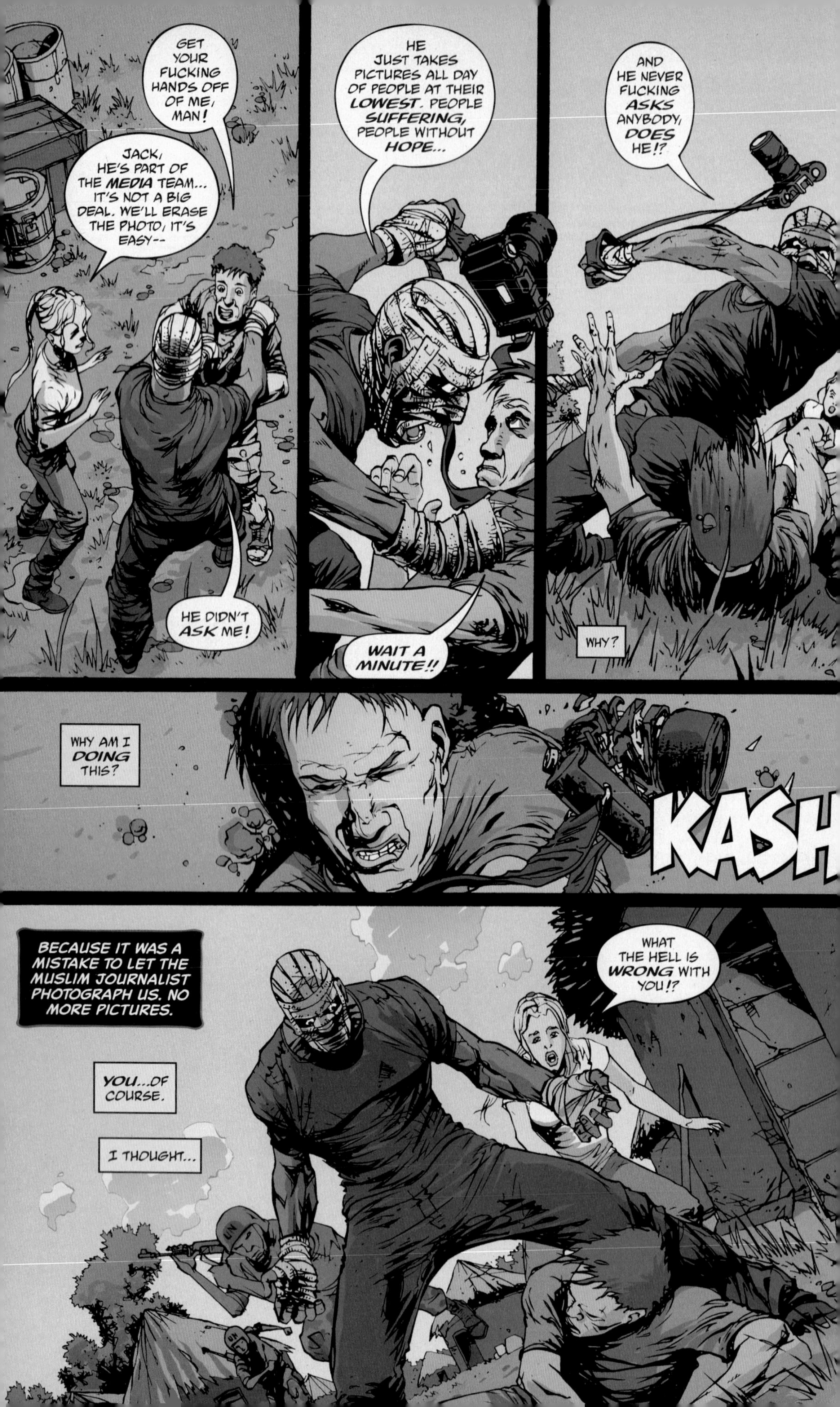

GET YOUR FUCKING HANDS OFF OF ME, MAN!
JACK, HE'S PART OF THE MEDIA TEAM... IT'S NOT A BIG DEAL. WE'LL ERASE THE PHOTO, IT'S EASY--
HE DIDN'T ASK ME!
HE JUST TAKES PICTURES ALL DAY OF PEOPLE AT THEIR LOWEST. PEOPLE SUFFERING, PEOPLE WITHOUT HOPE...
WAIT A MINUTE!!
AND HE NEVER FUCKING ASKS ANYBODY, DOES HE!?
WHY?
WHY AM I DOING THIS?
KASH
BECAUSE IT WAS A MISTAKE TO LET THE MUSLIM JOURNALIST PHOTOGRAPH US. NO MORE PICTURES.
WHAT THE HELL IS WRONG WITH YOU!?
YOU...OF COURSE.
I THOUGHT...

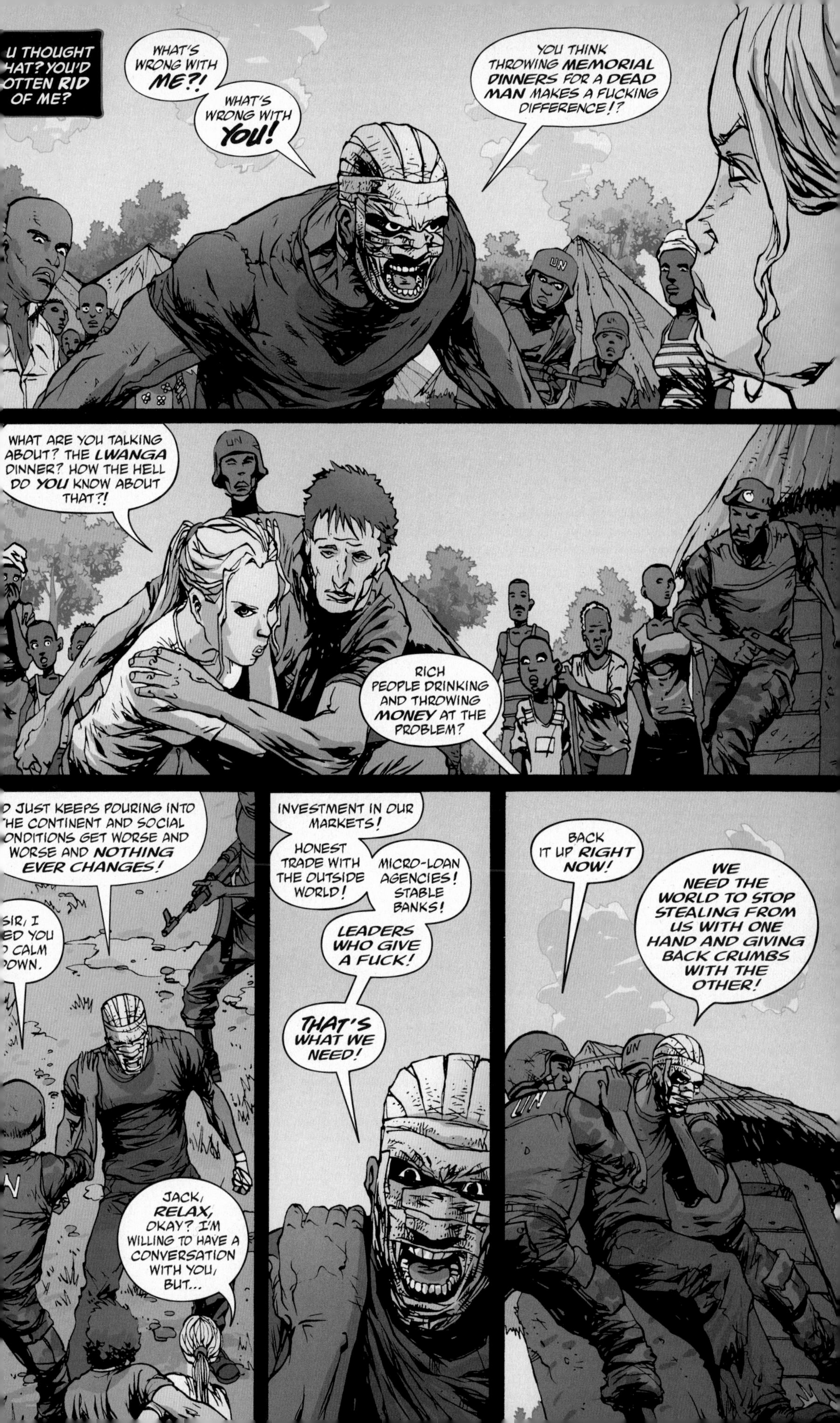
U THOUGHT
HAT? YOU'D
OTTEN RID
OF ME?
WHAT'S WRONG WITH ME?!
WHAT'S WRONG WITH YOU!
YOU THINK THROWING MEMORIAL DINNERS FOR A DEAD MAN MAKES A FUCKING DIFFERENCE!?
WHAT ARE YOU TALKING ABOUT? THE LWANGA DINNER? HOW THE HELL DO YOU KNOW ABOUT THAT?!
RICH PEOPLE DRINKING AND THROWING MONEY AT THE PROBLEM?
D JUST KEEPS POURING INTO THE CONTINENT AND SOCIAL ONDITIONS GET WORSE AND WORSE AND NOTHING EVER CHANGES!
SIR, I ED YOU CALM OWN.
JACK, RELAX, OKAY? I'M WILLING TO HAVE A CONVERSATION WITH YOU, BUT...
INVESTMENT IN OUR MARKETS!
HONEST TRADE WITH THE OUTSIDE WORLD!
MICRO-LOAN AGENCIES! STABLE BANKS!
LEADERS WHO GIVE A FUCK!
THAT'S WHAT WE NEED!
BACK IT UP RIGHT NOW!
WE NEED THE WORLD TO STOP STEALING FROM US WITH ONE HAND AND GIVING BACK CRUMBS WITH THE OTHER!

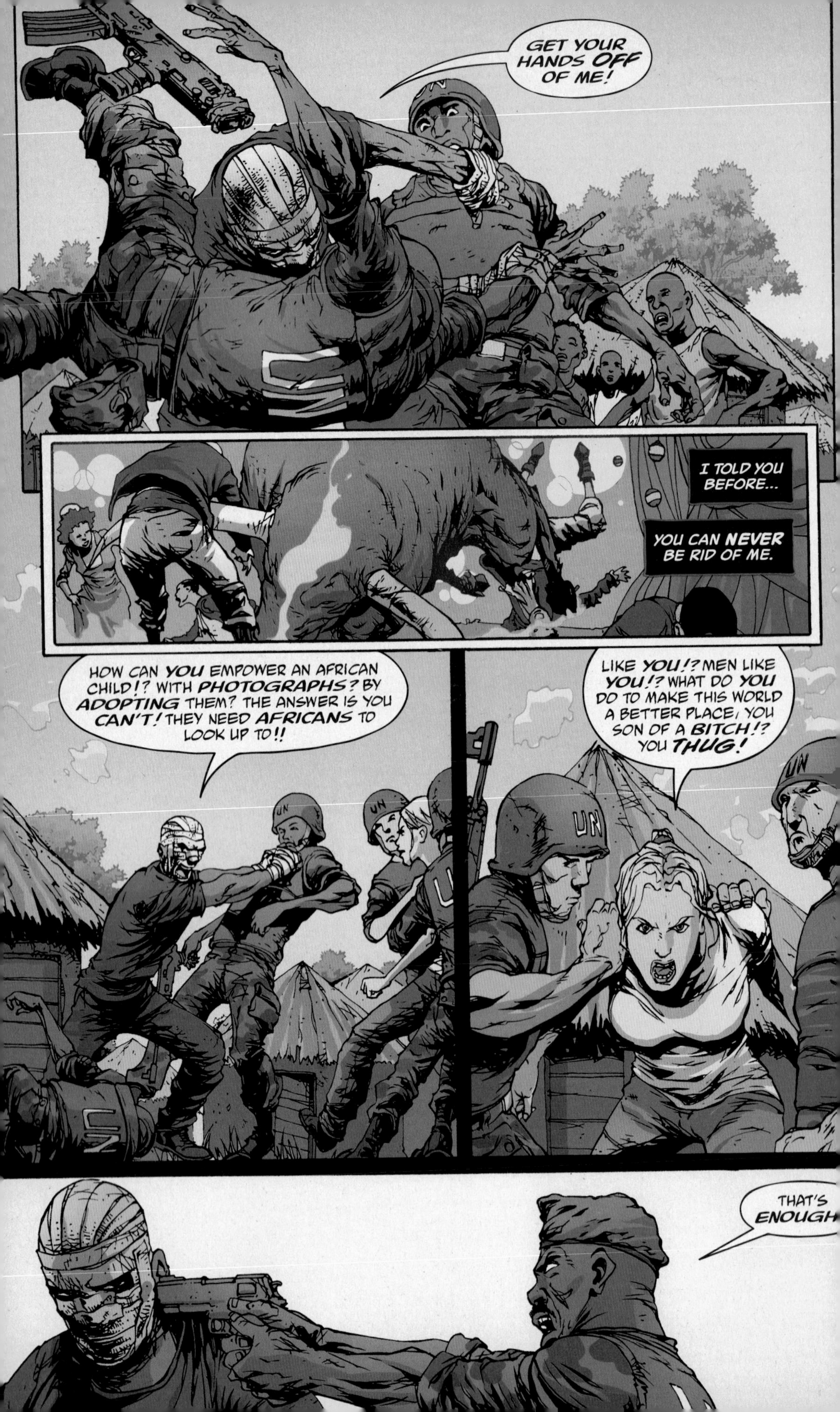
GET YOUR HANDS OFF OF ME!
I TOLD YOU BEFORE...
YOU CAN NEVER BE RID OF ME.
HOW CAN YOU EMPOWER AN AFRICAN CHILD!? WITH PHOTOGRAPHS? BY ADOPTING THEM? THE ANSWER IS YOU CAN'T! THEY NEED AFRICANS TO LOOK UP TO!!
LIKE YOU!? MEN LIKE YOU!? WHAT DO YOU DO TO MAKE THIS WORLD A BETTER PLACE, YOU SON OF A BITCH!? YOU THUG!
THAT'S ENOUGH

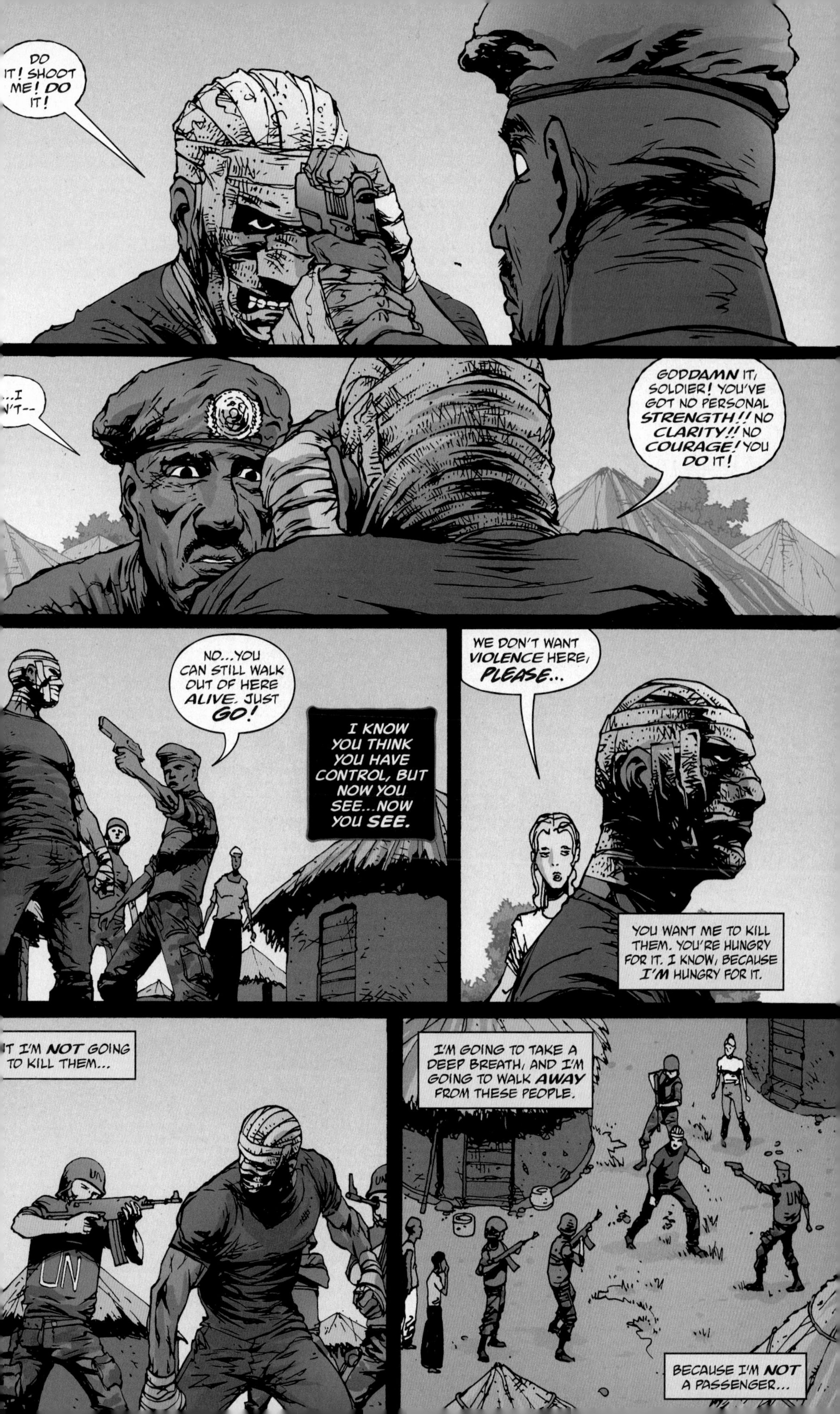
DO IT! SHOOT ME! DO IT!
...I N'T--
GODDAMN IT, SOLDIER! YOU'VE GOT NO PERSONAL STRENGTH!! NO CLARITY!! NO COURAGE! YOU DO IT!
NO...YOU CAN STILL WALK OUT OF HERE ALIVE. JUST GO!
I KNOW YOU THINK YOU HAVE CONTROL, BUT NOW YOU SEE...NOW YOU SEE.
WE DON'T WANT VIOLENCE HERE, PLEASE...
YOU WANT ME TO KILL THEM. YOU'RE HUNGRY FOR IT. I KNOW, BECAUSE I'M HUNGRY FOR IT.
T I'M NOT GOING TO KILL THEM...
I'M GOING TO TAKE A DEEP BREATH, AND I'M GOING TO WALK AWAY FROM THESE PEOPLE.
BECAUSE I'M NOT A PASSENGER...
UN
UN

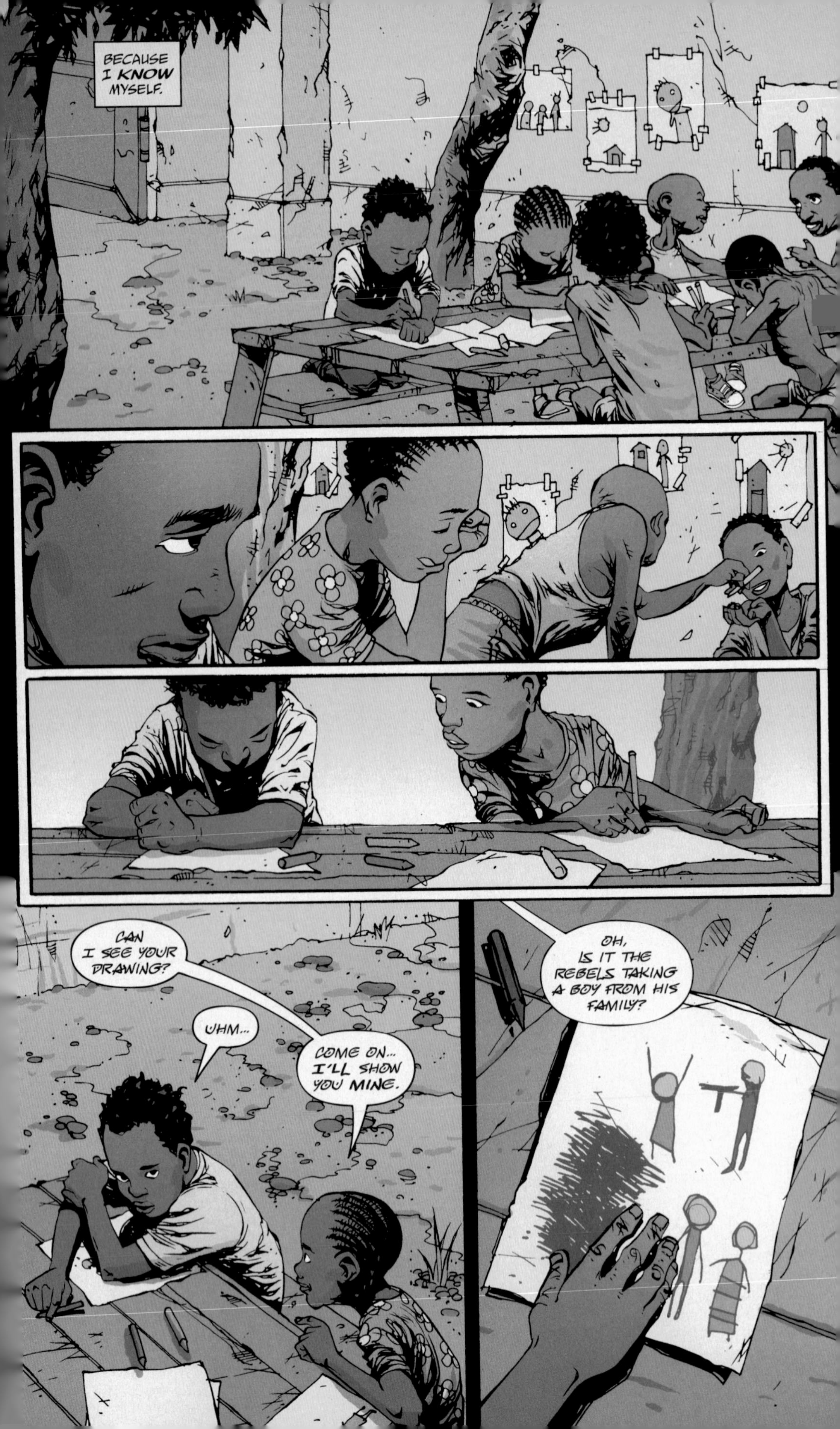
BECAUSE I KNOW MYSELF.
CAN I SEE YOUR DRAWING?
UHM...
COME ON... I'LL SHOW YOU MINE.
OH, IS IT THE REBELS TAKING A BOY FROM HIS FAMILY?

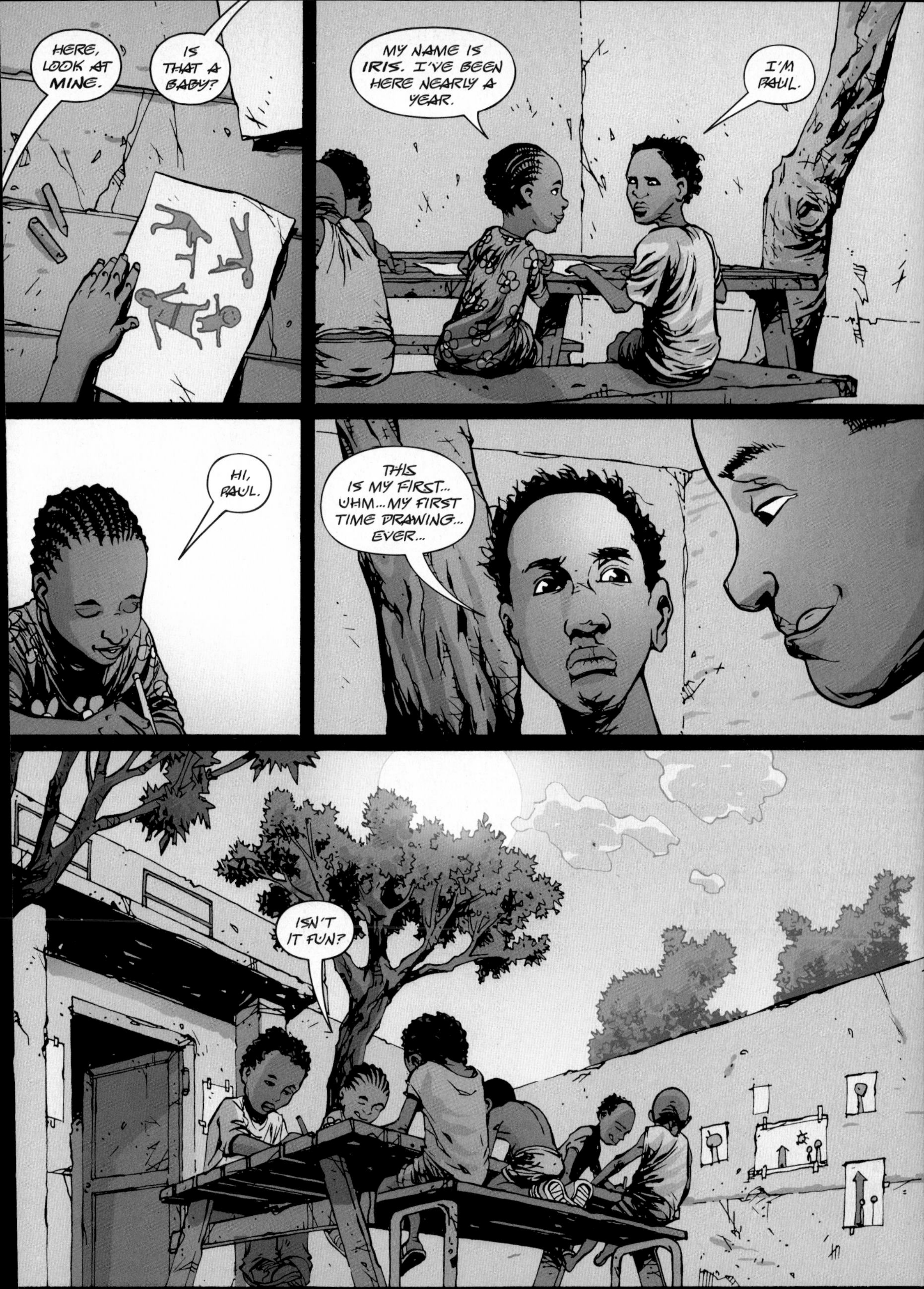
HERE, LOOK AT MINE.
IS THAT A BABY?
MY NAME IS IRIS. I'VE BEEN HERE NEARLY A YEAR.
I'M PAUL.
HI, PAUL.
THIS IS MY FIRST... UHM... MY FIRST TIME DRAWING... EVER...
ISN'T IT FUN?

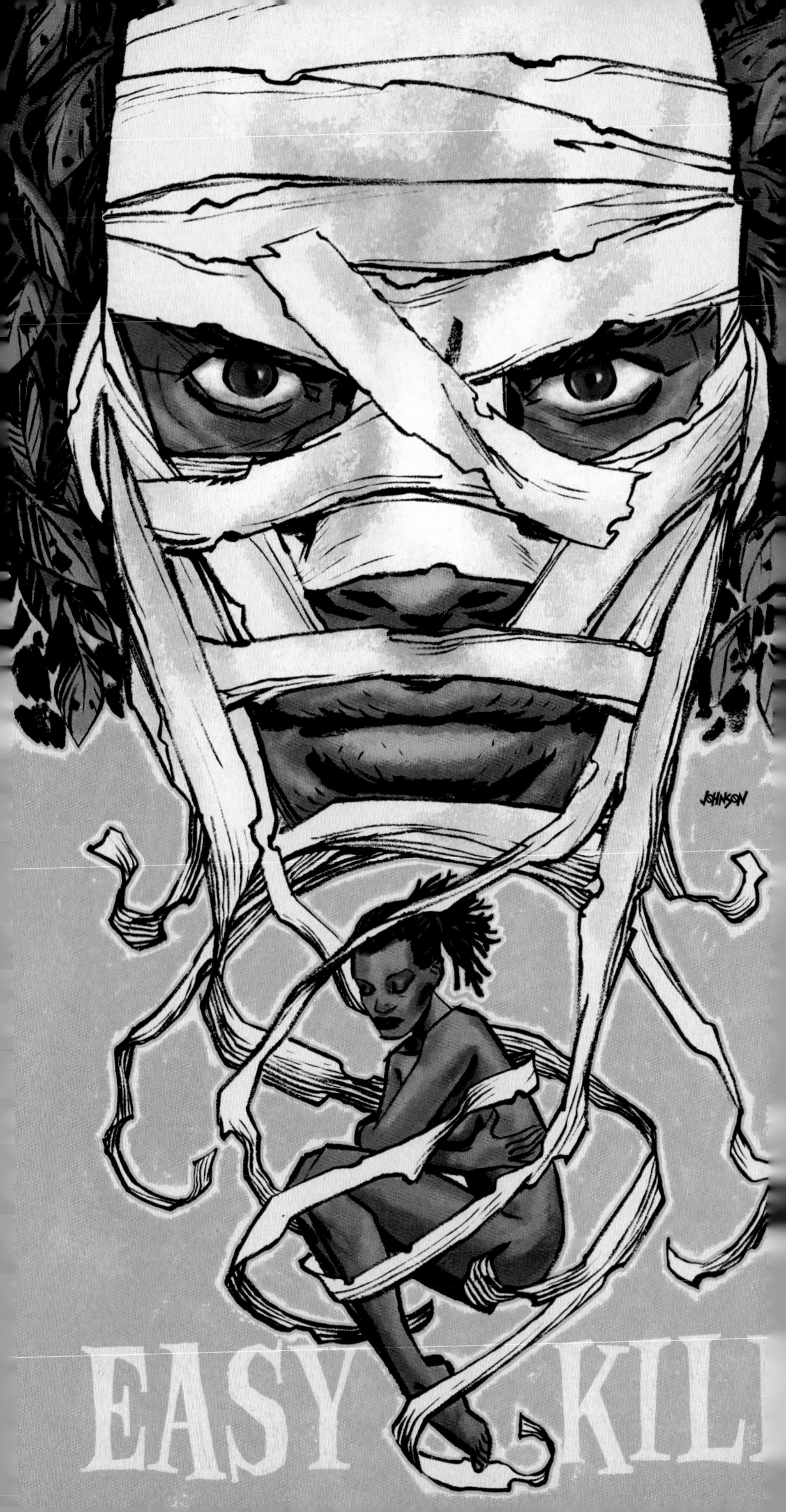
JOHNSON
EASY KIL

I WISH TO TELL
YOU A STORY, MOSES.
PERHAPS I HAVE TOLD
IT TO YOU BEFORE.
I CANNOT RECALL.

WHEN I WAS LITTLE, IN
KAMPALA, MY GRAND-
MOTHER WOULD TAKE
ME TO CHURCH EVERY
SUNDAY.

ON THE WAY HOME
WE WOULD ALWAYS
CROSS THE SAME
EMPTY LOT. AND
SHE WOULD SAY...

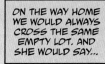

COME,
SERA, LISTEN...
A *WITCH* WAS
BURNED ON THIS
PATCH OF LAND
MANY YEARS
AGO...

IT WAS EASY TO
BELIEVE IN A WORLD
STITCHED TOGETHER
BY *EDDOGO*, BY
MAGIC, BACK THEN...

THROW
SOME GRASS SO
THAT HIS GHOST
DOES NOT FOLLOW
US HOME, SO WE
MAY PASS
SAFELY.

THAT
IS IT! THROW
THE GRASS ON
THE LAND!

EVERY SPELL HAD A
COUNTERSPELL.
EVERY HORROR COULD
BE UNDONE. EVERY
PROBLEM SOLVED.

IF YOU
ONLY HAD THE
KNOWLEDGE...

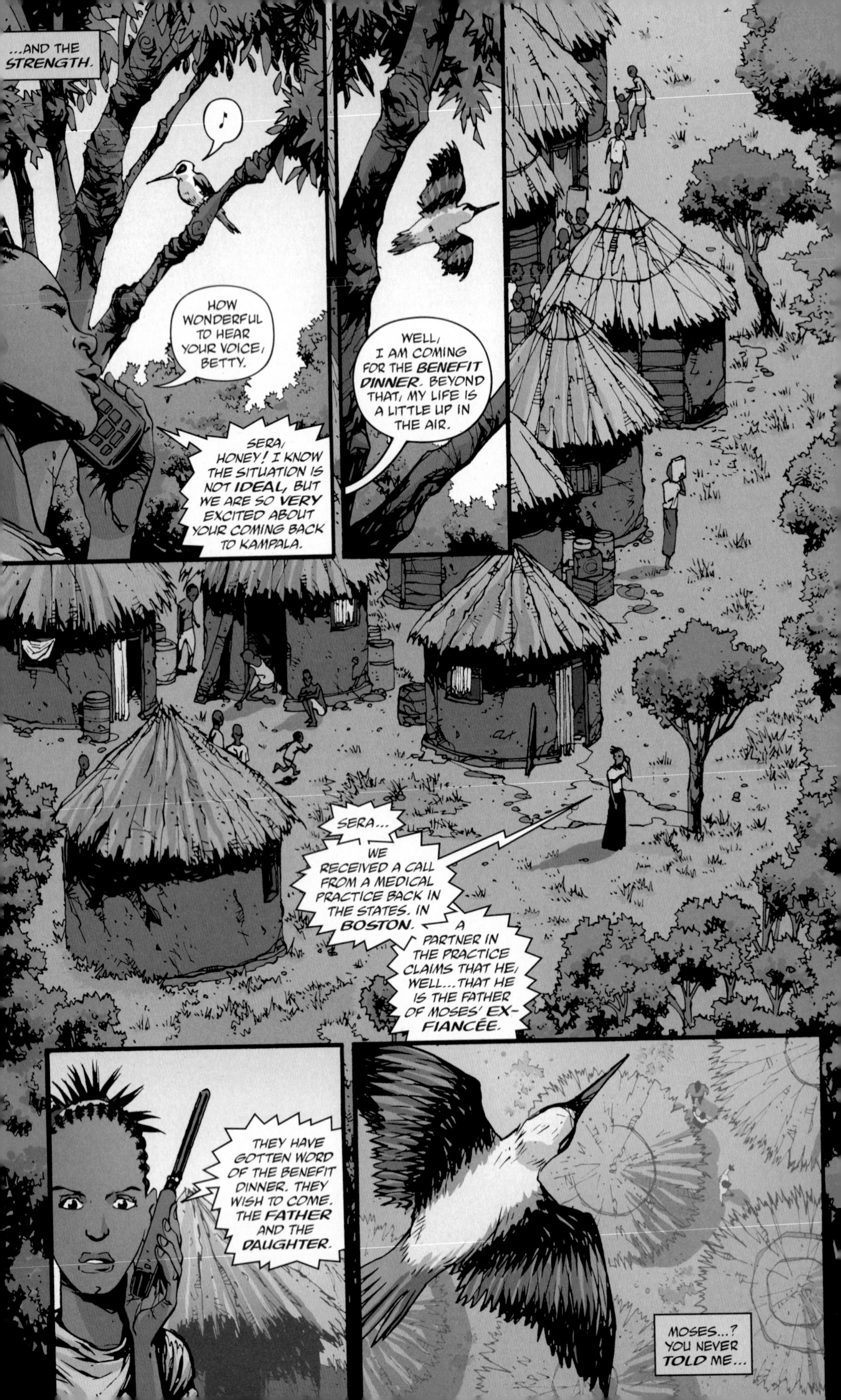
...AND THE STRENGTH.
♪
HOW WONDERFUL TO HEAR YOUR VOICE, BETTY.
SERA, HONEY! I KNOW THE SITUATION IS NOT IDEAL, BUT WE ARE SO VERY EXCITED ABOUT YOUR COMING BACK TO KAMPALA.
WELL, I AM COMING FOR THE BENEFIT DINNER. BEYOND THAT, MY LIFE IS A LITTLE UP IN THE AIR.
SERA...
WE RECEIVED A CALL FROM A MEDICAL PRACTICE BACK IN THE STATES. IN BOSTON.
A PARTNER IN THE PRACTICE CLAIMS THAT HE, WELL...THAT HE IS THE FATHER OF MOSES' EX-FIANCÉE.
THEY HAVE GOTTEN WORD OF THE BENEFIT DINNER. THEY WISH TO COME. THE FATHER AND THE DAUGHTER.
MOSES...? YOU NEVER TOLD ME...

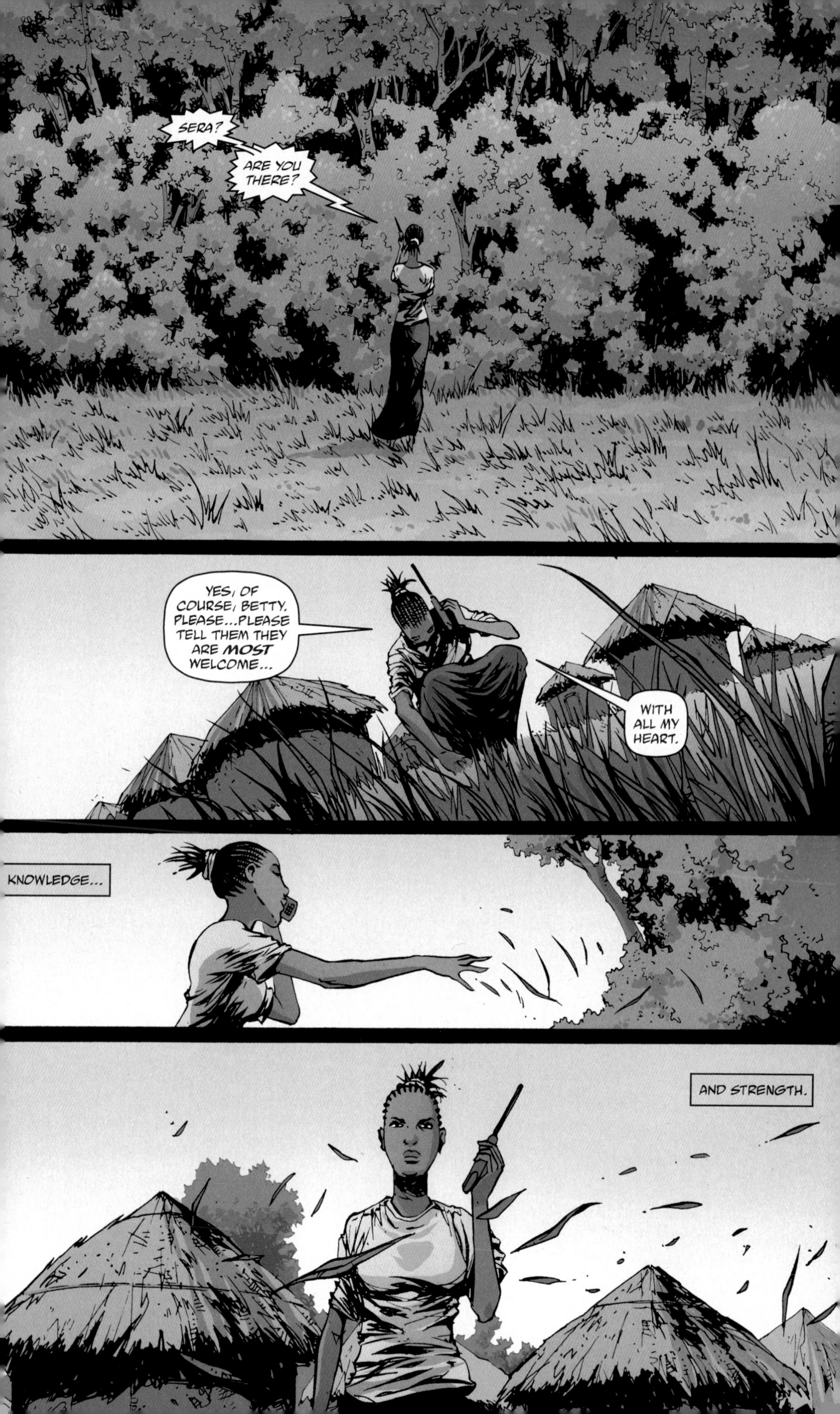
SERA?
ARE YOU THERE?
YES, OF COURSE, BETTY. PLEASE...PLEASE TELL THEM THEY ARE MOST WELCOME...
WITH ALL MY HEART.
KNOWLEDGE...
AND STRENGTH.

BANG
BANG BANG

KIWANJA!
OPEN THE
DOOR!

KIWANJA!

KRAK

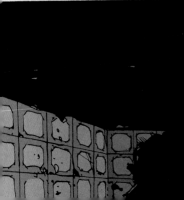

SORRY,
THERE'S NOBODY
HERE BUT US
CHICKENS...

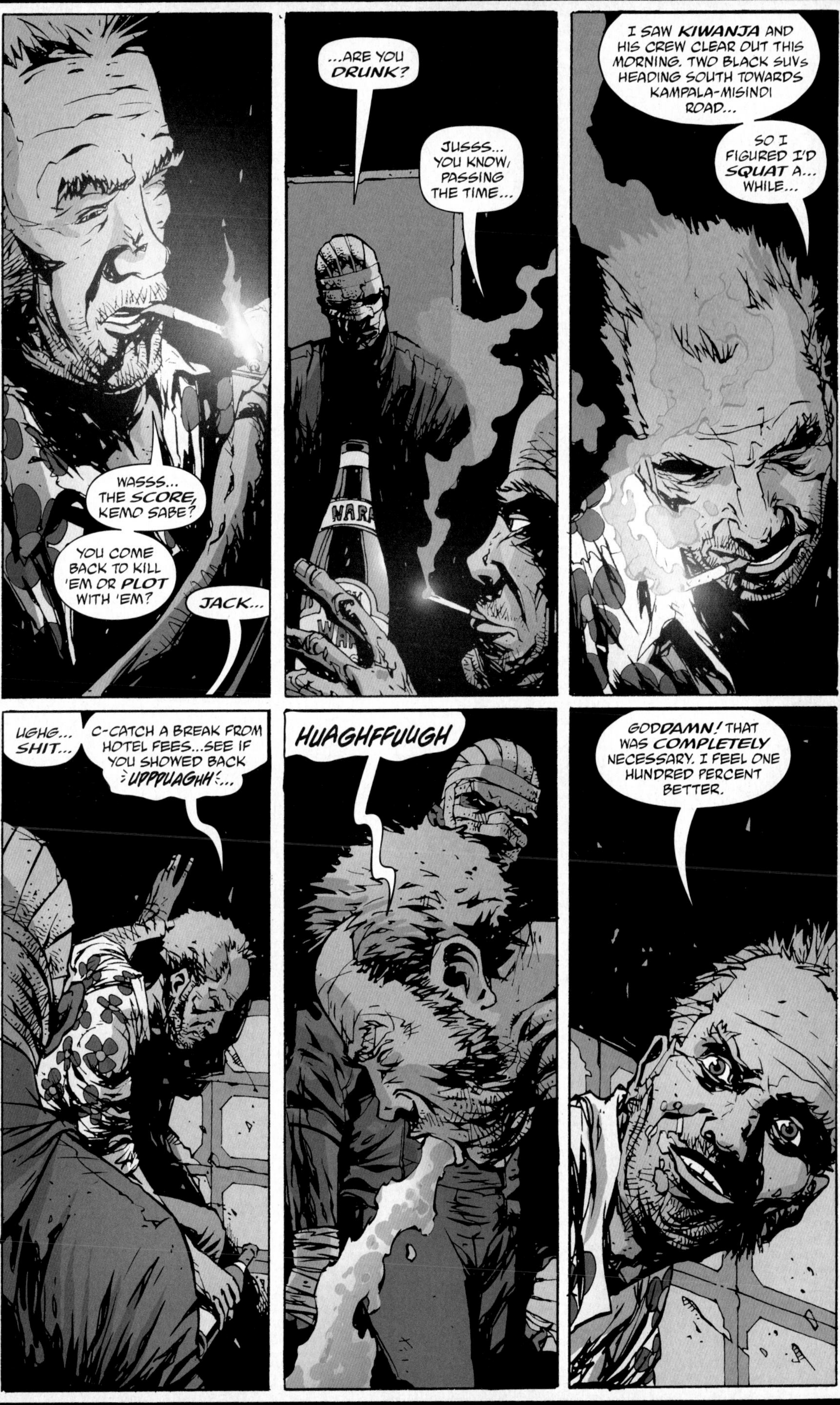
WASSS... THE SCORE, KEMO SABE?
YOU COME BACK TO KILL 'EM OR PLOT WITH 'EM?
JACK...
...ARE YOU DRUNK?
JUSSS... YOU KNOW, PASSING THE TIME...
I SAW KIWANJA AND HIS CREW CLEAR OUT THIS MORNING. TWO BLACK SUVS HEADING SOUTH TOWARDS KAMPALA-MISINDI ROAD...
SO I FIGURED I'D SQUAT A... WHILE...
UGHG... SHIT...
C-CATCH A BREAK FROM HOTEL FEES...SEE IF YOU SHOWED BACK UPPPUAGHH...
HUAGHFFUUGH
GODDAMN! THAT WAS COMPLETELY NECESSARY. I FEEL ONE HUNDRED PERCENT BETTER.

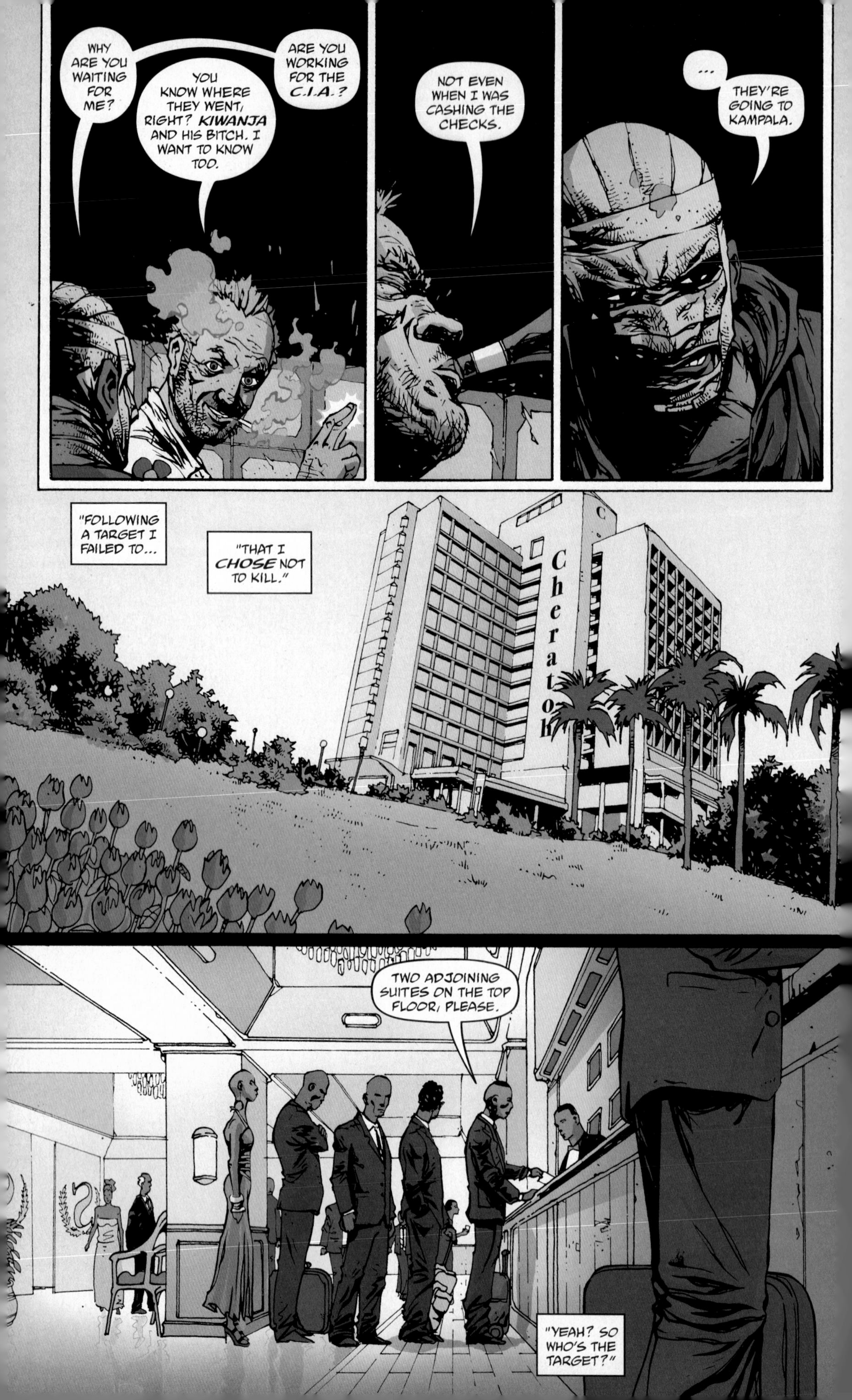
WHY ARE YOU WAITING FOR ME?
ARE YOU WORKING FOR THE C.I.A.?
YOU KNOW WHERE THEY WENT, RIGHT? KIWANJA AND HIS BITCH. I WANT TO KNOW TOO.
NOT EVEN WHEN I WAS CASHING THE CHECKS.
...
THEY'RE GOING TO KAMPALA.
"FOLLOWING A TARGET I FAILED TO...
"THAT I CHOSE NOT TO KILL."
Cheraton
TWO ADJOINING SUITES ON THE TOP FLOOR, PLEASE.
"YEAH? SO WHO'S THE TARGET?"

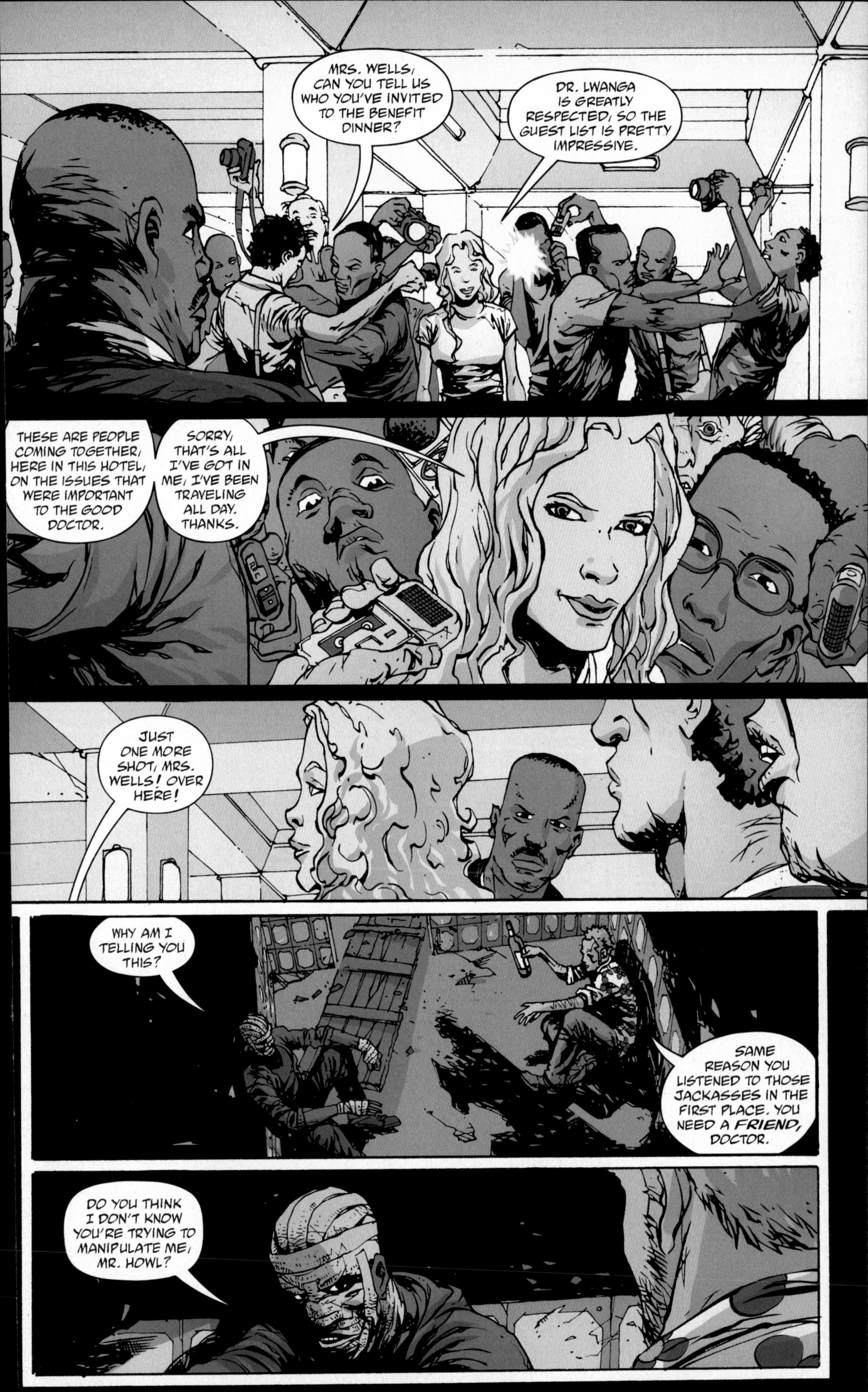
MRS. WELLS, CAN YOU TELL US WHO YOU'VE INVITED TO THE BENEFIT DINNER?
DR. LWANGA IS GREATLY RESPECTED, SO THE GUEST LIST IS PRETTY IMPRESSIVE.
THESE ARE PEOPLE COMING TOGETHER, HERE IN THIS HOTEL, ON THE ISSUES THAT WERE IMPORTANT TO THE GOOD DOCTOR.
SORRY, THAT'S ALL I'VE GOT IN ME, I'VE BEEN TRAVELING ALL DAY. THANKS.
JUST ONE MORE SHOT, MRS. WELLS! OVER HERE!
WHY AM I TELLING YOU THIS?
SAME REASON YOU LISTENED TO THOSE JACKASSES IN THE FIRST PLACE. YOU NEED A FRIEND, DOCTOR.
DO YOU THINK I DON'T KNOW YOU'RE TRYING TO MANIPULATE ME, MR. HOWL?

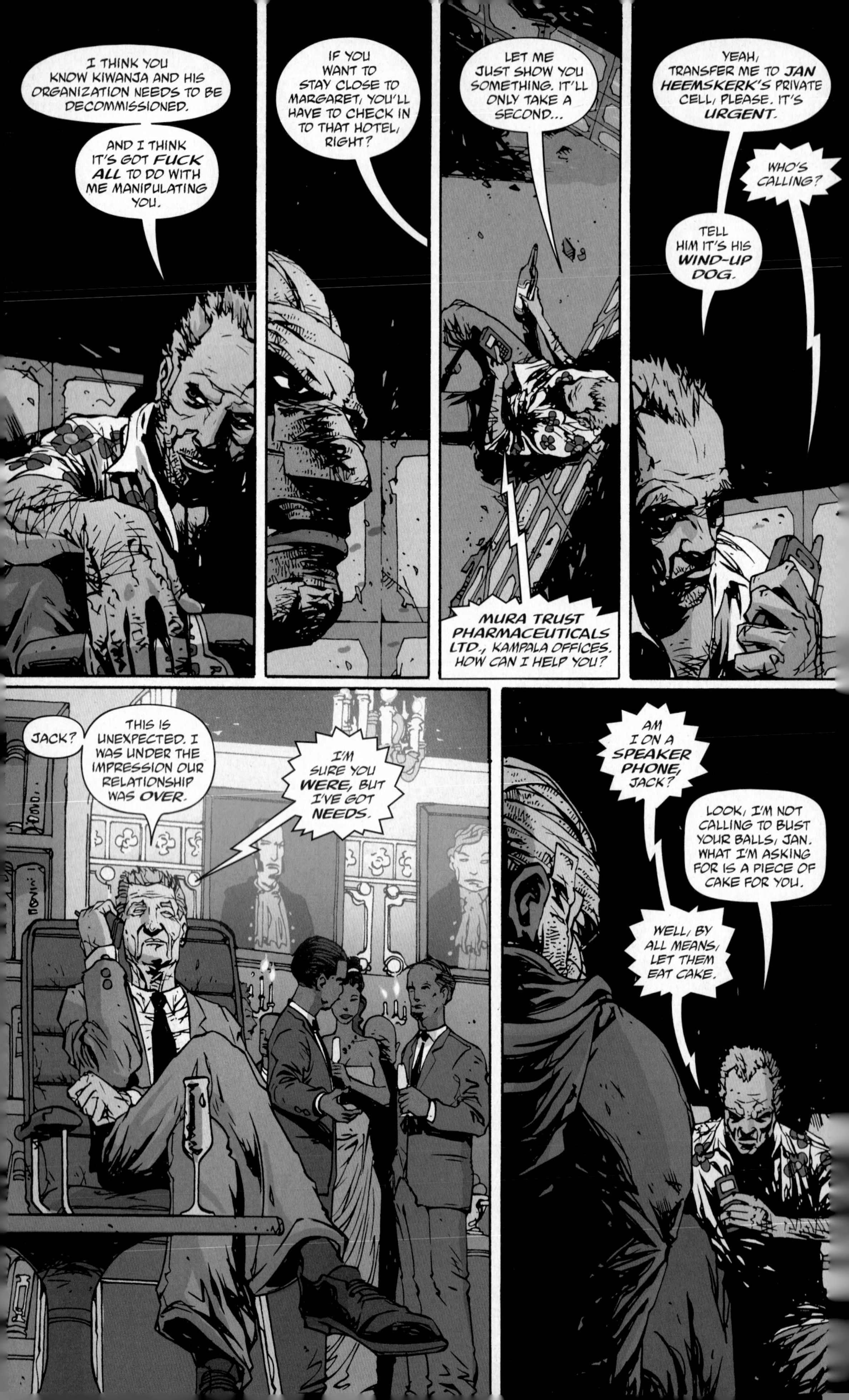
I THINK YOU KNOW KIWANJA AND HIS ORGANIZATION NEEDS TO BE DECOMMISSIONED.
AND I THINK IT'S GOT FUCK ALL TO DO WITH ME MANIPULATING YOU.
IF YOU WANT TO STAY CLOSE TO MARGARET, YOU'LL HAVE TO CHECK IN TO THAT HOTEL, RIGHT?
LET ME JUST SHOW YOU SOMETHING. IT'LL ONLY TAKE A SECOND...
MURA TRUST PHARMACEUTICALS LTD., KAMPALA OFFICES. HOW CAN I HELP YOU?
YEAH, TRANSFER ME TO JAN HEEMSKERK'S PRIVATE CELL, PLEASE. IT'S URGENT.
WHO'S CALLING?
TELL HIM IT'S HIS WIND-UP DOG.
JACK?
THIS IS UNEXPECTED. I WAS UNDER THE IMPRESSION OUR RELATIONSHIP WAS OVER.
I'M SURE YOU WERE, BUT I'VE GOT NEEDS.
AM I ON A SPEAKER PHONE, JACK?
LOOK, I'M NOT CALLING TO BUST YOUR BALLS, JAN. WHAT I'M ASKING FOR IS A PIECE OF CAKE FOR YOU.
WELL, BY ALL MEANS, LET THEM EAT CAKE.

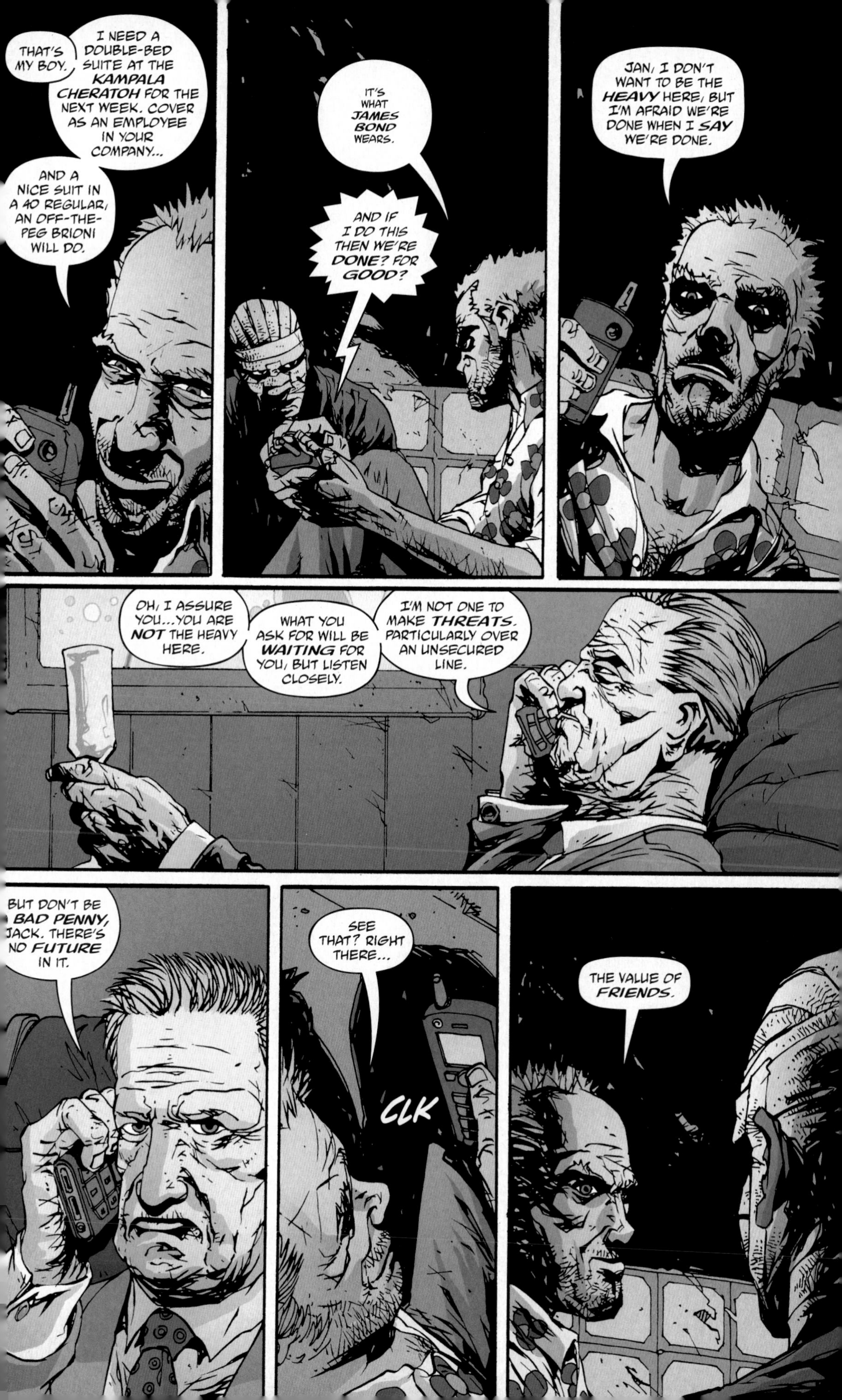

I NEED A DOUBLE-BED SUITE AT THE KAMPALA CHERATOH FOR THE NEXT WEEK. COVER AS AN EMPLOYEE IN YOUR COMPANY...
THAT'S MY BOY.
AND A NICE SUIT IN A 40 REGULAR, AN OFF-THE-PEG BRIONI WILL DO.
IT'S WHAT JAMES BOND WEARS.
AND IF I DO THIS THEN WE'RE DONE? FOR GOOD?
JAN, I DON'T WANT TO BE THE HEAVY HERE, BUT I'M AFRAID WE'RE DONE WHEN I SAY WE'RE DONE.
OH, I ASSURE YOU...YOU ARE NOT THE HEAVY HERE.
WHAT YOU ASK FOR WILL BE WAITING FOR YOU, BUT LISTEN CLOSELY.
I'M NOT ONE TO MAKE THREATS. PARTICULARLY OVER AN UNSECURED LINE.
BUT DON'T BE BAD PENNY, JACK. THERE'S NO FUTURE IN IT.
SEE THAT? RIGHT THERE...
CLK
THE VALUE OF FRIENDS.

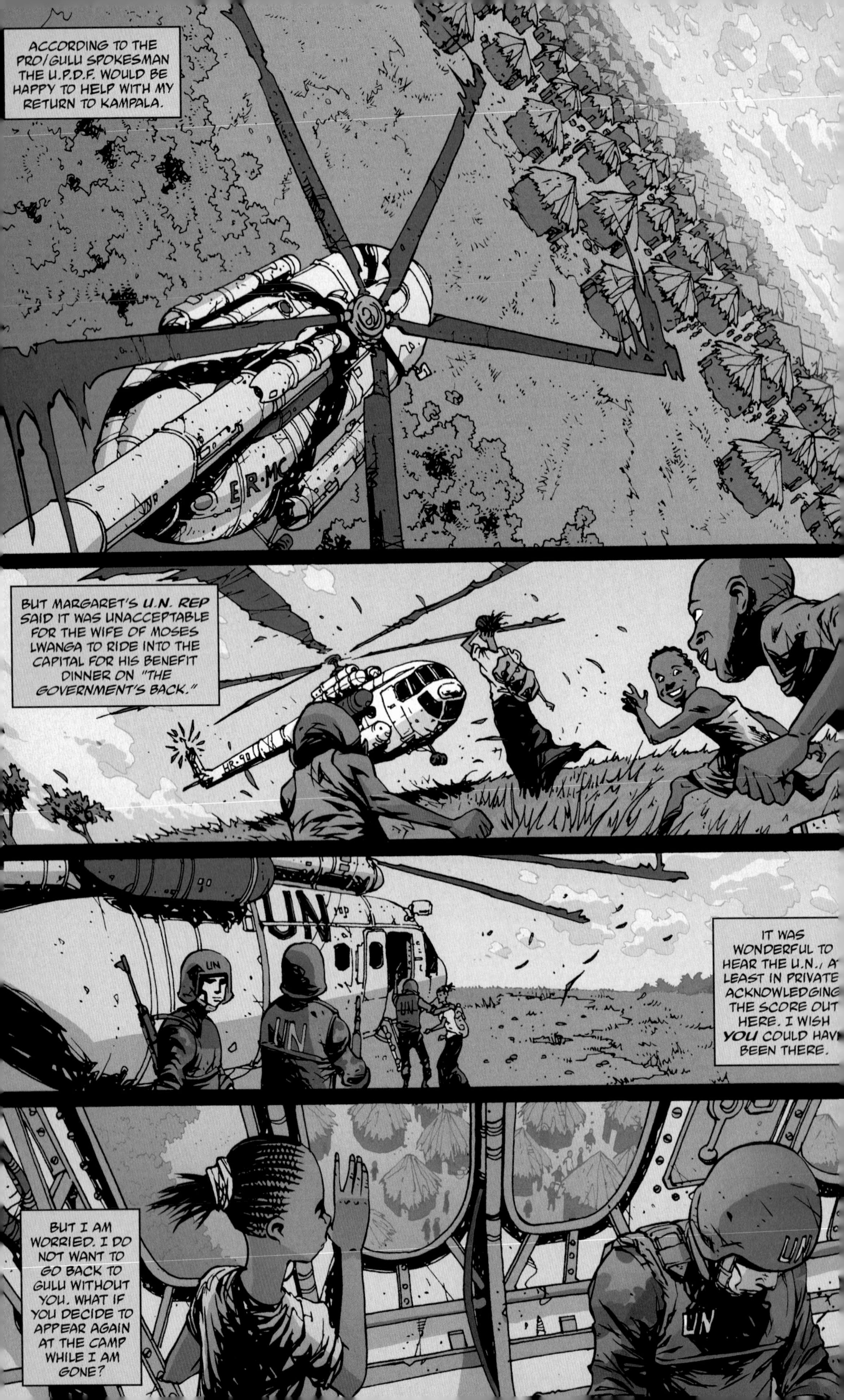
ACCORDING TO THE PRO/GULU SPOKESMAN THE U.P.D.F. WOULD BE HAPPY TO HELP WITH MY RETURN TO KAMPALA.
ER·MC
BUT MARGARET'S U.N. REP SAID IT WAS UNACCEPTABLE FOR THE WIFE OF MOSES LWANGA TO RIDE INTO THE CAPITAL FOR HIS BENEFIT DINNER ON "THE GOVERNMENT'S BACK."
UN
IT WAS WONDERFUL TO HEAR THE U.N., A LEAST IN PRIVATE ACKNOWLEDGING THE SCORE OUT HERE. I WISH YOU COULD HAV BEEN THERE.
BUT I AM WORRIED. I DO NOT WANT TO GO BACK TO GULU WITHOUT YOU. WHAT IF YOU DECIDE TO APPEAR AGAIN AT THE CAMP WHILE I AM GONE?

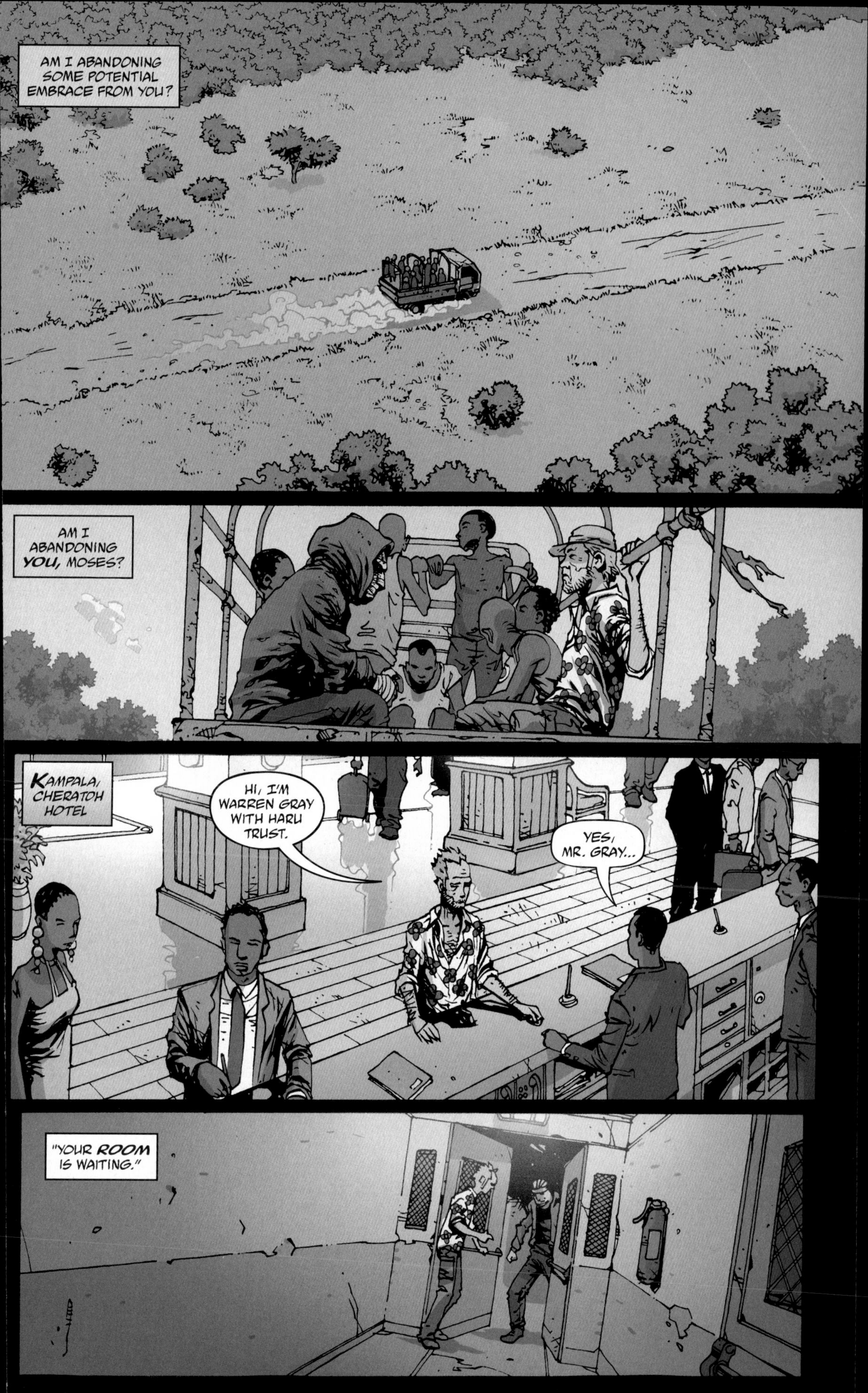
AM I ABANDONING SOME POTENTIAL EMBRACE FROM YOU?
AM I ABANDONING YOU, MOSES?
KAMPALA, CHERATON HOTEL
HI, I'M WARREN GRAY WITH HARU TRUST.
YES, MR. GRAY...
"YOUR ROOM IS WAITING."

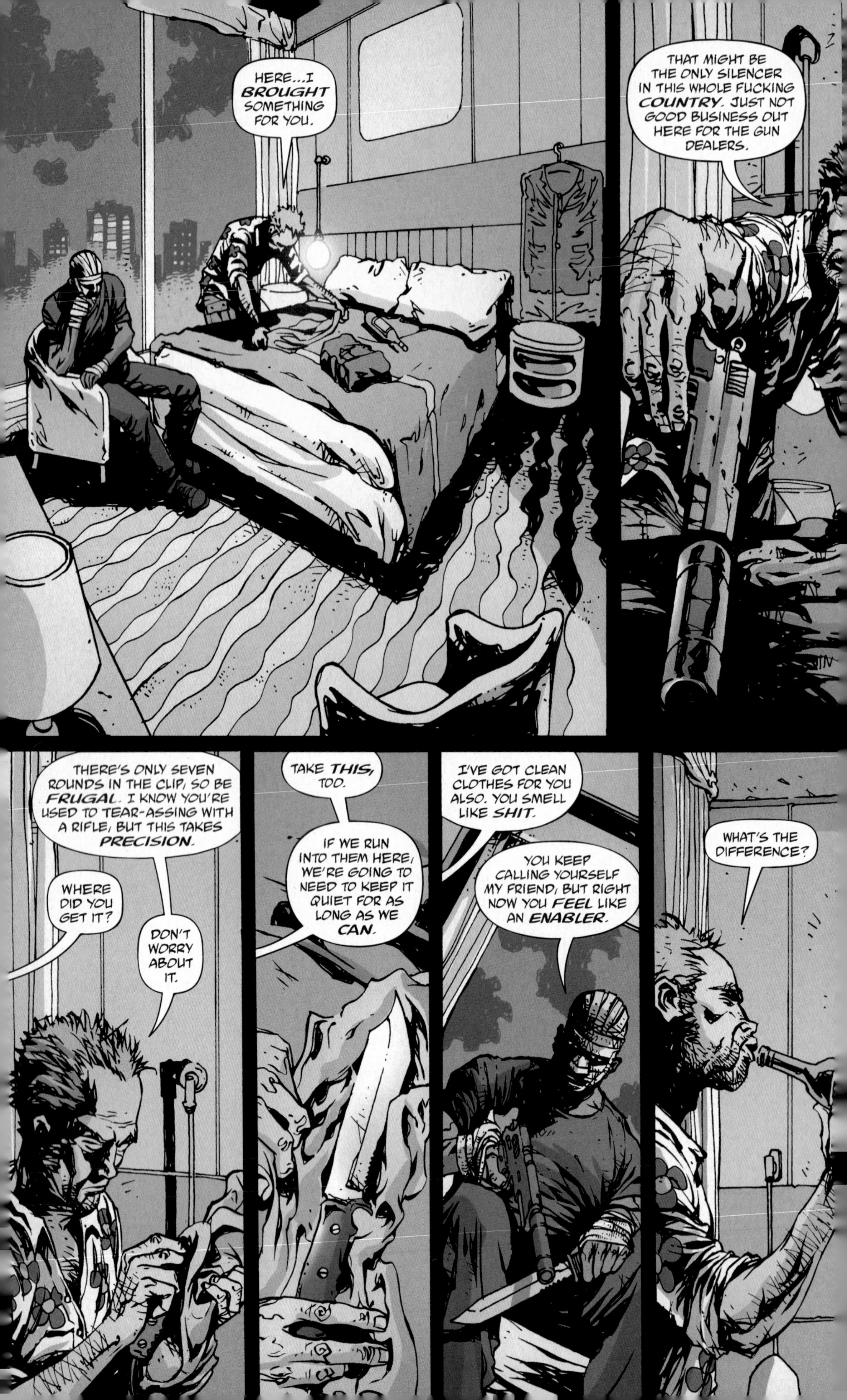
HERE...I BROUGHT SOMETHING FOR YOU.
THAT MIGHT BE THE ONLY SILENCER IN THIS WHOLE FUCKING COUNTRY. JUST NOT GOOD BUSINESS OUT HERE FOR THE GUN DEALERS.
THERE'S ONLY SEVEN ROUNDS IN THE CLIP, SO BE FRUGAL. I KNOW YOU'RE USED TO TEAR-ASSING WITH A RIFLE, BUT THIS TAKES PRECISION.
WHERE DID YOU GET IT?
DON'T WORRY ABOUT IT.
TAKE THIS, TOO.
IF WE RUN INTO THEM HERE, WE'RE GOING TO NEED TO KEEP IT QUIET FOR AS LONG AS WE CAN.
I'VE GOT CLEAN CLOTHES FOR YOU ALSO. YOU SMELL LIKE SHIT.
YOU KEEP CALLING YOURSELF MY FRIEND, BUT RIGHT NOW YOU FEEL LIKE AN ENABLER.
WHAT'S THE DIFFERENCE?

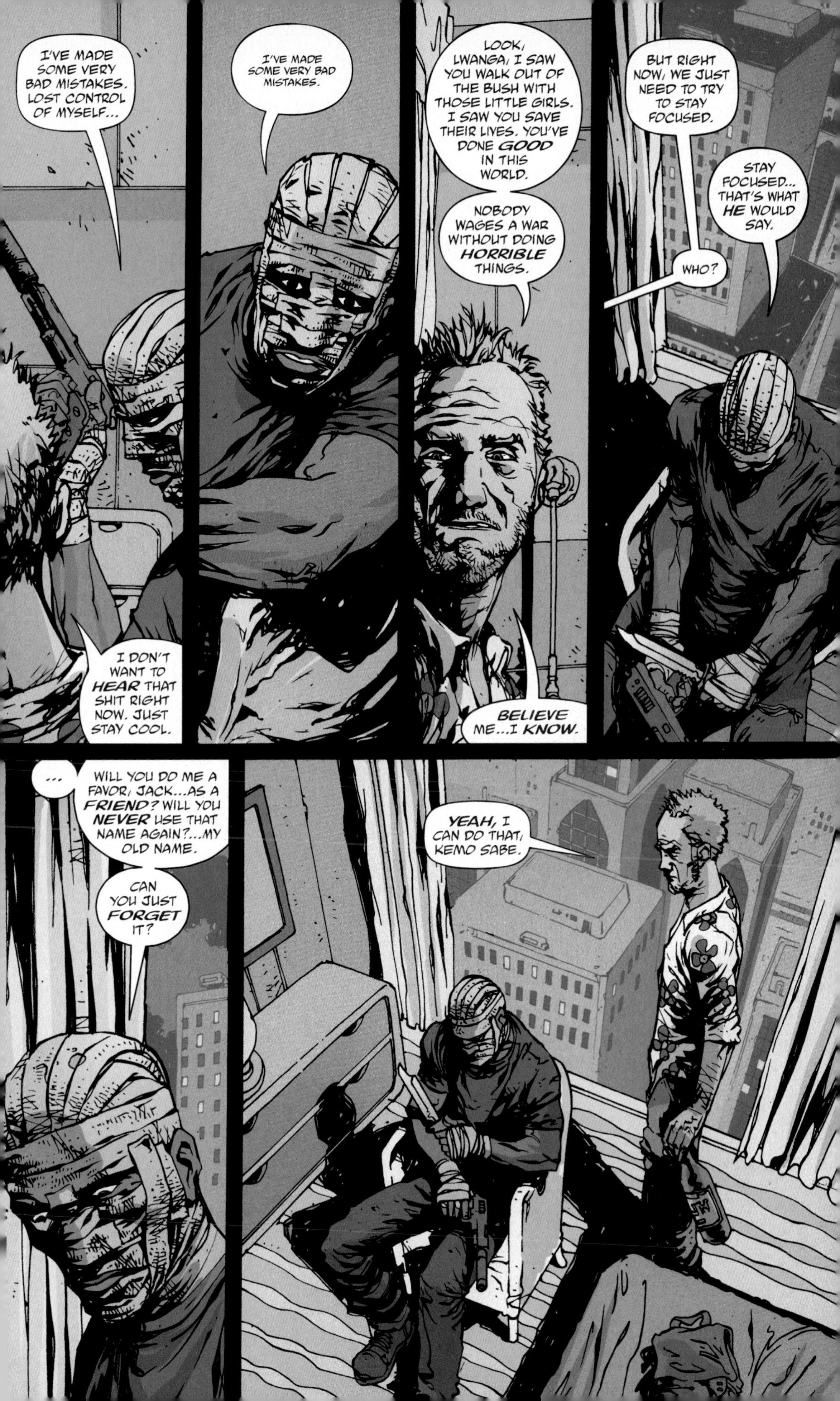

I'VE MADE SOME VERY BAD MISTAKES. LOST CONTROL OF MYSELF...
I DON'T WANT TO HEAR THAT SHIT RIGHT NOW. JUST STAY COOL.
I'VE MADE SOME VERY BAD MISTAKES.
LOOK, LWANGA, I SAW YOU WALK OUT OF THE BUSH WITH THOSE LITTLE GIRLS. I SAW YOU SAVE THEIR LIVES. YOU'VE DONE GOOD IN THIS WORLD.
NOBODY WAGES A WAR WITHOUT DOING HORRIBLE THINGS.
BELIEVE ME...I KNOW.
BUT RIGHT NOW, WE JUST NEED TO TRY TO STAY FOCUSED.
STAY FOCUSED... THAT'S WHAT HE WOULD SAY.
WHO?
...
WILL YOU DO ME A FAVOR, JACK...AS A FRIEND? WILL YOU NEVER USE THAT NAME AGAIN?...MY OLD NAME.
CAN YOU JUST FORGET IT?
YEAH, I CAN DO THAT, KEMO SABE.

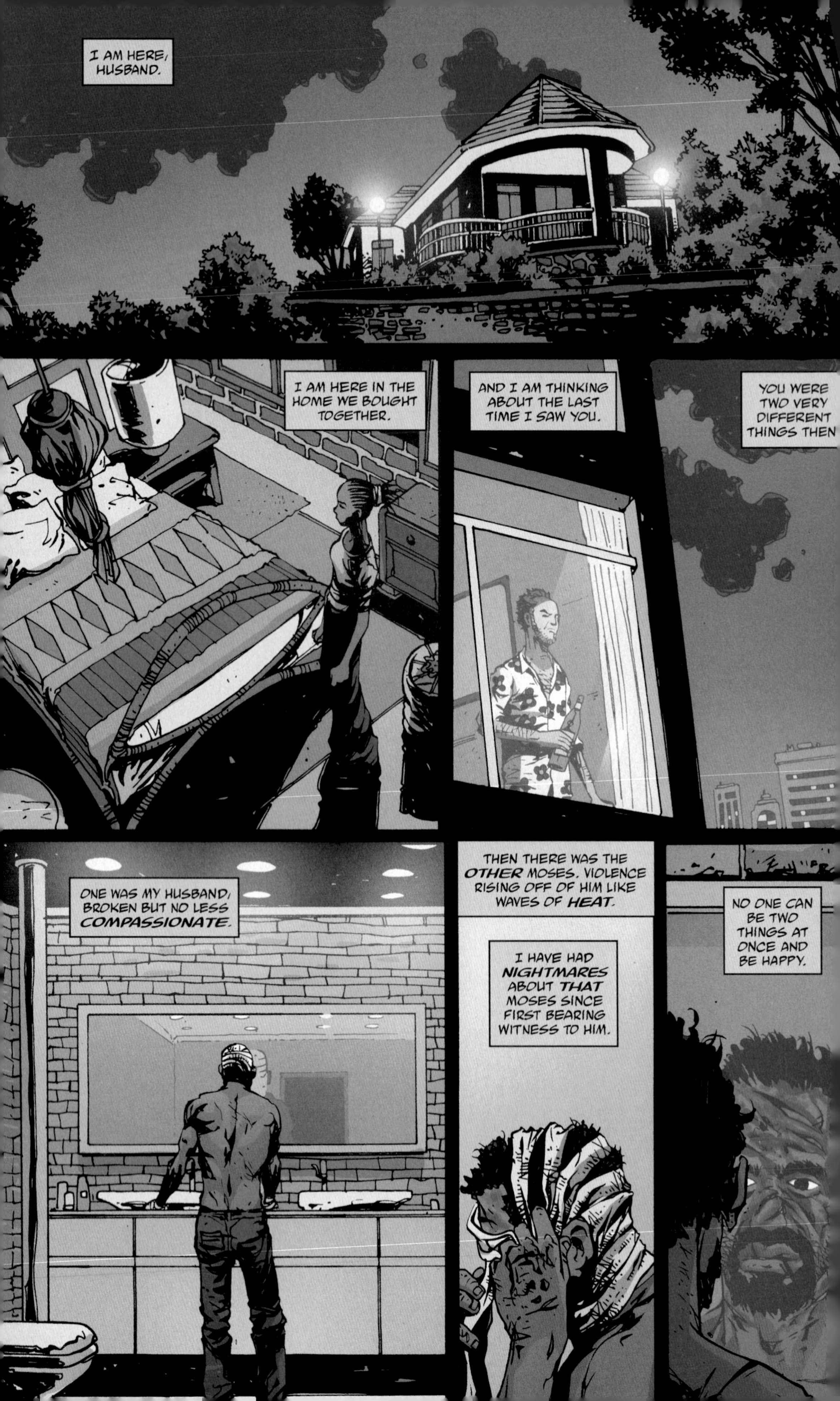
I AM HERE, HUSBAND.
I AM HERE IN THE HOME WE BOUGHT TOGETHER.
AND I AM THINKING ABOUT THE LAST TIME I SAW YOU.
YOU WERE TWO VERY DIFFERENT THINGS THEN
ONE WAS MY HUSBAND, BROKEN BUT NO LESS COMPASSIONATE.
THEN THERE WAS THE OTHER MOSES. VIOLENCE RISING OFF OF HIM LIKE WAVES OF HEAT.
I HAVE HAD NIGHTMARES ABOUT THAT MOSES SINCE FIRST BEARING WITNESS TO HIM.
NO ONE CAN BE TWO THINGS AT ONCE AND BE HAPPY.

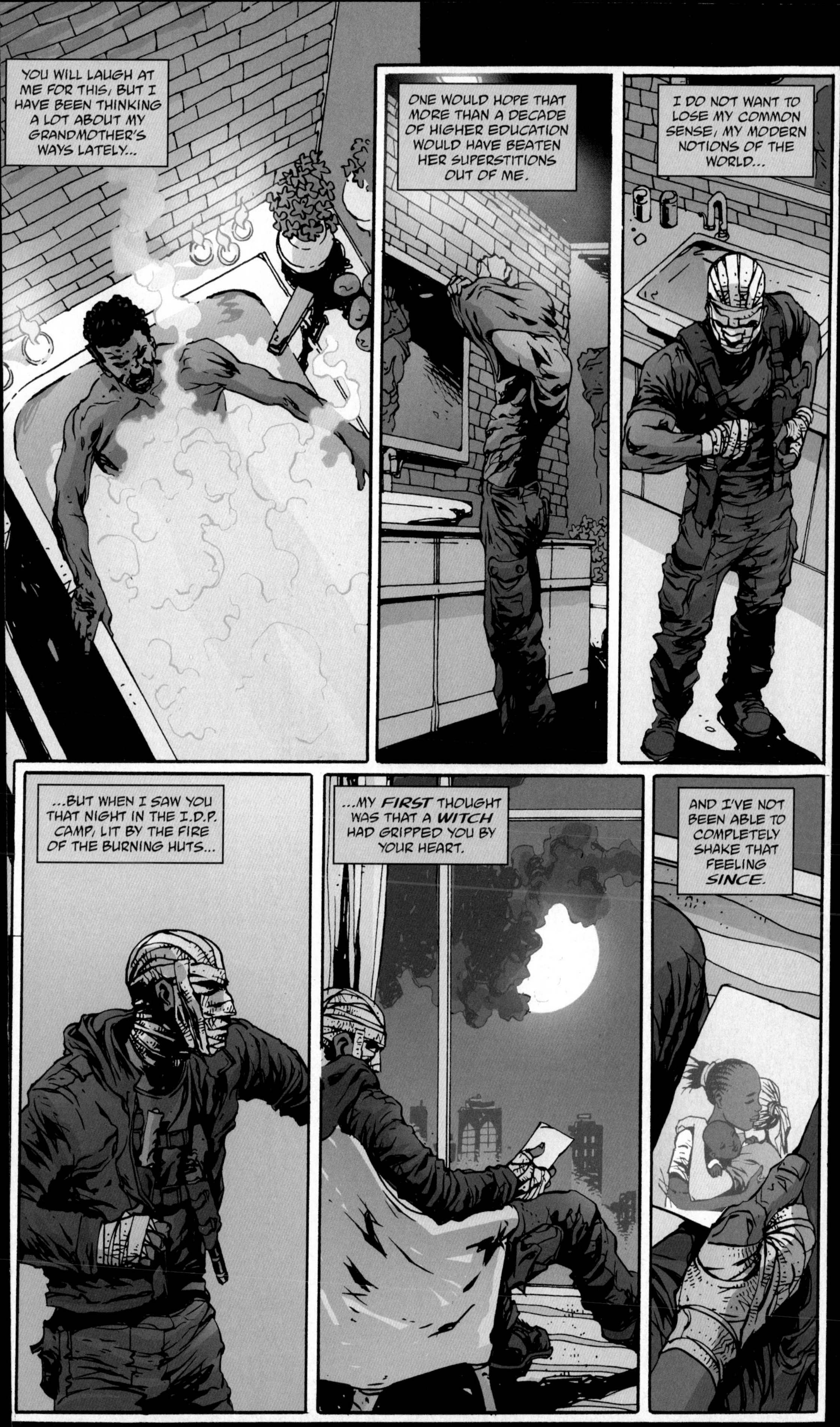
YOU WILL LAUGH AT ME FOR THIS, BUT I HAVE BEEN THINKING A LOT ABOUT MY GRANDMOTHER'S WAYS LATELY...
ONE WOULD HOPE THAT MORE THAN A DECADE OF HIGHER EDUCATION WOULD HAVE BEATEN HER SUPERSTITIONS OUT OF ME.
I DO NOT WANT TO LOSE MY COMMON SENSE, MY MODERN NOTIONS OF THE WORLD...
...BUT WHEN I SAW YOU THAT NIGHT IN THE I.D.P. CAMP, LIT BY THE FIRE OF THE BURNING HUTS...
...MY FIRST THOUGHT WAS THAT A WITCH HAD GRIPPED YOU BY YOUR HEART.
AND I'VE NOT BEEN ABLE TO COMPLETELY SHAKE THAT FEELING SINCE.

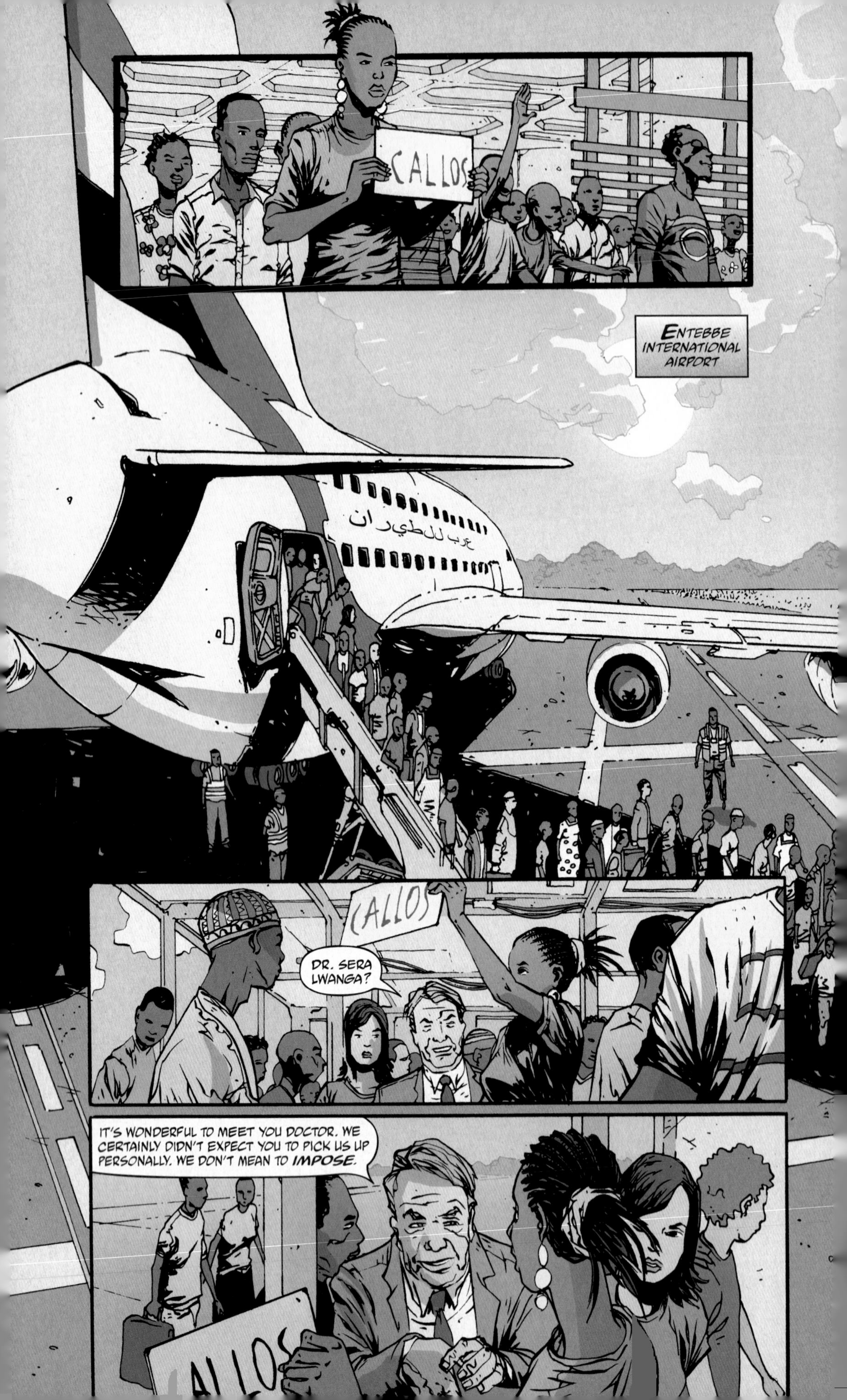
CALLOS
ENTEBBE INTERNATIONAL AIRPORT
CALLOS
DR. SERA LWANGA?
IT'S WONDERFUL TO MEET YOU DOCTOR. WE CERTAINLY DIDN'T EXPECT YOU TO PICK US UP PERSONALLY. WE DON'T MEAN TO *IMPOSE*.

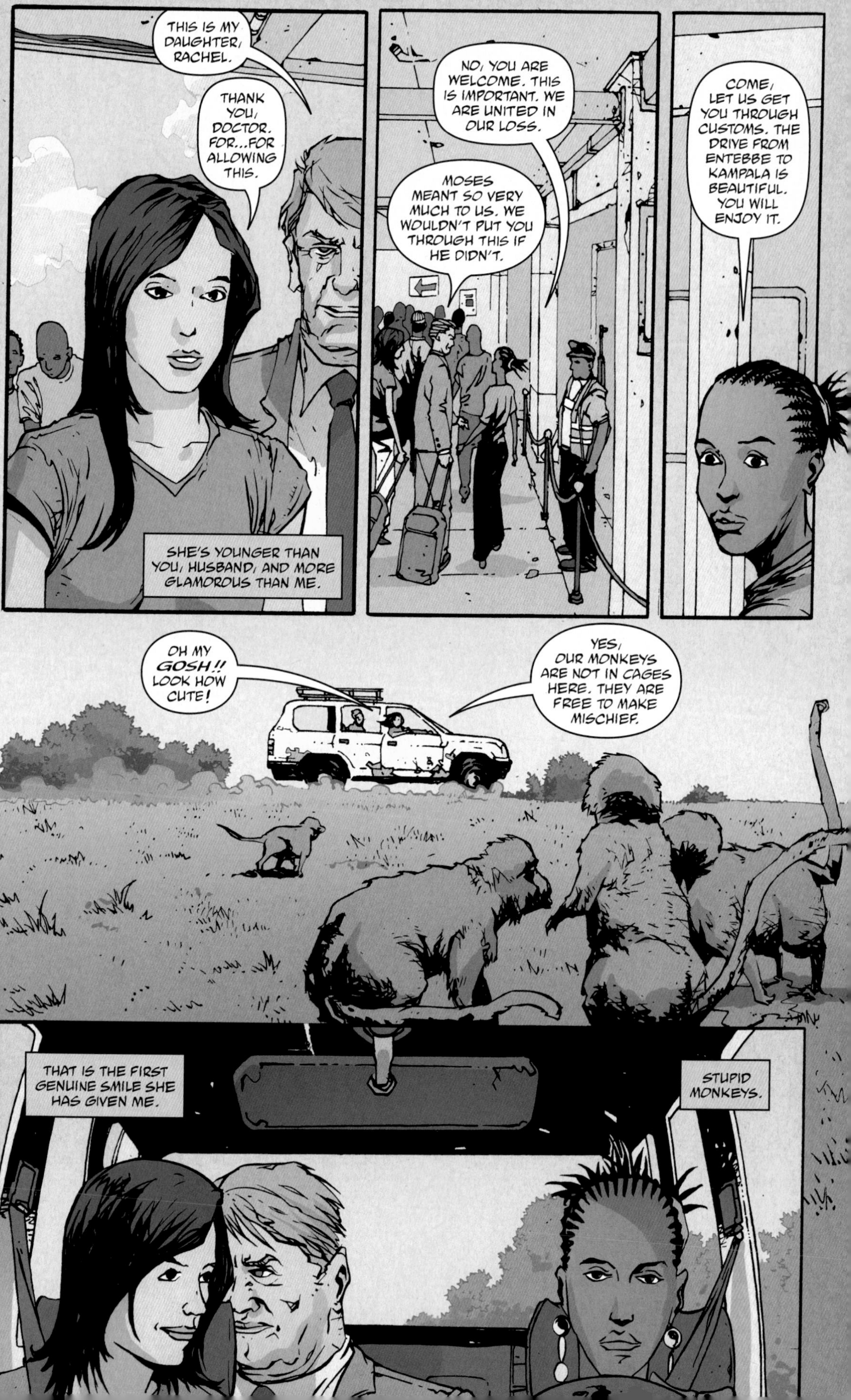
THIS IS MY DAUGHTER, RACHEL.
THANK YOU, DOCTOR. FOR...FOR ALLOWING THIS.
SHE'S YOUNGER THAN YOU, HUSBAND, AND MORE GLAMOROUS THAN ME.
NO, YOU ARE WELCOME. THIS IS IMPORTANT. WE ARE UNITED IN OUR LOSS.
MOSES MEANT SO VERY MUCH TO US. WE WOULDN'T PUT YOU THROUGH THIS IF HE DIDN'T.
COME, LET US GET YOU THROUGH CUSTOMS. THE DRIVE FROM ENTEBBE TO KAMPALA IS BEAUTIFUL. YOU WILL ENJOY IT.
OH MY GOSH!! LOOK HOW CUTE!
YES, OUR MONKEYS ARE NOT IN CAGES HERE. THEY ARE FREE TO MAKE MISCHIEF.
THAT IS THE FIRST GENUINE SMILE SHE HAS GIVEN ME.
STUPID MONKEYS.

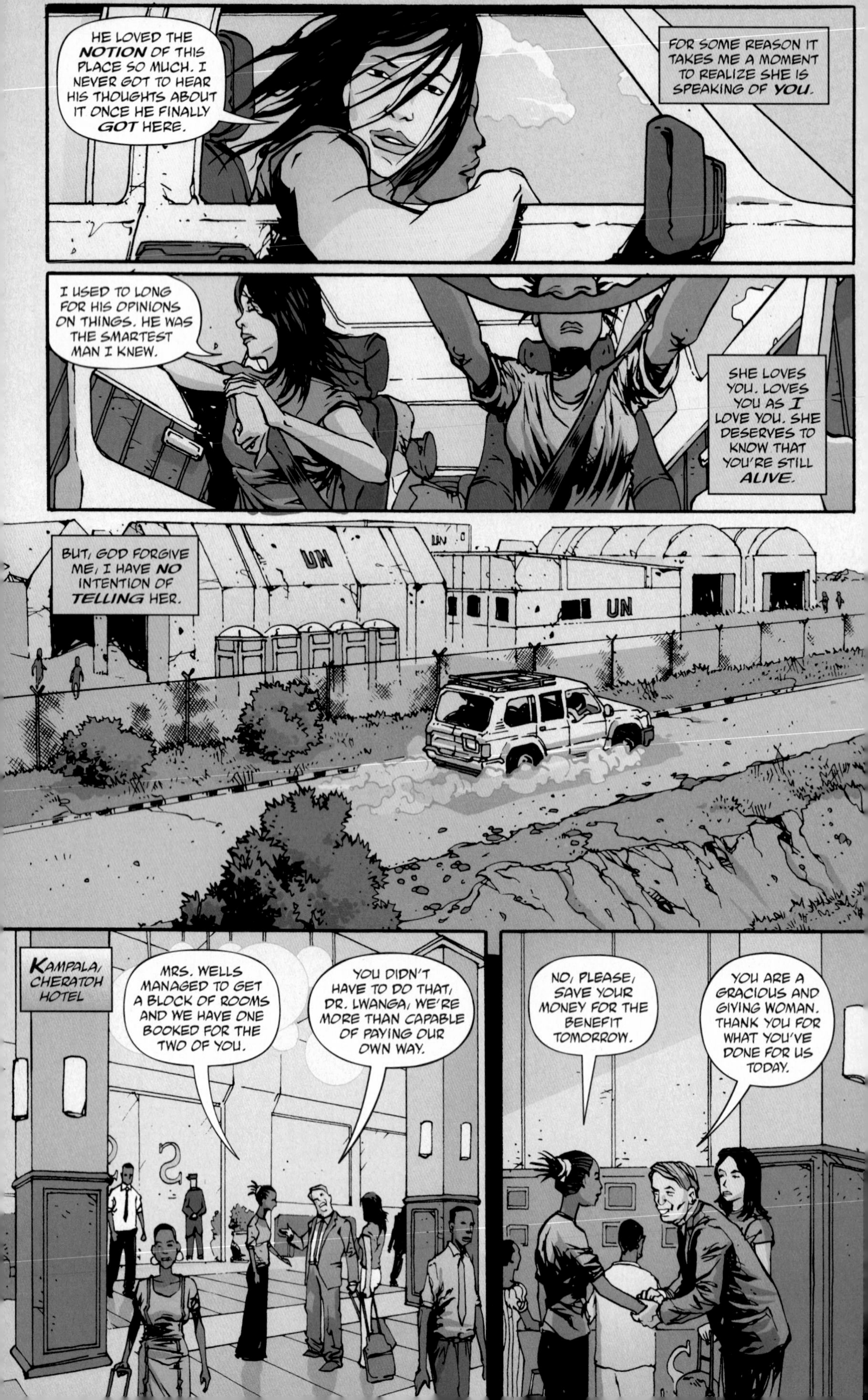
HE LOVED THE NOTION OF THIS PLACE SO MUCH. I NEVER GOT TO HEAR HIS THOUGHTS ABOUT IT ONCE HE FINALLY GOT HERE.
FOR SOME REASON IT TAKES ME A MOMENT TO REALIZE SHE IS SPEAKING OF YOU.
I USED TO LONG FOR HIS OPINIONS ON THINGS. HE WAS THE SMARTEST MAN I KNEW.
SHE LOVES YOU. LOVES YOU AS I LOVE YOU. SHE DESERVES TO KNOW THAT YOU'RE STILL ALIVE.
BUT, GOD FORGIVE ME, I HAVE NO INTENTION OF TELLING HER.
UN
UN
KAMPALA, CHERATON HOTEL
MRS. WELLS MANAGED TO GET A BLOCK OF ROOMS AND WE HAVE ONE BOOKED FOR THE TWO OF YOU.
YOU DIDN'T HAVE TO DO THAT, DR. LWANGA, WE'RE MORE THAN CAPABLE OF PAYING OUR OWN WAY.
NO, PLEASE, SAVE YOUR MONEY FOR THE BENEFIT TOMORROW.
YOU ARE A GRACIOUS AND GIVING WOMAN. THANK YOU FOR WHAT YOU'VE DONE FOR US TODAY.

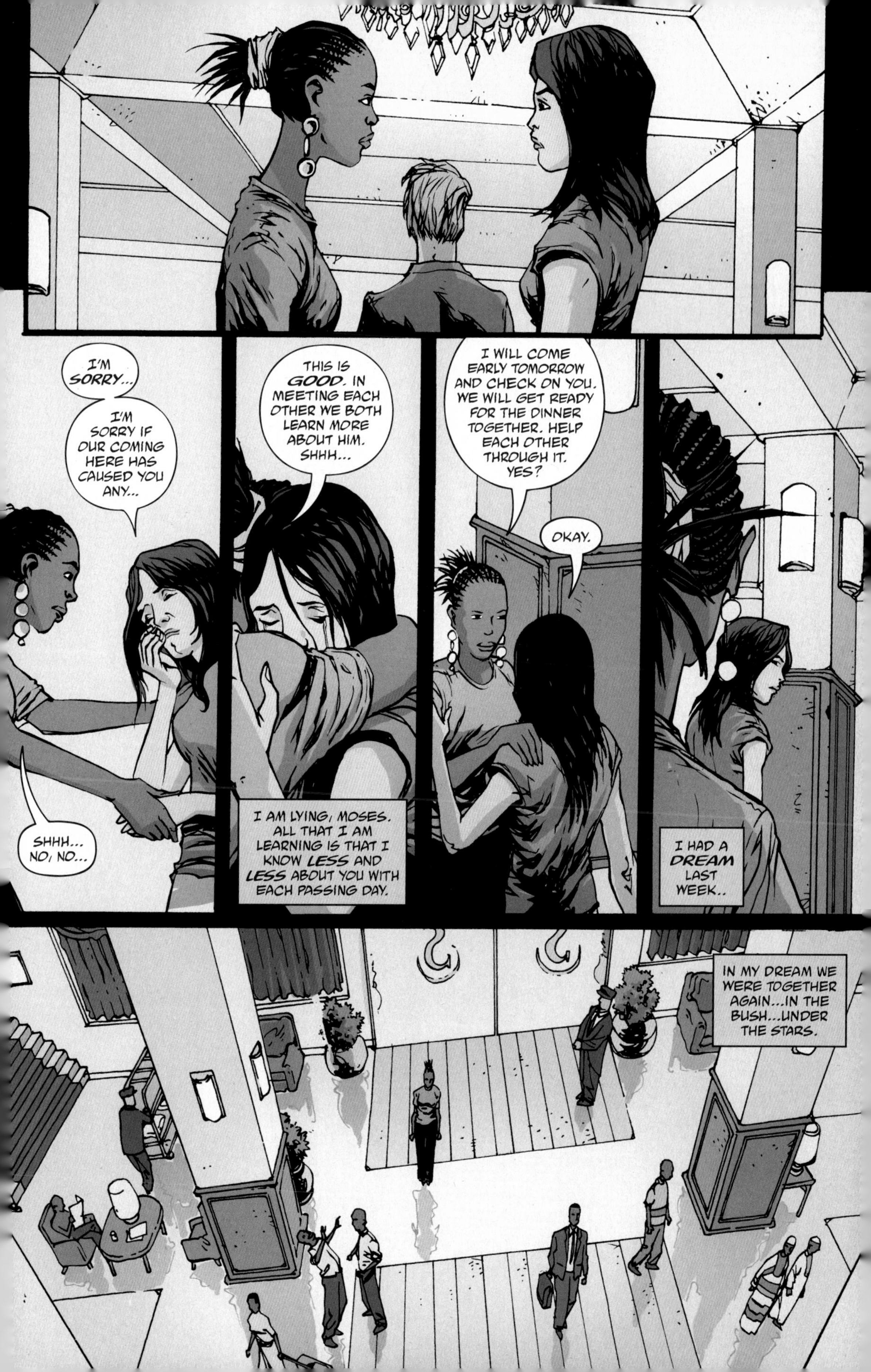
I'M SORRY...
I'M SORRY IF OUR COMING HERE HAS CAUSED YOU ANY...
SHHH... NO, NO...
THIS IS GOOD. IN MEETING EACH OTHER WE BOTH LEARN MORE ABOUT HIM. SHHH...
I AM LYING, MOSES. ALL THAT I AM LEARNING IS THAT I KNOW LESS AND LESS ABOUT YOU WITH EACH PASSING DAY.
I WILL COME EARLY TOMORROW AND CHECK ON YOU. WE WILL GET READY FOR THE DINNER TOGETHER. HELP EACH OTHER THROUGH IT. YES?
OKAY.
I HAD A DREAM LAST WEEK..
IN MY DREAM WE WERE TOGETHER AGAIN...IN THE BUSH...UNDER THE STARS.

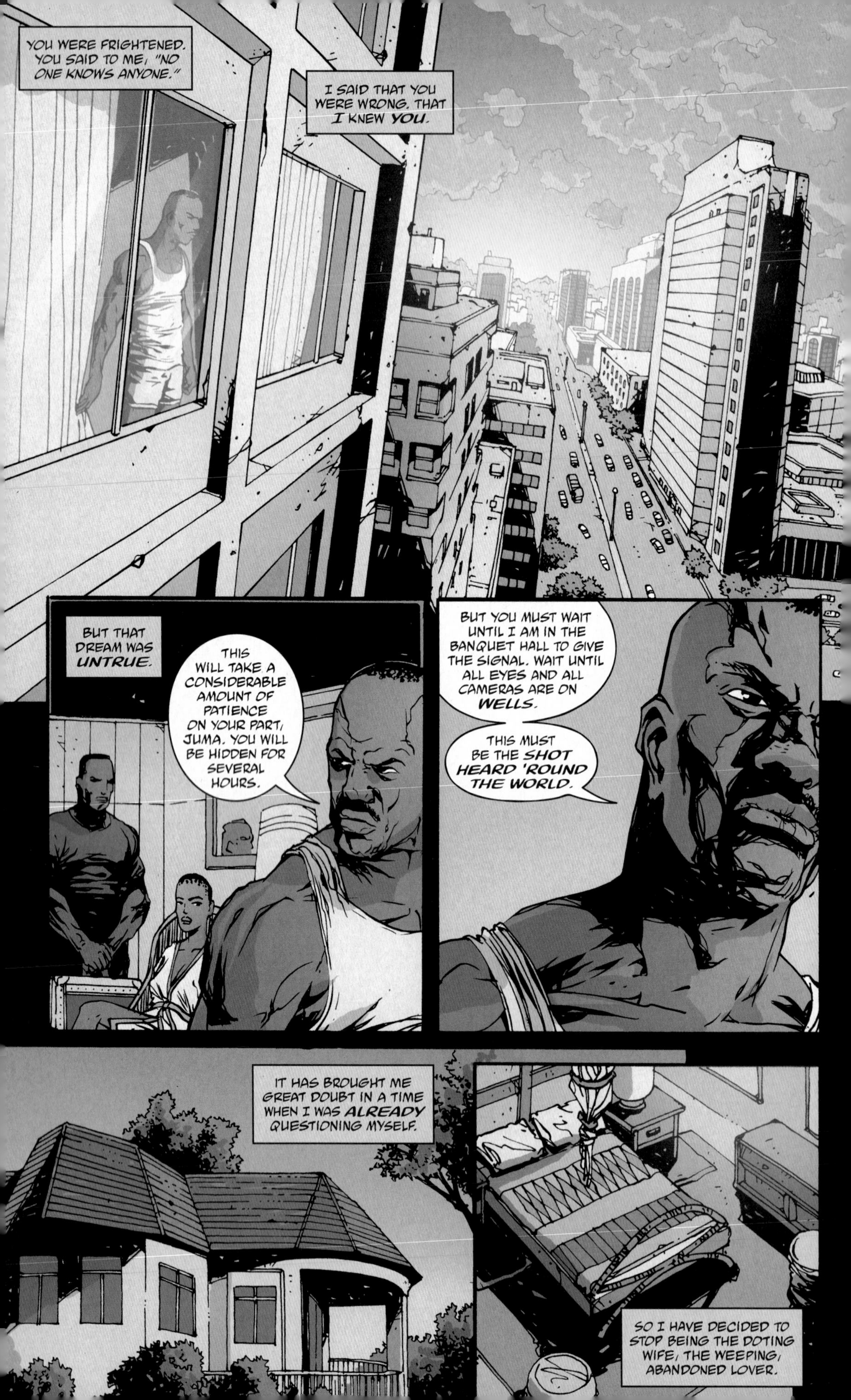
YOU WERE FRIGHTENED. YOU SAID TO ME, "NO ONE KNOWS ANYONE."
I SAID THAT YOU WERE WRONG. THAT I KNEW YOU.
BUT THAT DREAM WAS UNTRUE.
THIS WILL TAKE A CONSIDERABLE AMOUNT OF PATIENCE ON YOUR PART, JUMA. YOU WILL BE HIDDEN FOR SEVERAL HOURS.
BUT YOU MUST WAIT UNTIL I AM IN THE BANQUET HALL TO GIVE THE SIGNAL. WAIT UNTIL ALL EYES AND ALL CAMERAS ARE ON WELLS.
THIS MUST BE THE SHOT HEARD 'ROUND THE WORLD.
IT HAS BROUGHT ME GREAT DOUBT IN A TIME WHEN I WAS ALREADY QUESTIONING MYSELF.
SO I HAVE DECIDED TO STOP BEING THE DOTING WIFE, THE WEEPING, ABANDONED LOVER.

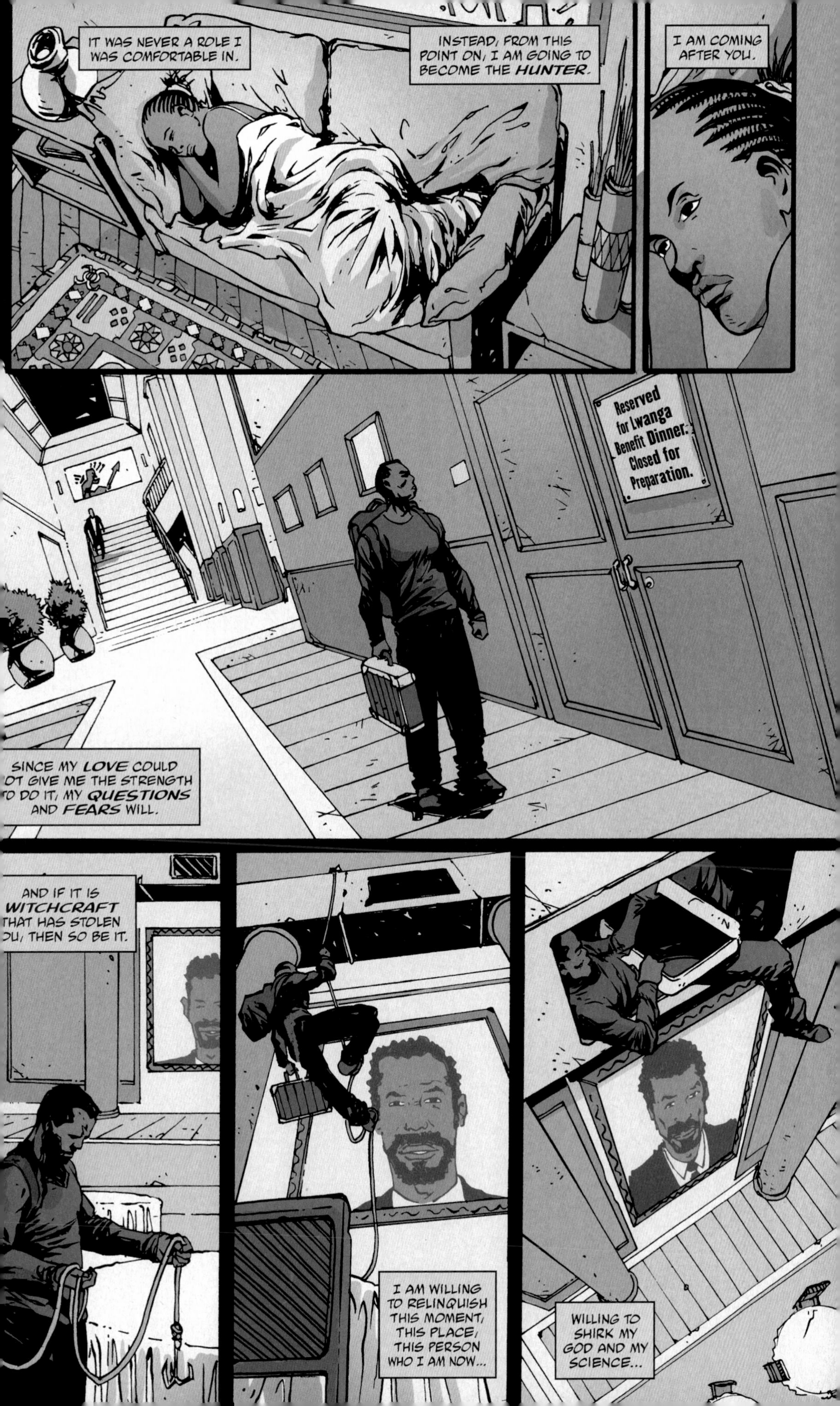
IT WAS NEVER A ROLE I WAS COMFORTABLE IN.
INSTEAD, FROM THIS POINT ON, I AM GOING TO BECOME THE HUNTER.
I AM COMING AFTER YOU.
Reserved for Lwanga Benefit Dinner: Closed for Preparation.
SINCE MY LOVE COULD OT GIVE ME THE STRENGTH TO DO IT, MY QUESTIONS AND FEARS WILL.
AND IF IT IS WITCHCRAFT THAT HAS STOLEN OU, THEN SO BE IT.
I AM WILLING TO RELINQUISH THIS MOMENT, THIS PLACE, THIS PERSON WHO I AM NOW...
WILLING TO SHIRK MY GOD AND MY SCIENCE...

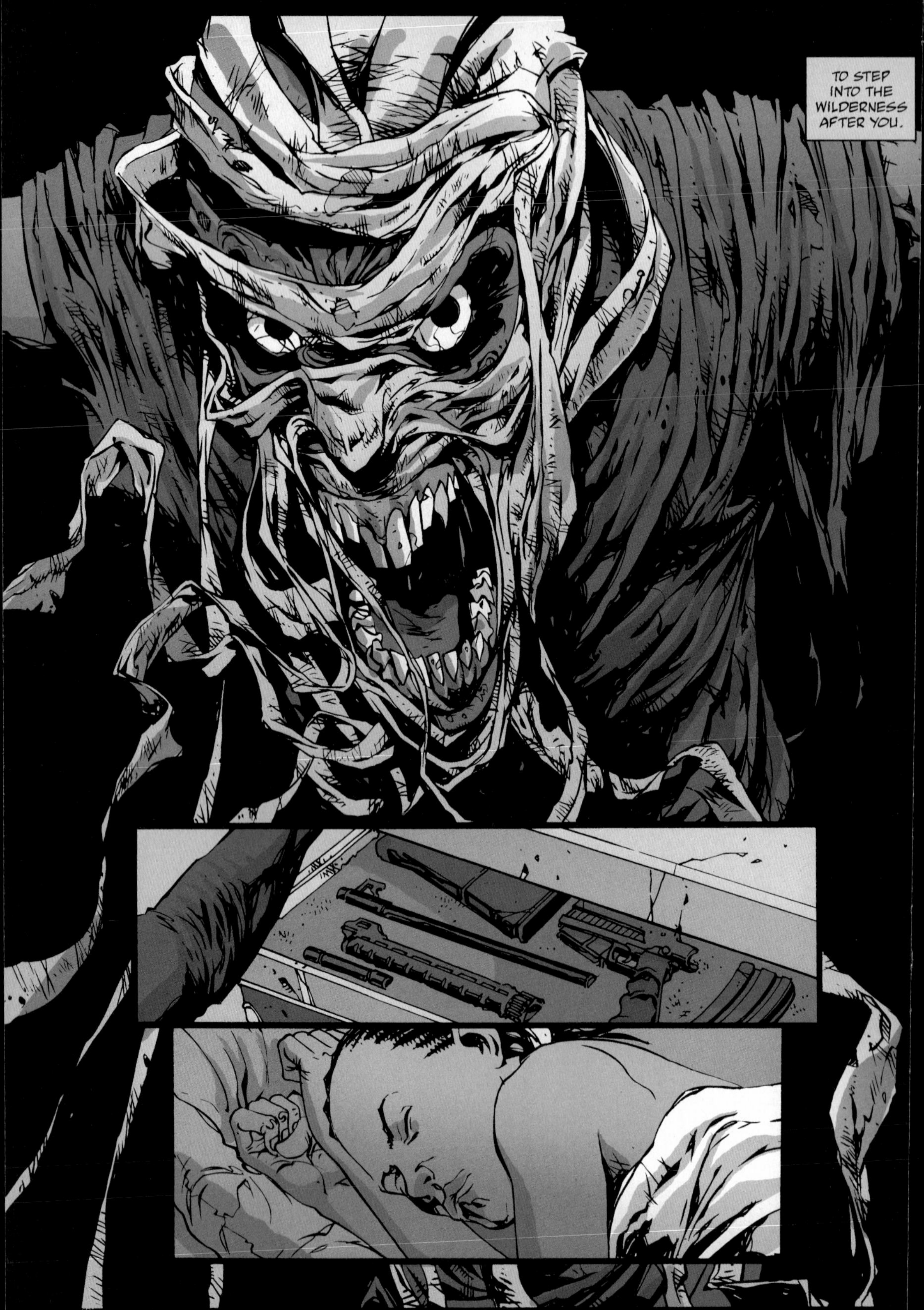
TO STEP INTO THE WILDERNESS AFTER YOU.

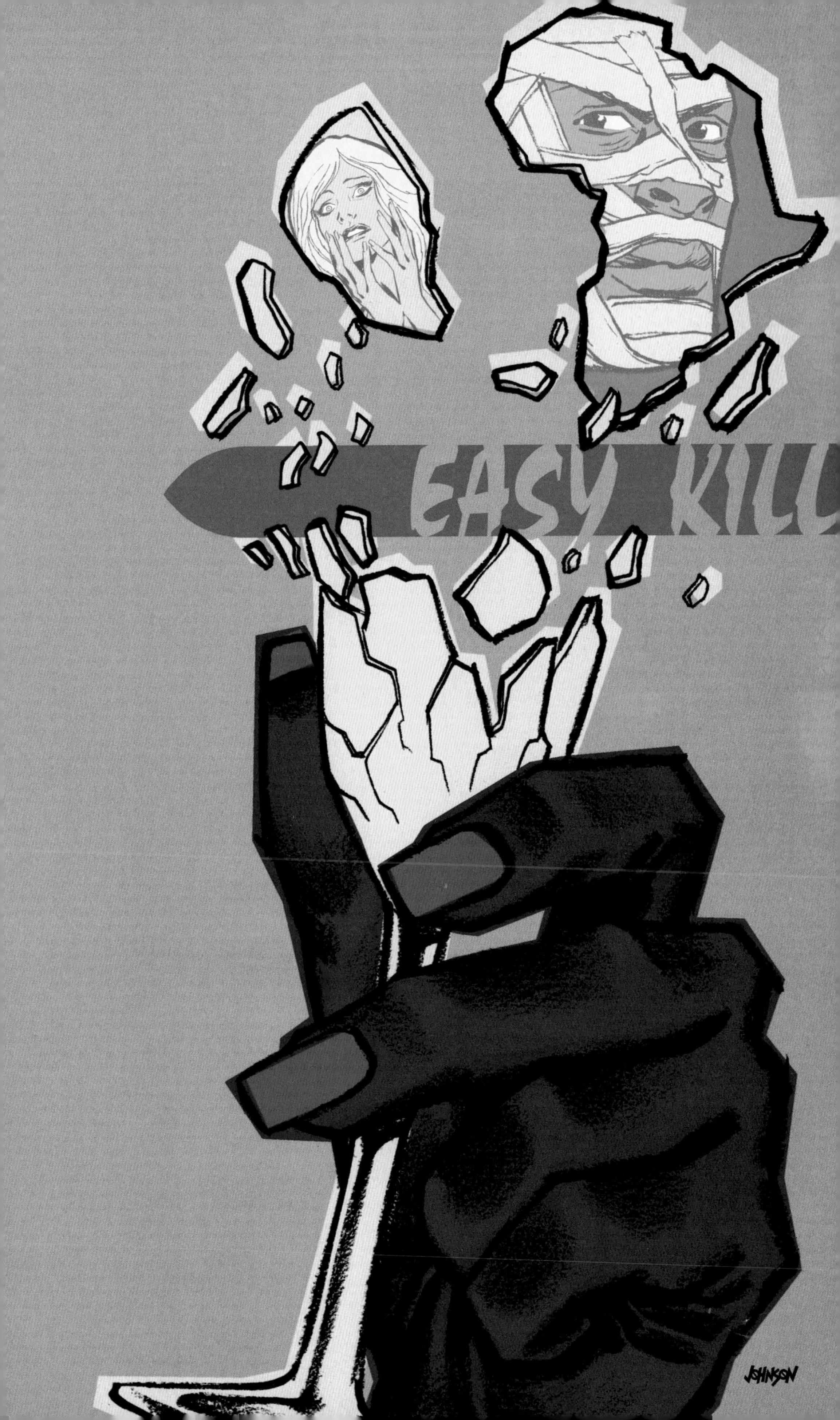
EASY KILL
JOHNSON

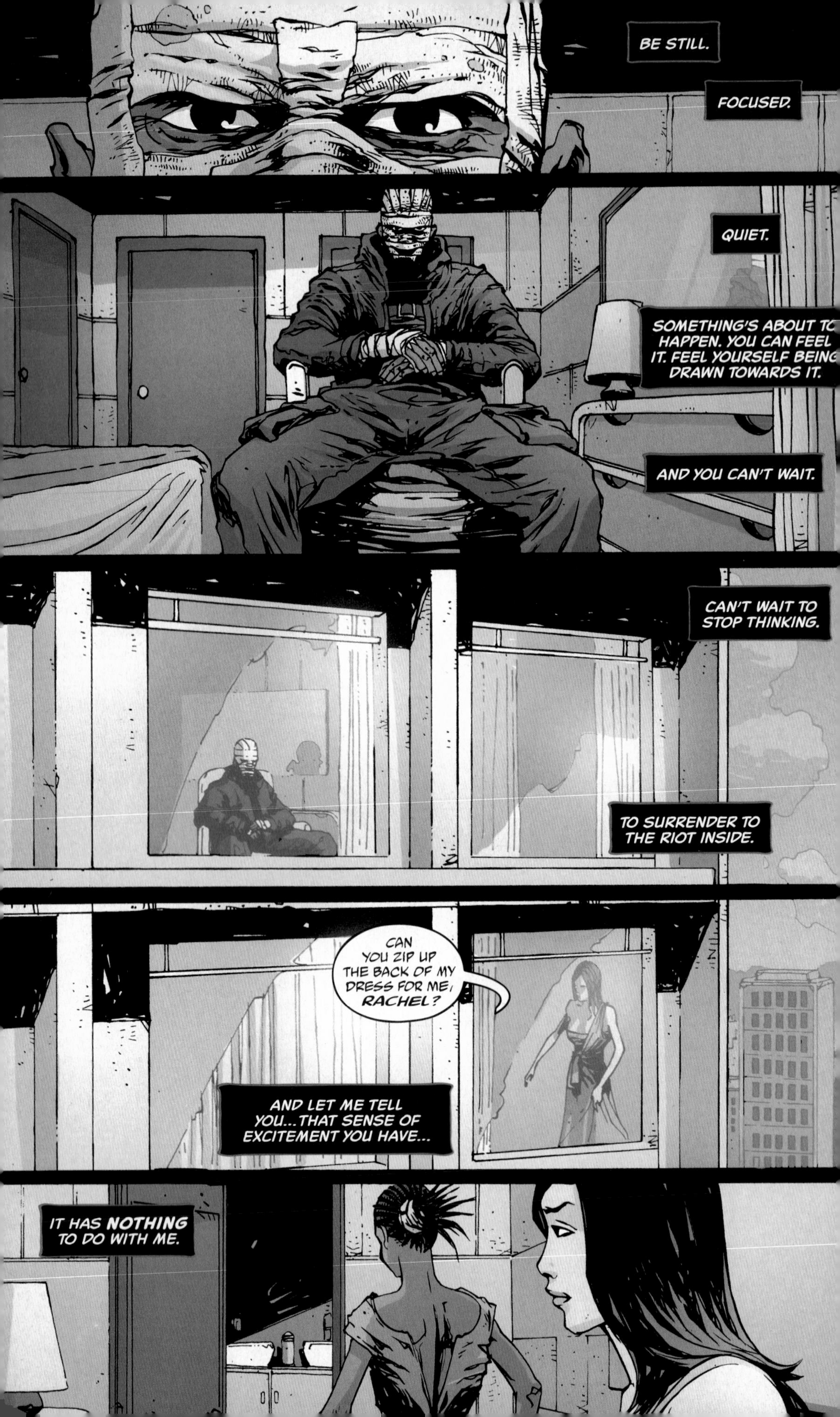
BE STILL.
FOCUSED.
QUIET.
SOMETHING'S ABOUT TO HAPPEN. YOU CAN FEEL IT. FEEL YOURSELF BEING DRAWN TOWARDS IT.
AND YOU CAN'T WAIT.
CAN'T WAIT TO STOP THINKING.
TO SURRENDER TO THE RIOT INSIDE.
CAN YOU ZIP UP THE BACK OF MY DRESS FOR ME, RACHEL?
AND LET ME TELL YOU...THAT SENSE OF EXCITEMENT YOU HAVE...
IT HAS NOTHING TO DO WITH ME.

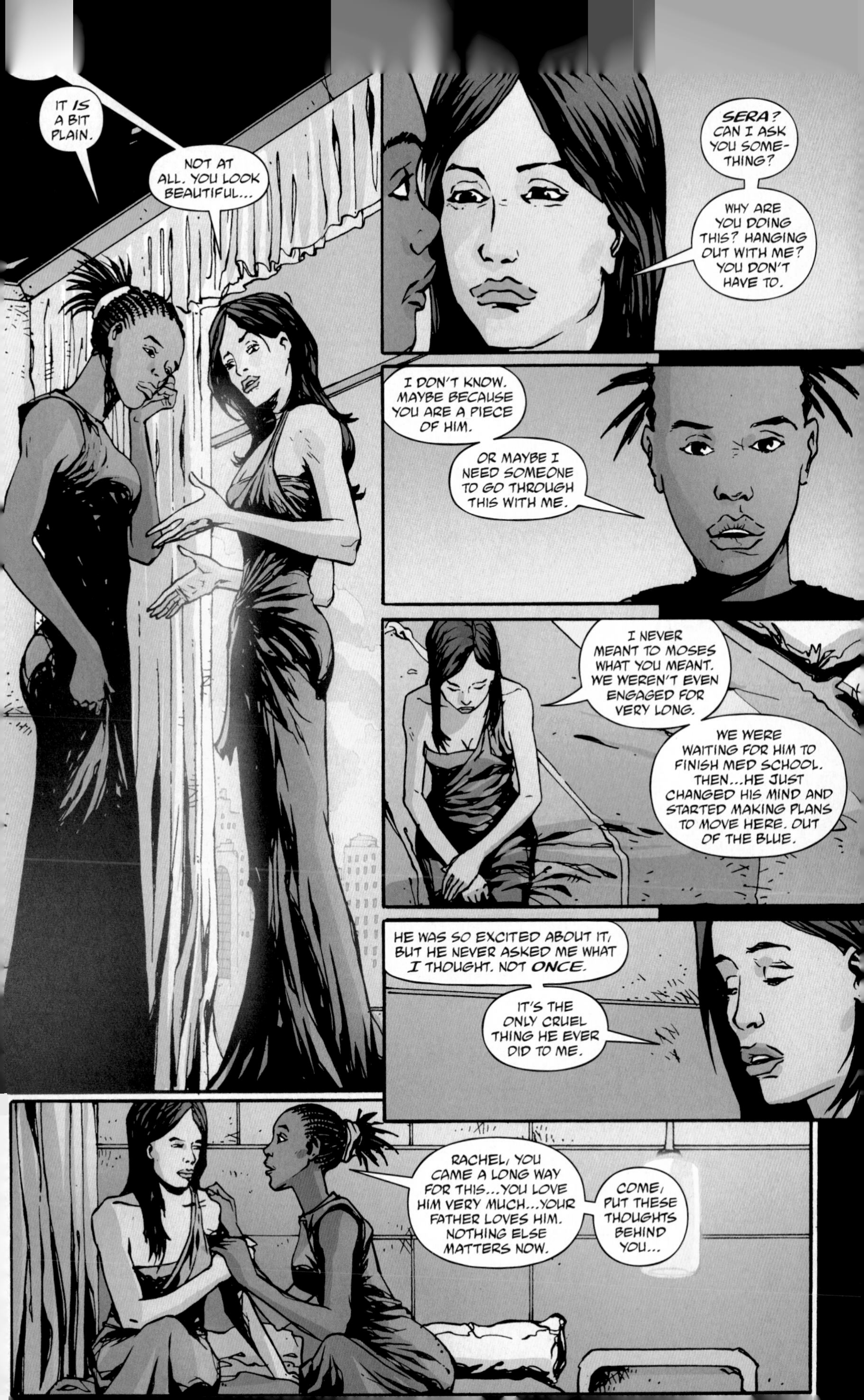
IT IS A BIT PLAIN.
NOT AT ALL. YOU LOOK BEAUTIFUL...
SERA? CAN I ASK YOU SOME-THING?
WHY ARE YOU DOING THIS? HANGING OUT WITH ME? YOU DON'T HAVE TO.
I DON'T KNOW. MAYBE BECAUSE YOU ARE A PIECE OF HIM.
OR MAYBE I NEED SOMEONE TO GO THROUGH THIS WITH ME.
I NEVER MEANT TO MOSES WHAT YOU MEANT. WE WEREN'T EVEN ENGAGED FOR VERY LONG.
WE WERE WAITING FOR HIM TO FINISH MED SCHOOL. THEN...HE JUST CHANGED HIS MIND AND STARTED MAKING PLANS TO MOVE HERE. OUT OF THE BLUE.
HE WAS SO EXCITED ABOUT IT, BUT HE NEVER ASKED ME WHAT I THOUGHT. NOT ONCE.
IT'S THE ONLY CRUEL THING HE EVER DID TO ME.
RACHEL, YOU CAME A LONG WAY FOR THIS...YOU LOVE HIM VERY MUCH...YOUR FATHER LOVES HIM. NOTHING ELSE MATTERS NOW.
COME, PUT THESE THOUGHTS BEHIND YOU...

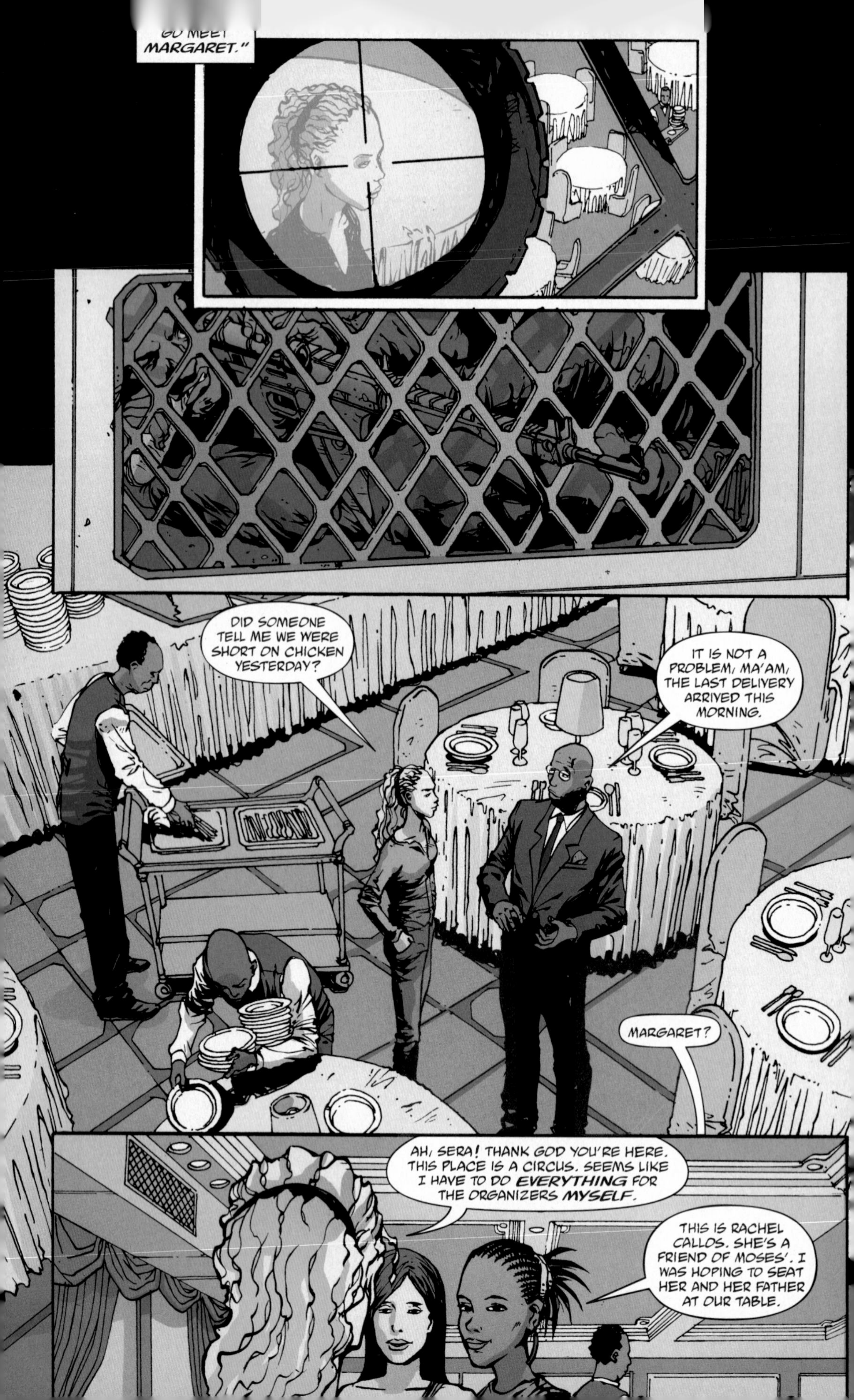
GO MEET MARGARET."
DID SOMEONE TELL ME WE WERE SHORT ON CHICKEN YESTERDAY?
IT IS NOT A PROBLEM, MA'AM, THE LAST DELIVERY ARRIVED THIS MORNING.
MARGARET?
AH, SERA! THANK GOD YOU'RE HERE. THIS PLACE IS A CIRCUS. SEEMS LIKE I HAVE TO DO EVERYTHING FOR THE ORGANIZERS MYSELF.
THIS IS RACHEL CALLOS. SHE'S A FRIEND OF MOSES'. I WAS HOPING TO SEAT HER AND HER FATHER AT OUR TABLE.

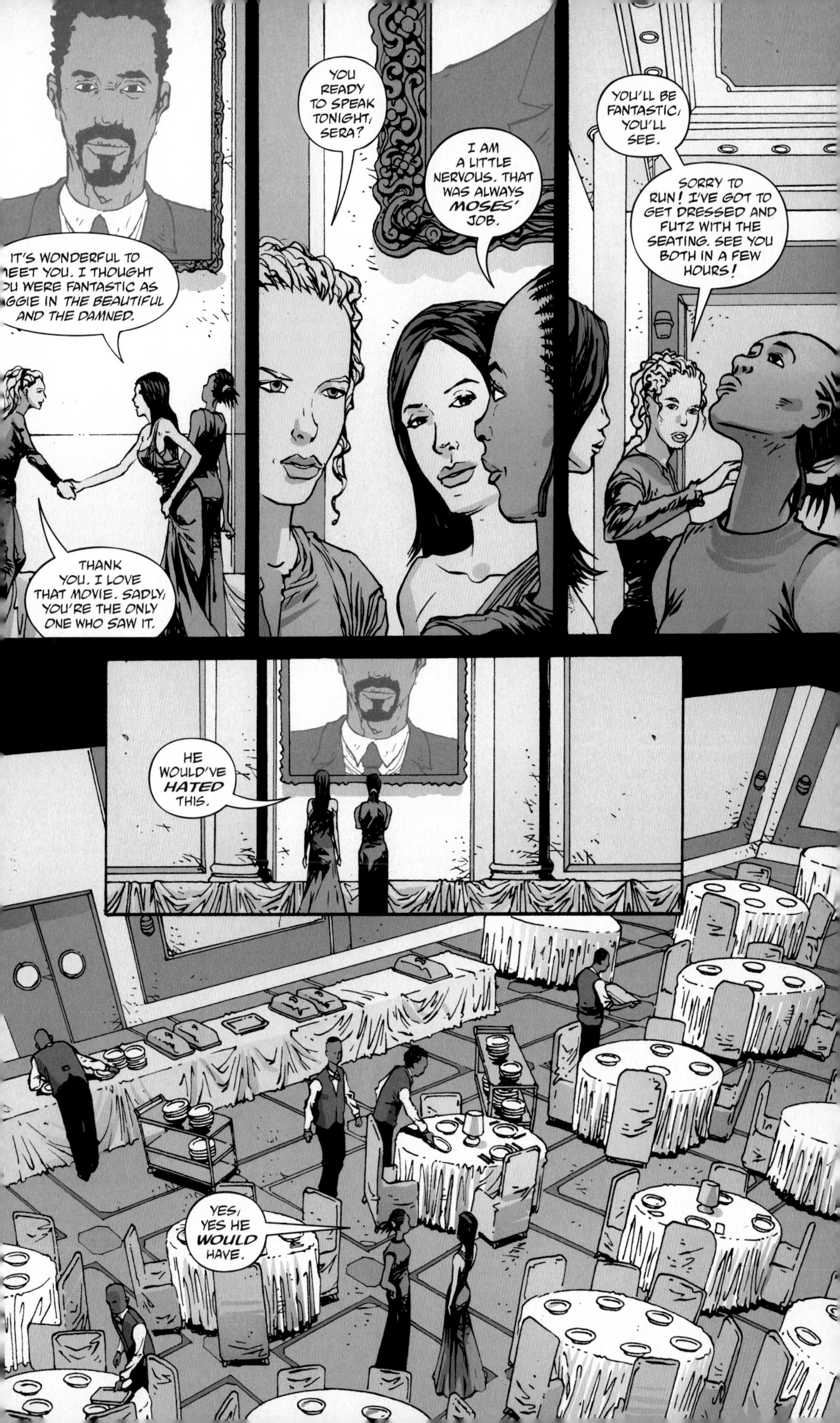
IT'S WONDERFUL TO MEET YOU. I THOUGHT YOU WERE FANTASTIC AS GGIE IN THE BEAUTIFUL AND THE DAMNED.
THANK YOU. I LOVE THAT MOVIE. SADLY, YOU'RE THE ONLY ONE WHO SAW IT.
YOU READY TO SPEAK TONIGHT, SERA?
I AM A LITTLE NERVOUS. THAT WAS ALWAYS MOSES' JOB.
YOU'LL BE FANTASTIC, YOU'LL SEE.
SORRY TO RUN! I'VE GOT TO GET DRESSED AND FUTZ WITH THE SEATING. SEE YOU BOTH IN A FEW HOURS!
HE WOULD'VE HATED THIS.
YES, YES HE WOULD HAVE.

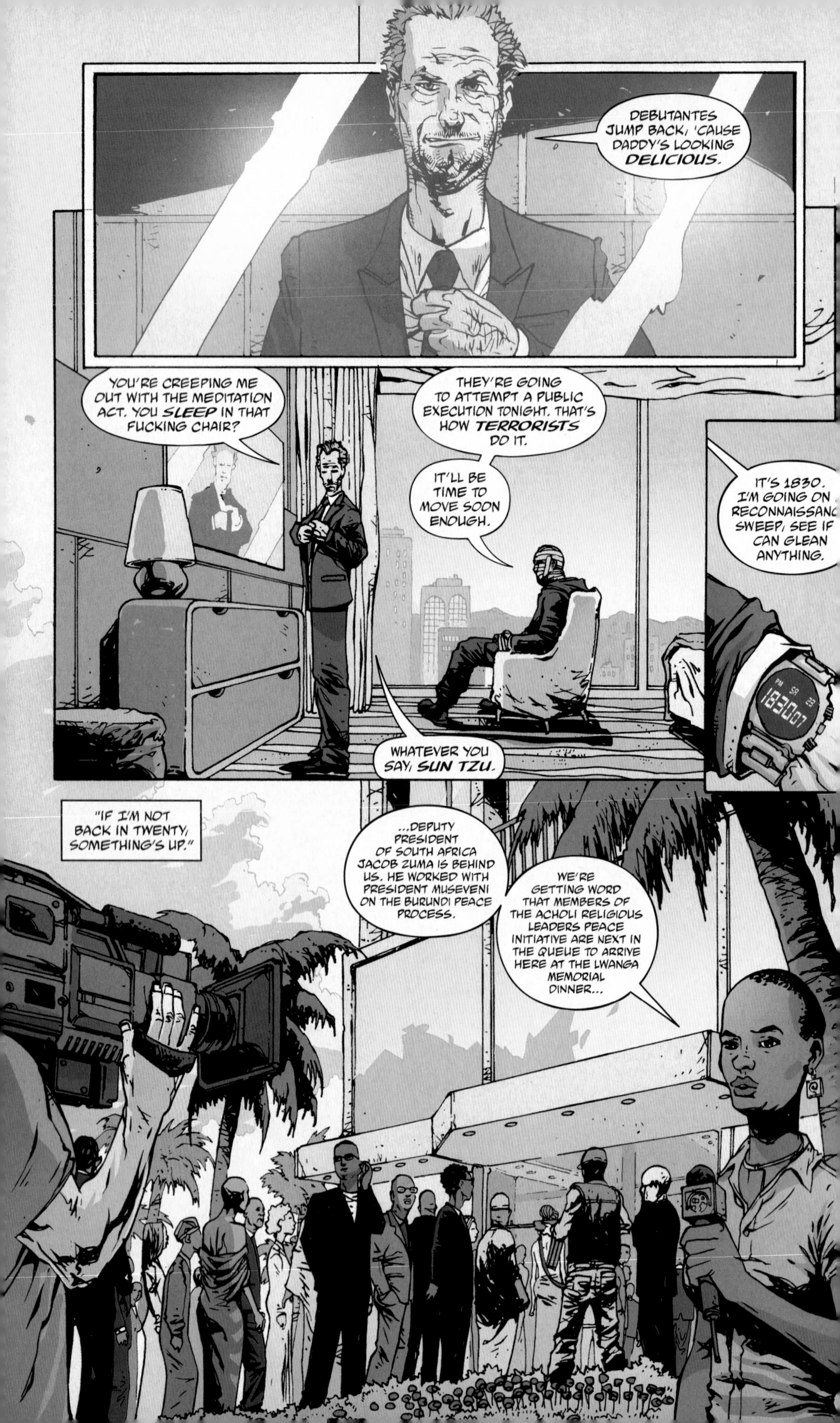
DEBUTANTES JUMP BACK, 'CAUSE DADDY'S LOOKING DELICIOUS.
YOU'RE CREEPING ME OUT WITH THE MEDITATION ACT. YOU SLEEP IN THAT FUCKING CHAIR?
THEY'RE GOING TO ATTEMPT A PUBLIC EXECUTION TONIGHT. THAT'S HOW TERRORISTS DO IT.
IT'LL BE TIME TO MOVE SOON ENOUGH.
WHATEVER YOU SAY, SUN TZU.
IT'S 1830. I'M GOING ON RECONNAISSANC SWEEP, SEE IF CAN GLEAN ANYTHING.
"IF I'M NOT BACK IN TWENTY, SOMETHING'S UP."
...DEPUTY PRESIDENT OF SOUTH AFRICA JACOB ZUMA IS BEHIND US. HE WORKED WITH PRESIDENT MUSEVENI ON THE BURUNDI PEACE PROCESS.
WE'RE GETTING WORD THAT MEMBERS OF THE ACHOLI RELIGIOUS LEADERS PEACE INITIATIVE ARE NEXT IN THE QUEUE TO ARRIVE HERE AT THE LWANGA MEMORIAL DINNER...

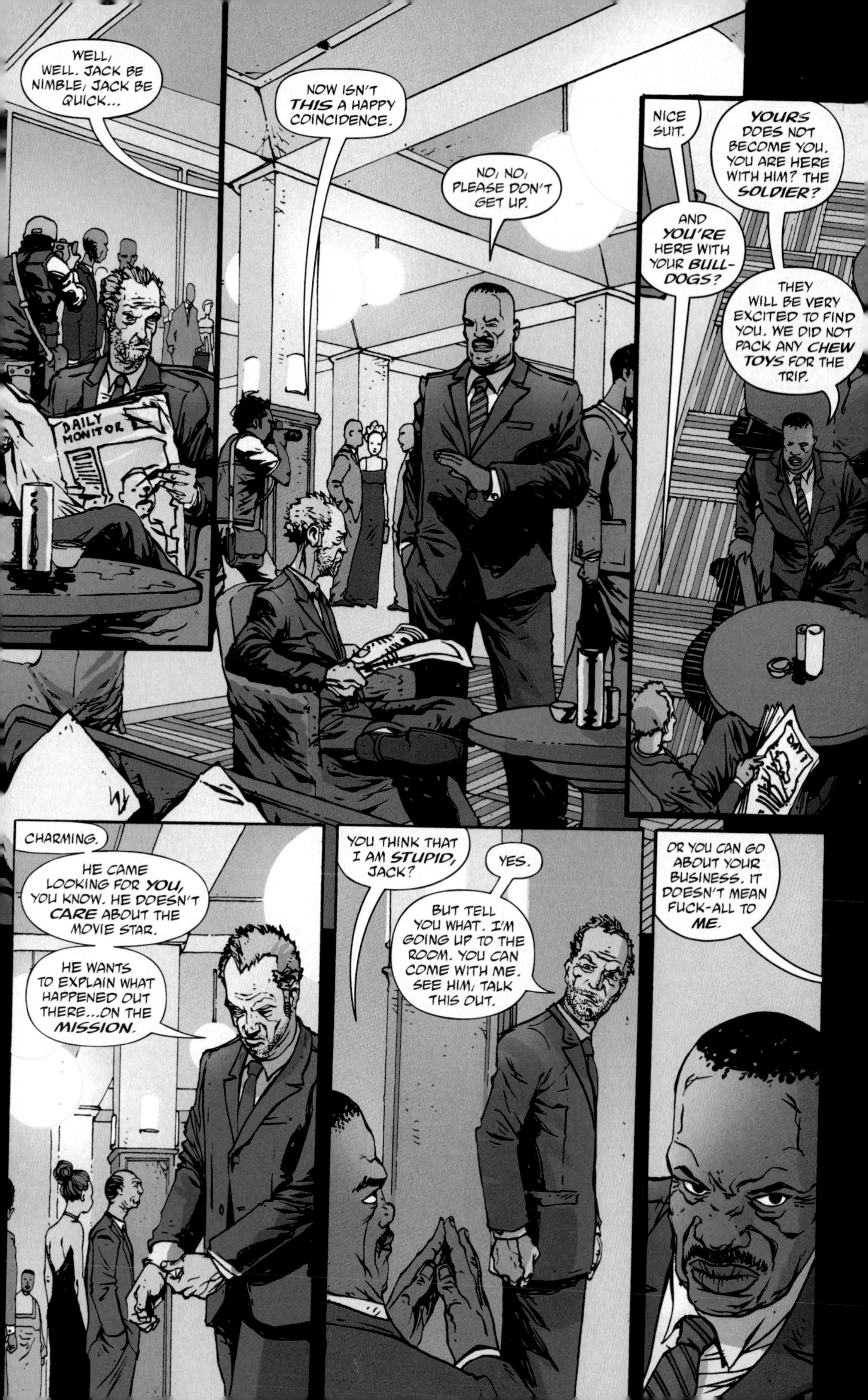

WELL, WELL. JACK BE NIMBLE, JACK BE QUICK...
NOW ISN'T THIS A HAPPY COINCIDENCE.
NO, NO, PLEASE DON'T GET UP.
NICE SUIT.
YOURS DOES NOT BECOME YOU. YOU ARE HERE WITH HIM? THE SOLDIER?
AND YOU'RE HERE WITH YOUR BULL-DOGS?
THEY WILL BE VERY EXCITED TO FIND YOU. WE DID NOT PACK ANY CHEW TOYS FOR THE TRIP.
DAILY MONITOR
CHARMING.
HE CAME LOOKING FOR YOU, YOU KNOW. HE DOESN'T CARE ABOUT THE MOVIE STAR.
HE WANTS TO EXPLAIN WHAT HAPPENED OUT THERE...ON THE MISSION.
YOU THINK THAT I AM STUPID, JACK?
YES.
BUT TELL YOU WHAT. I'M GOING UP TO THE ROOM. YOU CAN COME WITH ME. SEE HIM, TALK THIS OUT.
OR YOU CAN GO ABOUT YOUR BUSINESS. IT DOESN'T MEAN FUCK-ALL TO ME.

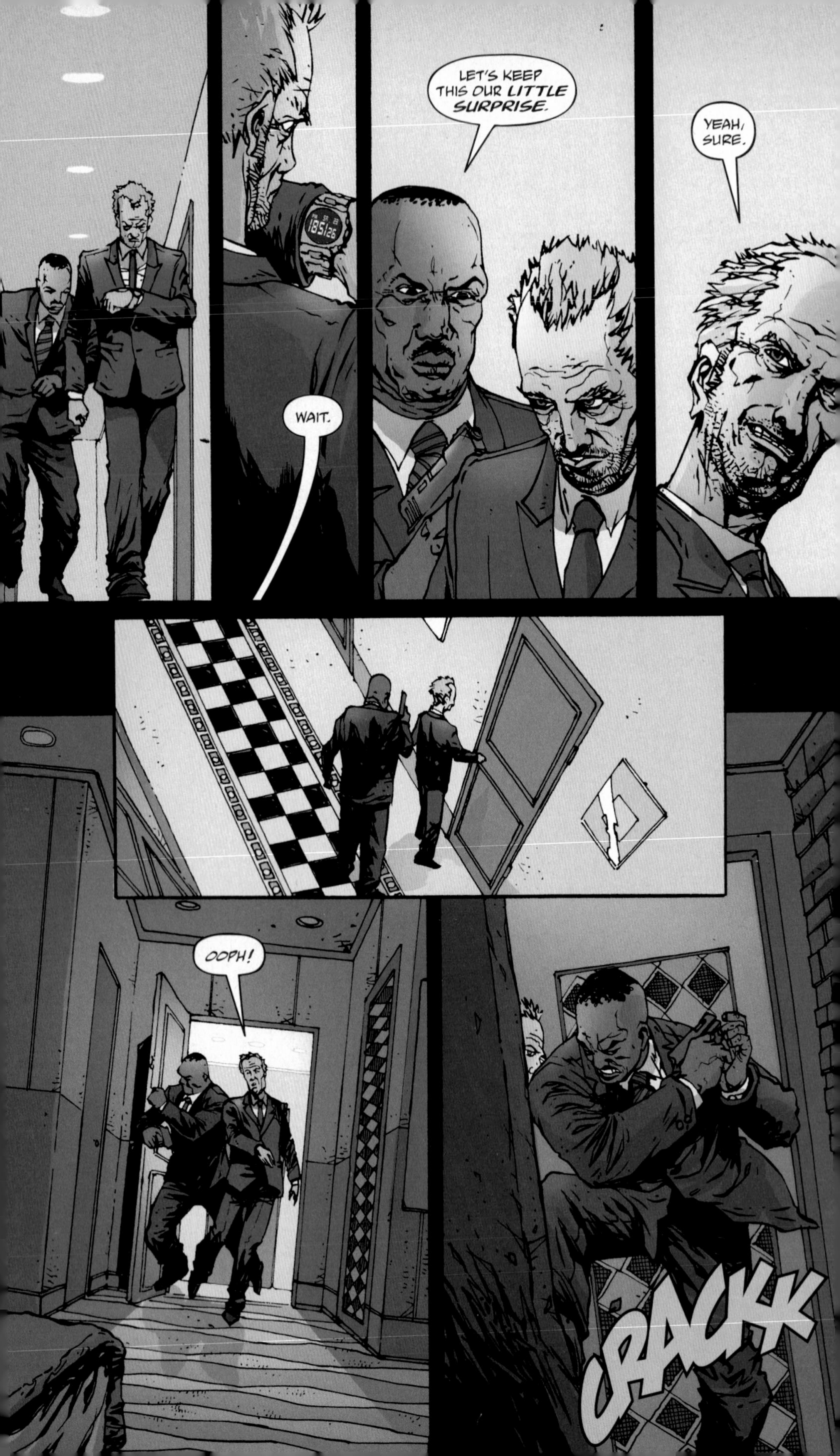
WAIT.
LET'S KEEP THIS OUR LITTLE SURPRISE.
YEAH, SURE.
OOPH!
CRACKK

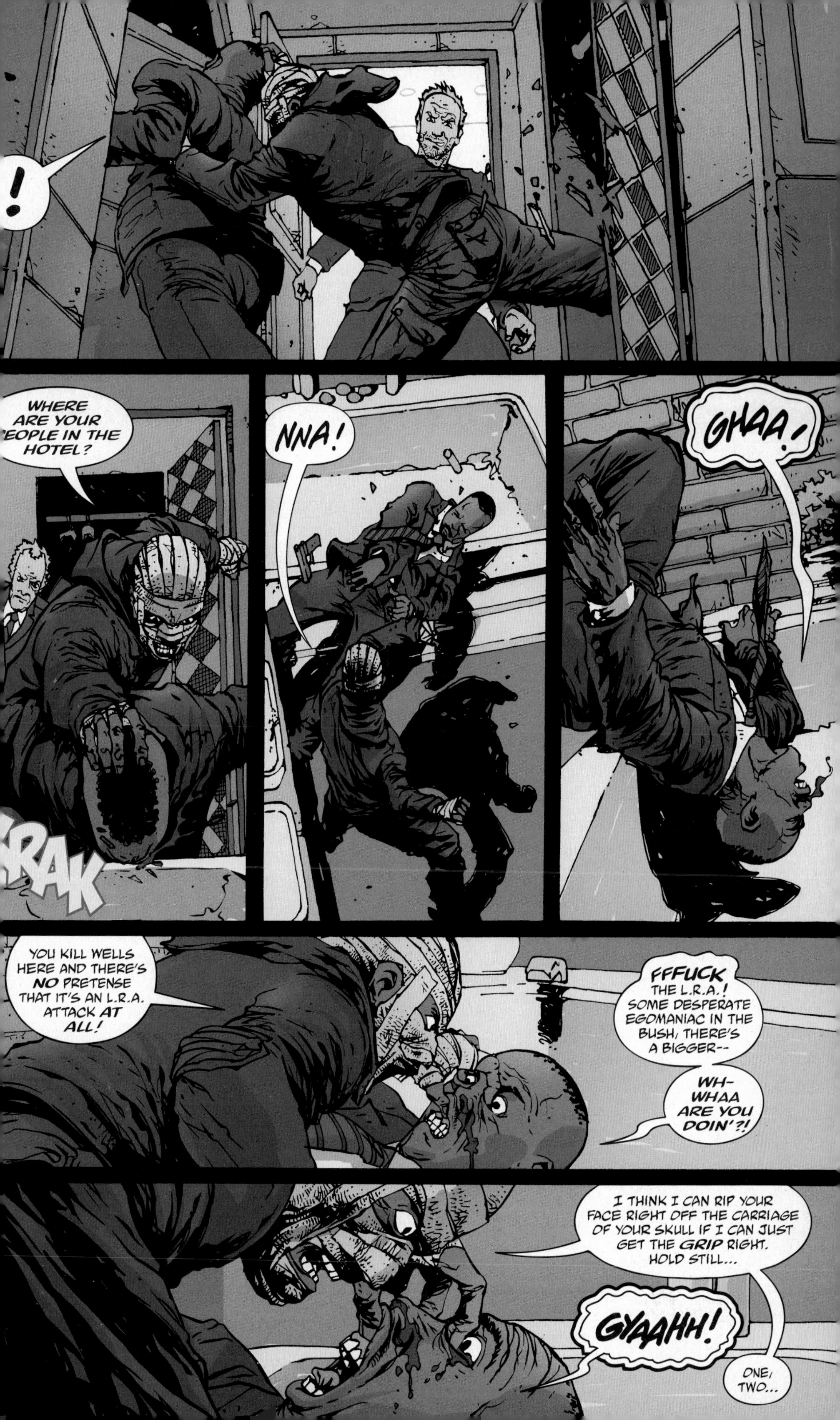
!
WHERE ARE YOUR PEOPLE IN THE HOTEL?
KRAK
NNA!
GHAA!
YOU KILL WELLS HERE AND THERE'S NO PRETENSE THAT IT'S AN L.R.A. ATTACK AT ALL!
FFFUCK THE L.R.A.! SOME DESPERATE EGOMANIAC IN THE BUSH, THERE'S A BIGGER--
WH-WHAA ARE YOU DOIN'?!
I THINK I CAN RIP YOUR FACE RIGHT OFF THE CARRIAGE OF YOUR SKULL IF I CAN JUST GET THE GRIP RIGHT. HOLD STILL...
GYAAHH!
ONE, TWO...

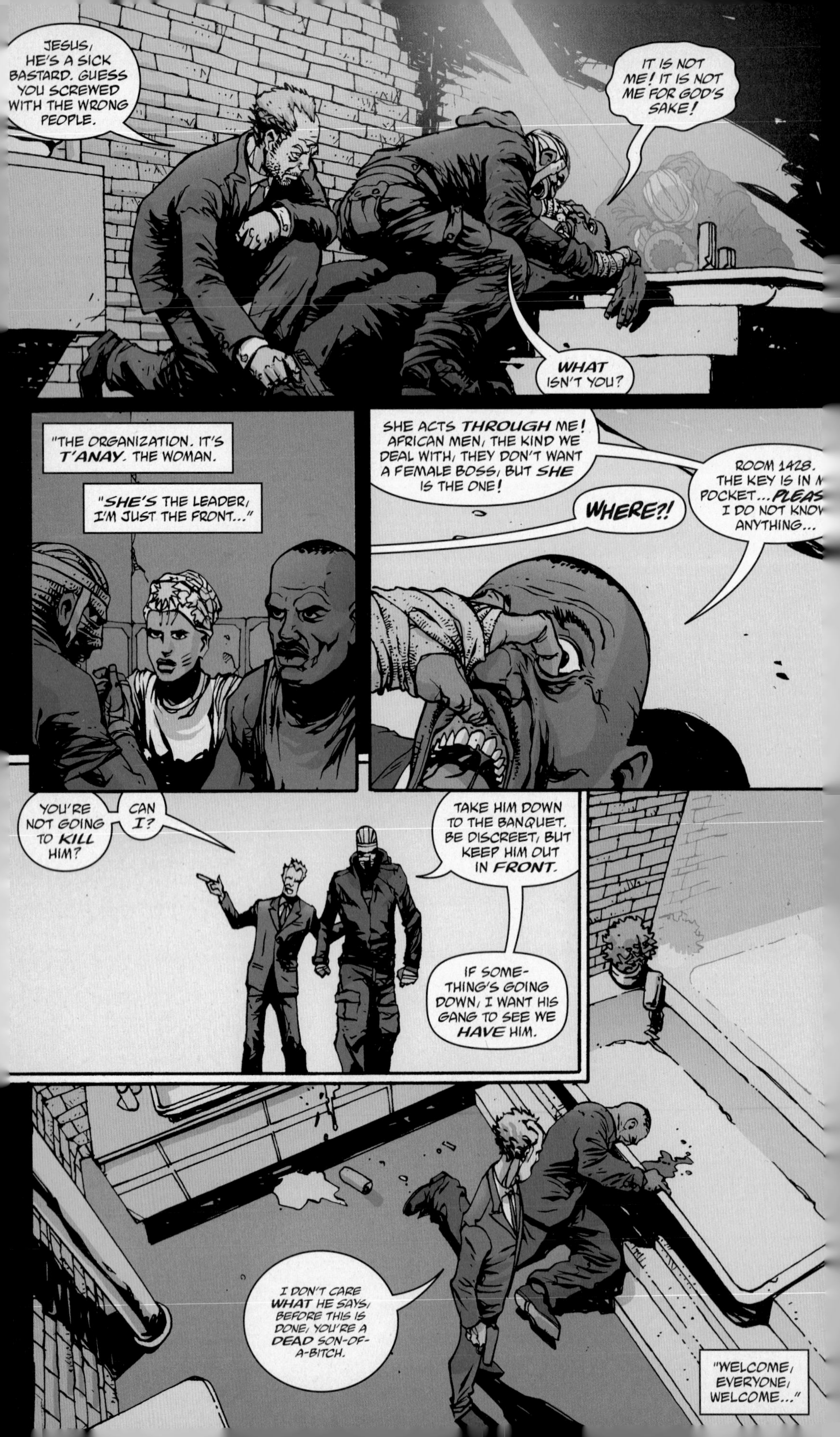
JESUS, HE'S A SICK BASTARD. GUESS YOU SCREWED WITH THE WRONG PEOPLE.
IT IS NOT ME! IT IS NOT ME FOR GOD'S SAKE!
WHAT ISN'T YOU?
"THE ORGANIZATION. IT'S T'ANAY. THE WOMAN.
"SHE'S THE LEADER, I'M JUST THE FRONT..."
SHE ACTS THROUGH ME! AFRICAN MEN, THE KIND WE DEAL WITH, THEY DON'T WANT A FEMALE BOSS, BUT SHE IS THE ONE!
WHERE?!
ROOM 1428. THE KEY IS IN M POCKET...PLEAS I DO NOT KNOW ANYTHING...
YOU'RE NOT GOING TO KILL HIM?
CAN I?
TAKE HIM DOWN TO THE BANQUET. BE DISCREET, BUT KEEP HIM OUT IN FRONT.
IF SOMETHING'S GOING DOWN, I WANT HIS GANG TO SEE WE HAVE HIM.
I DON'T CARE WHAT HE SAYS, BEFORE THIS IS DONE, YOU'RE A DEAD SON-OF-A-BITCH.
"WELCOME, EVERYONE, WELCOME..."

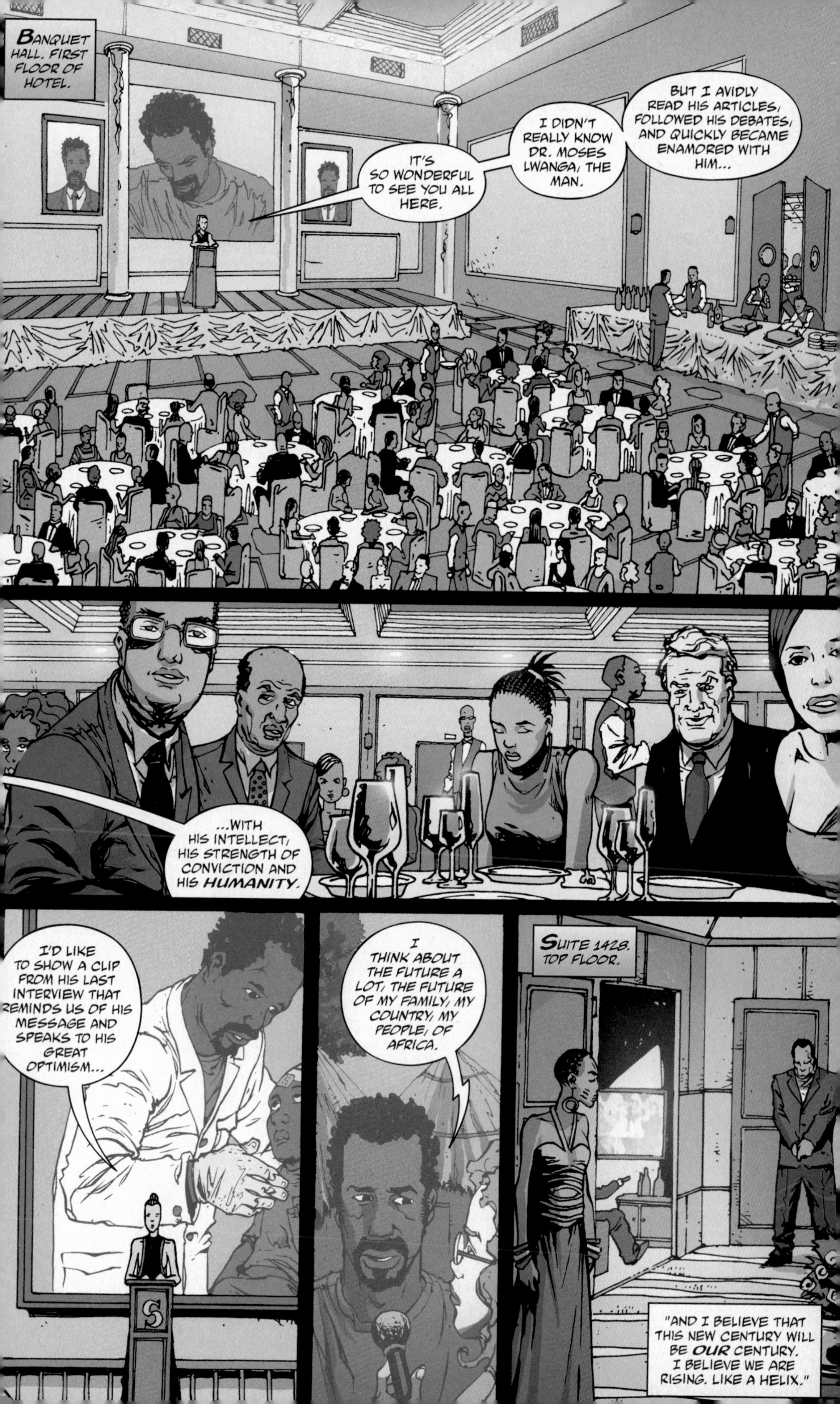

BANQUET HALL. FIRST FLOOR OF HOTEL.
IT'S SO WONDERFUL TO SEE YOU ALL HERE.
I DIDN'T REALLY KNOW DR. MOSES LWANGA, THE MAN.
BUT I AVIDLY READ HIS ARTICLES, FOLLOWED HIS DEBATES, AND QUICKLY BECAME ENAMORED WITH HIM...
...WITH HIS INTELLECT, HIS STRENGTH OF CONVICTION AND HIS HUMANITY.
I'D LIKE TO SHOW A CLIP FROM HIS LAST INTERVIEW THAT REMINDS US OF HIS MESSAGE AND SPEAKS TO HIS GREAT OPTIMISM...
I THINK ABOUT THE FUTURE A LOT, THE FUTURE OF MY FAMILY, MY COUNTRY, MY PEOPLE, OF AFRICA.
SUITE 1428. TOP FLOOR.
"AND I BELIEVE THAT THIS NEW CENTURY WILL BE OUR CENTURY. I BELIEVE WE ARE RISING. LIKE A HELIX."

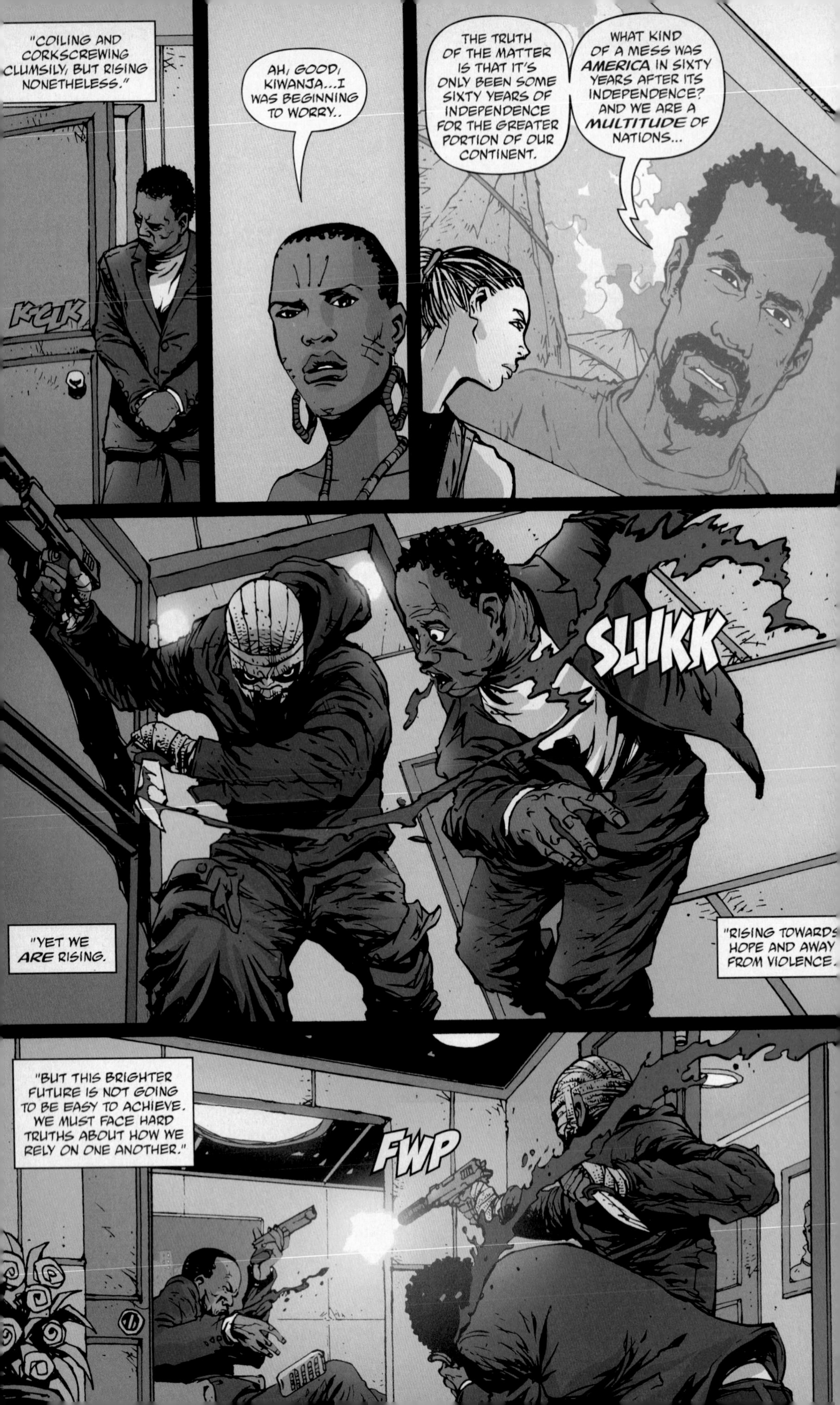
"COILING AND CORKSCREWING CLUMSILY, BUT RISING NONETHELESS."
AH, GOOD, KIWANJA...I WAS BEGINNING TO WORRY..
KRCLK
THE TRUTH OF THE MATTER IS THAT IT'S ONLY BEEN SOME SIXTY YEARS OF INDEPENDENCE FOR THE GREATER PORTION OF OUR CONTINENT.
WHAT KIND OF A MESS WAS AMERICA IN SIXTY YEARS AFTER ITS INDEPENDENCE? AND WE ARE A MULTITUDE OF NATIONS...
SLIKK
"YET WE ARE RISING.
"RISING TOWARDS HOPE AND AWAY FROM VIOLENCE.
"BUT THIS BRIGHTER FUTURE IS NOT GOING TO BE EASY TO ACHIEVE. WE MUST FACE HARD TRUTHS ABOUT HOW WE RELY ON ONE ANOTHER."
FWP

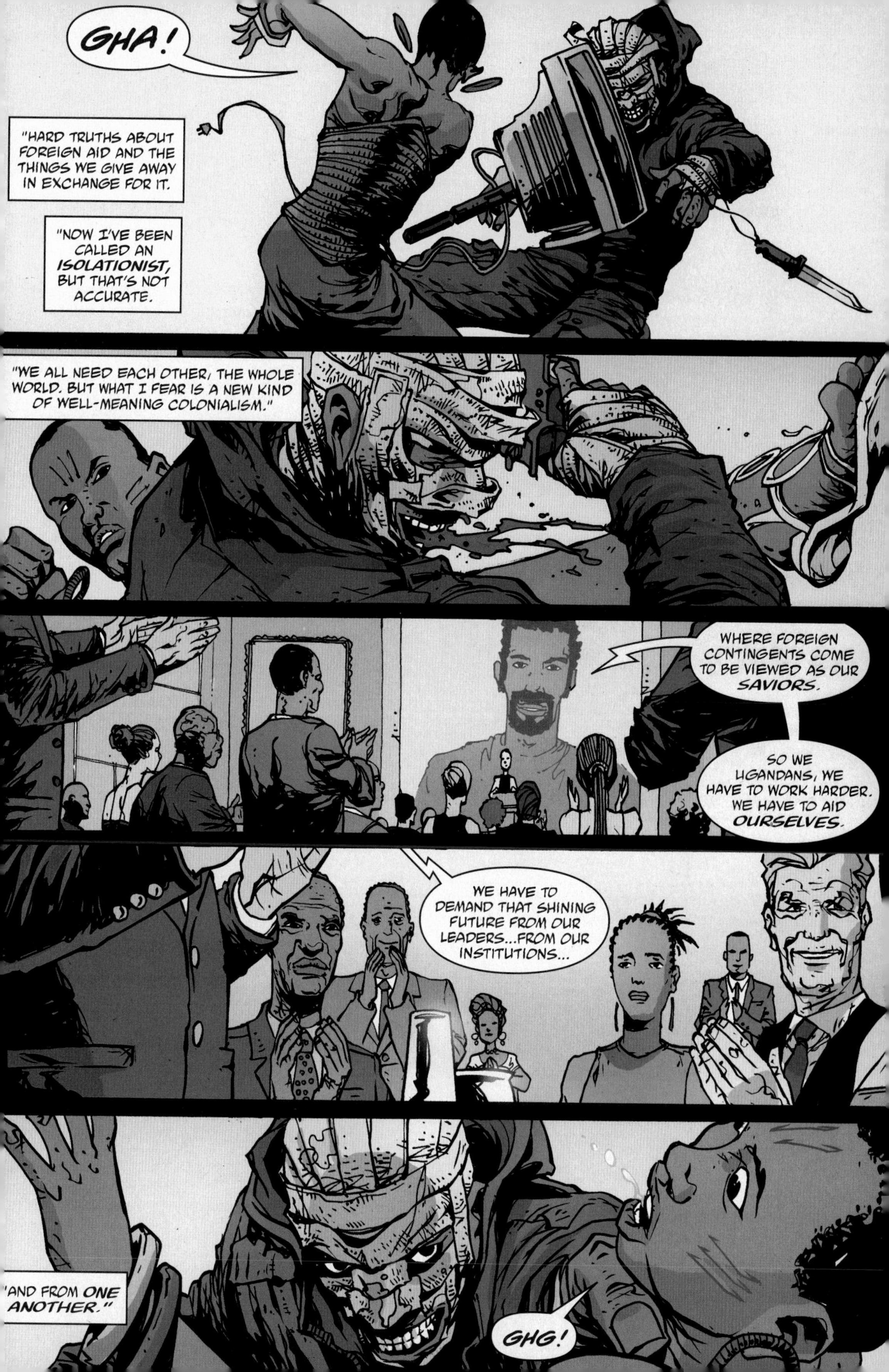
GHA!
"HARD TRUTHS ABOUT FOREIGN AID AND THE THINGS WE GIVE AWAY IN EXCHANGE FOR IT.
"NOW I'VE BEEN CALLED AN ISOLATIONIST, BUT THAT'S NOT ACCURATE.
"WE ALL NEED EACH OTHER, THE WHOLE WORLD. BUT WHAT I FEAR IS A NEW KIND OF WELL-MEANING COLONIALISM."
WHERE FOREIGN CONTINGENTS COME TO BE VIEWED AS OUR SAVIORS.
SO WE UGANDANS, WE HAVE TO WORK HARDER. WE HAVE TO AID OURSELVES.
WE HAVE TO DEMAND THAT SHINING FUTURE FROM OUR LEADERS...FROM OUR INSTITUTIONS...
"AND FROM ONE ANOTHER."
GHG!

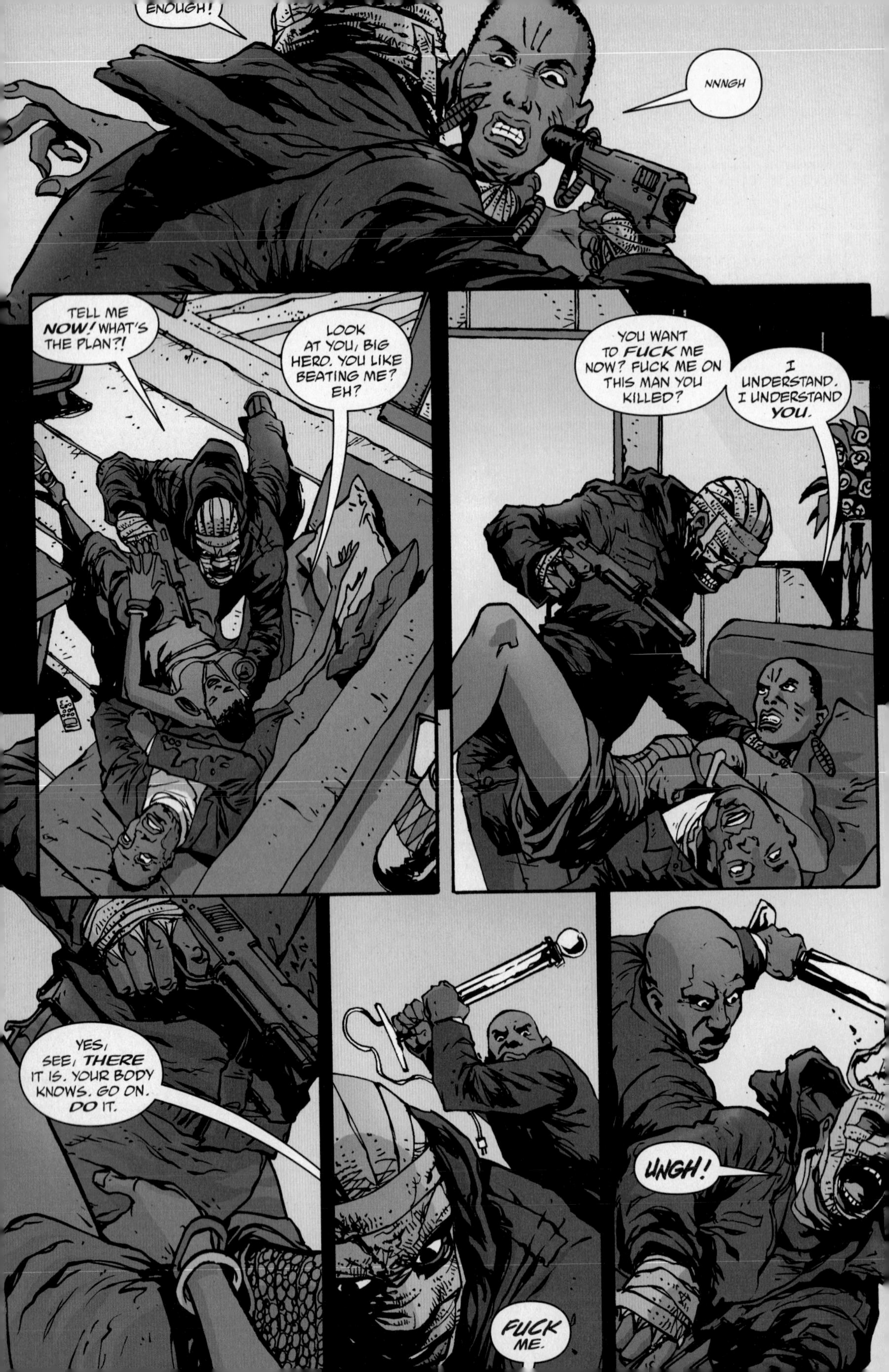

ENOUGH!
NNNGH
TELL ME NOW! WHAT'S THE PLAN?!
LOOK AT YOU, BIG HERO. YOU LIKE BEATING ME? EH?
YOU WANT TO FUCK ME NOW? FUCK ME ON THIS MAN YOU KILLED?
I UNDERSTAND. I UNDERSTAND YOU.
YES, SEE, THERE IT IS. YOUR BODY KNOWS. GO ON. DO IT.
FUCK ME.
UNGH!

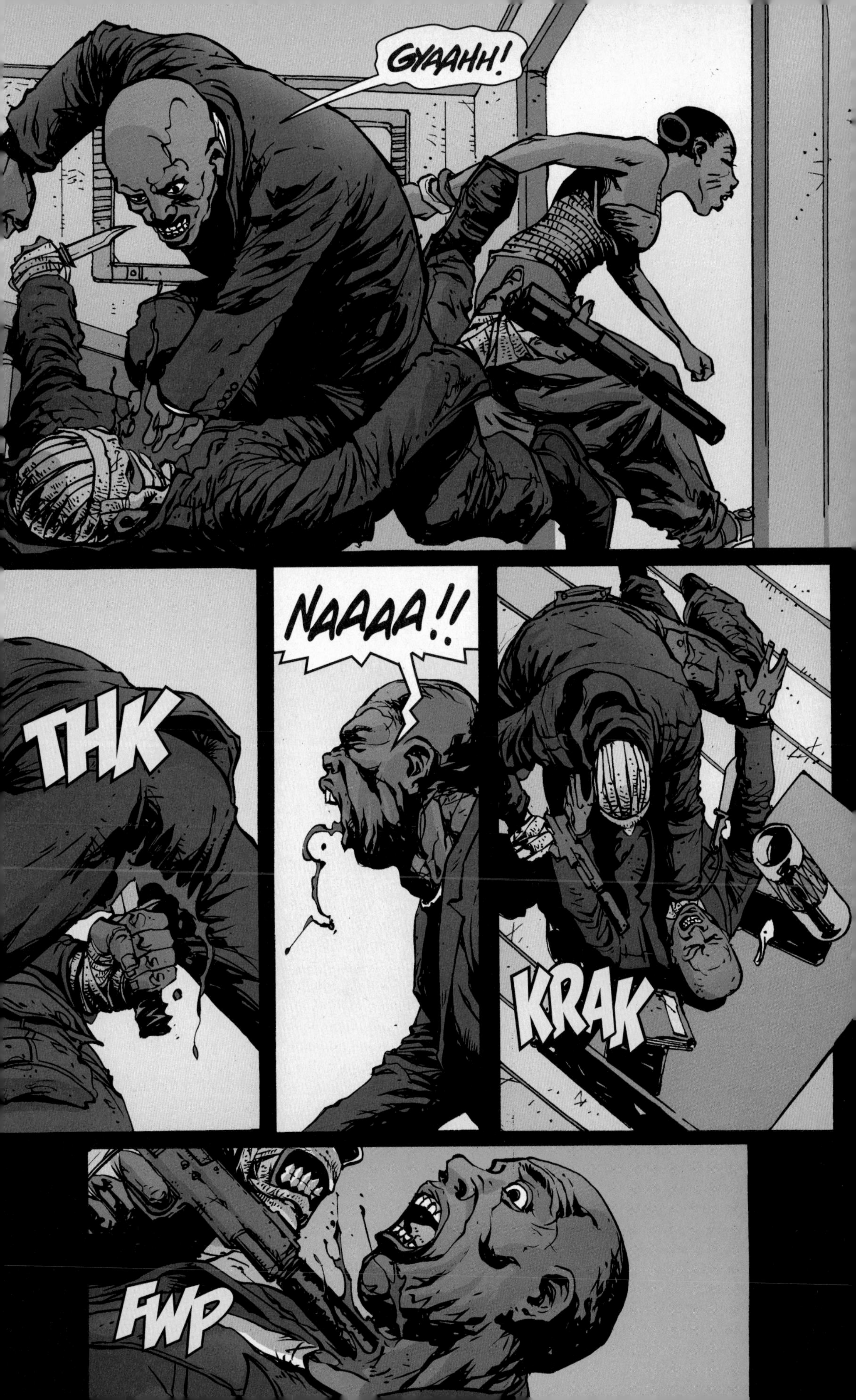
GYAAHH!
THK
NAAAA!!
KRAK
FWP

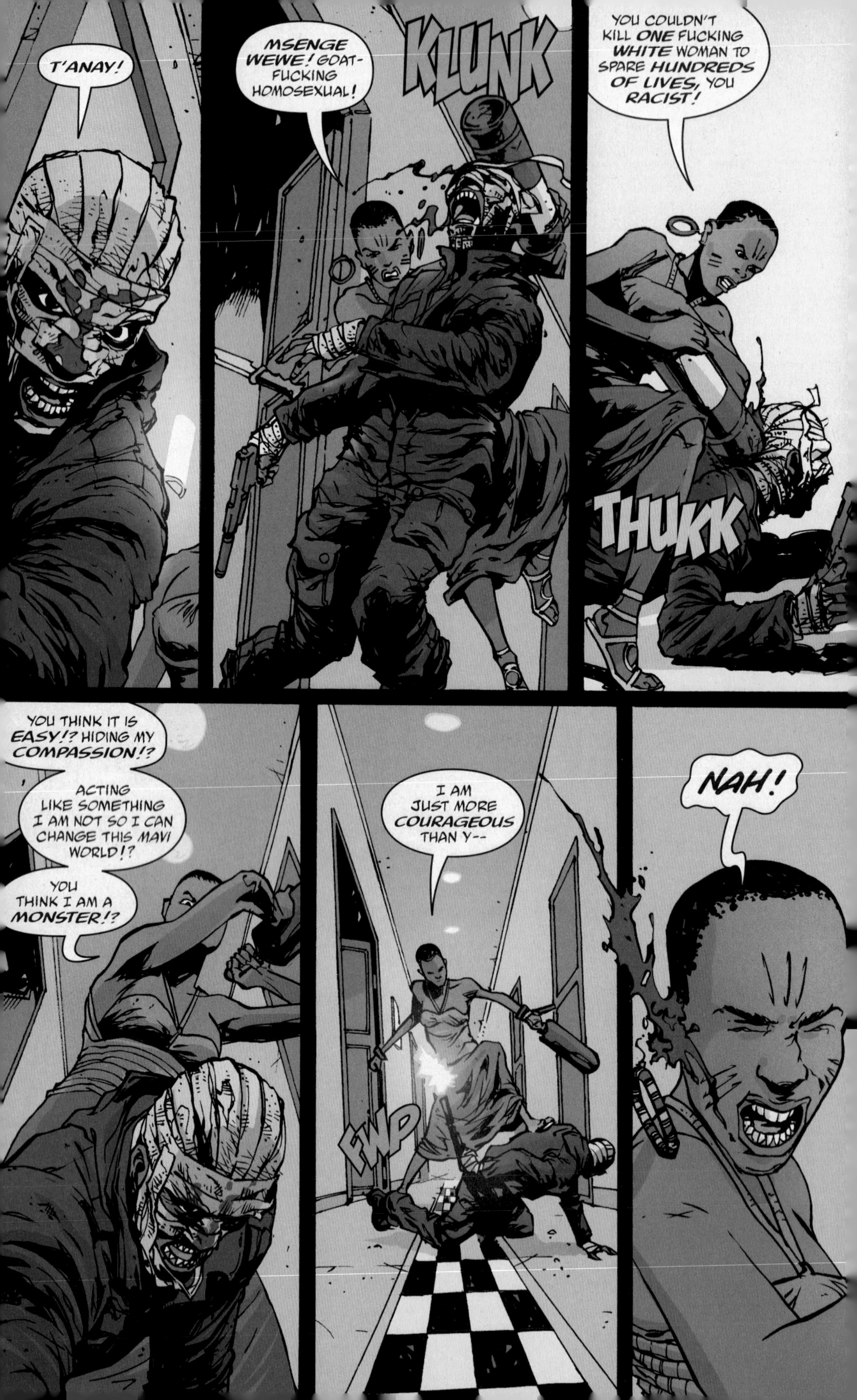
T'ANAY!
MSENGE WEWE! GOAT-FUCKING HOMOSEXUAL!
KLUNK
YOU COULDN'T KILL ONE FUCKING WHITE WOMAN TO SPARE HUNDREDS OF LIVES, YOU RACIST!
THUKK
YOU THINK IT IS EASY!? HIDING MY COMPASSION!?
ACTING LIKE SOMETHING I AM NOT SO I CAN CHANGE THIS MAVI WORLD!?
YOU THINK I AM A MONSTER!?
I AM JUST MORE COURAGEOUS THAN Y--
FWP
NAH!

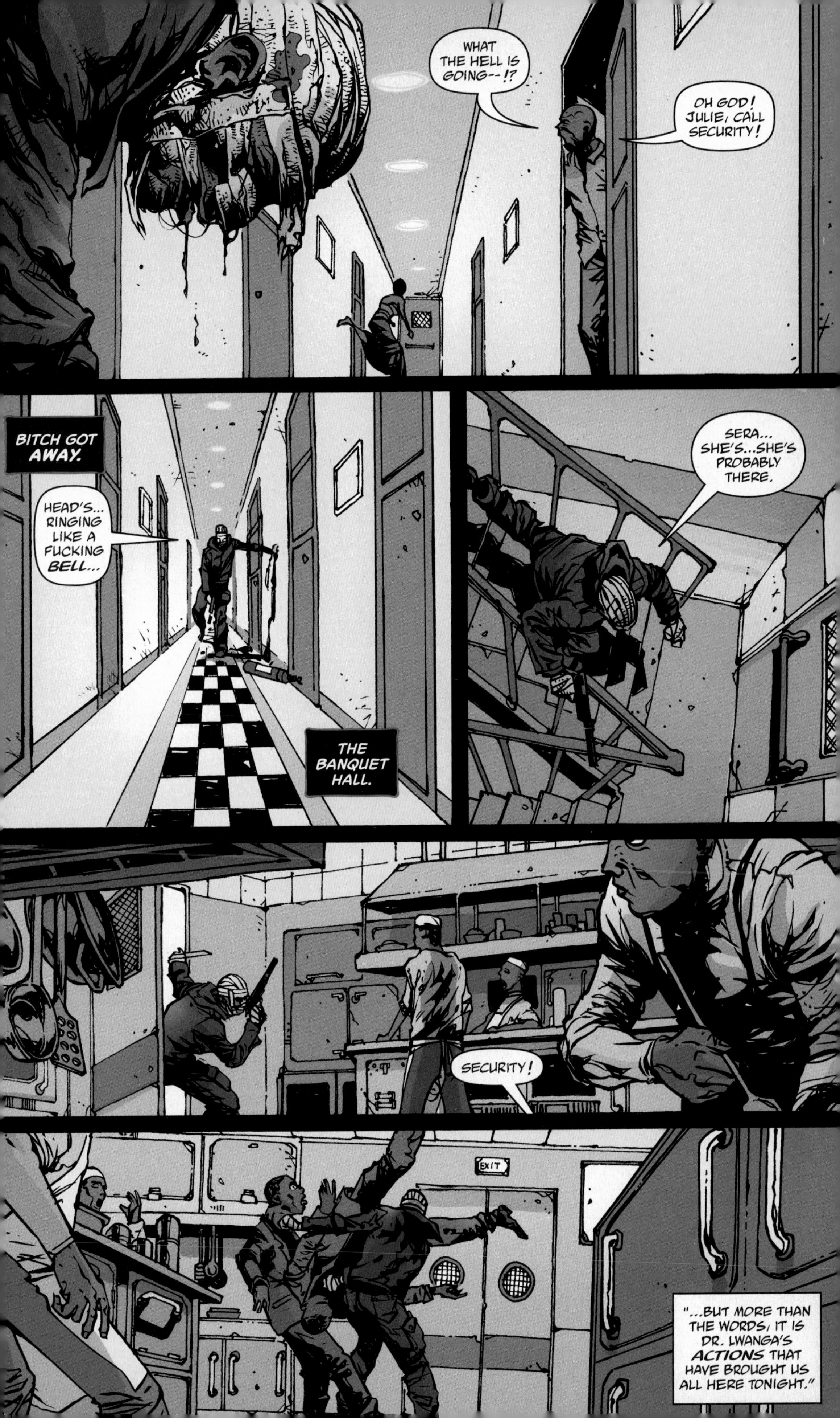
WHAT THE HELL IS GOING--!?
OH GOD! JULIE, CALL SECURITY!
BITCH GOT AWAY.
HEAD'S... RINGING LIKE A FUCKING BELL...
THE BANQUET HALL.
SERA... SHE'S...SHE'S PROBABLY THERE.
SECURITY!
EXIT
"...BUT MORE THAN THE WORDS, IT IS DR. LWANGA'S ACTIONS THAT HAVE BROUGHT US ALL HERE TONIGHT."

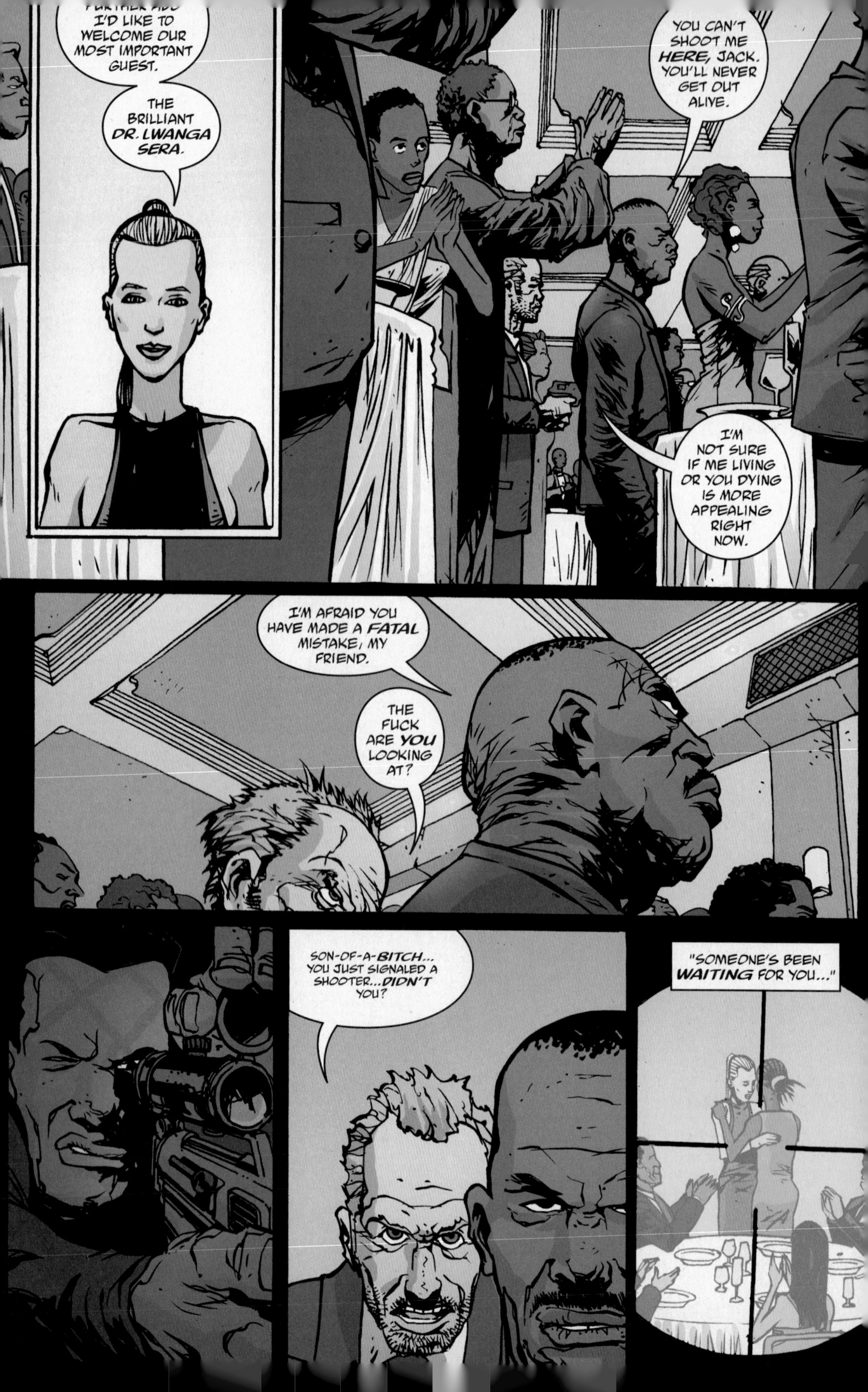
I'D LIKE TO WELCOME OUR MOST IMPORTANT GUEST.
THE BRILLIANT DR. LWANGA SERA.
YOU CAN'T SHOOT ME HERE, JACK. YOU'LL NEVER GET OUT ALIVE.
I'M NOT SURE IF ME LIVING OR YOU DYING IS MORE APPEALING RIGHT NOW.
I'M AFRAID YOU HAVE MADE A FATAL MISTAKE, MY FRIEND.
THE FUCK ARE YOU LOOKING AT?
SON-OF-A-BITCH... YOU JUST SIGNALED A SHOOTER... DIDN'T YOU?
"SOMEONE'S BEEN WAITING FOR YOU..."

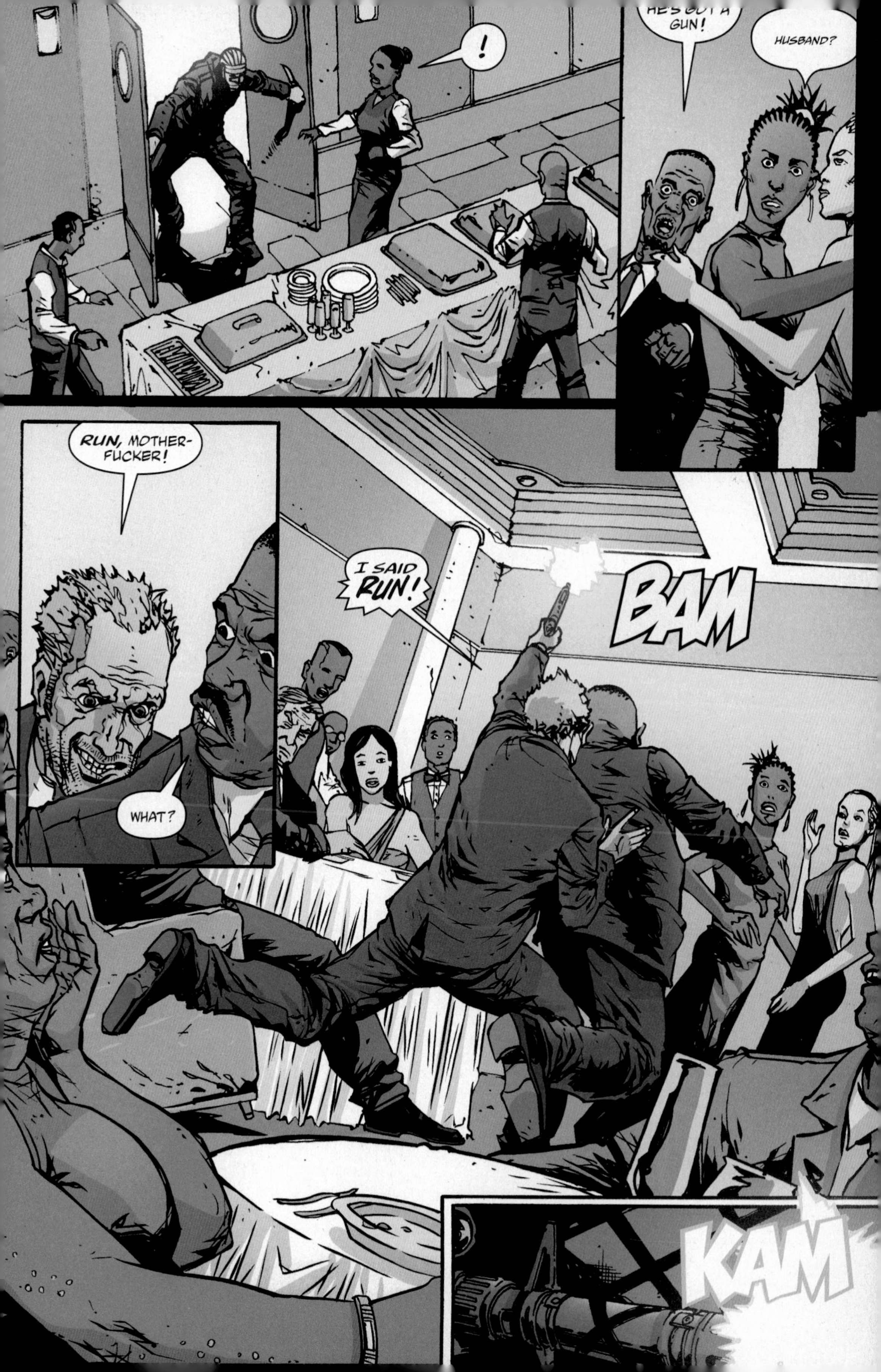
!
HE'S GOT A GUN!
HUSBAND?
RUN, MOTHER-FUCKER!
WHAT?
I SAID RUN!
BAM
KAM

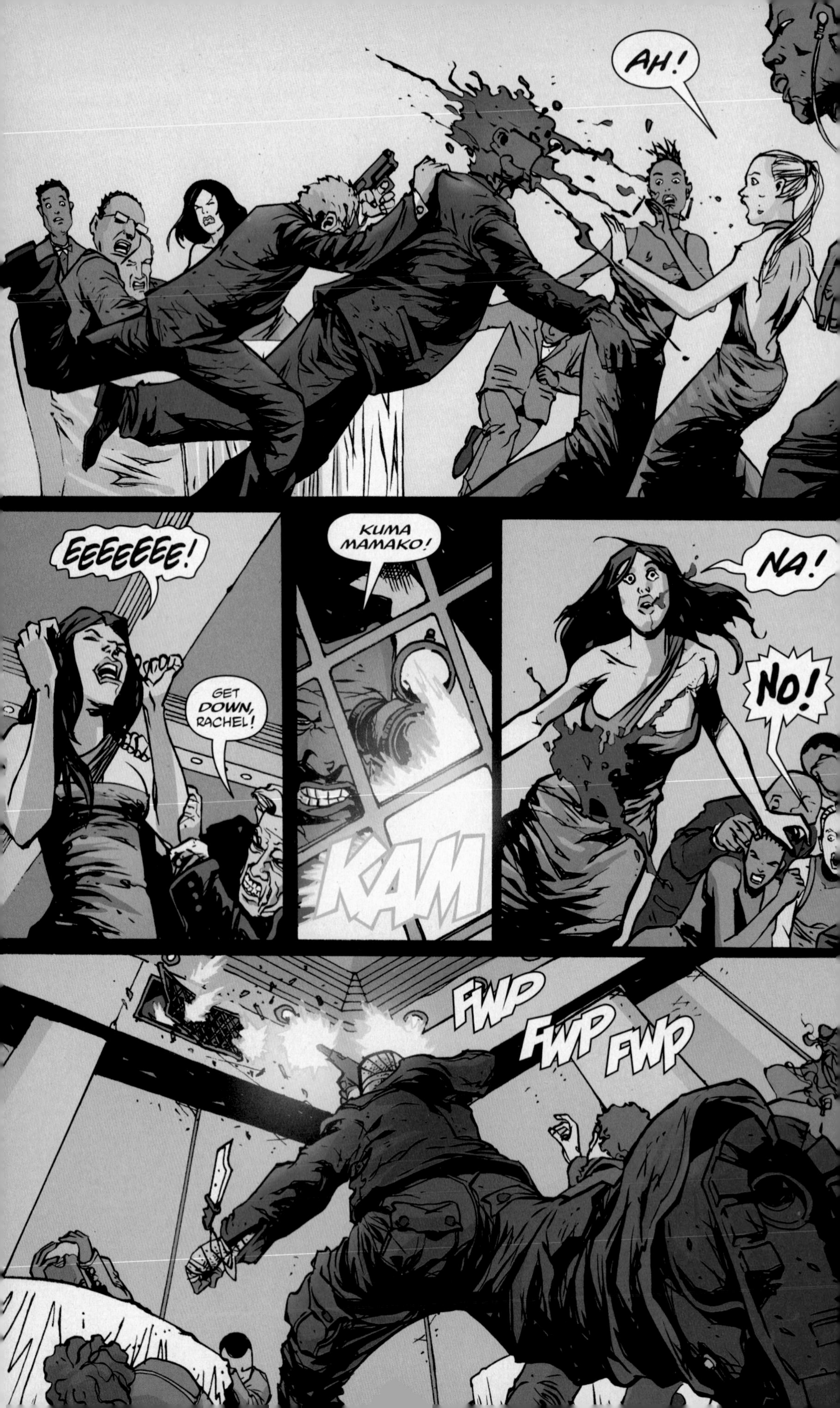
AH!
EEEEEEEE!
GET DOWN, RACHEL!
KUMA MAMAKO!
KAM
NA!
NO!
FWP
FWP
FWP

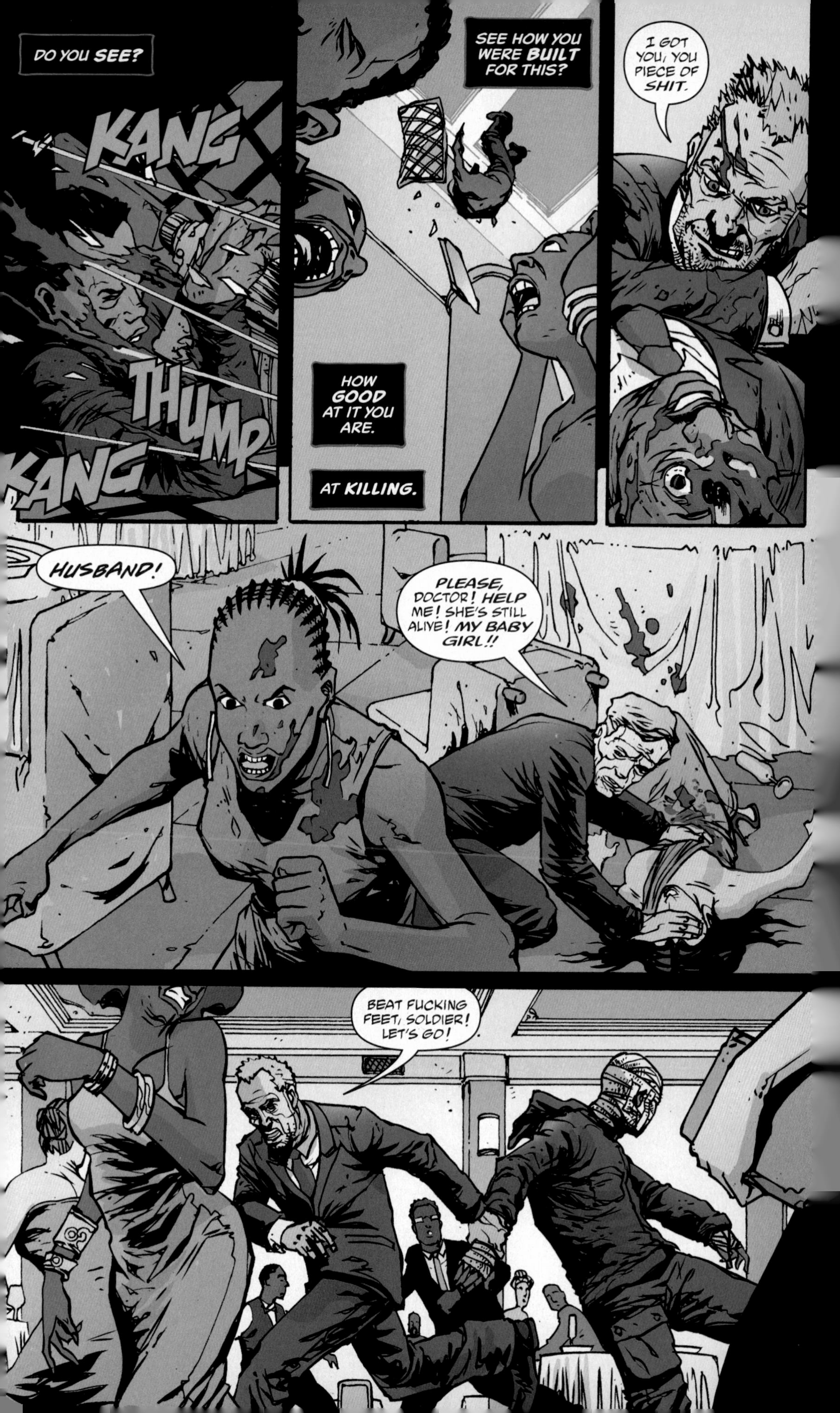
DO YOU SEE?
KANG
THUMP
KANG
SEE HOW YOU WERE BUILT FOR THIS?
HOW GOOD AT IT YOU ARE.
AT KILLING.
I GOT YOU, YOU PIECE OF SHIT.
HUSBAND!
PLEASE, DOCTOR! HELP ME! SHE'S STILL ALIVE! MY BABY GIRL!!
BEAT FUCKING FEET, SOLDIER! LET'S GO!

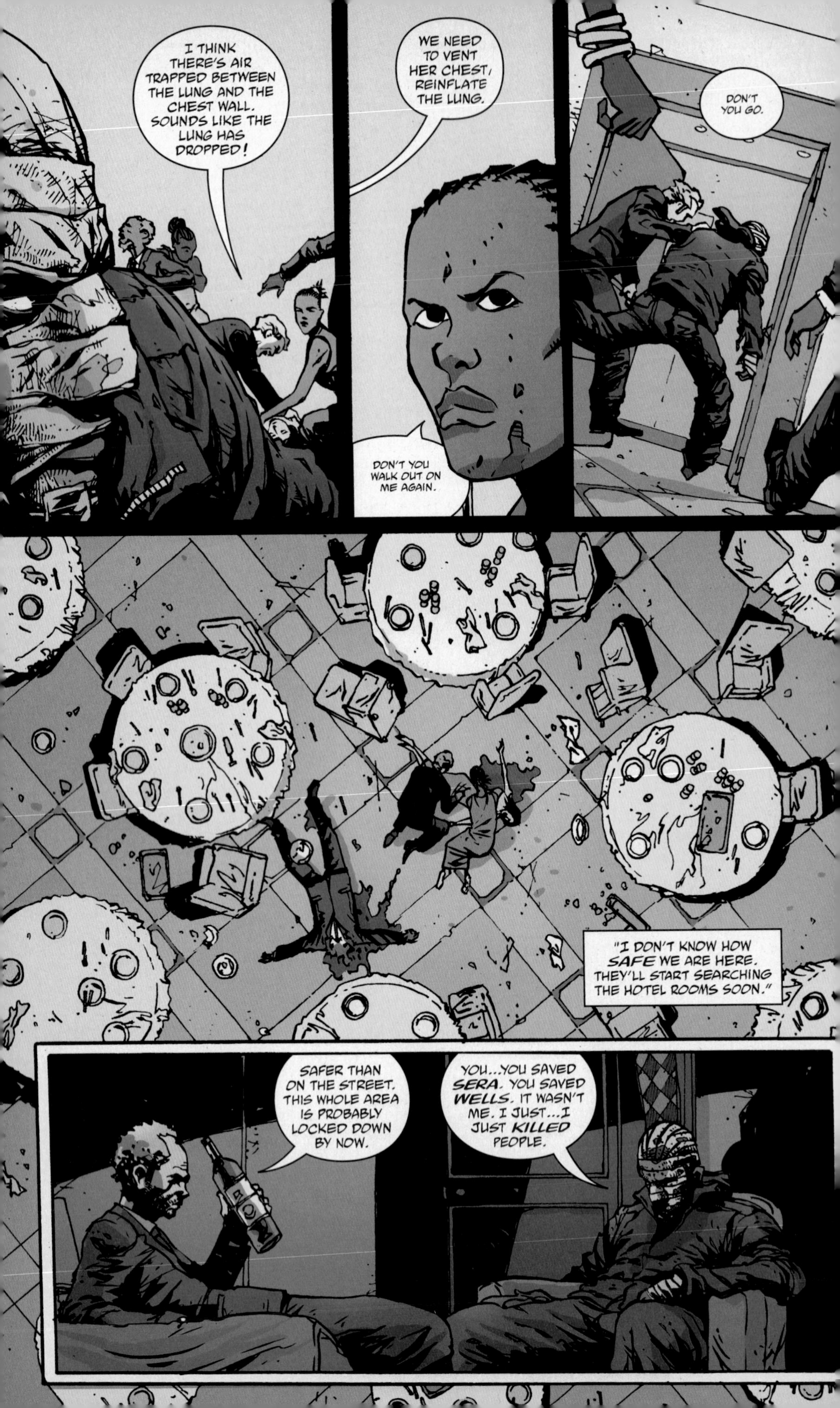
I THINK THERE'S AIR TRAPPED BETWEEN THE LUNG AND THE CHEST WALL. SOUNDS LIKE THE LUNG HAS DROPPED!
WE NEED TO VENT HER CHEST, REINFLATE THE LUNG.
DON'T YOU WALK OUT ON ME AGAIN.
DON'T YOU GO.
"I DON'T KNOW HOW SAFE WE ARE HERE. THEY'LL START SEARCHING THE HOTEL ROOMS SOON."
SAFER THAN ON THE STREET. THIS WHOLE AREA IS PROBABLY LOCKED DOWN BY NOW.
YOU...YOU SAVED SERA. YOU SAVED WELLS. IT WASN'T ME. I JUST...I JUST KILLED PEOPLE.

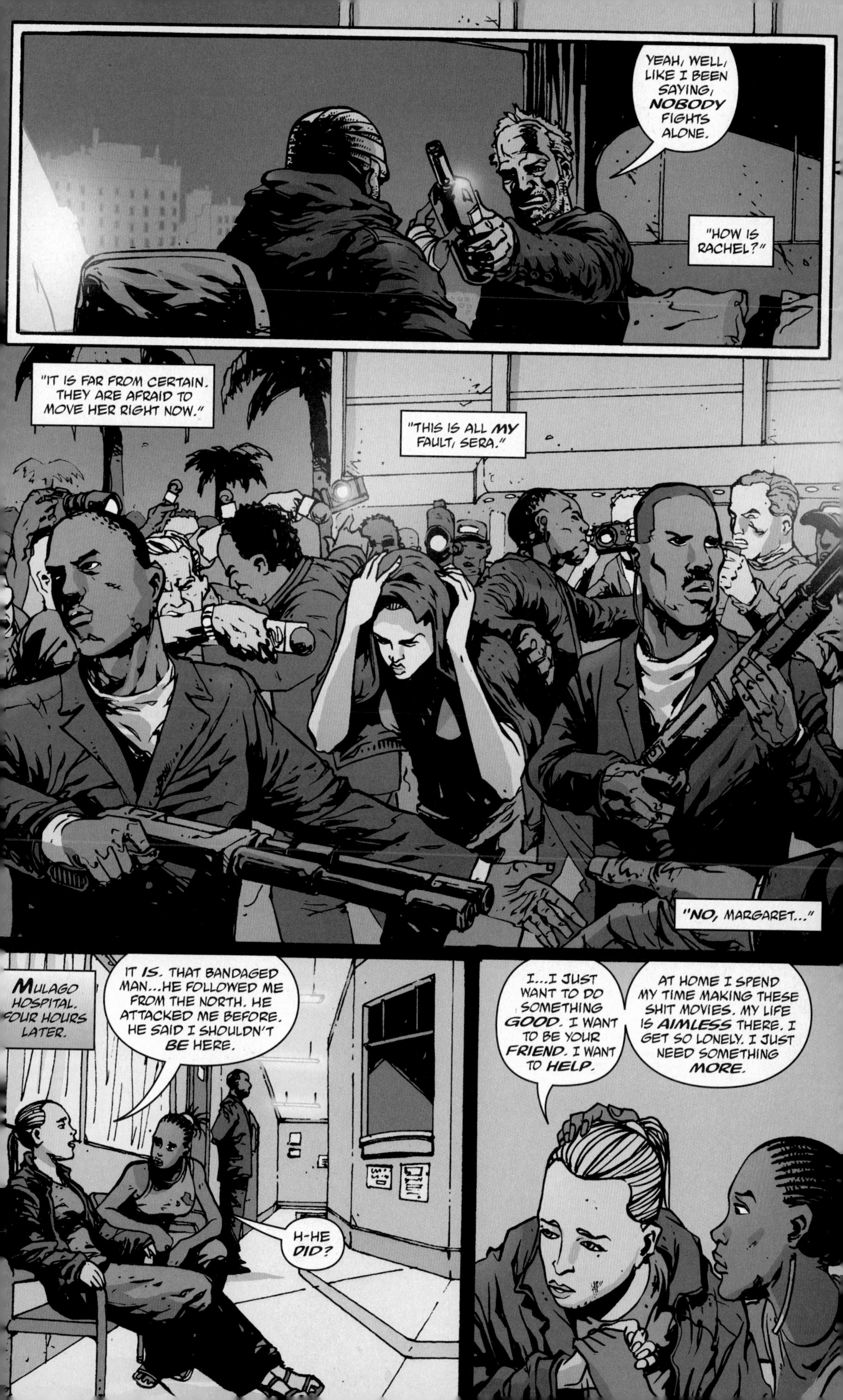
YEAH, WELL, LIKE I BEEN SAYING, NOBODY FIGHTS ALONE.
"HOW IS RACHEL?"
"IT IS FAR FROM CERTAIN. THEY ARE AFRAID TO MOVE HER RIGHT NOW."
"THIS IS ALL MY FAULT, SERA."
"NO, MARGARET..."
MULAGO HOSPITAL. FOUR HOURS LATER.
IT IS. THAT BANDAGED MAN...HE FOLLOWED ME FROM THE NORTH. HE ATTACKED ME BEFORE. HE SAID I SHOULDN'T BE HERE.
H-HE DID?
I...I JUST WANT TO DO SOMETHING GOOD. I WANT TO BE YOUR FRIEND. I WANT TO HELP.
AT HOME I SPEND MY TIME MAKING THESE SHIT MOVIES. MY LIFE IS AIMLESS THERE. I GET SO LONELY. I JUST NEED SOMETHING MORE.

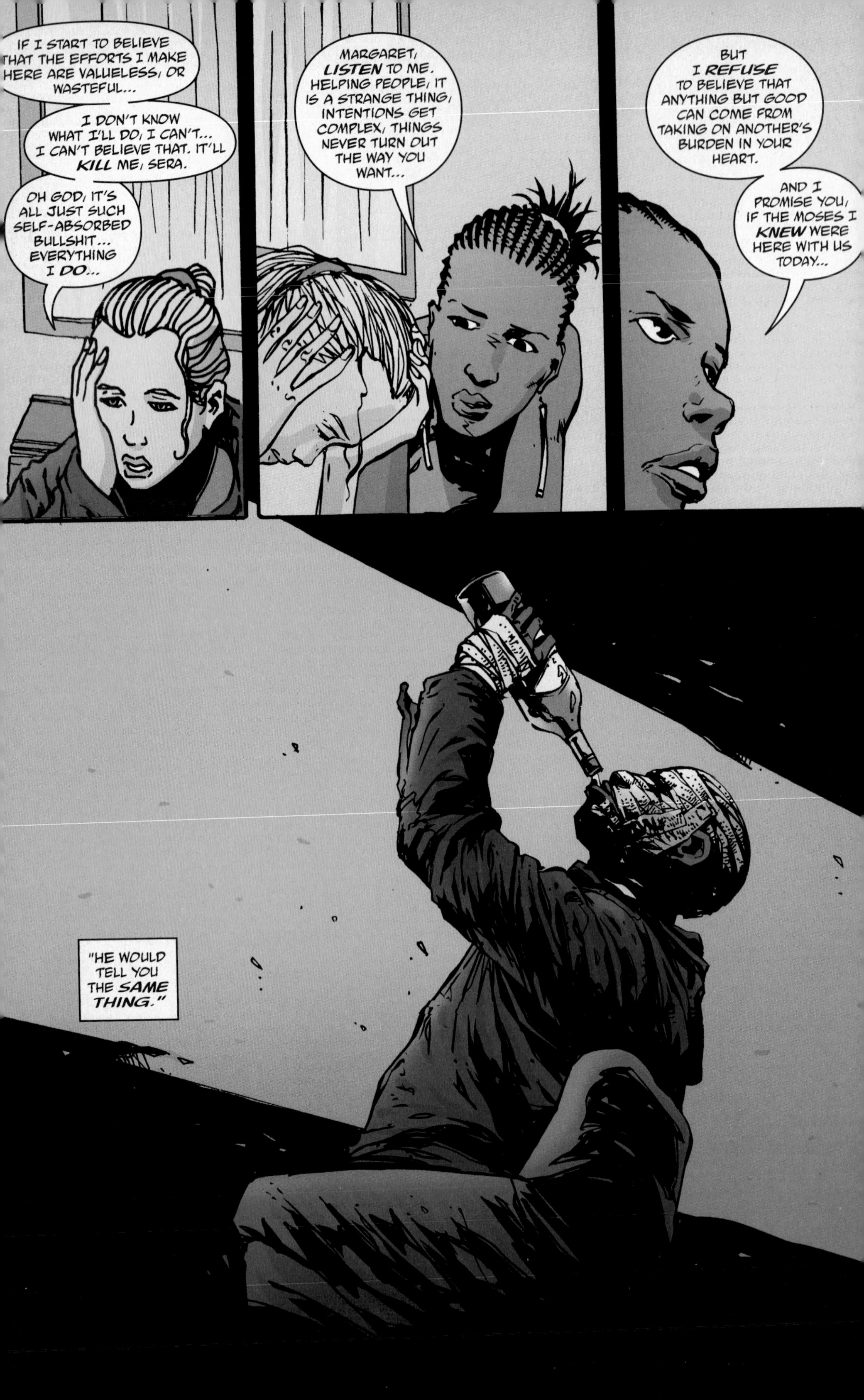

IF I START TO BELIEVE THAT THE EFFORTS I MAKE HERE ARE VALUELESS, OR WASTEFUL...
I DON'T KNOW WHAT I'LL DO, I CAN'T... I CAN'T BELIEVE THAT. IT'LL KILL ME, SERA.
OH GOD, IT'S ALL JUST SUCH SELF-ABSORBED BULLSHIT... EVERYTHING I DO...
MARGARET, LISTEN TO ME. HELPING PEOPLE, IT IS A STRANGE THING, INTENTIONS GET COMPLEX, THINGS NEVER TURN OUT THE WAY YOU WANT...
BUT I REFUSE TO BELIEVE THAT ANYTHING BUT GOOD CAN COME FROM TAKING ON ANOTHER'S BURDEN IN YOUR HEART.
AND I PROMISE YOU, IF THE MOSES I KNEW WERE HERE WITH US TODAY...
"HE WOULD TELL YOU THE SAME THING."

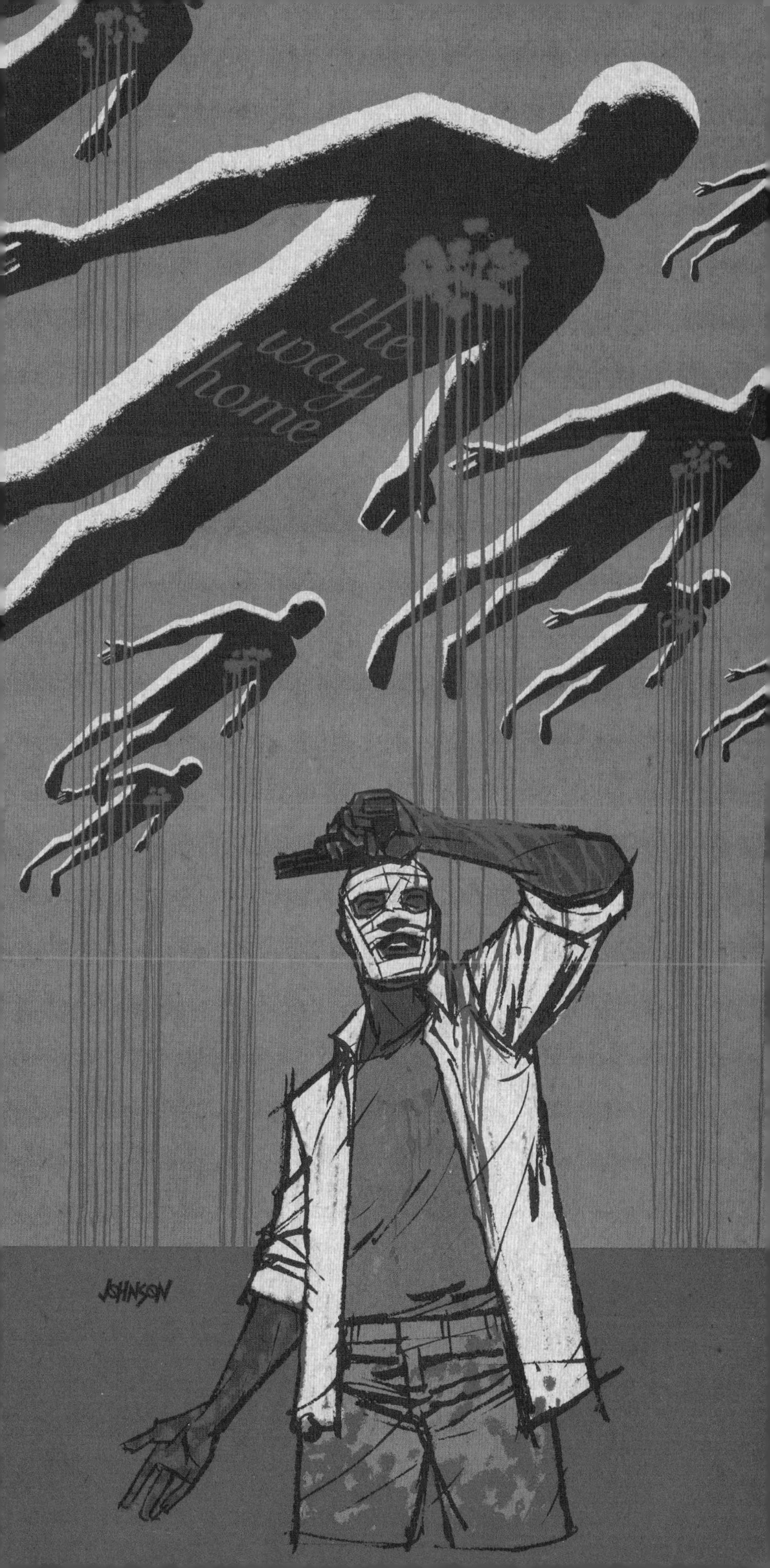
the way home
JOHNSON

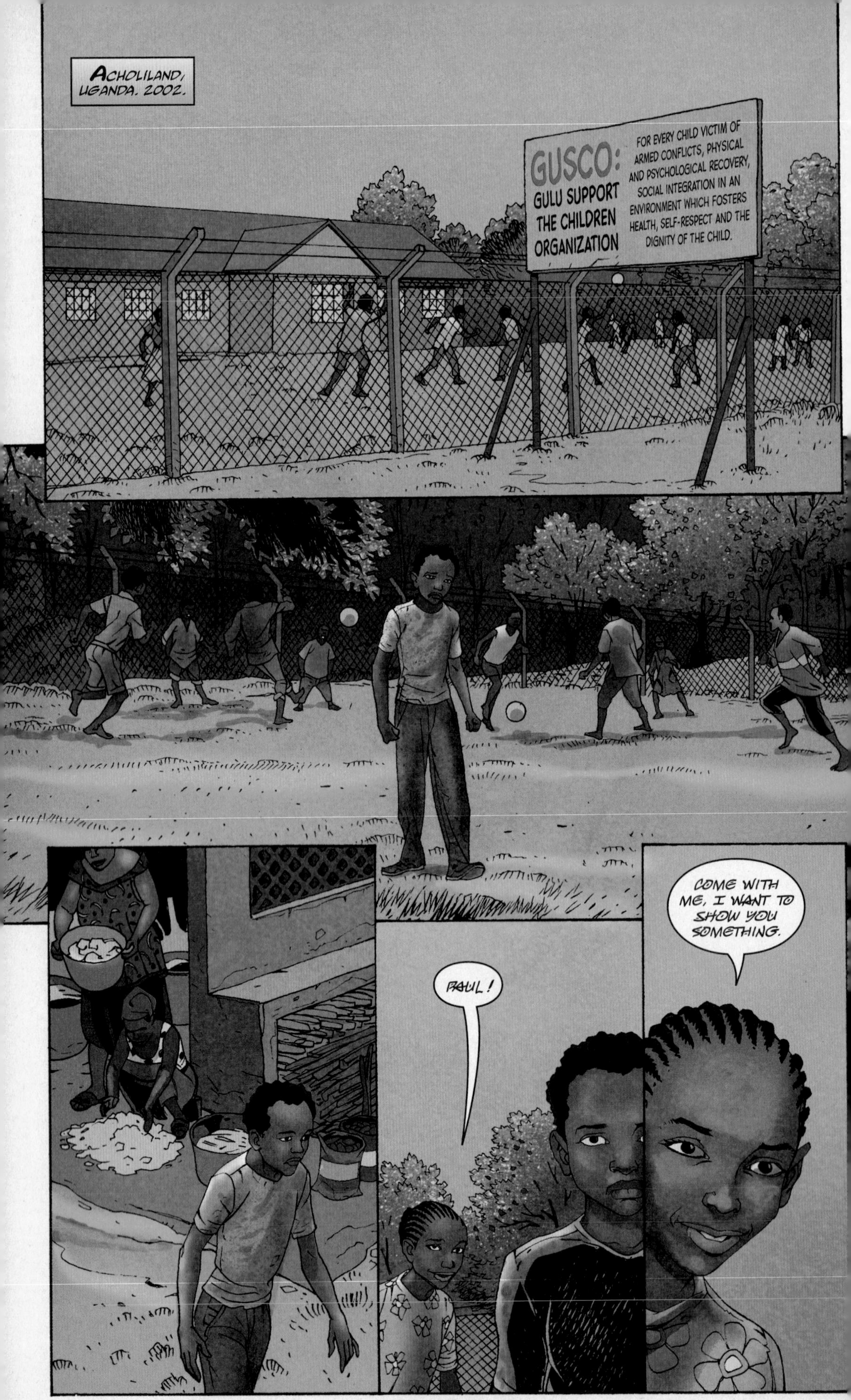

ACHOLILAND, UGANDA. 2002.
GUSCO: GULU SUPPORT THE CHILDREN ORGANIZATION
FOR EVERY CHILD VICTIM OF ARMED CONFLICTS, PHYSICAL AND PSYCHOLOGICAL RECOVERY, SOCIAL INTEGRATION IN AN ENVIRONMENT WHICH FOSTERS HEALTH, SELF-RESPECT AND THE DIGNITY OF THE CHILD.
PAUL!
COME WITH ME, I WANT TO SHOW YOU SOMETHING.

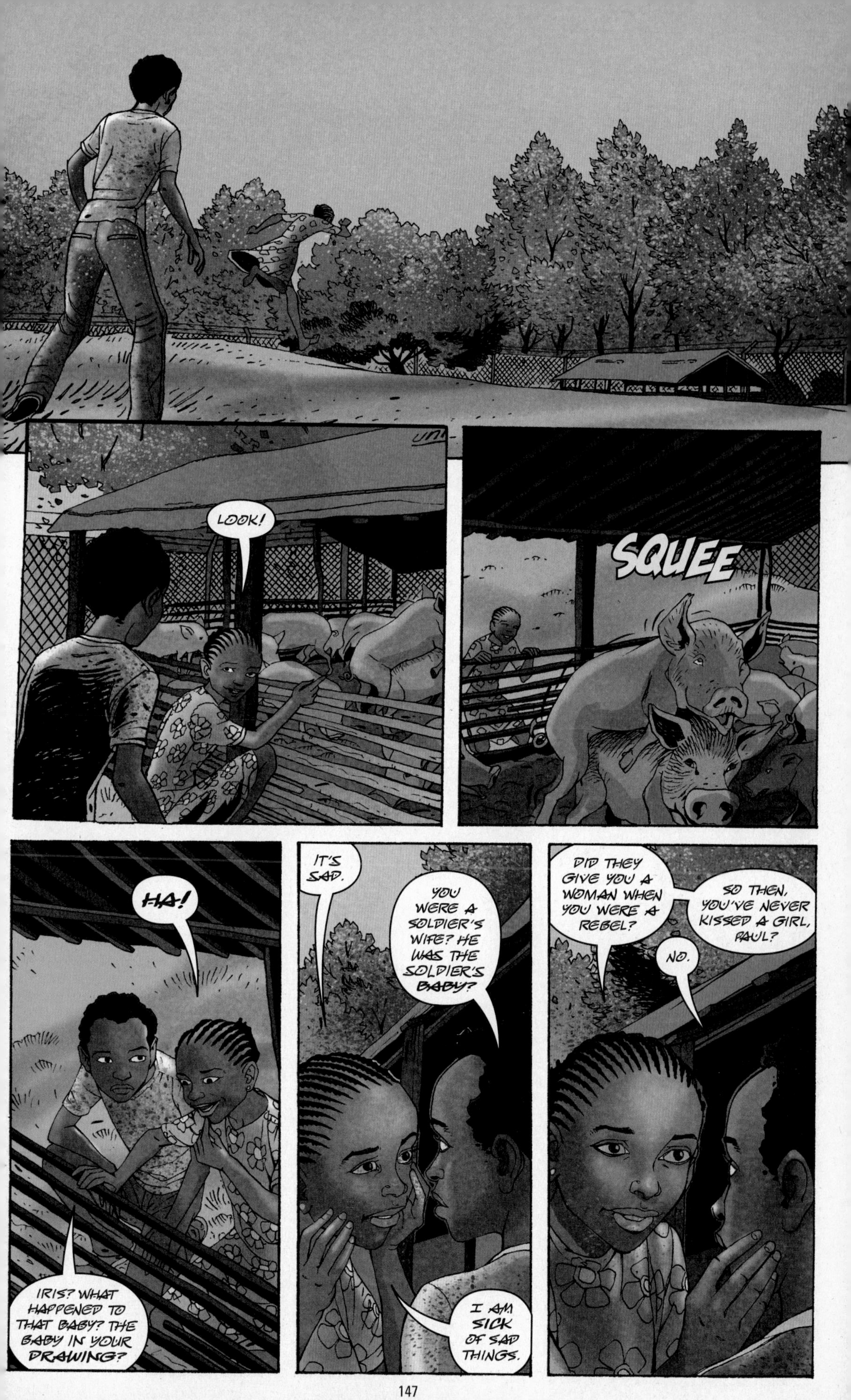
LOOK!
SQUEE
HA!
IRIS? WHAT HAPPENED TO THAT BABY? THE BABY IN YOUR DRAWING?
IT'S SAD.
YOU WERE A SOLDIER'S WIFE? HE WAS THE SOLDIER'S BABY?
I AM SICK OF SAD THINGS.
DID THEY GIVE YOU A WOMAN WHEN YOU WERE A REBEL?
NO.
SO THEN, YOU'VE NEVER KISSED A GIRL, PAUL?

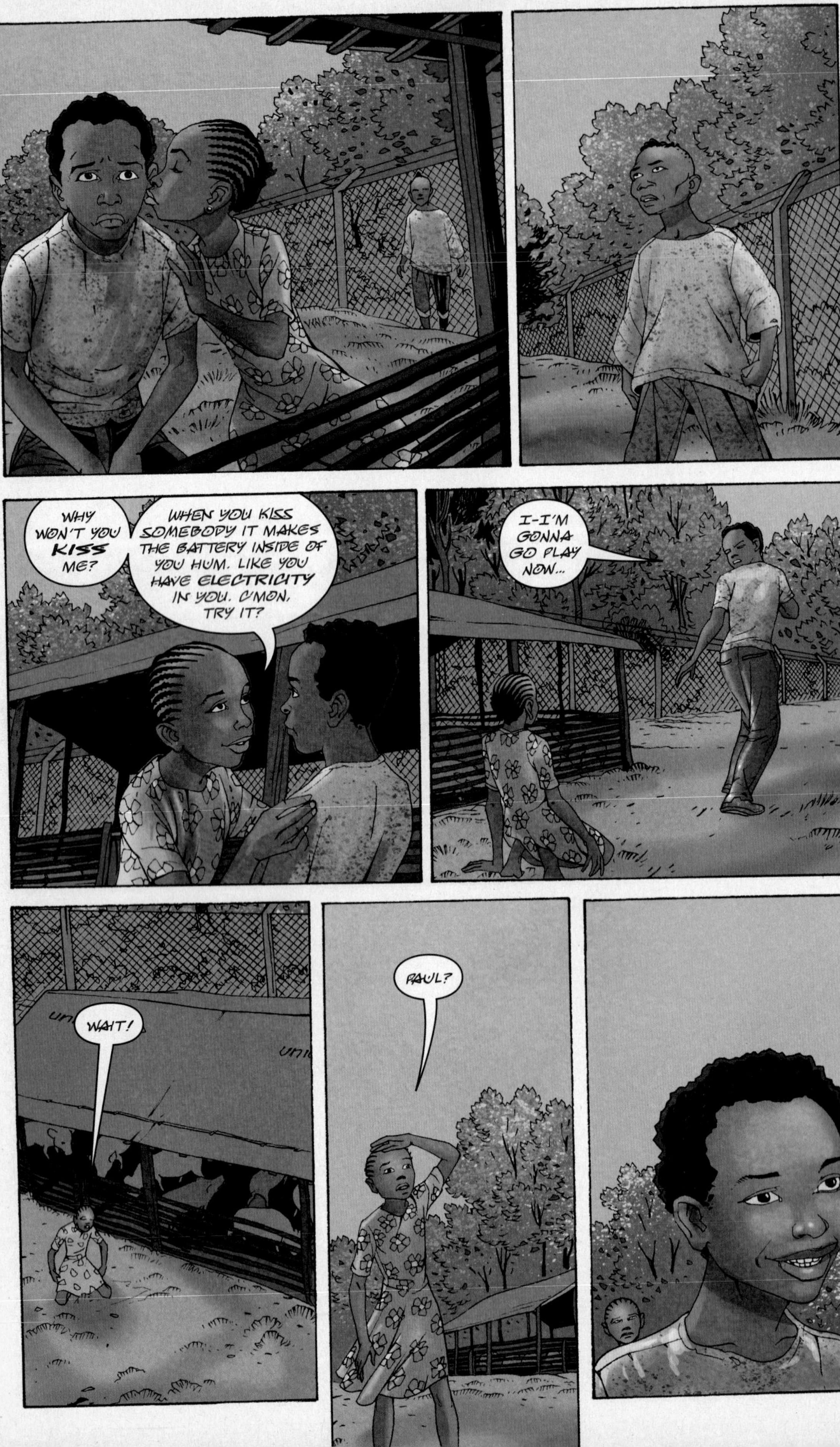
WHY WON'T YOU KISS ME?
WHEN YOU KISS SOMEBODY IT MAKES THE BATTERY INSIDE OF YOU HUM. LIKE YOU HAVE ELECTRICITY IN YOU. C'MON, TRY IT?
I-I'M GONNA GO PLAY NOW...
WAIT!
PAUL?

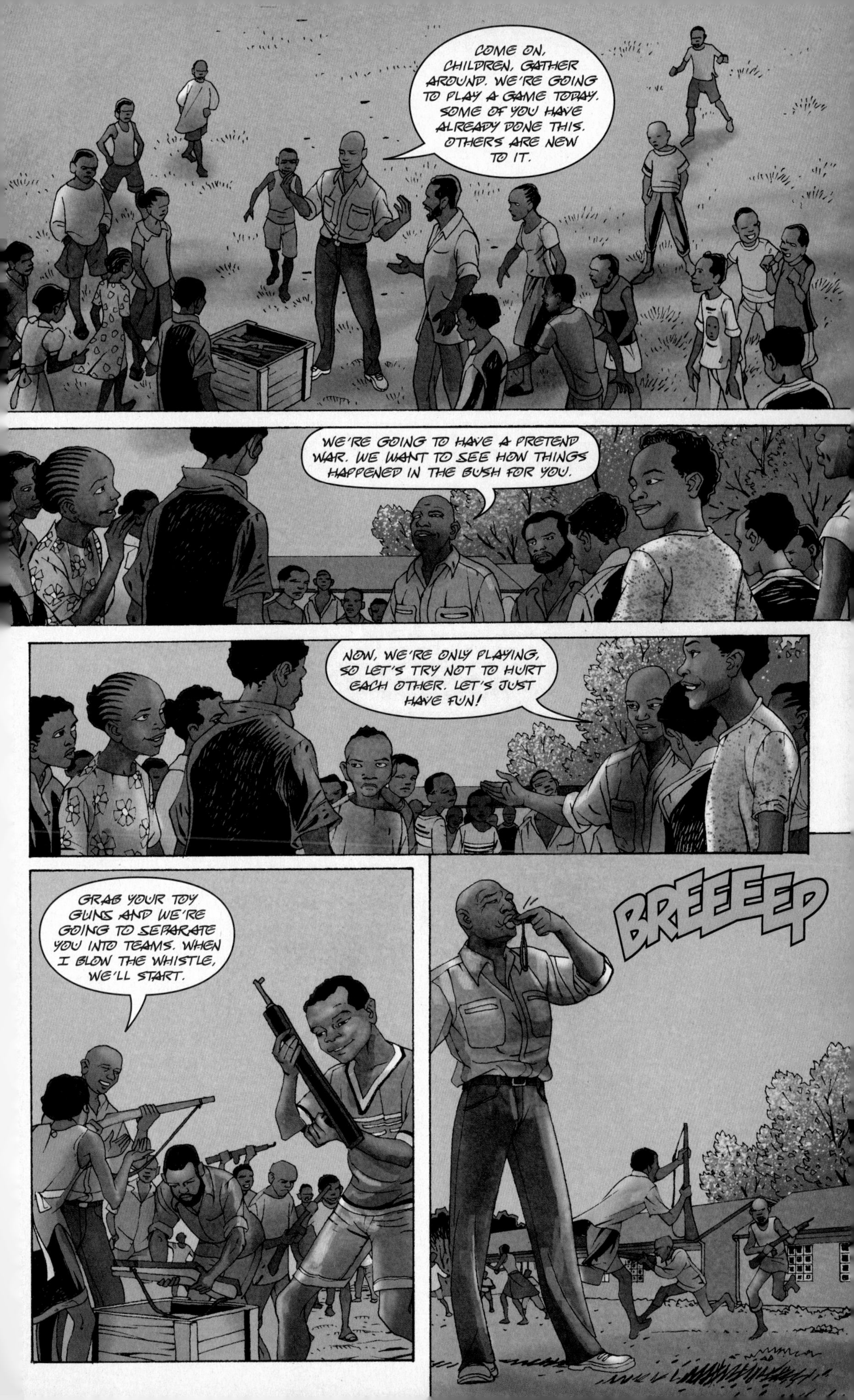
COME ON, CHILDREN, GATHER AROUND. WE'RE GOING TO PLAY A GAME TODAY. SOME OF YOU HAVE ALREADY DONE THIS. OTHERS ARE NEW TO IT.
WE'RE GOING TO HAVE A PRETEND WAR. WE WANT TO SEE HOW THINGS HAPPENED IN THE BUSH FOR YOU.
NOW, WE'RE ONLY PLAYING, SO LET'S TRY NOT TO HURT EACH OTHER. LET'S JUST HAVE FUN!
GRAB YOUR TOY GUNS AND WE'RE GOING TO SEPARATE YOU INTO TEAMS. WHEN I BLOW THE WHISTLE, WE'LL START.
BREEEEP

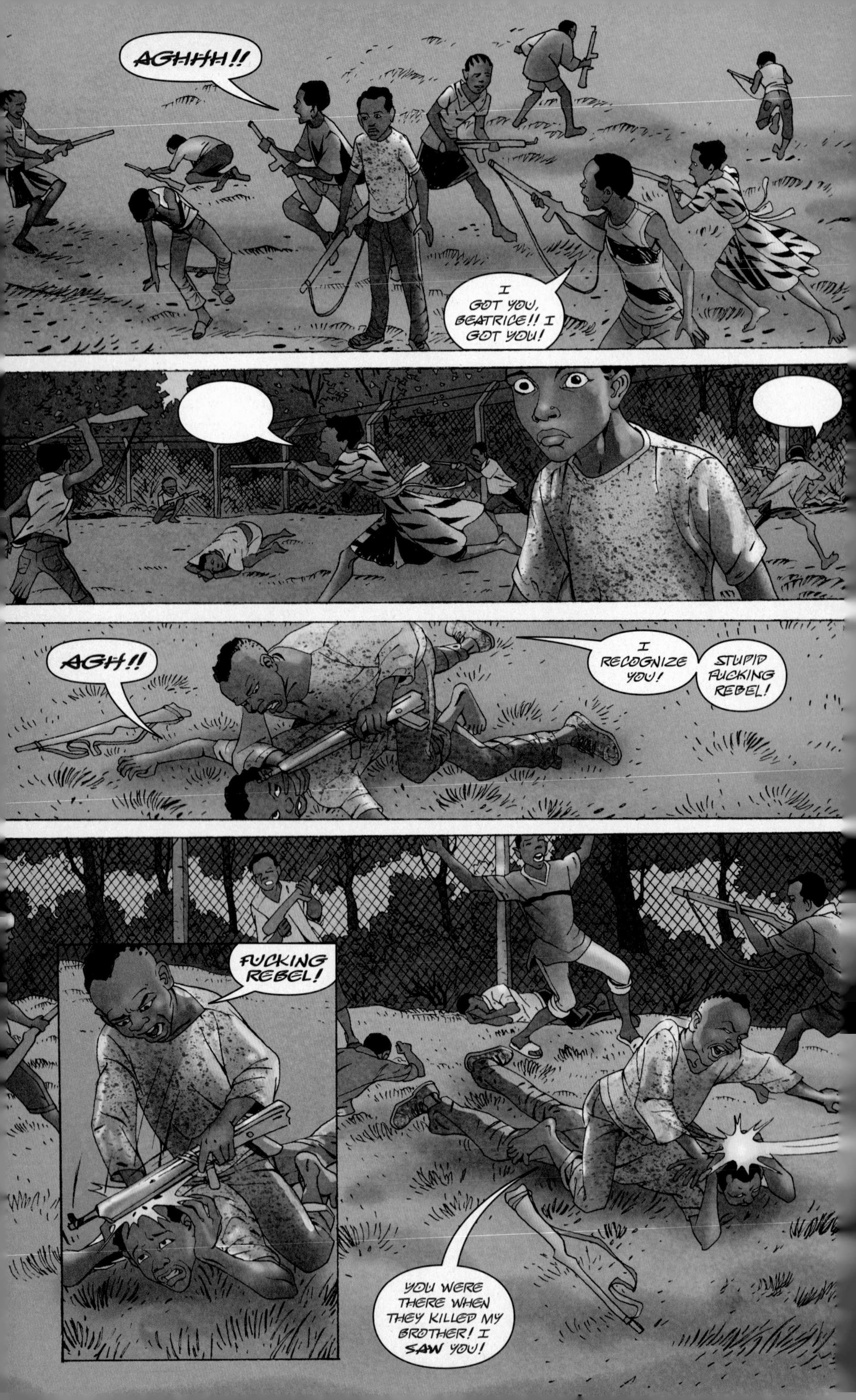
AGHHH!!
I GOT YOU, BEATRICE!! I GOT YOU!
AGH!!
I RECOGNIZE YOU!
STUPID FUCKING REBEL!
FUCKING REBEL!
YOU WERE THERE WHEN THEY KILLED MY BROTHER! I SAW YOU!

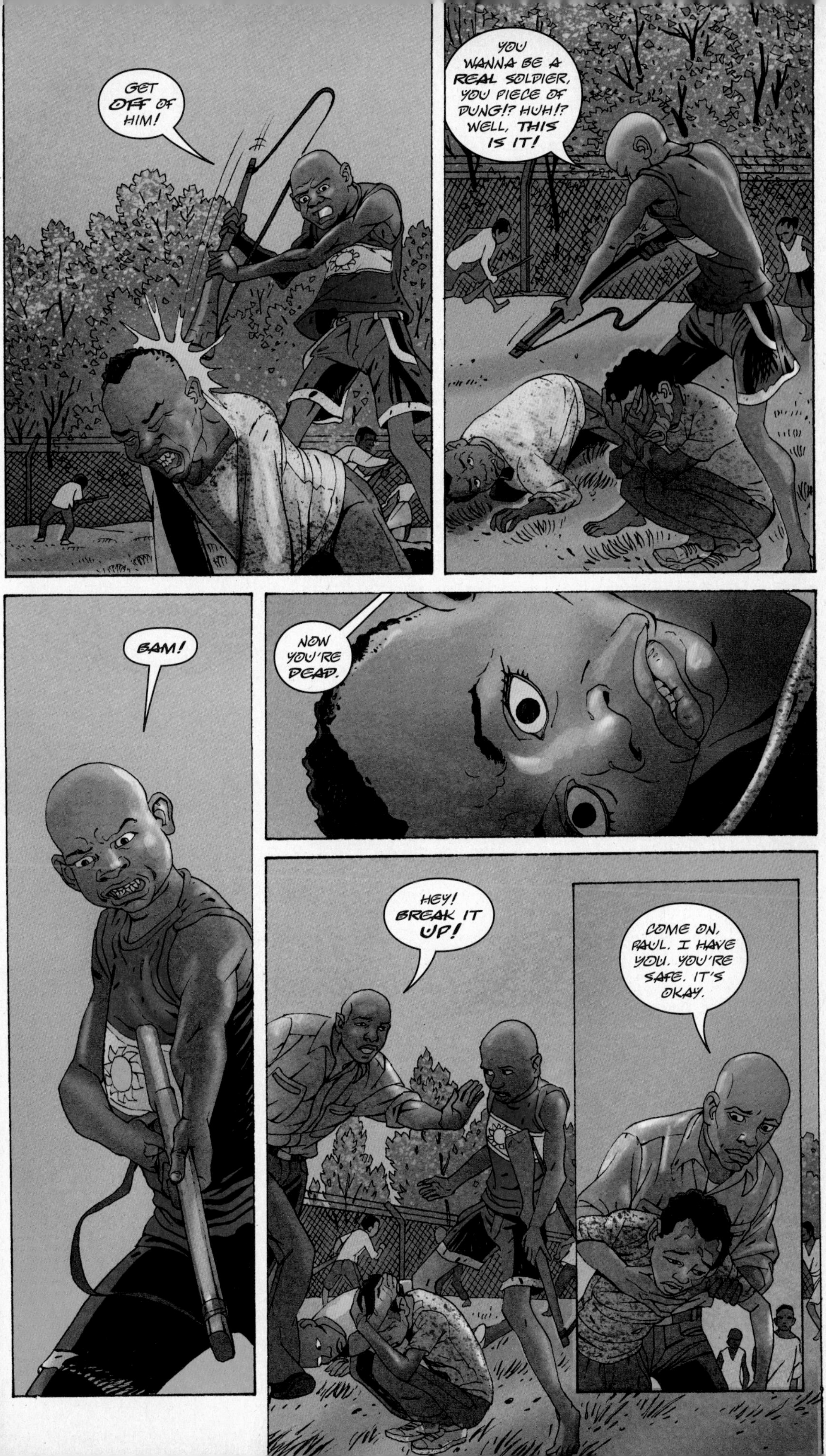
GET OFF OF HIM!
YOU WANNA BE A REAL SOLDIER, YOU PIECE OF DUNG!? HUH!? WELL, THIS IS IT!
BAM!
NOW YOU'RE DEAD.
HEY! BREAK IT UP!
COME ON, PAUL. I HAVE YOU. YOU'RE SAFE. IT'S OKAY.

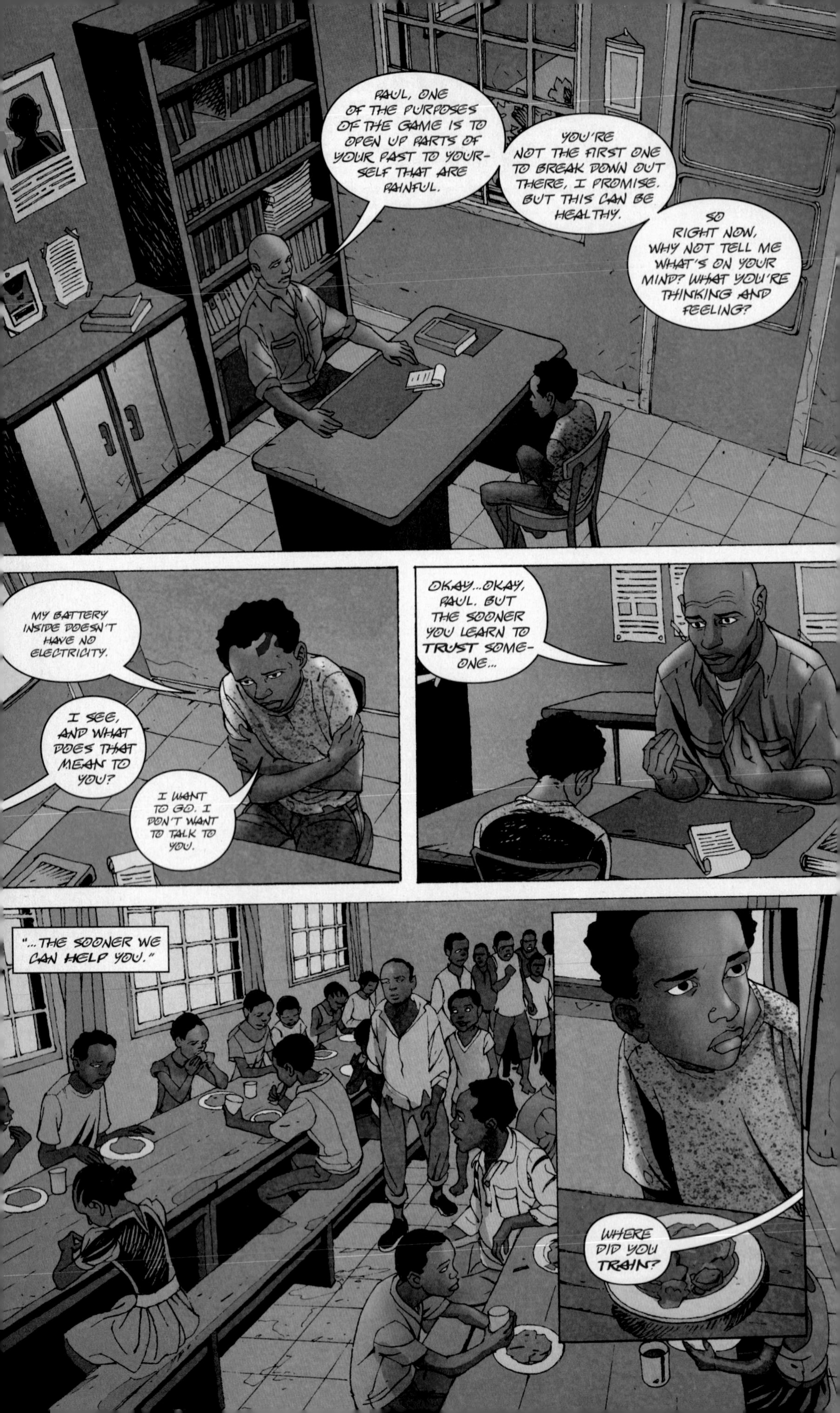
PAUL, ONE OF THE PURPOSES OF THE GAME IS TO OPEN UP PARTS OF YOUR PAST TO YOURSELF THAT ARE PAINFUL.
YOU'RE NOT THE FIRST ONE TO BREAK DOWN OUT THERE, I PROMISE. BUT THIS CAN BE HEALTHY.
SO RIGHT NOW, WHY NOT TELL ME WHAT'S ON YOUR MIND? WHAT YOU'RE THINKING AND FEELING?
MY BATTERY INSIDE DOESN'T HAVE NO ELECTRICITY.
I SEE, AND WHAT DOES THAT MEAN TO YOU?
I WANT TO GO. I DON'T WANT TO TALK TO YOU.
OKAY...OKAY, PAUL. BUT THE SOONER YOU LEARN TO TRUST SOMEONE...
"...THE SOONER WE CAN HELP YOU."
WHERE DID YOU TRAIN?

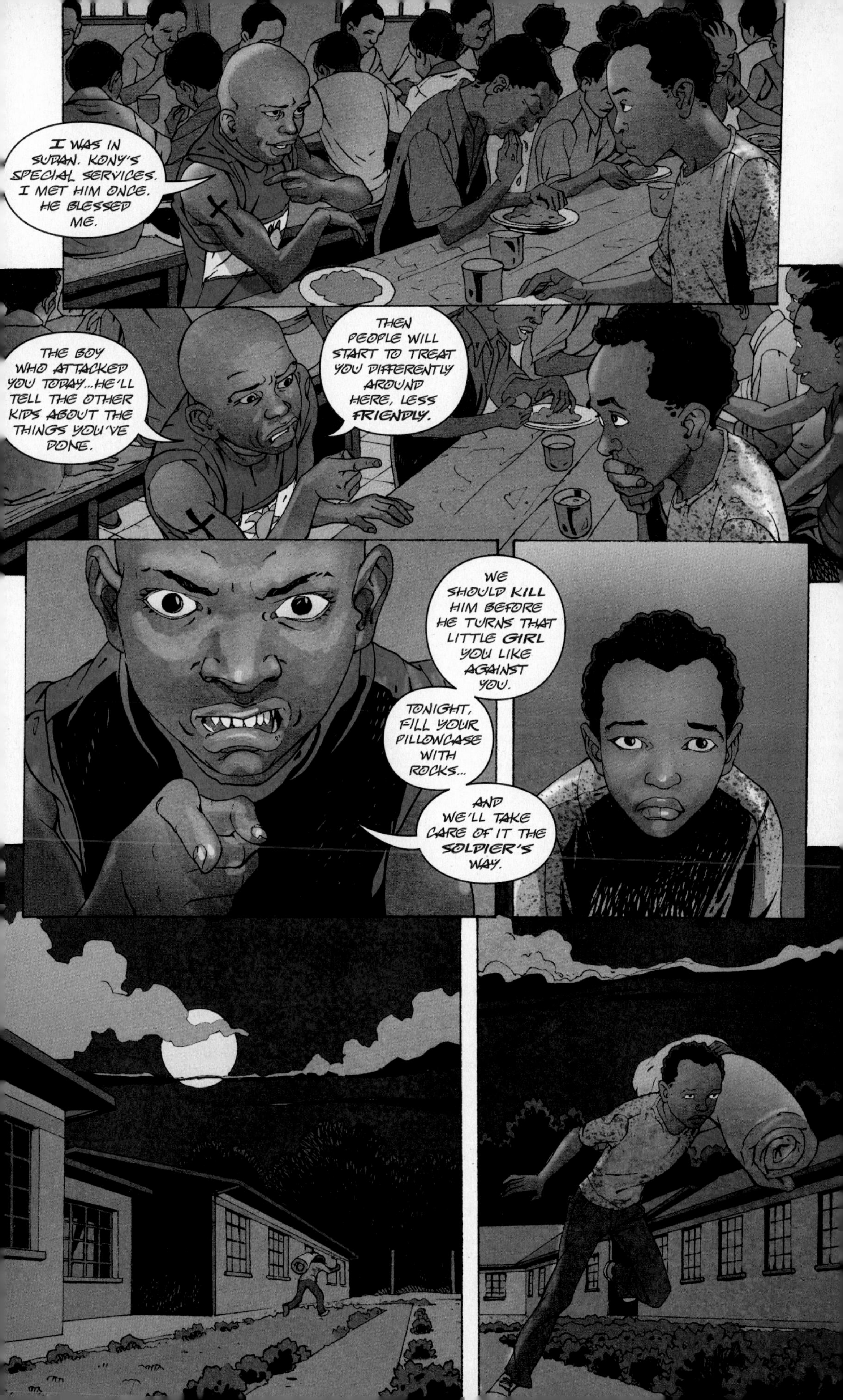
I WAS IN SUDAN. KONY'S SPECIAL SERVICES. I MET HIM ONCE. HE BLESSED ME.
THE BOY WHO ATTACKED YOU TODAY...HE'LL TELL THE OTHER KIDS ABOUT THE THINGS YOU'VE DONE.
THEN PEOPLE WILL START TO TREAT YOU DIFFERENTLY AROUND HERE, LESS FRIENDLY.
WE SHOULD KILL HIM BEFORE HE TURNS THAT LITTLE GIRL YOU LIKE AGAINST YOU.
TONIGHT, FILL YOUR PILLOWCASE WITH ROCKS...
AND WE'LL TAKE CARE OF IT THE SOLDIER'S WAY.

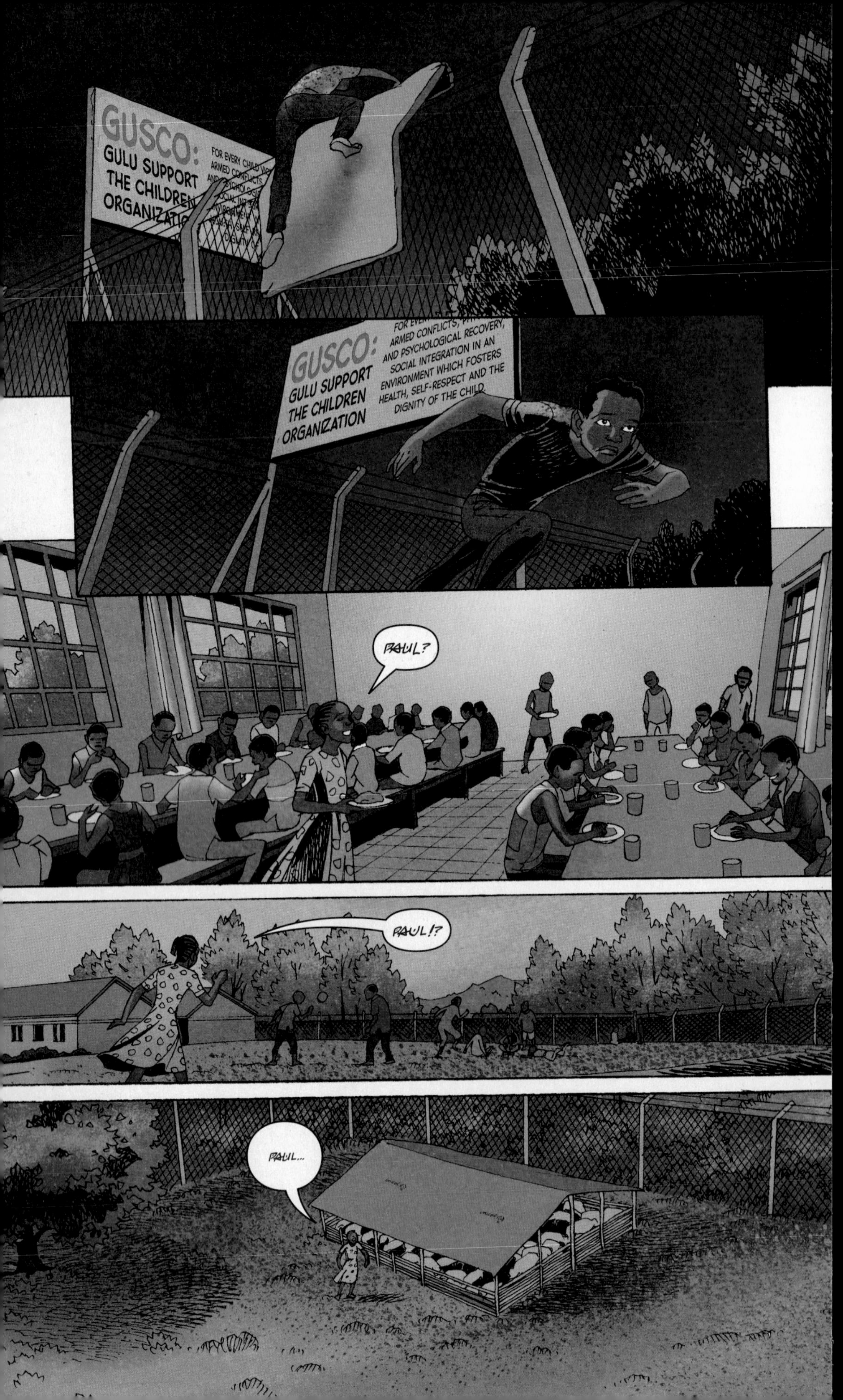
GUSCO:
GULU SUPPORT
THE CHILDREN
GUSCO:
GULU SUPPORT
THE CHILDREN
ORGANIZATION
ARMED CONFLICTS,
AND PSYCHOLOGICAL RECOVERY,
SOCIAL INTEGRATION IN AN
ENVIRONMENT WHICH FOSTERS
HEALTH, SELF-RESPECT AND THE
DIGNITY OF THE CHILD.
PAUL?
PAUL!?
PAUL...

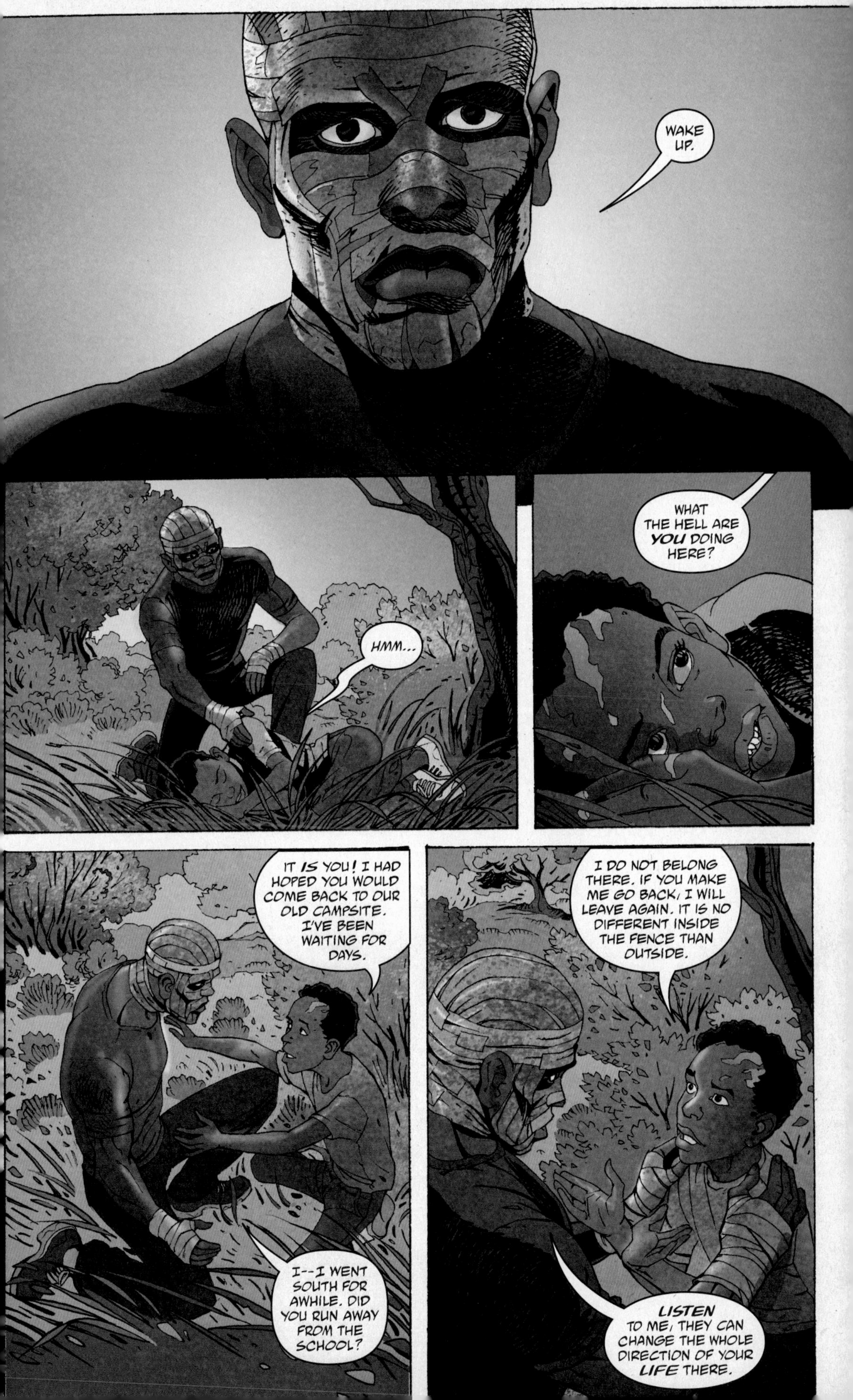
WAKE UP.
HMM...
WHAT THE HELL ARE YOU DOING HERE?
IT IS YOU! I HAD HOPED YOU WOULD COME BACK TO OUR OLD CAMPSITE. I'VE BEEN WAITING FOR DAYS.
I--I WENT SOUTH FOR AWHILE. DID YOU RUN AWAY FROM THE SCHOOL?
I DO NOT BELONG THERE. IF YOU MAKE ME GO BACK, I WILL LEAVE AGAIN. IT IS NO DIFFERENT INSIDE THE FENCE THAN OUTSIDE.
LISTEN TO ME, THEY CAN CHANGE THE WHOLE DIRECTION OF YOUR LIFE THERE.

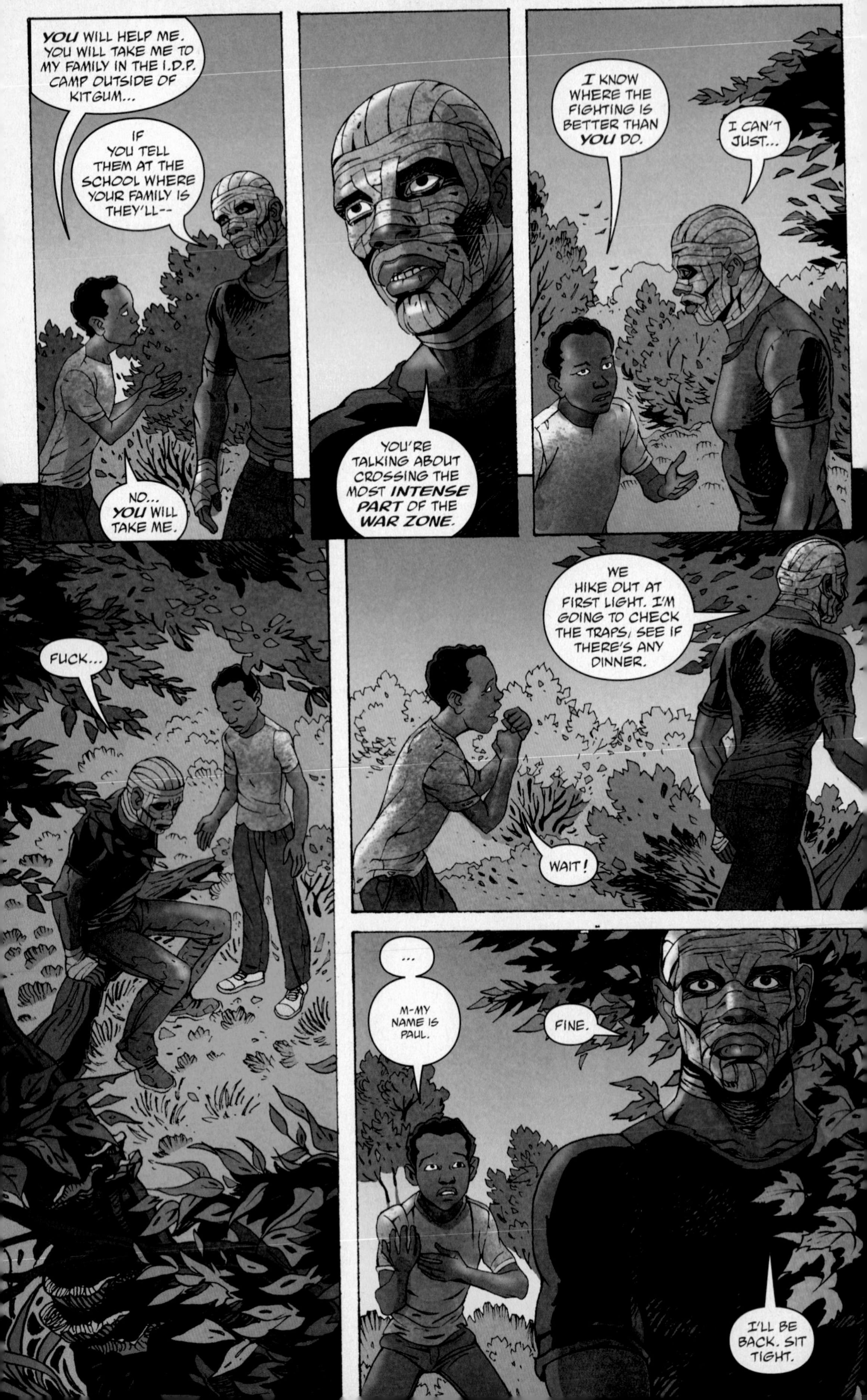
YOU WILL HELP ME. YOU WILL TAKE ME TO MY FAMILY IN THE I.D.P. CAMP OUTSIDE OF KITGUM...
IF YOU TELL THEM AT THE SCHOOL WHERE YOUR FAMILY IS THEY'LL--
NO... YOU WILL TAKE ME.
YOU'RE TALKING ABOUT CROSSING THE MOST INTENSE PART OF THE WAR ZONE.
I KNOW WHERE THE FIGHTING IS BETTER THAN YOU DO.
I CAN'T JUST...
FUCK...
WE HIKE OUT AT FIRST LIGHT. I'M GOING TO CHECK THE TRAPS, SEE IF THERE'S ANY DINNER.
WAIT!
...
M-MY NAME IS PAUL.
FINE.
I'LL BE BACK. SIT TIGHT.

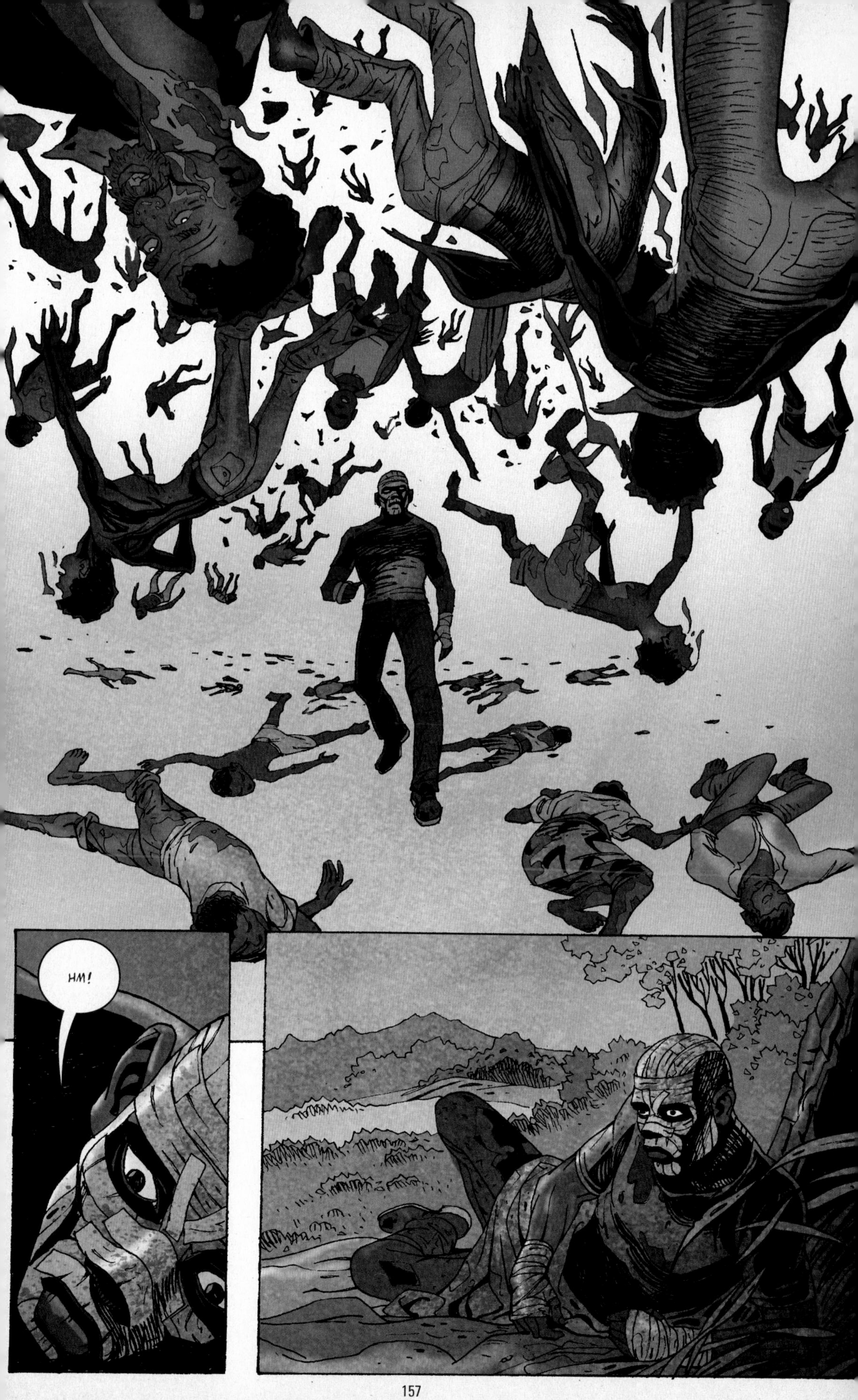
HM!

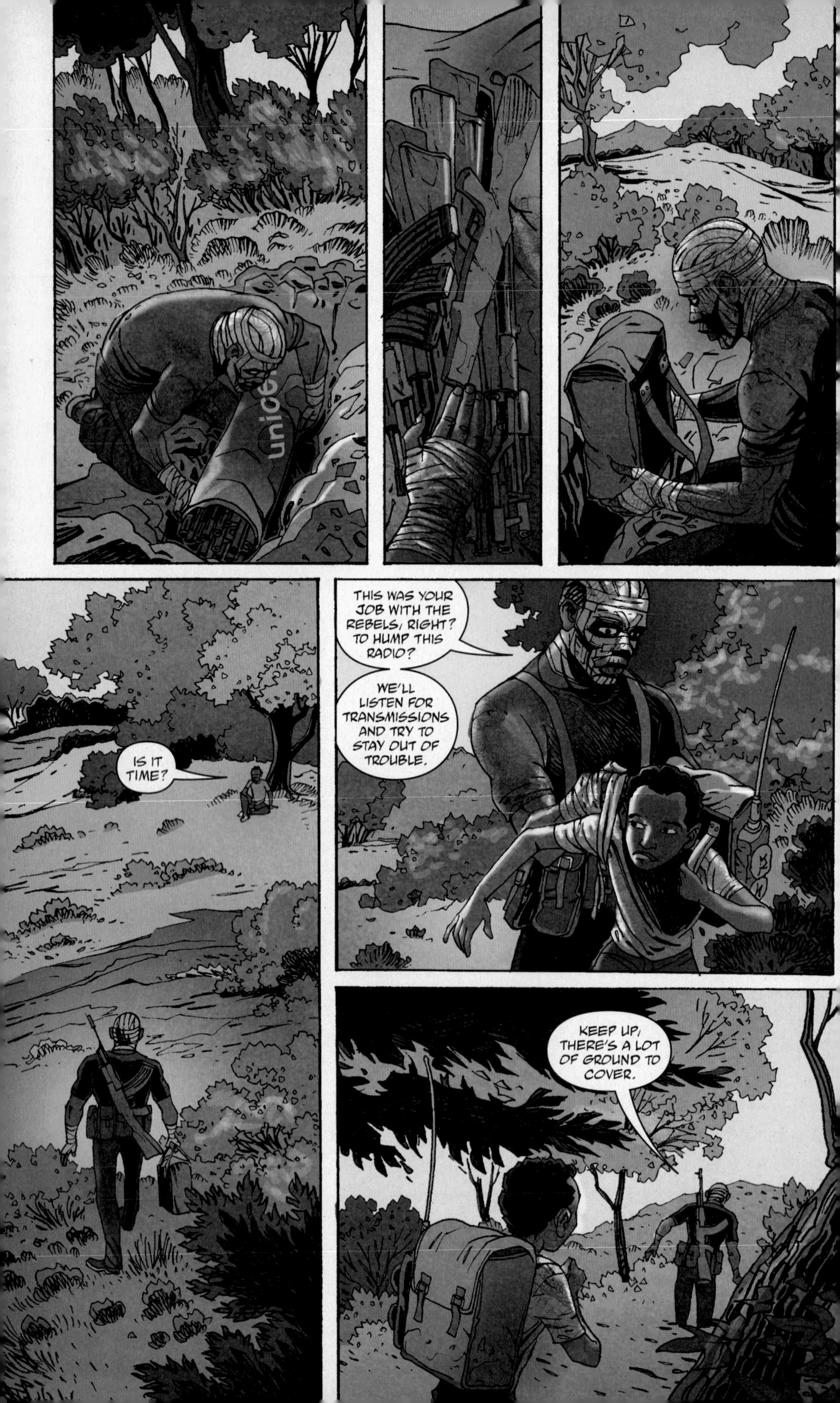
IS IT TIME?
THIS WAS YOUR JOB WITH THE REBELS, RIGHT? TO HUMP THIS RADIO?
WE'LL LISTEN FOR TRANSMISSIONS AND TRY TO STAY OUT OF TROUBLE.
KEEP UP, THERE'S A LOT OF GROUND TO COVER.

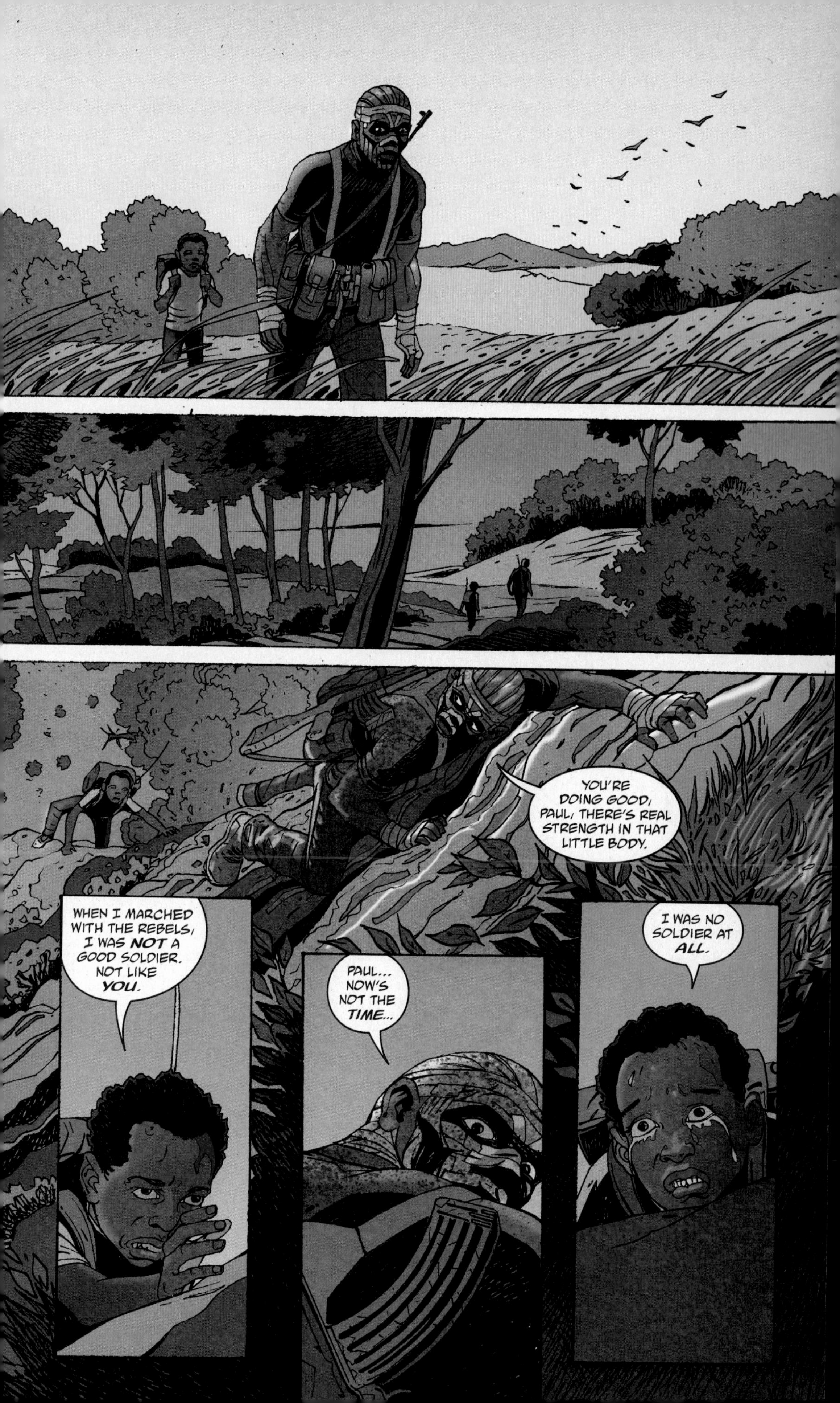
YOU'RE DOING GOOD, PAUL, THERE'S REAL STRENGTH IN THAT LITTLE BODY.
WHEN I MARCHED WITH THE REBELS, I WAS NOT A GOOD SOLDIER. NOT LIKE YOU.
PAUL... NOW'S NOT THE TIME...
I WAS NO SOLDIER AT ALL.

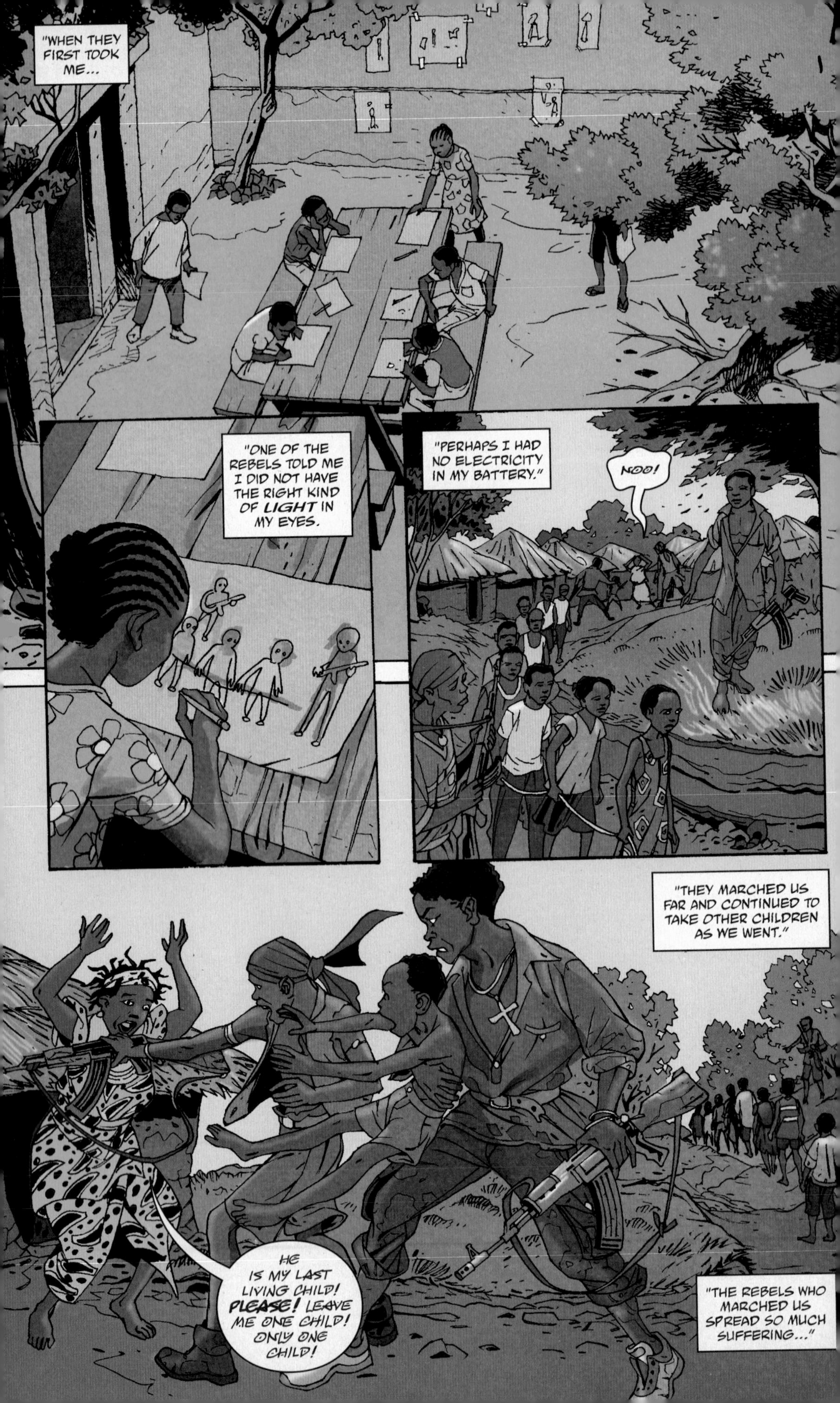
"WHEN THEY FIRST TOOK ME...
"ONE OF THE REBELS TOLD ME I DID NOT HAVE THE RIGHT KIND OF LIGHT IN MY EYES.
"PERHAPS I HAD NO ELECTRICITY IN MY BATTERY."
NOO!
"THEY MARCHED US FAR AND CONTINUED TO TAKE OTHER CHILDREN AS WE WENT."
HE IS MY LAST LIVING CHILD! PLEASE! LEAVE ME ONE CHILD! ONLY ONE CHILD!
"THE REBELS WHO MARCHED US SPREAD SO MUCH SUFFERING..."

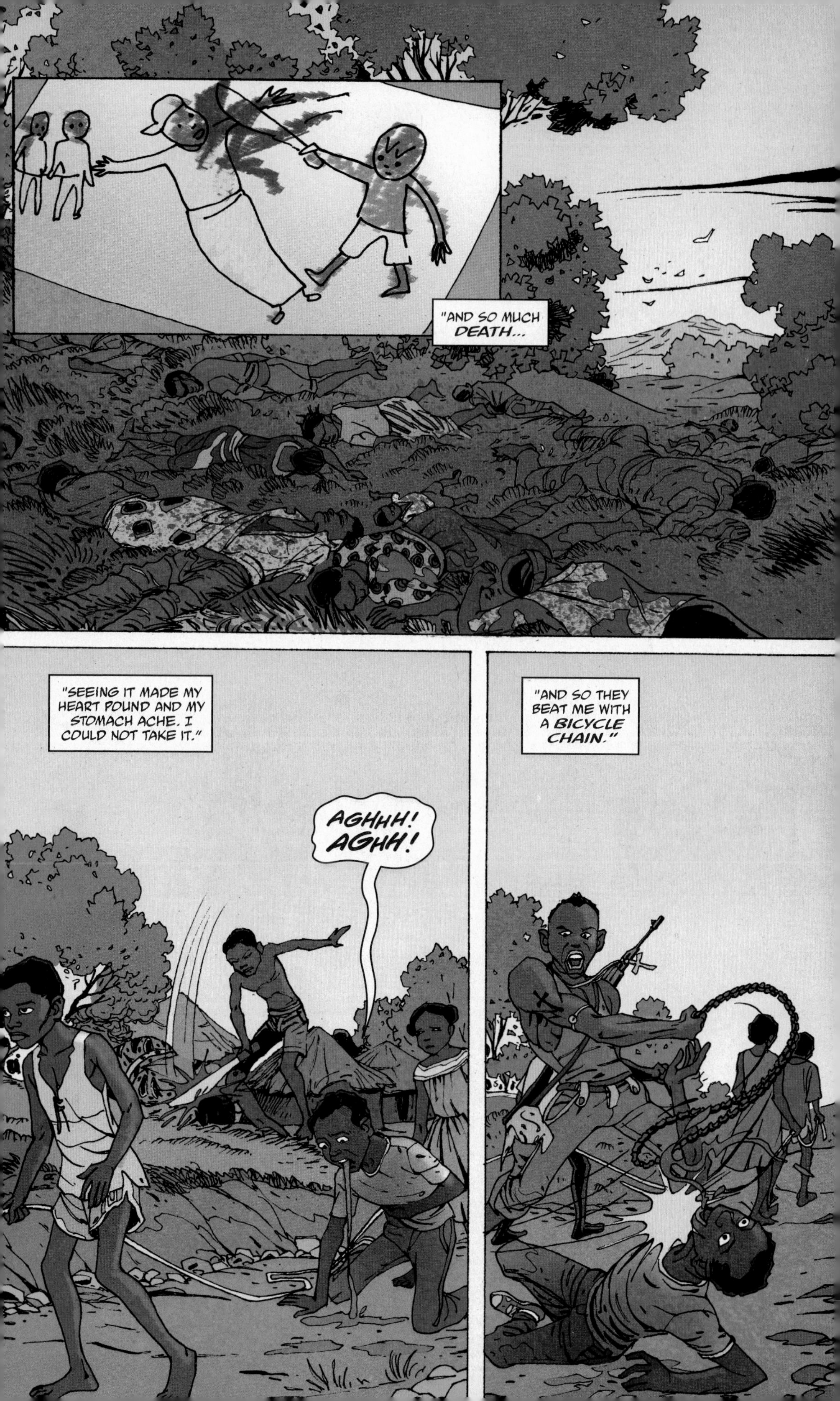
"AND SO MUCH DEATH...
"SEEING IT MADE MY HEART POUND AND MY STOMACH ACHE. I COULD NOT TAKE IT."
AGHHH! AGHH!
"AND SO THEY BEAT ME WITH A BICYCLE CHAIN."

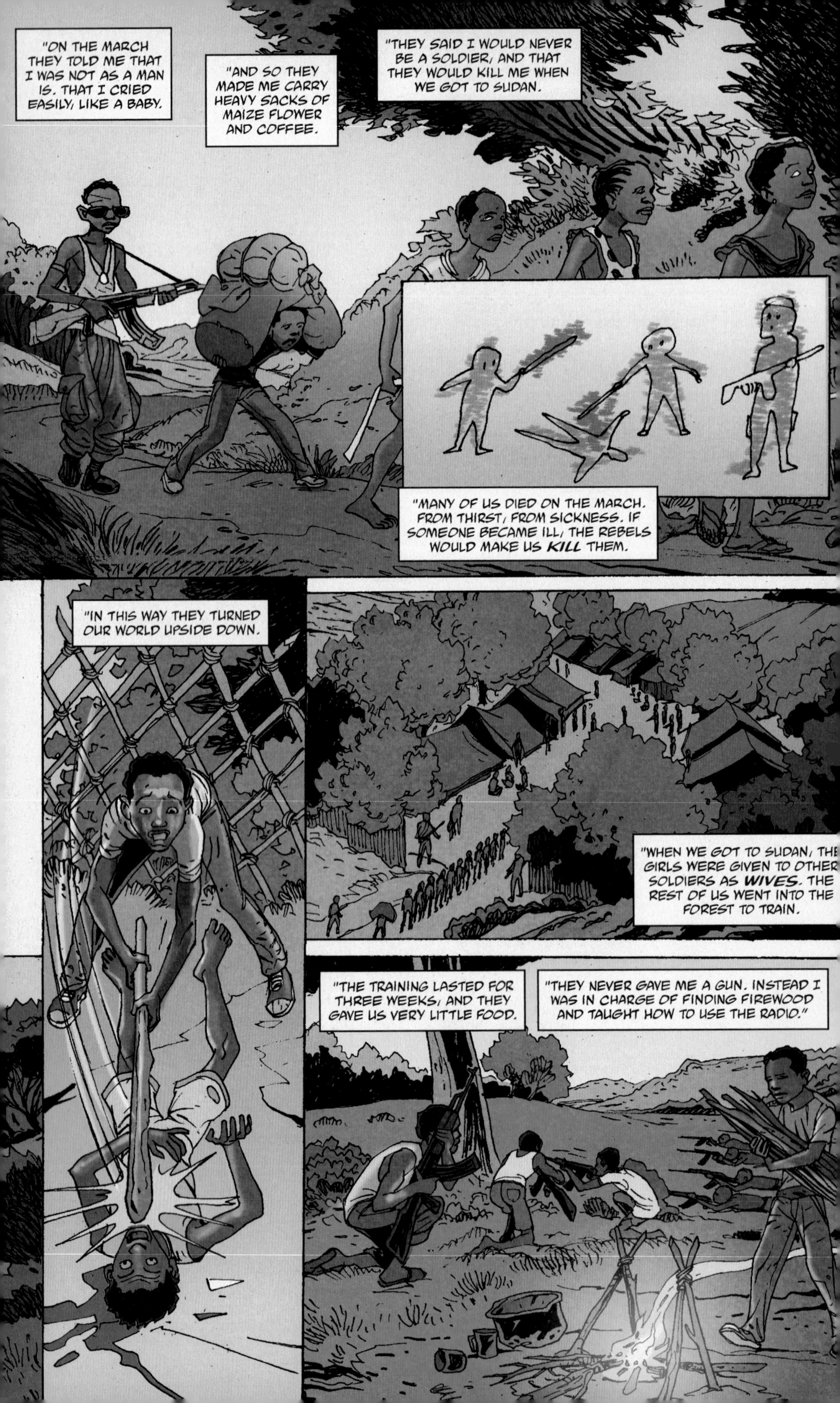
"ON THE MARCH THEY TOLD ME THAT I WAS NOT AS A MAN IS. THAT I CRIED EASILY, LIKE A BABY.
"AND SO THEY MADE ME CARRY HEAVY SACKS OF MAIZE FLOWER AND COFFEE.
"THEY SAID I WOULD NEVER BE A SOLDIER, AND THAT THEY WOULD KILL ME WHEN WE GOT TO SUDAN.
"MANY OF US DIED ON THE MARCH. FROM THIRST, FROM SICKNESS. IF SOMEONE BECAME ILL, THE REBELS WOULD MAKE US KILL THEM.
"IN THIS WAY THEY TURNED OUR WORLD UPSIDE DOWN.
"WHEN WE GOT TO SUDAN, THE GIRLS WERE GIVEN TO OTHER SOLDIERS AS WIVES. THE REST OF US WENT INTO THE FOREST TO TRAIN.
"THE TRAINING LASTED FOR THREE WEEKS, AND THEY GAVE US VERY LITTLE FOOD.
"THEY NEVER GAVE ME A GUN. INSTEAD I WAS IN CHARGE OF FINDING FIREWOOD AND TAUGHT HOW TO USE THE RADIO."

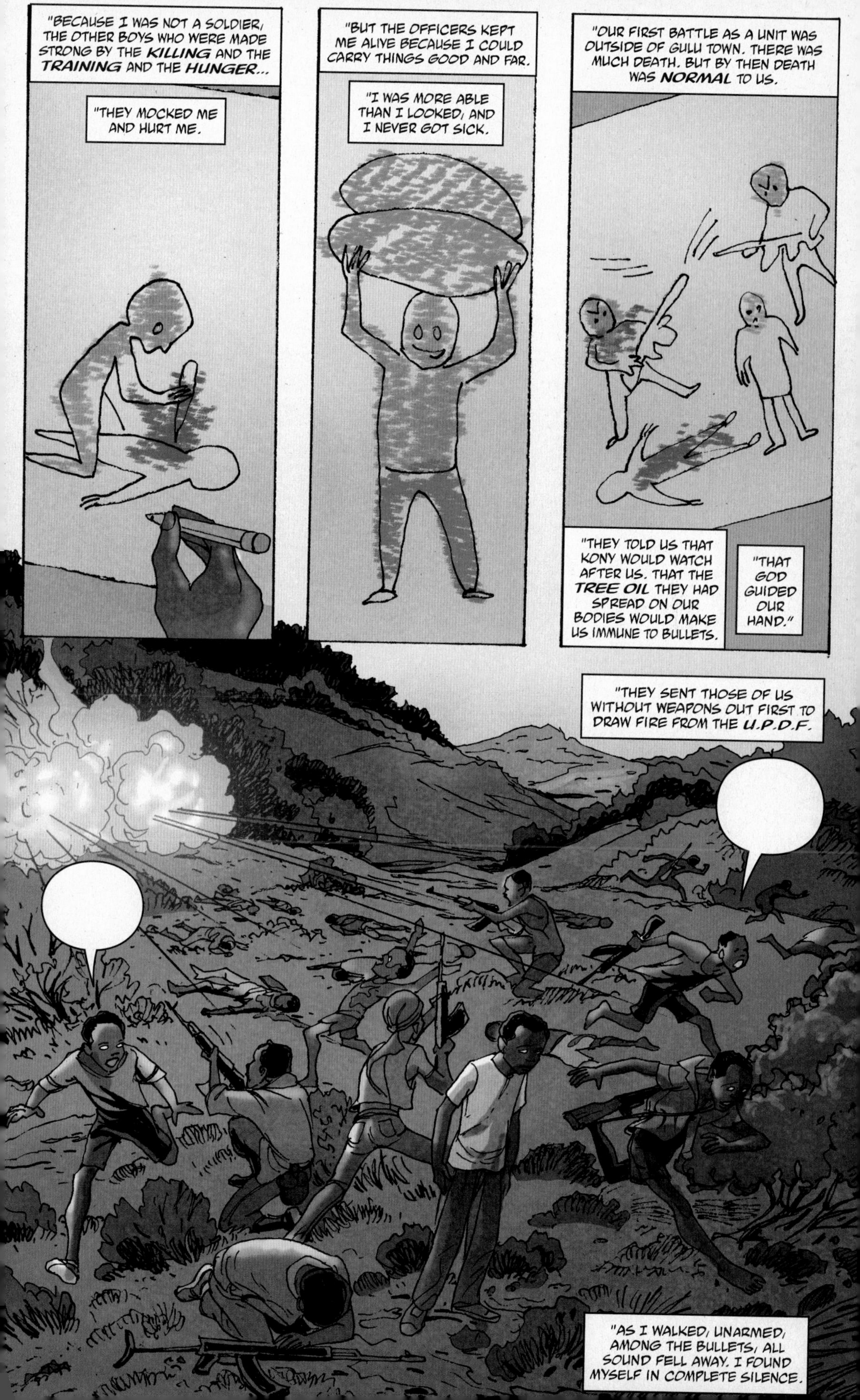
"BECAUSE I WAS NOT A SOLDIER, THE OTHER BOYS WHO WERE MADE STRONG BY THE KILLING AND THE TRAINING AND THE HUNGER...
"THEY MOCKED ME AND HURT ME.
"BUT THE OFFICERS KEPT ME ALIVE BECAUSE I COULD CARRY THINGS GOOD AND FAR.
"I WAS MORE ABLE THAN I LOOKED, AND I NEVER GOT SICK.
"OUR FIRST BATTLE AS A UNIT WAS OUTSIDE OF GULU TOWN. THERE WAS MUCH DEATH. BUT BY THEN DEATH WAS NORMAL TO US.
"THEY TOLD US THAT KONY WOULD WATCH AFTER US. THAT THE TREE OIL THEY HAD SPREAD ON OUR BODIES WOULD MAKE US IMMUNE TO BULLETS.
"THAT GOD GUIDED OUR HAND."
"THEY SENT THOSE OF US WITHOUT WEAPONS OUT FIRST TO DRAW FIRE FROM THE U.P.D.F.
"AS I WALKED, UNARMED, AMONG THE BULLETS, ALL SOUND FELL AWAY. I FOUND MYSELF IN COMPLETE SILENCE.

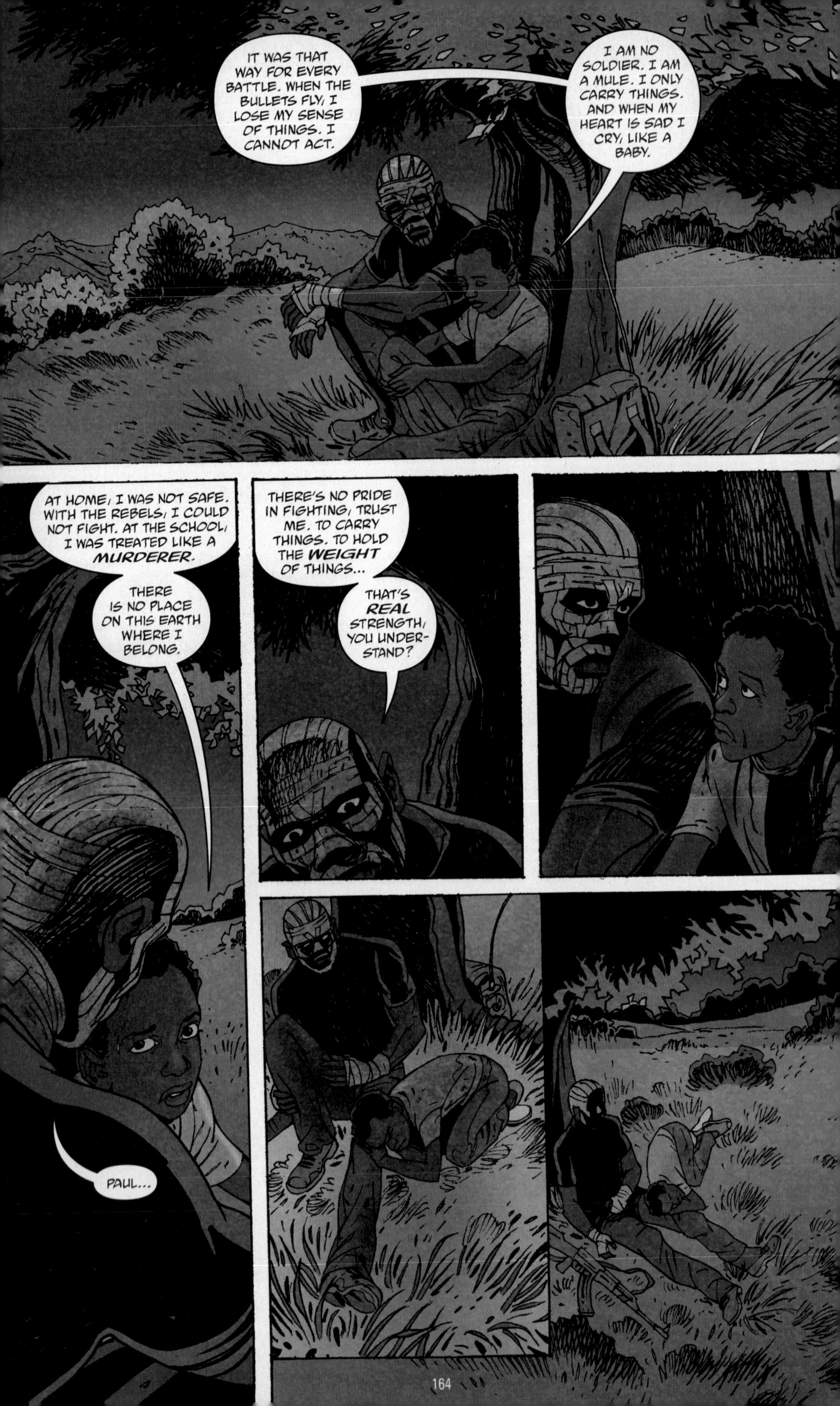
IT WAS THAT WAY FOR EVERY BATTLE. WHEN THE BULLETS FLY, I LOSE MY SENSE OF THINGS. I CANNOT ACT.
I AM NO SOLDIER. I AM A MULE. I ONLY CARRY THINGS. AND WHEN MY HEART IS SAD I CRY, LIKE A BABY.
AT HOME, I WAS NOT SAFE. WITH THE REBELS, I COULD NOT FIGHT. AT THE SCHOOL, I WAS TREATED LIKE A MURDERER.
THERE IS NO PLACE ON THIS EARTH WHERE I BELONG.
THERE'S NO PRIDE IN FIGHTING, TRUST ME. TO CARRY THINGS. TO HOLD THE WEIGHT OF THINGS...
THAT'S REAL STRENGTH, YOU UNDERSTAND?
PAUL...

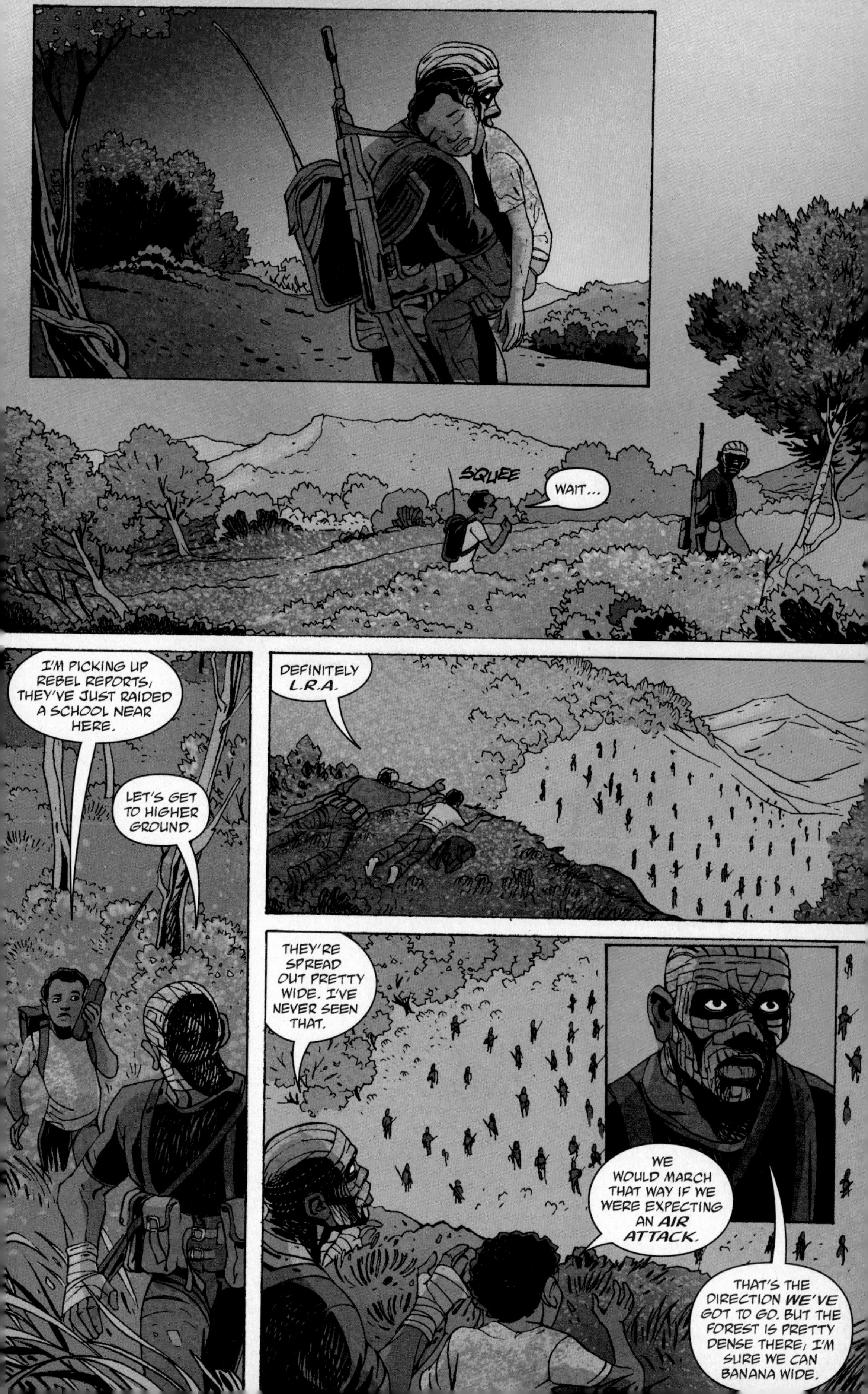
SQUEE
WAIT...
I'M PICKING UP REBEL REPORTS, THEY'VE JUST RAIDED A SCHOOL NEAR HERE.
LET'S GET TO HIGHER GROUND.
DEFINITELY L.R.A.
THEY'RE SPREAD OUT PRETTY WIDE. I'VE NEVER SEEN THAT.
WE WOULD MARCH THAT WAY IF WE WERE EXPECTING AN AIR ATTACK.
THAT'S THE DIRECTION WE'VE GOT TO GO. BUT THE FOREST IS PRETTY DENSE THERE, I'M SURE WE CAN BANANA WIDE.

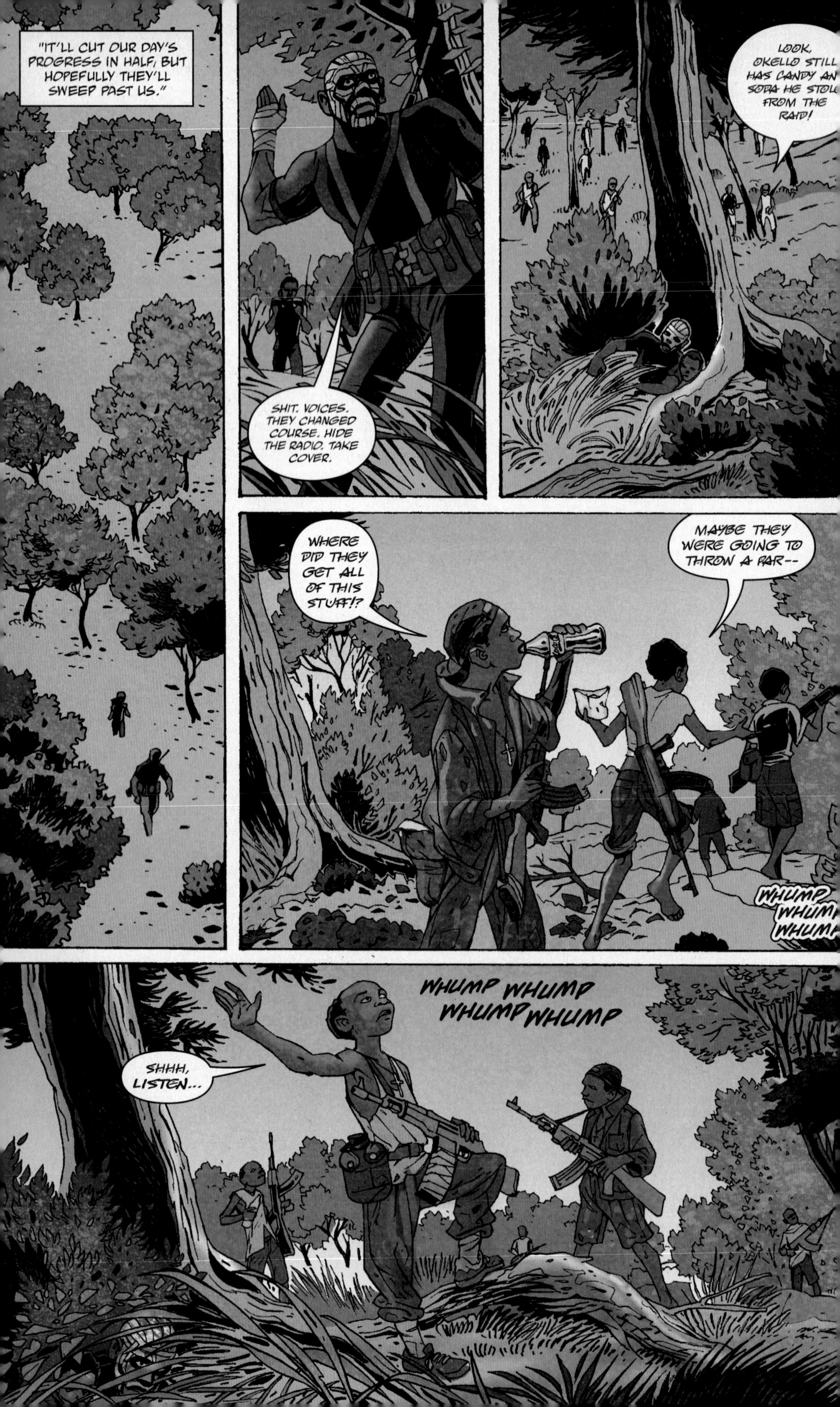
"IT'LL CUT OUR DAY'S PROGRESS IN HALF, BUT HOPEFULLY THEY'LL SWEEP PAST US."
SHIT. VOICES. THEY CHANGED COURSE. HIDE THE RADIO. TAKE COVER.
LOOK, OKELLO STILL HAS CANDY AN SODA HE STOL FROM THE RAID!
WHERE DID THEY GET ALL OF THIS STUFF!?
MAYBE THEY WERE GOING TO THROW A PAR--
WHUMP WHUM WHUM
WHUMP WHUMP WHUMP WHUMP
SHHH, LISTEN...

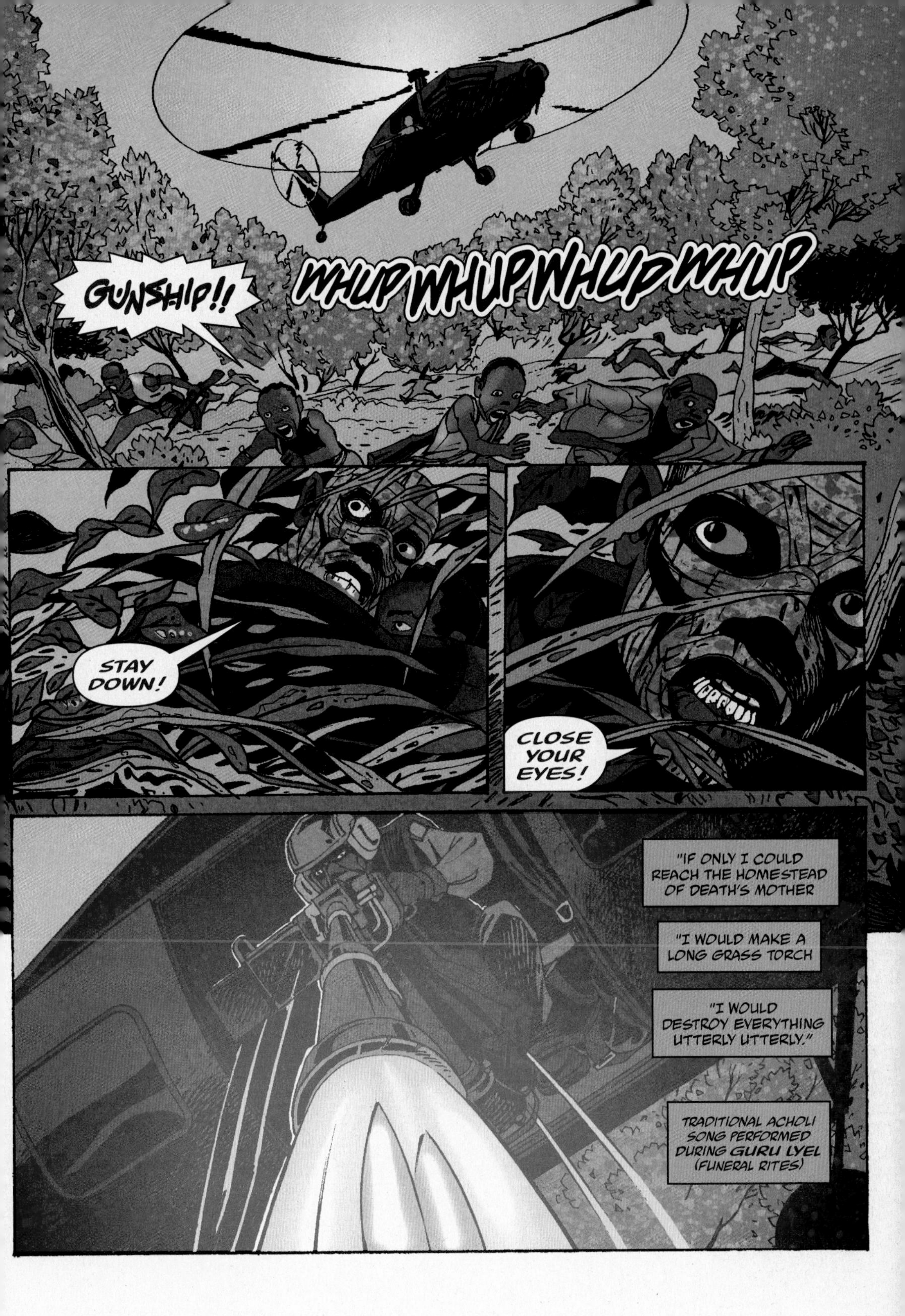
GUNSHIP!!
WHUP WHUP WHUP WHUP
STAY DOWN!
CLOSE YOUR EYES!
"IF ONLY I COULD REACH THE HOMESTEAD OF DEATH'S MOTHER
"I WOULD MAKE A LONG GRASS TORCH
"I WOULD DESTROY EVERYTHING UTTERLY UTTERLY."
TRADITIONAL ACHOLI SONG PERFORMED DURING GURU LYEL (FUNERAL RITES)

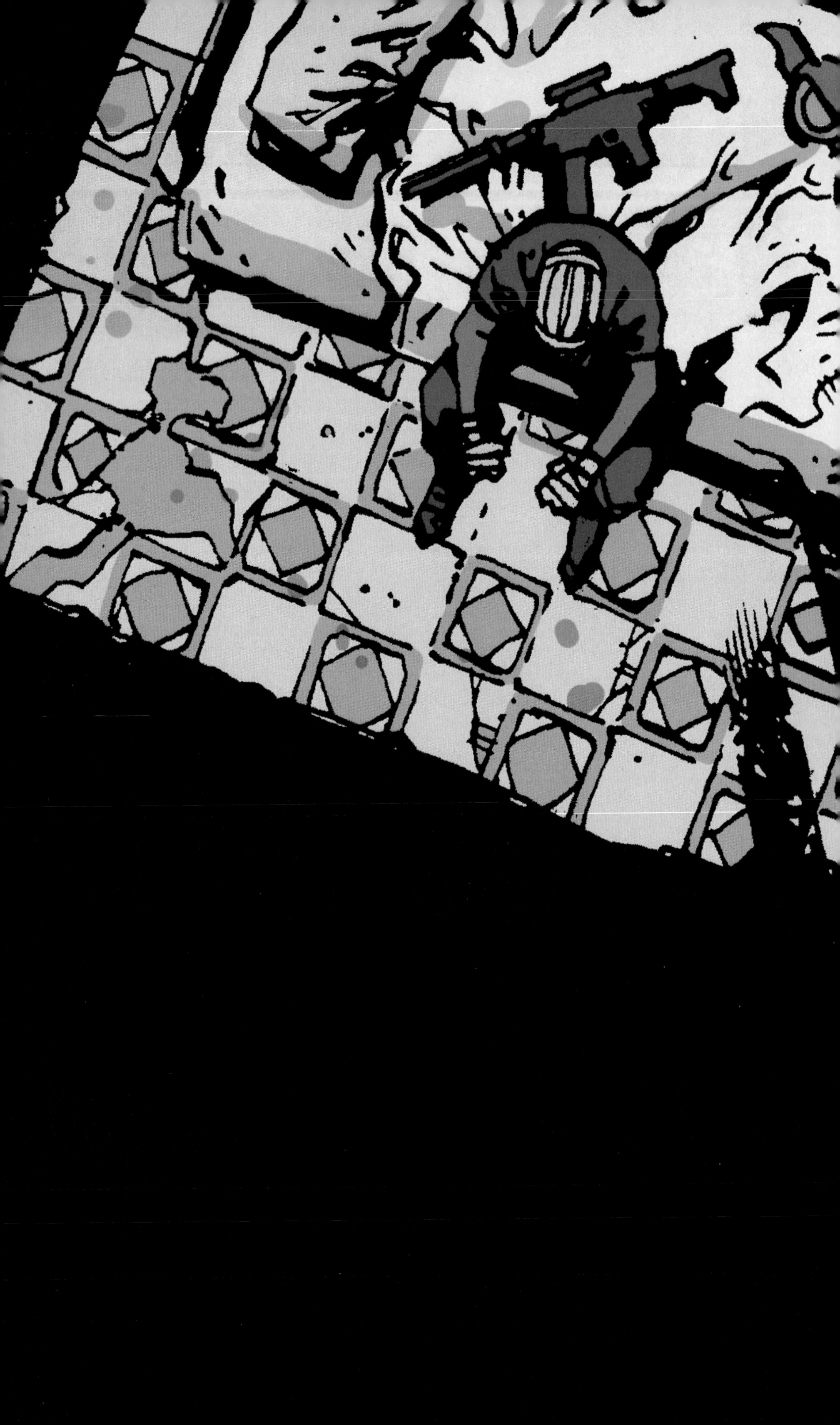

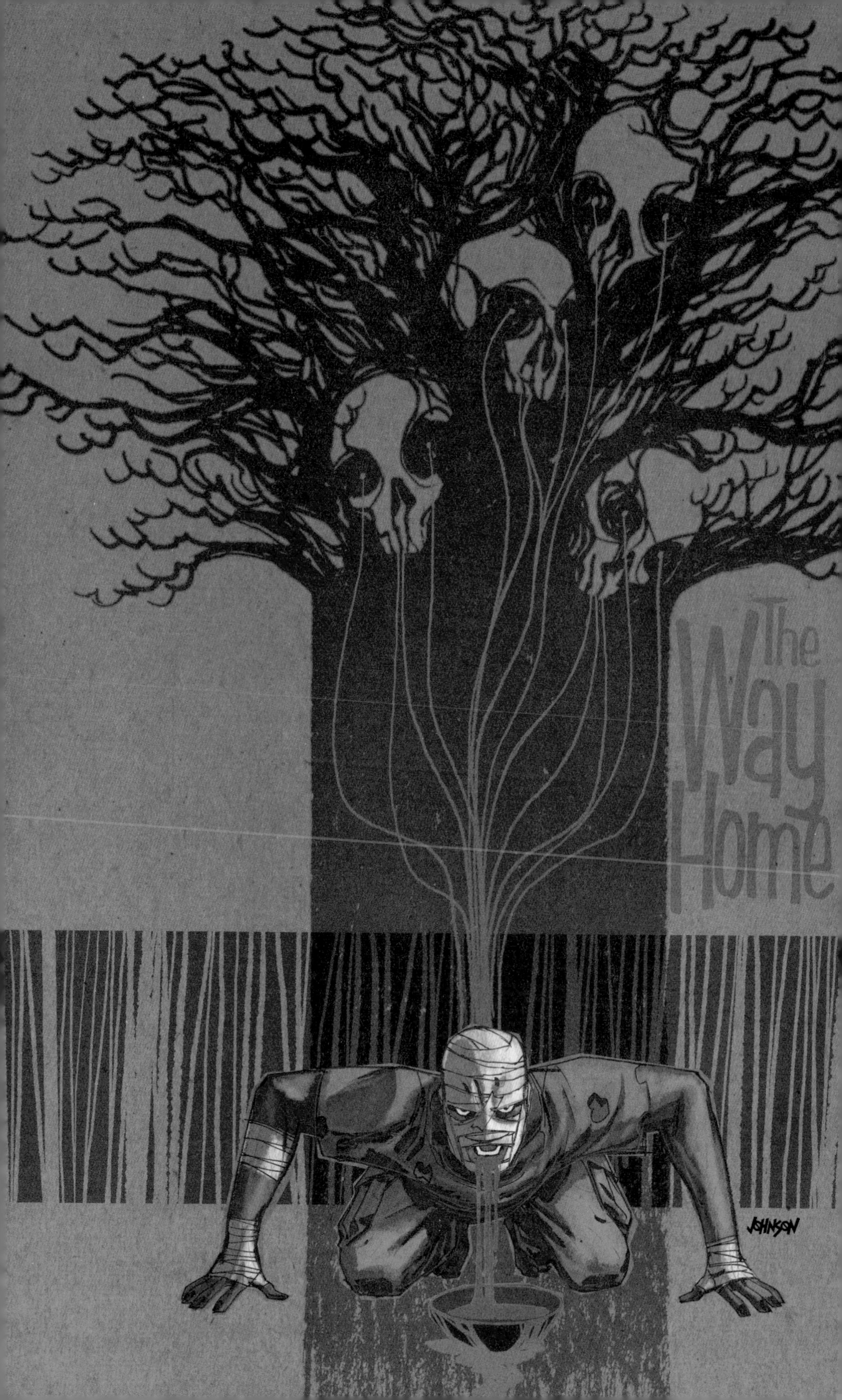
The Way Home
JOHNSON

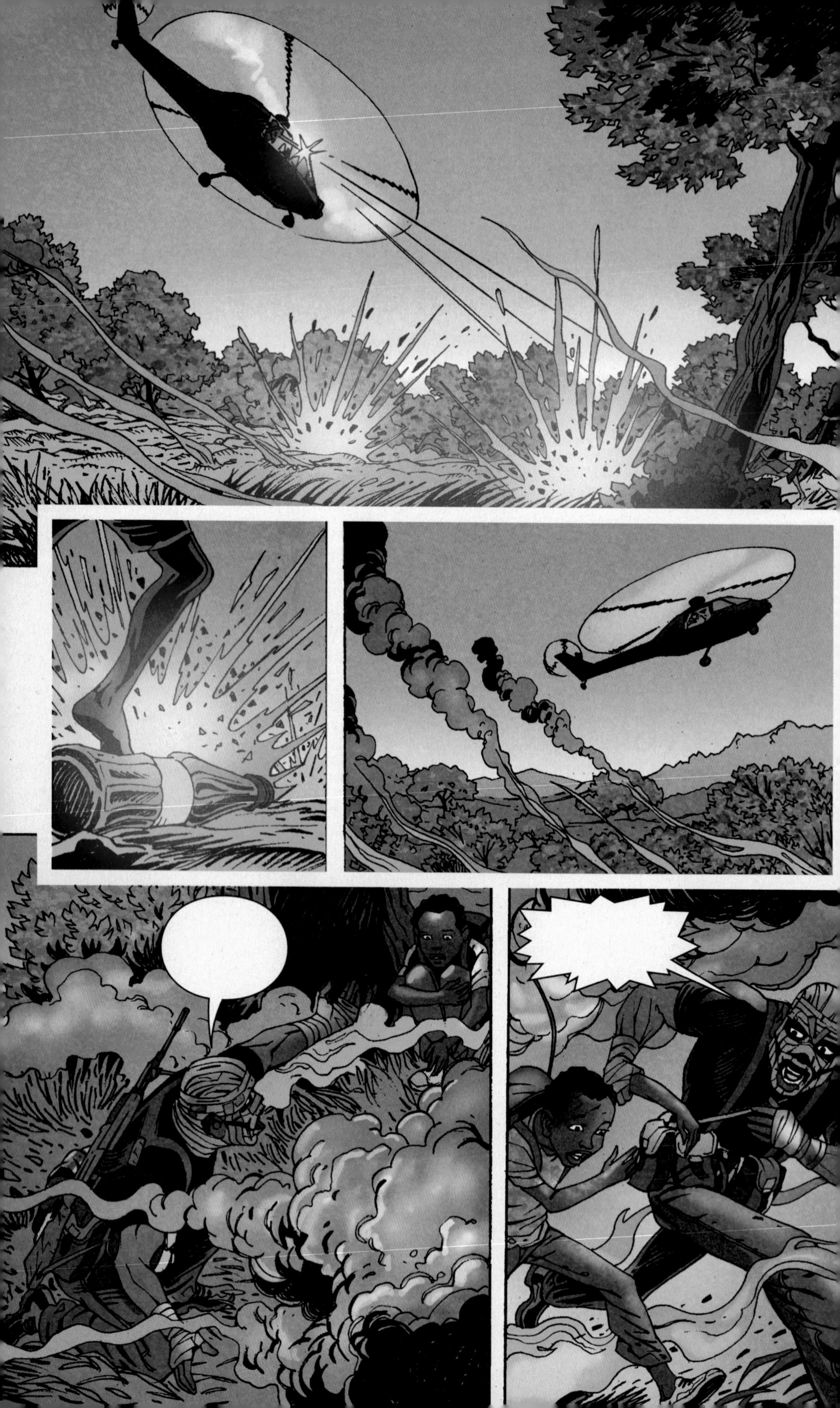

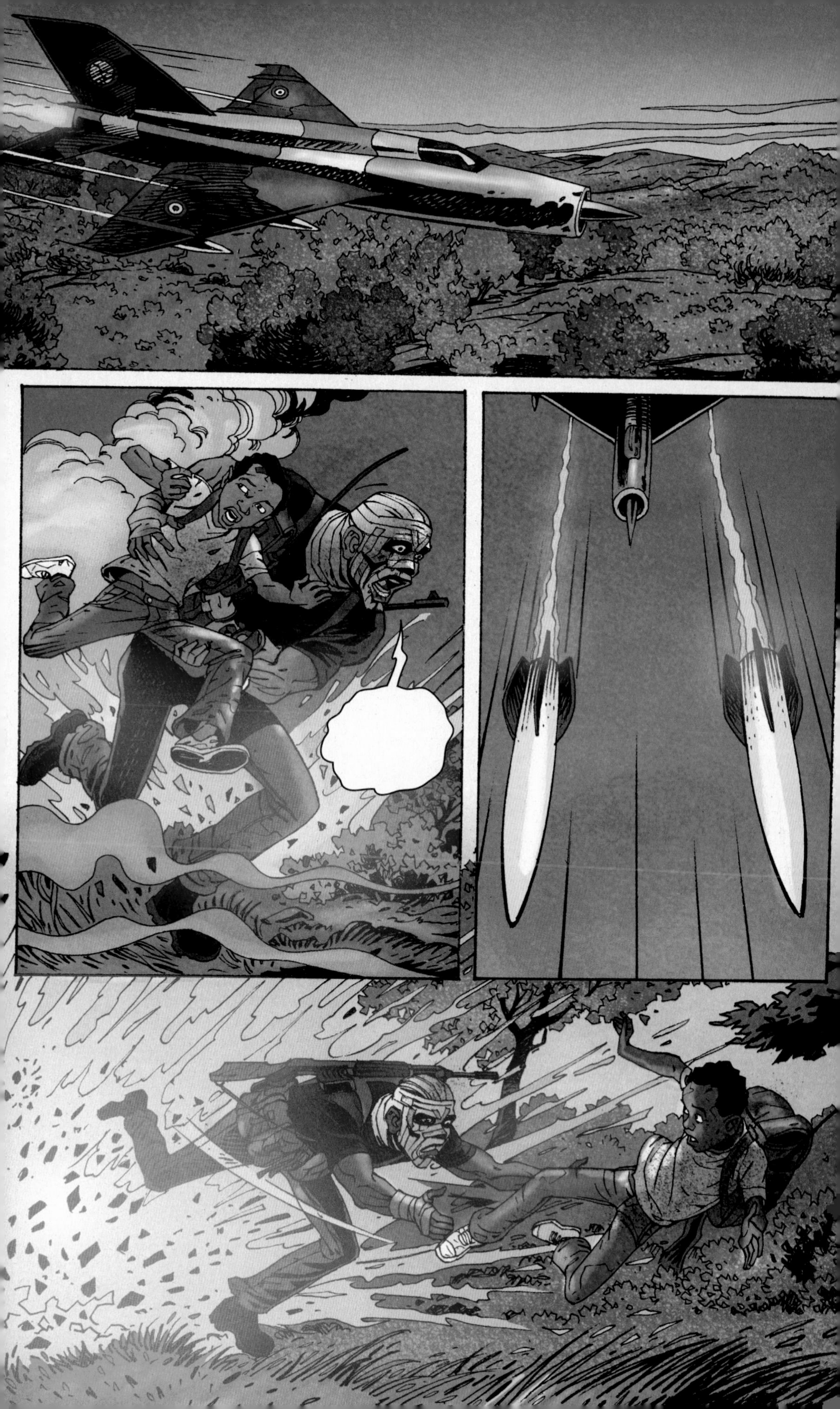

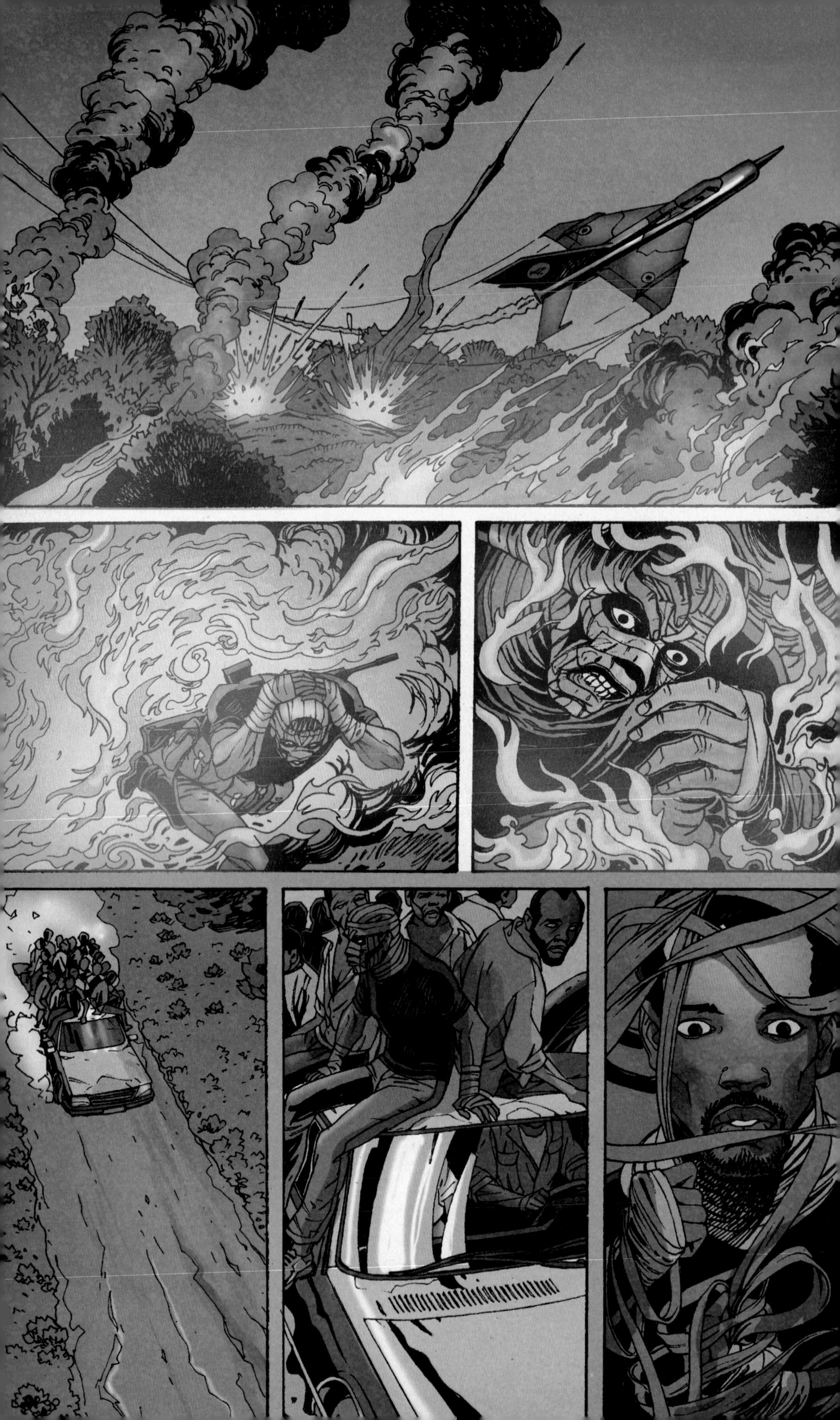

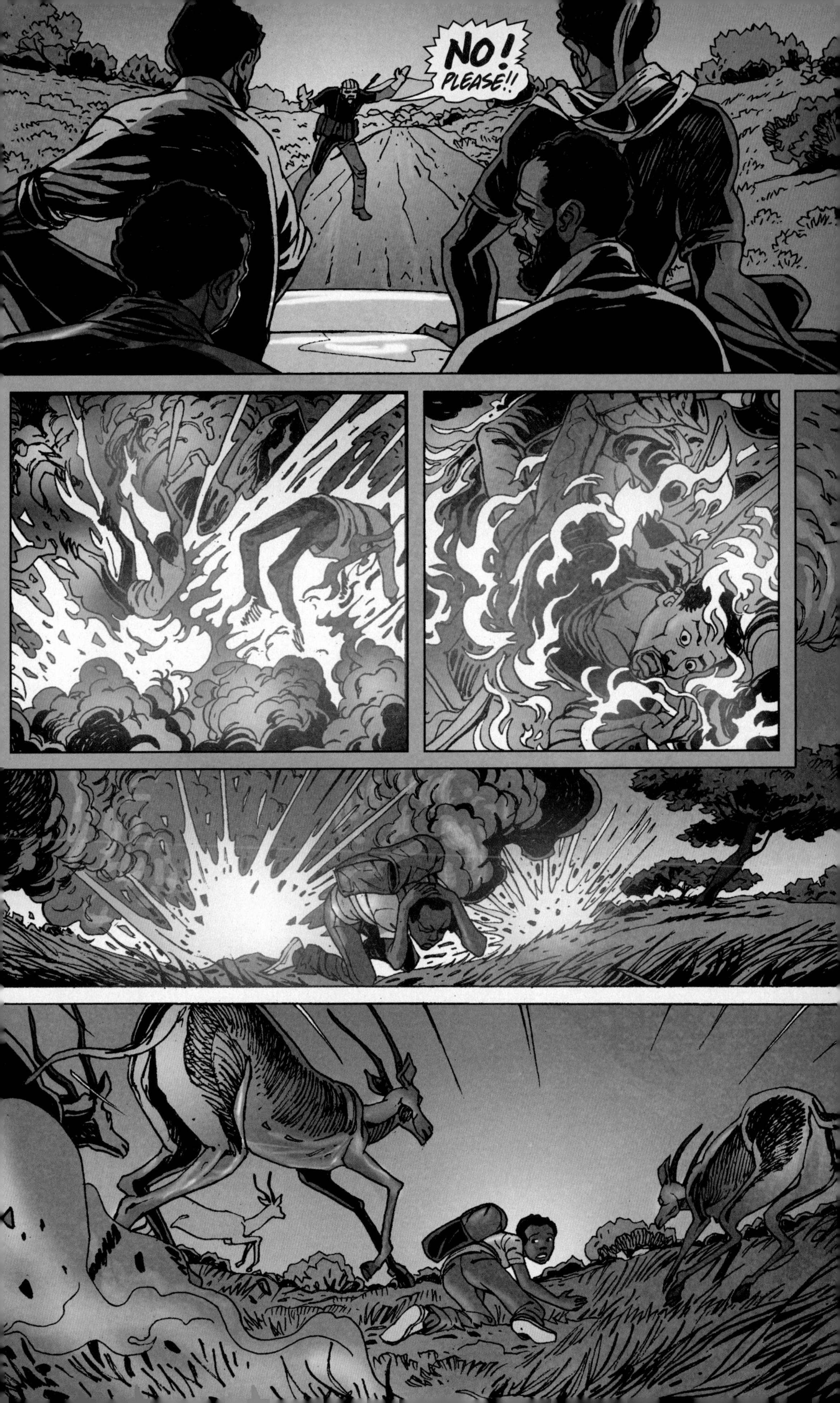
NO!
PLEASE!!

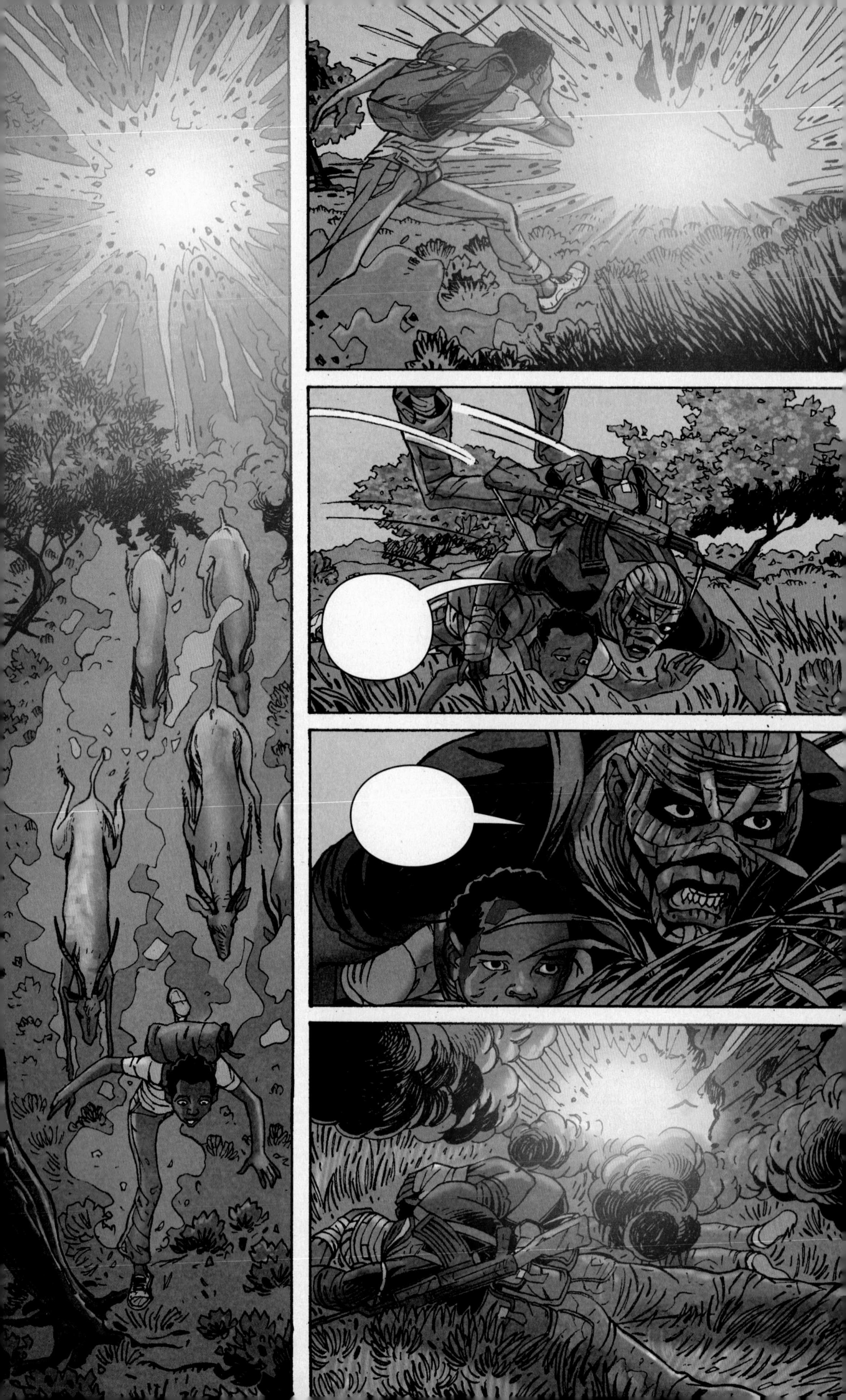

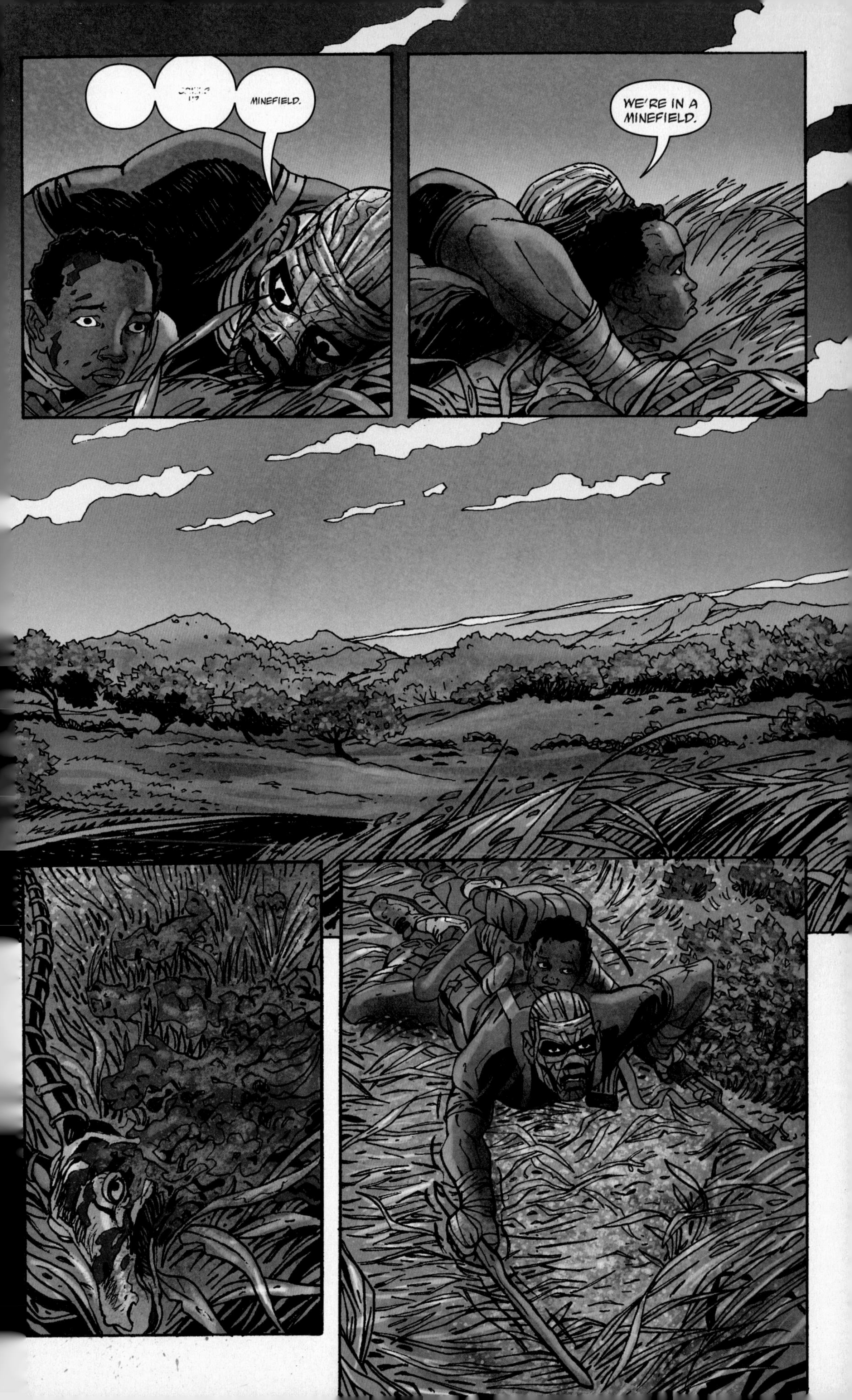
MINEFIELD.
WE'RE IN A MINEFIELD.

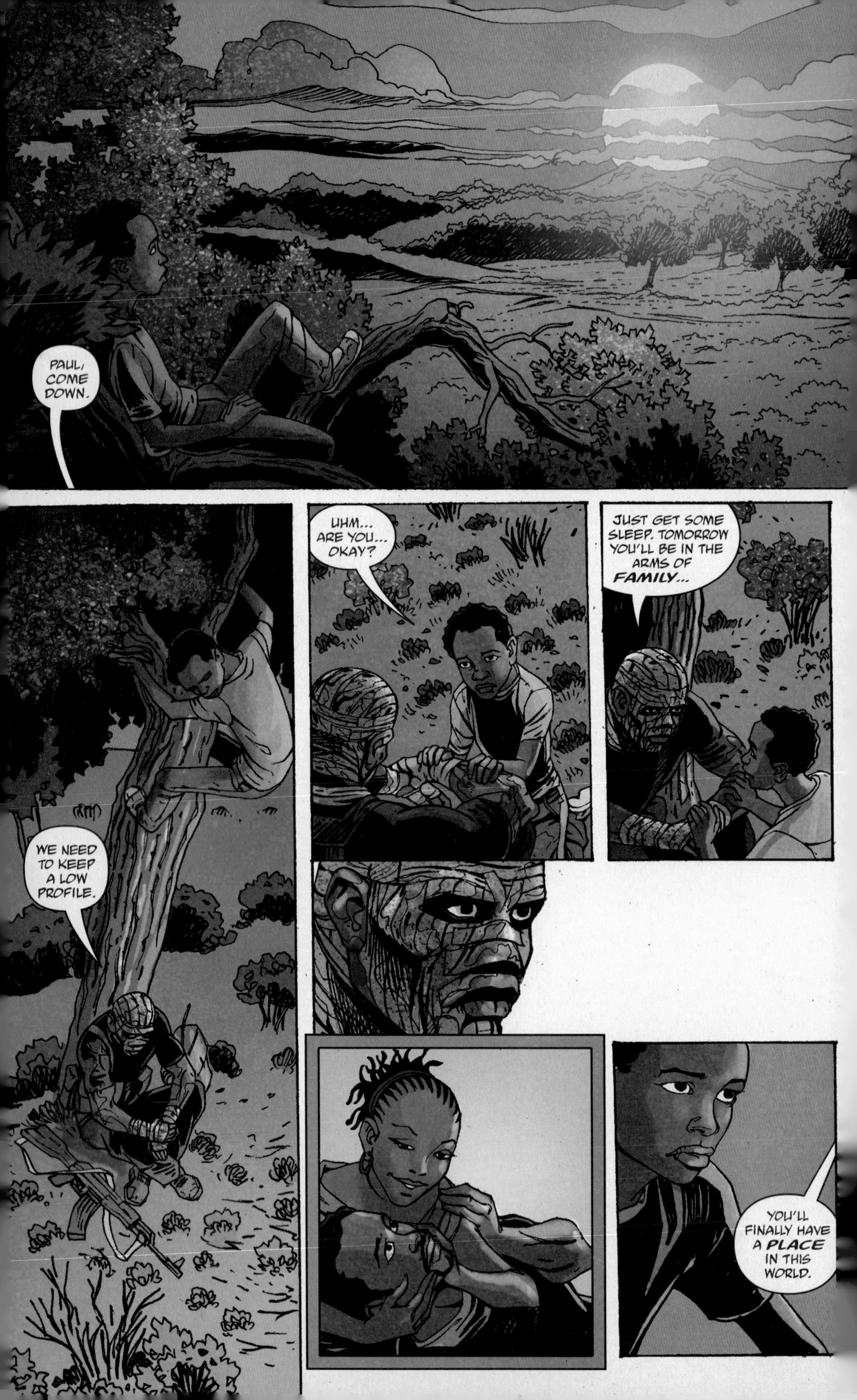
PAUL, COME DOWN.
WE NEED TO KEEP A LOW PROFILE.
UHM... ARE YOU... OKAY?
JUST GET SOME SLEEP. TOMORROW YOU'LL BE IN THE ARMS OF FAMILY...
YOU'LL FINALLY HAVE A PLACE IN THIS WORLD.

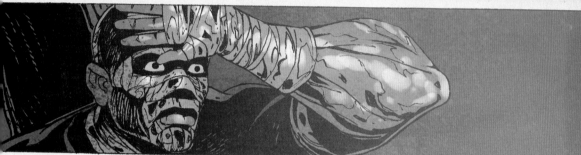

I'M
SORRY...

I--I KNOW
I KILLED THOSE
INNOCENT PEOPLE
ON THAT TRUCK...I
KNOW I SHOULD
SUFFER...

WHERE
ARE WE
GOING?

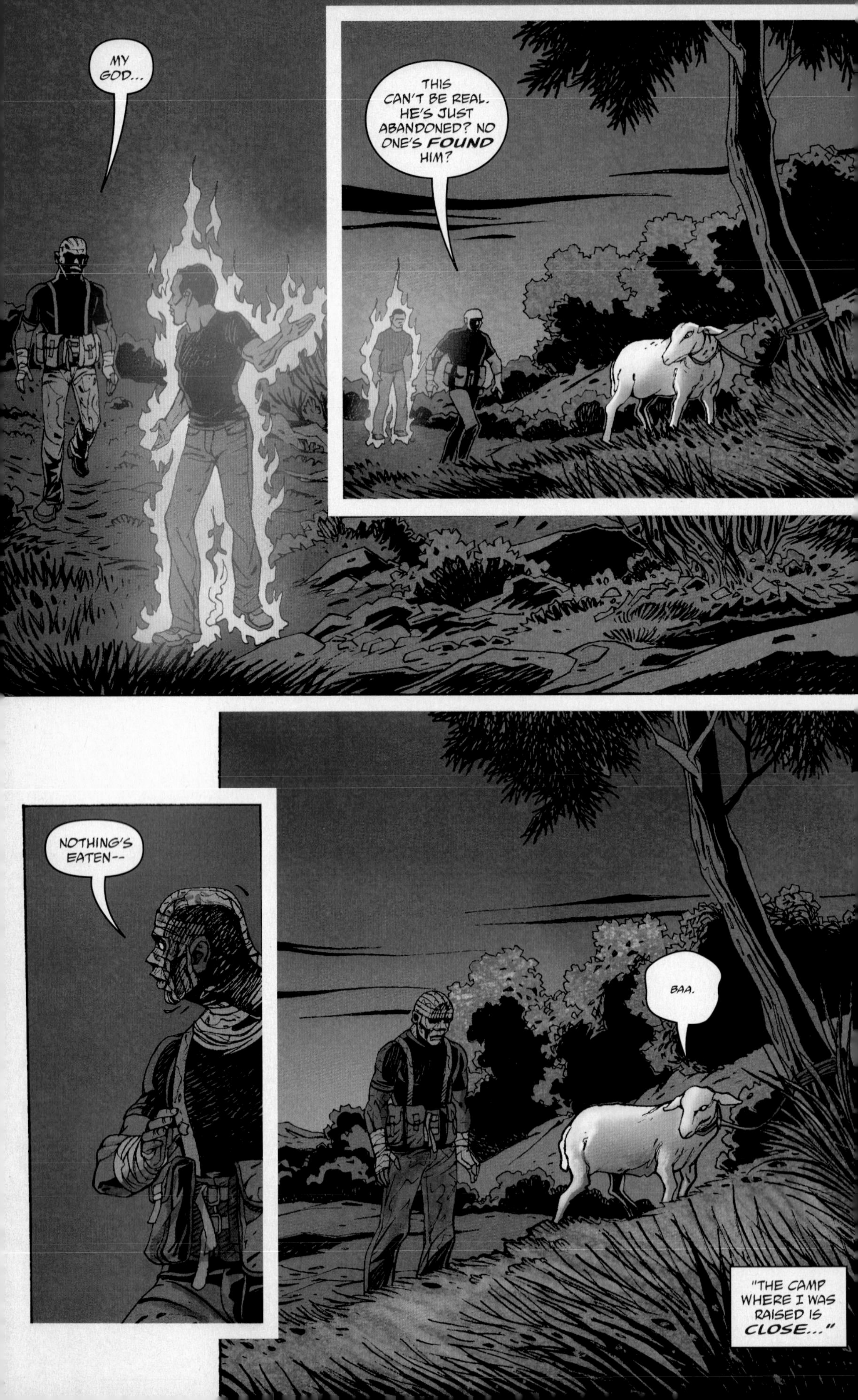
MY GOD...
THIS CAN'T BE REAL. HE'S JUST ABANDONED? NO ONE'S FOUND HIM?
NOTHING'S EATEN--
BAA.
"THE CAMP WHERE I WAS RAISED IS CLOSE..."

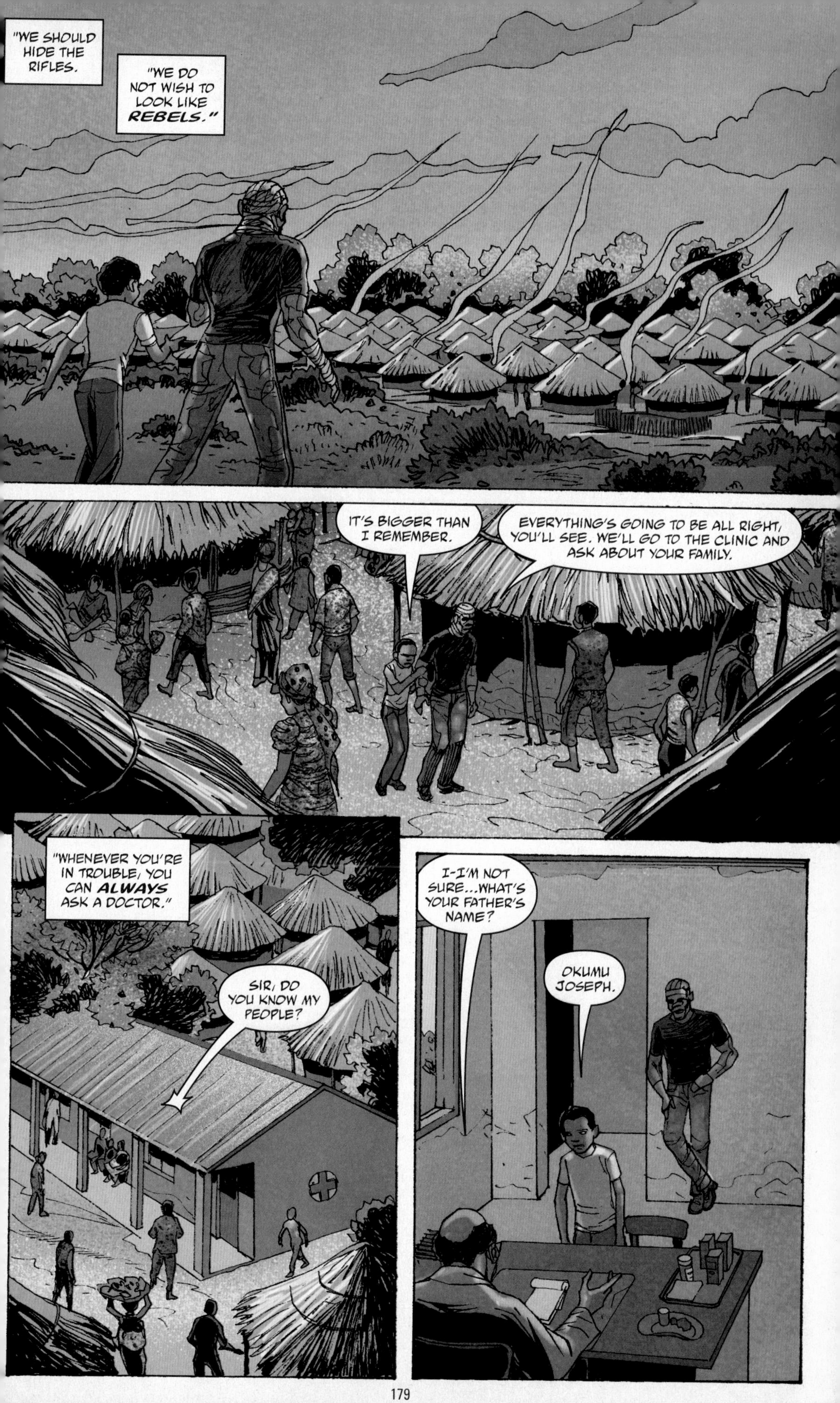
"WE SHOULD HIDE THE RIFLES.
"WE DO NOT WISH TO LOOK LIKE REBELS."
IT'S BIGGER THAN I REMEMBER.
EVERYTHING'S GOING TO BE ALL RIGHT, YOU'LL SEE. WE'LL GO TO THE CLINIC AND ASK ABOUT YOUR FAMILY.
"WHENEVER YOU'RE IN TROUBLE, YOU CAN ALWAYS ASK A DOCTOR."
SIR, DO YOU KNOW MY PEOPLE?
I-I'M NOT SURE...WHAT'S YOUR FATHER'S NAME?
OKUMU JOSEPH.

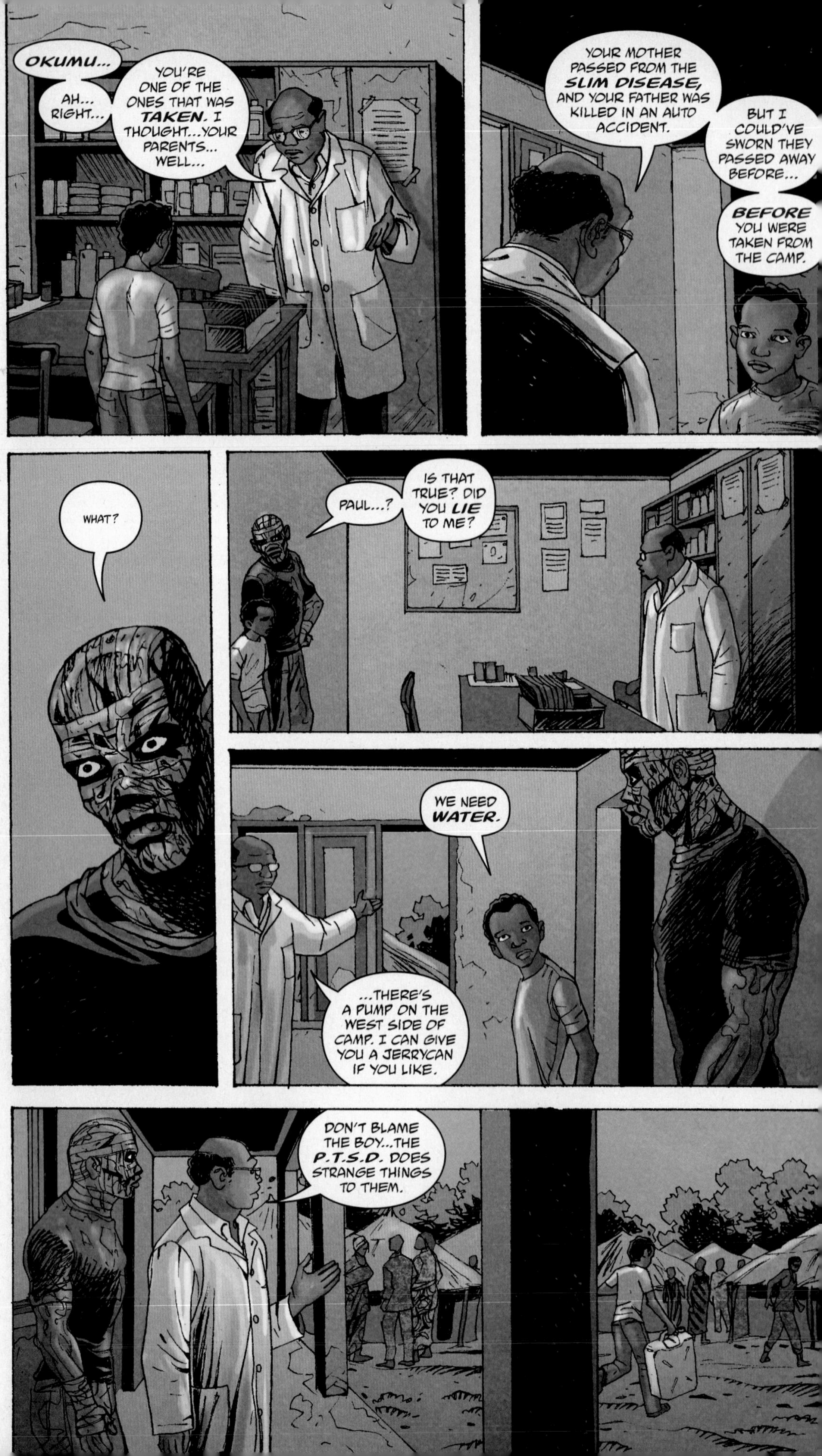

OKUMU...
AH... RIGHT...
YOU'RE ONE OF THE ONES THAT WAS TAKEN. I THOUGHT...YOUR PARENTS... WELL...
YOUR MOTHER PASSED FROM THE SLIM DISEASE, AND YOUR FATHER WAS KILLED IN AN AUTO ACCIDENT.
BUT I COULD'VE SWORN THEY PASSED AWAY BEFORE...
BEFORE YOU WERE TAKEN FROM THE CAMP.
WHAT?
PAUL...?
IS THAT TRUE? DID YOU LIE TO ME?
WE NEED WATER.
...THERE'S A PUMP ON THE WEST SIDE OF CAMP. I CAN GIVE YOU A JERRYCAN IF YOU LIKE.
DON'T BLAME THE BOY...THE P.T.S.D. DOES STRANGE THINGS TO THEM.

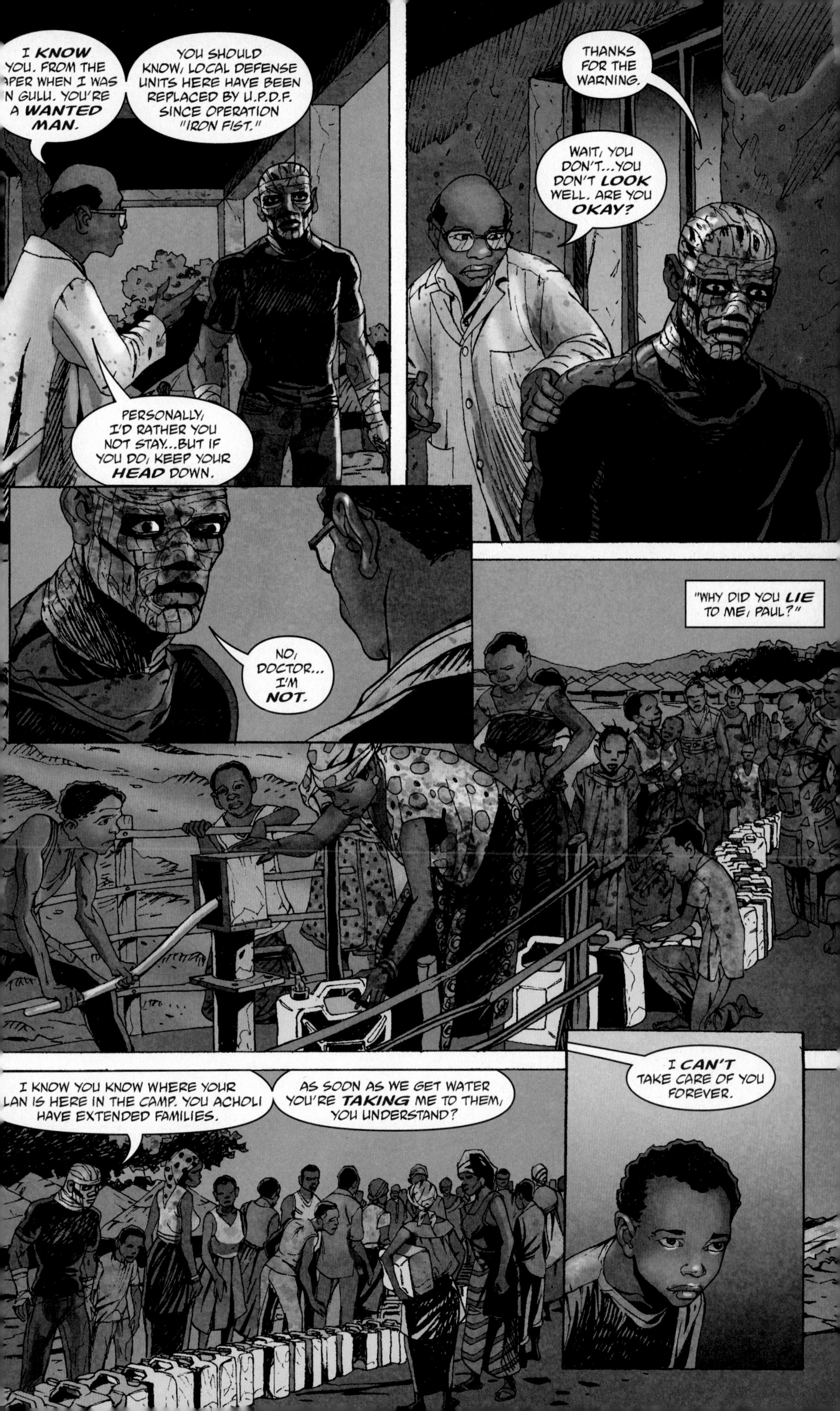
I KNOW YOU. FROM THE APER WHEN I WAS N GULU. YOU'RE A WANTED MAN.
YOU SHOULD KNOW, LOCAL DEFENSE UNITS HERE HAVE BEEN REPLACED BY U.P.D.F. SINCE OPERATION "IRON FIST."
PERSONALLY, I'D RATHER YOU NOT STAY...BUT IF YOU DO, KEEP YOUR HEAD DOWN.
THANKS FOR THE WARNING.
WAIT, YOU DON'T...YOU DON'T LOOK WELL. ARE YOU OKAY?
NO, DOCTOR... I'M NOT.
"WHY DID YOU LIE TO ME, PAUL?"
I KNOW YOU KNOW WHERE YOUR LAN IS HERE IN THE CAMP. YOU ACHOLI HAVE EXTENDED FAMILIES.
AS SOON AS WE GET WATER YOU'RE TAKING ME TO THEM, YOU UNDERSTAND?
I CAN'T TAKE CARE OF YOU FOREVER.

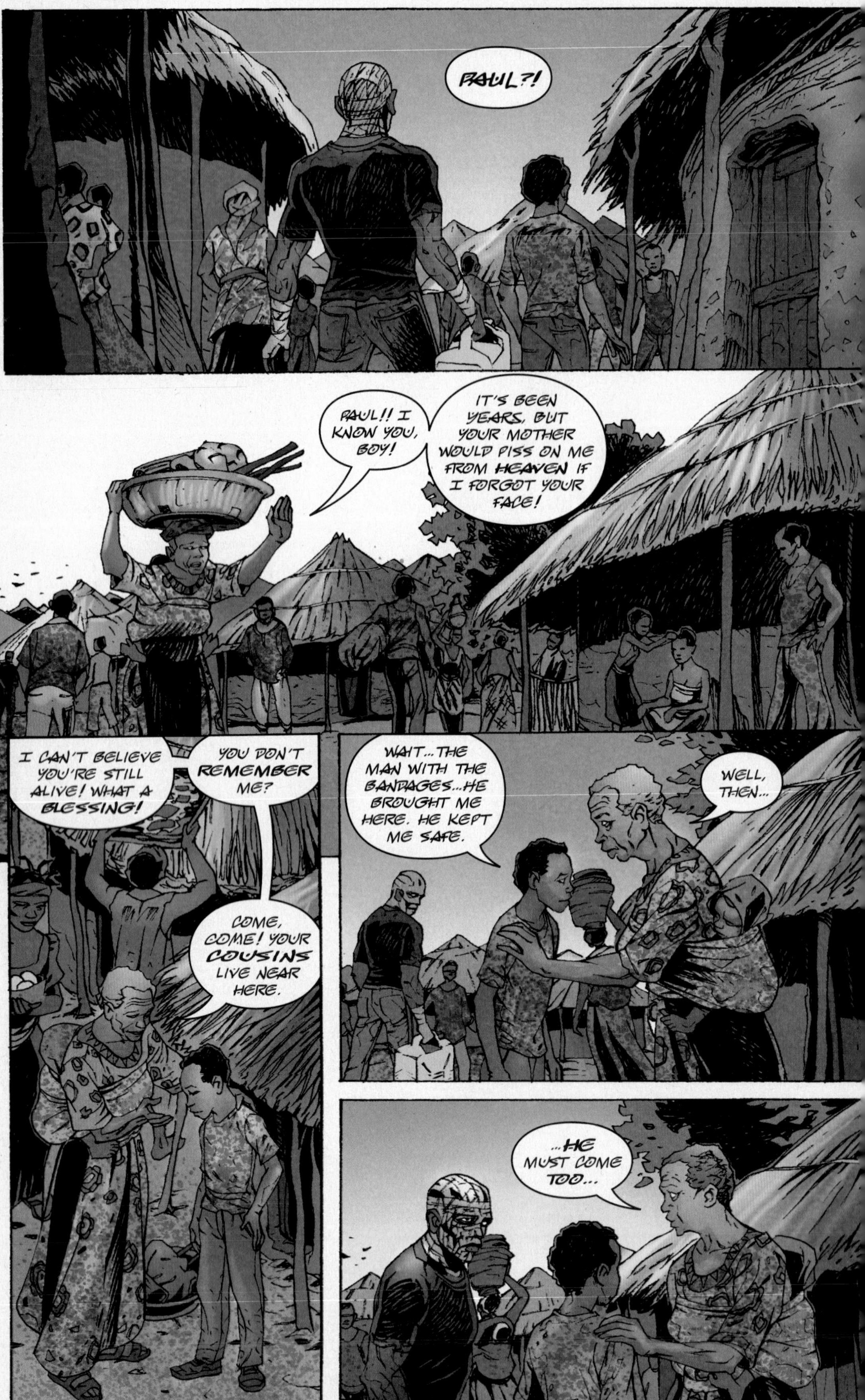
PAUL?!
PAUL!! I KNOW YOU, BOY!
IT'S BEEN YEARS, BUT YOUR MOTHER WOULD PISS ON ME FROM HEAVEN IF I FORGOT YOUR FACE!
I CAN'T BELIEVE YOU'RE STILL ALIVE! WHAT A BLESSING!
YOU DON'T REMEMBER ME?
COME, COME! YOUR COUSINS LIVE NEAR HERE.
WAIT... THE MAN WITH THE BANDAGES... HE BROUGHT ME HERE. HE KEPT ME SAFE.
WELL, THEN...
...HE MUST COME TOO...

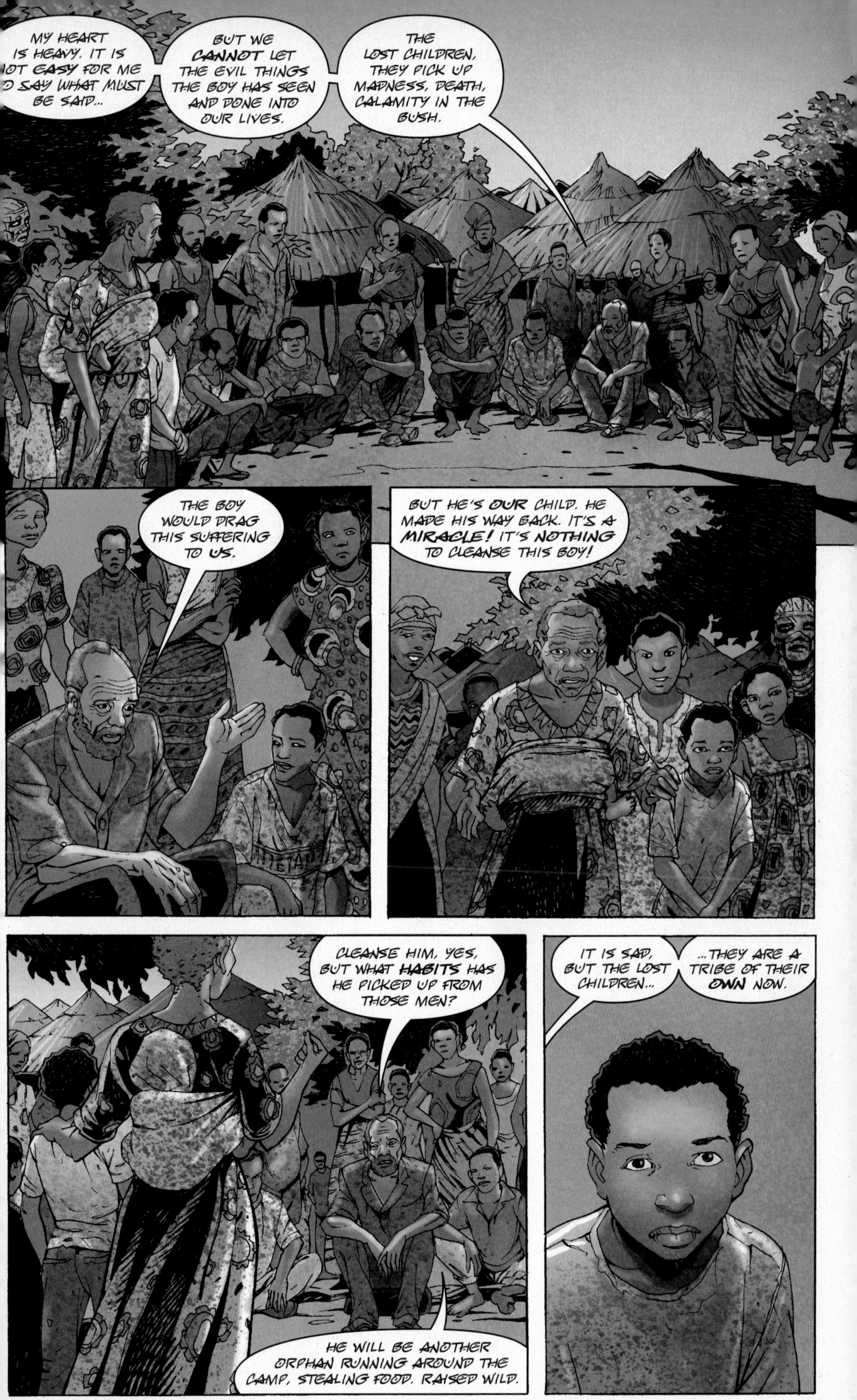
MY HEART IS HEAVY. IT IS NOT EASY FOR ME TO SAY WHAT MUST BE SAID...
BUT WE CANNOT LET THE EVIL THINGS THE BOY HAS SEEN AND DONE INTO OUR LIVES.
THE LOST CHILDREN, THEY PICK UP MADNESS, DEATH, CALAMITY IN THE BUSH.
THE BOY WOULD DRAG THIS SUFFERING TO US.
BUT HE'S OUR CHILD. HE MADE HIS WAY BACK. IT'S A MIRACLE! IT'S NOTHING TO CLEANSE THIS BOY!
CLEANSE HIM, YES, BUT WHAT HABITS HAS HE PICKED UP FROM THOSE MEN?
HE WILL BE ANOTHER ORPHAN RUNNING AROUND THE CAMP, STEALING FOOD. RAISED WILD.
IT IS SAD, BUT THE LOST CHILDREN...
...THEY ARE A TRIBE OF THEIR OWN NOW.

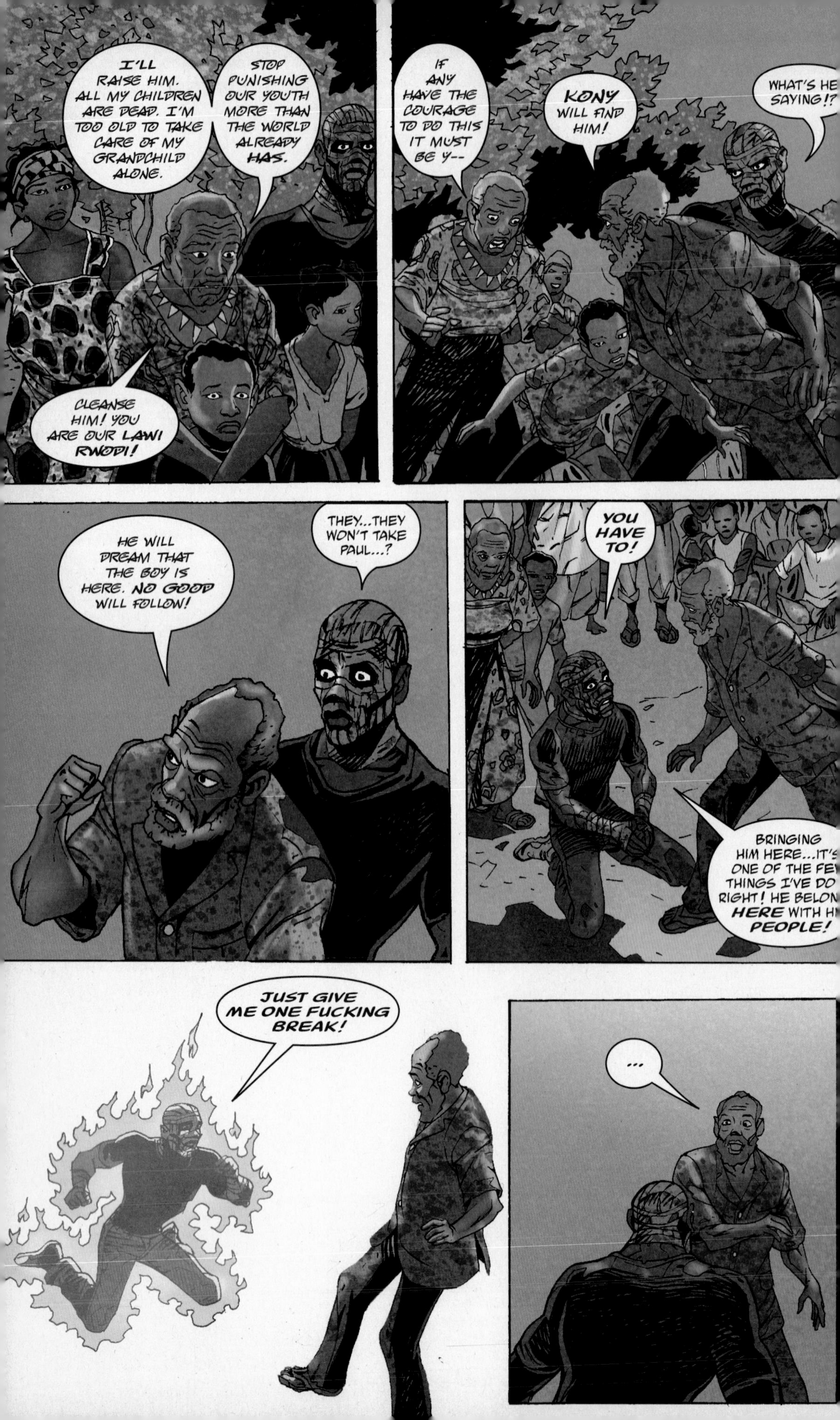
I'LL RAISE HIM. ALL MY CHILDREN ARE DEAD. I'M TOO OLD TO TAKE CARE OF MY GRANDCHILD ALONE.
STOP PUNISHING OUR YOUTH MORE THAN THE WORLD ALREADY HAS.
CLEANSE HIM! YOU ARE OUR LAWI RWODI!
IF ANY HAVE THE COURAGE TO DO THIS IT MUST BE Y--
KONY WILL FIND HIM!
WHAT'S HE SAYING!?
HE WILL DREAM THAT THE BOY IS HERE. NO GOOD WILL FOLLOW!
THEY...THEY WON'T TAKE PAUL...?
YOU HAVE TO!
BRINGING HIM HERE...IT'S ONE OF THE FE THINGS I'VE DO RIGHT! HE BELON HERE WITH H PEOPLE!
JUST GIVE ME ONE FUCKING BREAK!
...

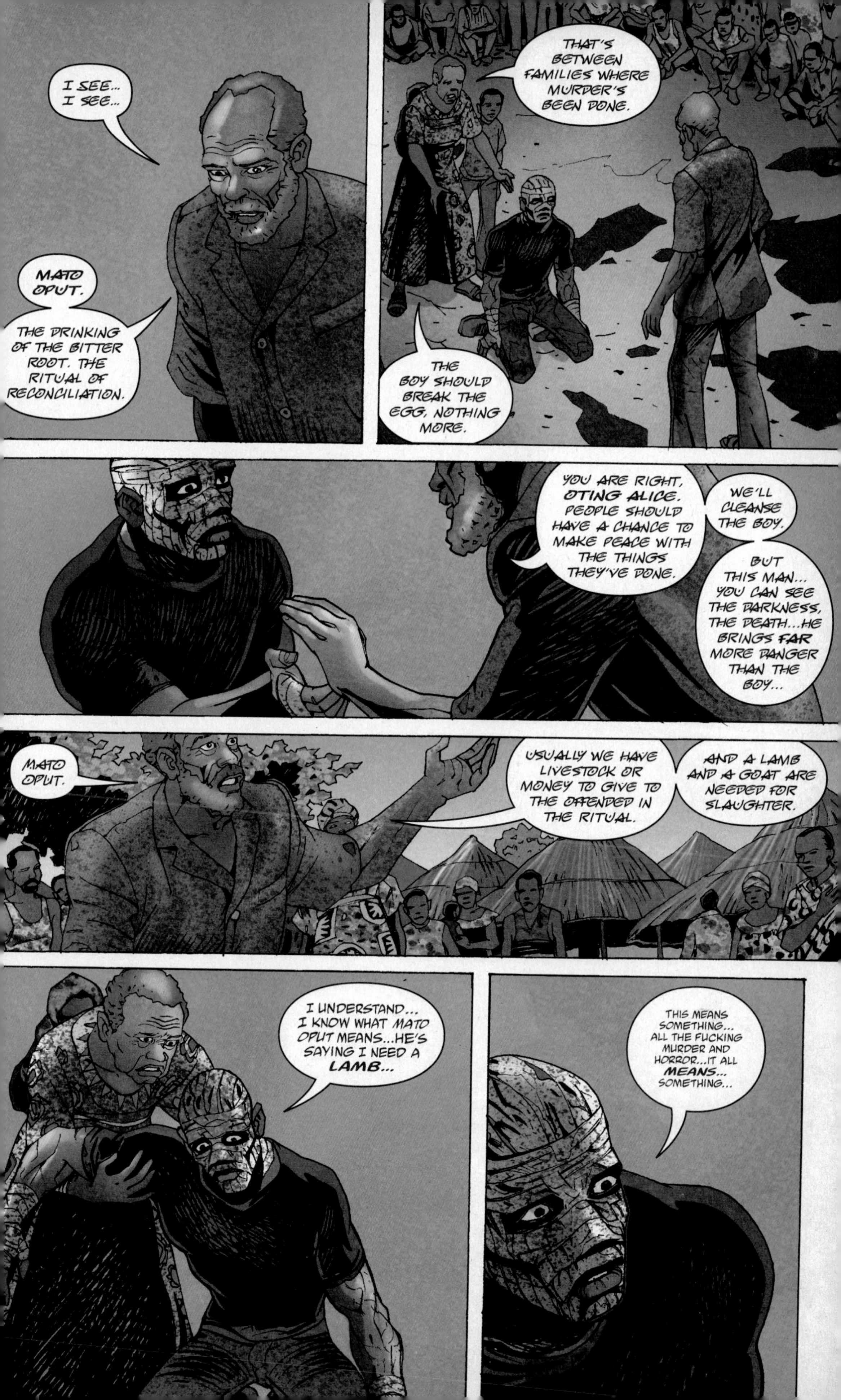
I SEE... I SEE...
MATO OPUT.
THE DRINKING OF THE BITTER ROOT. THE RITUAL OF RECONCILIATION.
THAT'S BETWEEN FAMILIES WHERE MURDER'S BEEN DONE.
THE BOY SHOULD BREAK THE EGG, NOTHING MORE.
YOU ARE RIGHT, OTING ALICE. PEOPLE SHOULD HAVE A CHANCE TO MAKE PEACE WITH THE THINGS THEY'VE DONE.
WE'LL CLEANSE THE BOY.
BUT THIS MAN... YOU CAN SEE THE DARKNESS, THE DEATH...HE BRINGS FAR MORE DANGER THAN THE BOY...
MATO OPUT.
USUALLY WE HAVE LIVESTOCK OR MONEY TO GIVE TO THE OFFENDED IN THE RITUAL.
AND A LAMB AND A GOAT ARE NEEDED FOR SLAUGHTER.
I UNDERSTAND... I KNOW WHAT MATO OPUT MEANS...HE'S SAYING I NEED A LAMB...
THIS MEANS SOMETHING... ALL THE FUCKING MURDER AND HORROR...IT ALL MEANS... SOMETHING...

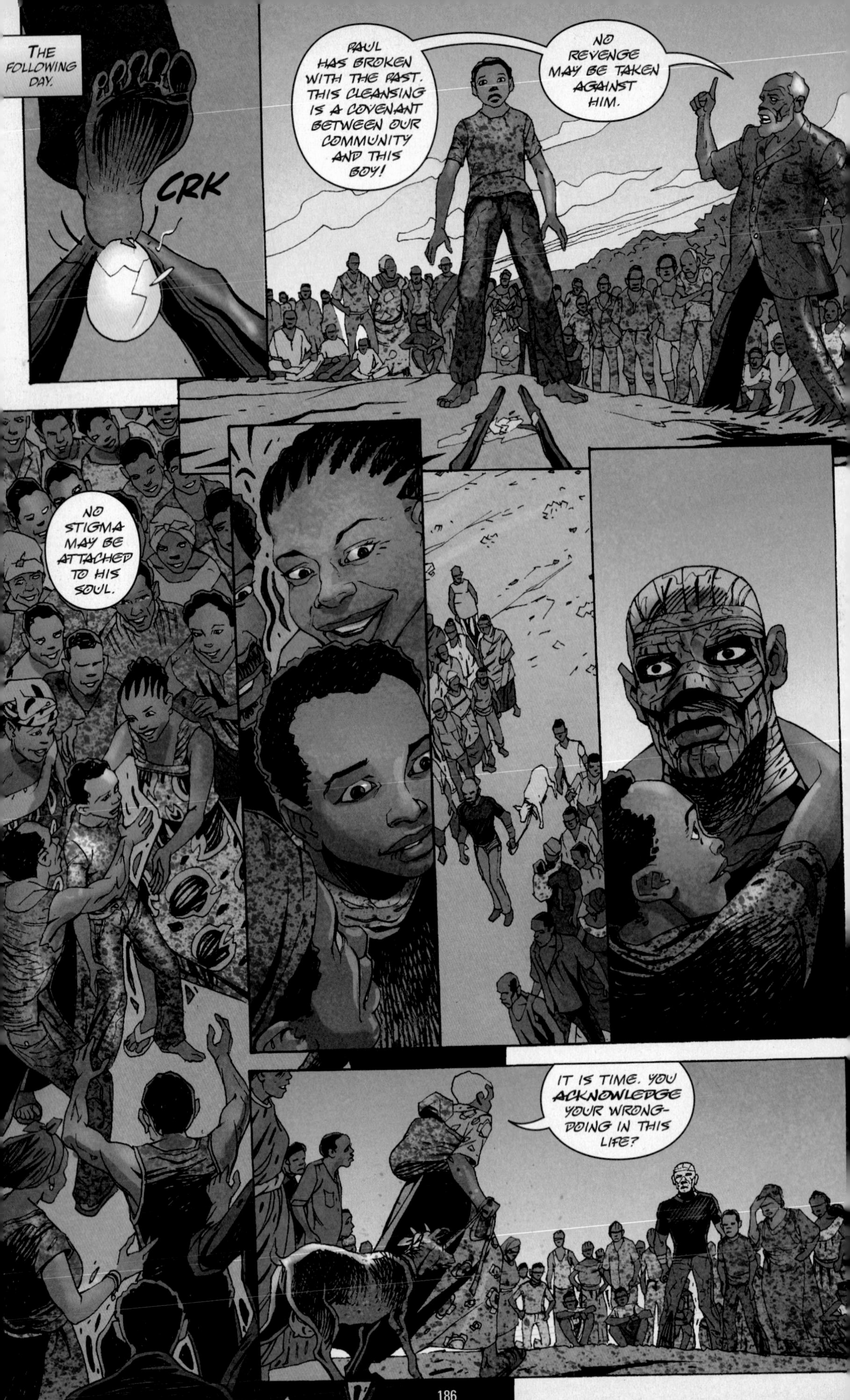
THE FOLLOWING DAY.
CRK
PAUL HAS BROKEN WITH THE PAST. THIS CLEANSING IS A COVENANT BETWEEN OUR COMMUNITY AND THIS BOY!
NO REVENGE MAY BE TAKEN AGAINST HIM.
NO STIGMA MAY BE ATTACHED TO HIS SOUL.
IT IS TIME. YOU ACKNOWLEDGE YOUR WRONG-DOING IN THIS LIFE?

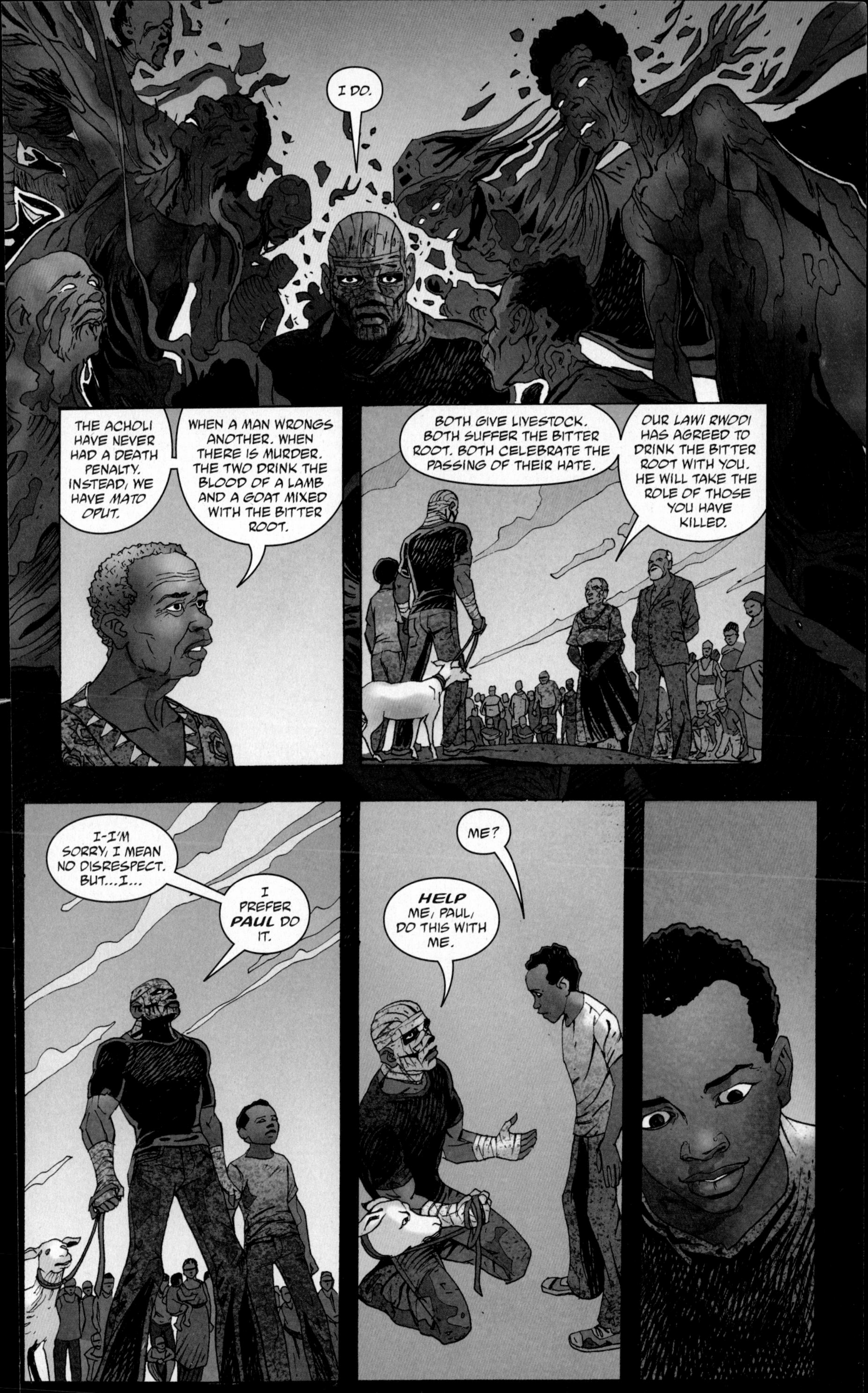
I DO.
THE ACHOLI HAVE NEVER HAD A DEATH PENALTY. INSTEAD, WE HAVE MATO OPUT.
WHEN A MAN WRONGS ANOTHER. WHEN THERE IS MURDER. THE TWO DRINK THE BLOOD OF A LAMB AND A GOAT MIXED WITH THE BITTER ROOT.
BOTH GIVE LIVESTOCK. BOTH SUFFER THE BITTER ROOT. BOTH CELEBRATE THE PASSING OF THEIR HATE.
OUR LAWI RWODI HAS AGREED TO DRINK THE BITTER ROOT WITH YOU. HE WILL TAKE THE ROLE OF THOSE YOU HAVE KILLED.
I-I'M SORRY, I MEAN NO DISRESPECT. BUT...I...
I PREFER **PAUL** DO IT.
ME?
HELP ME, PAUL, DO THIS WITH ME.

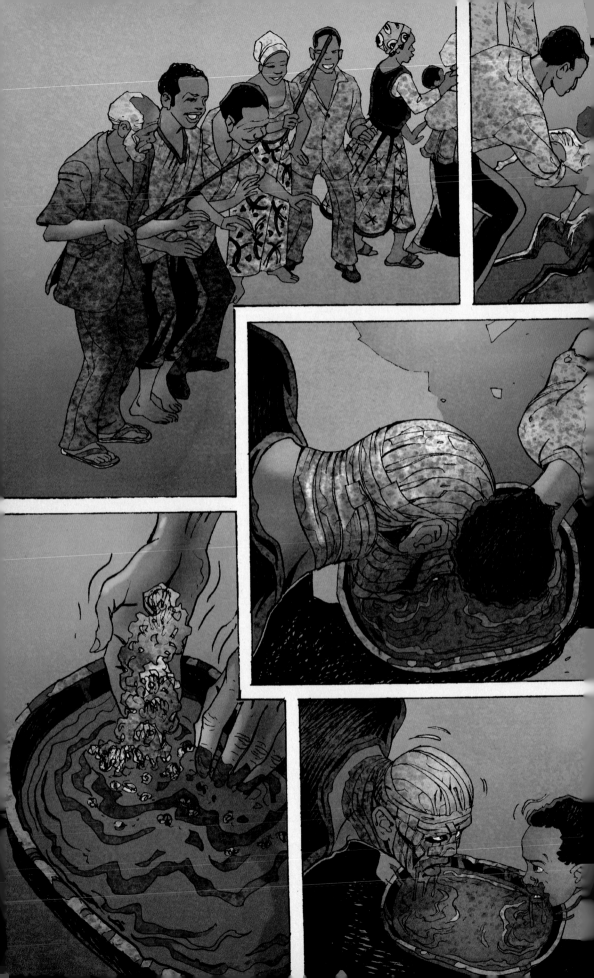

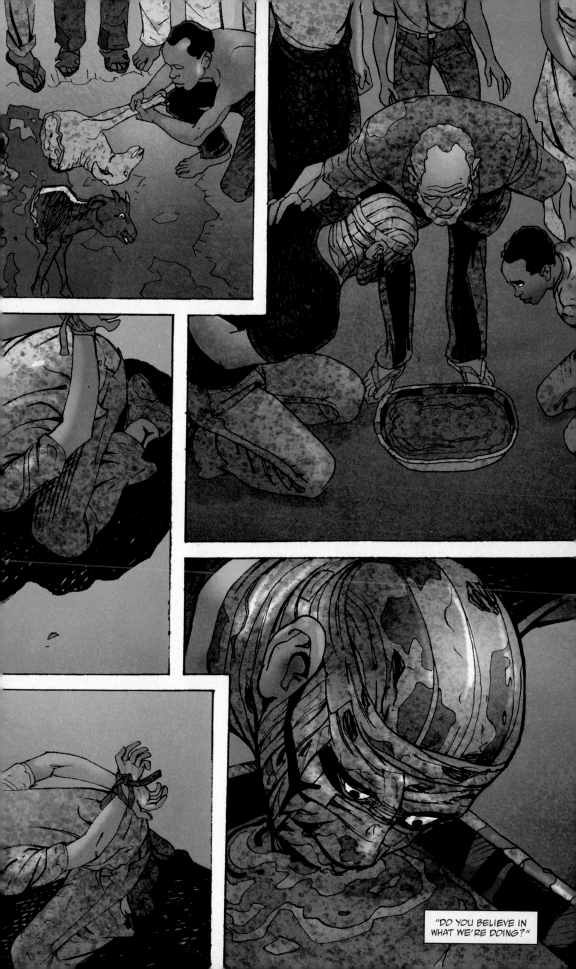

"DO YOU BELIEVE IN
WHAT WE'RE DOING?"

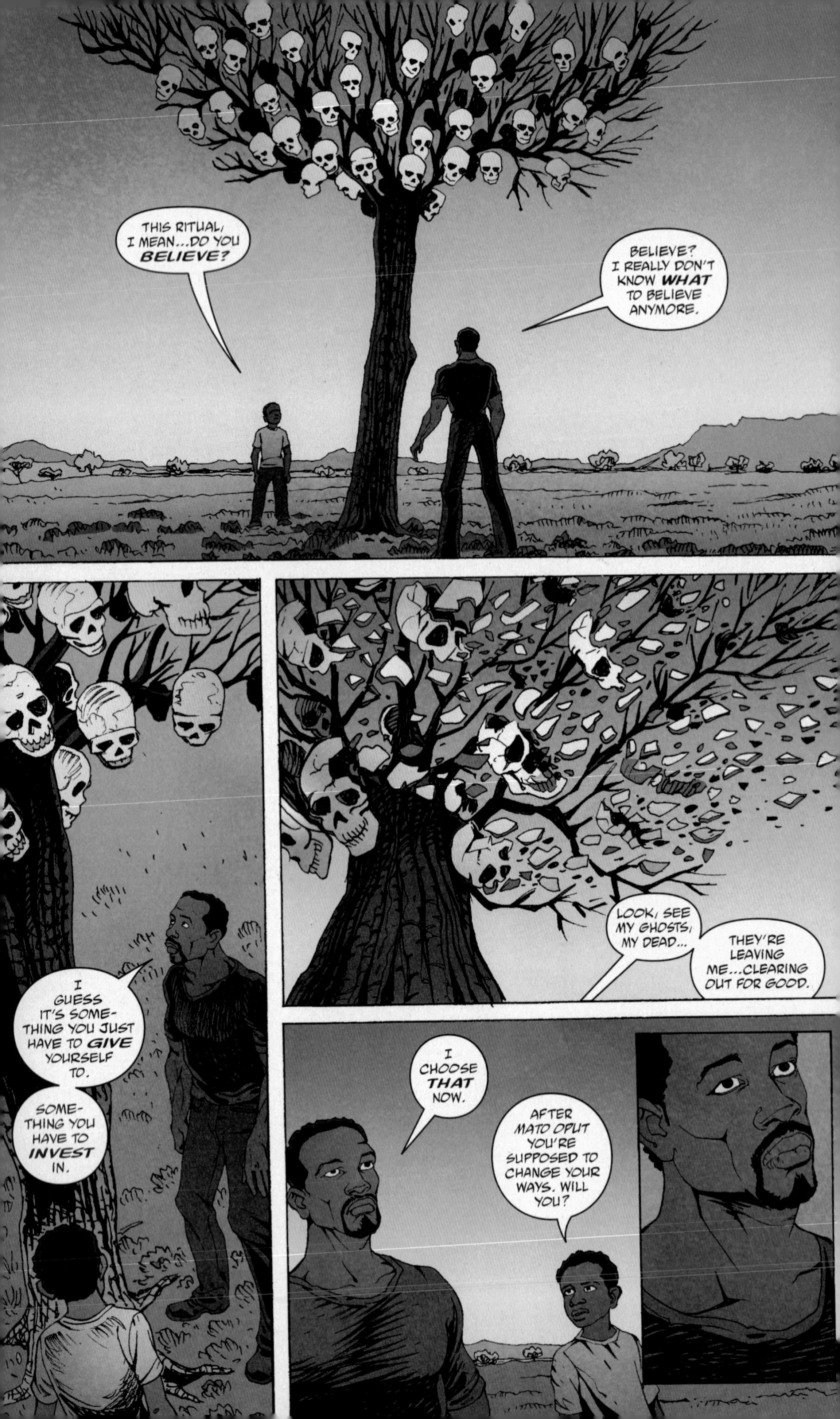

THIS RITUAL, I MEAN...DO YOU BELIEVE?
BELIEVE? I REALLY DON'T KNOW WHAT TO BELIEVE ANYMORE.
I GUESS IT'S SOMETHING YOU JUST HAVE TO GIVE YOURSELF TO.
SOMETHING YOU HAVE TO INVEST IN.
LOOK, SEE MY GHOSTS, MY DEAD...
THEY'RE LEAVING ME...CLEARING OUT FOR GOOD.
I CHOOSE THAT NOW.
AFTER MATO OPUT YOU'RE SUPPOSED TO CHANGE YOUR WAYS. WILL YOU?

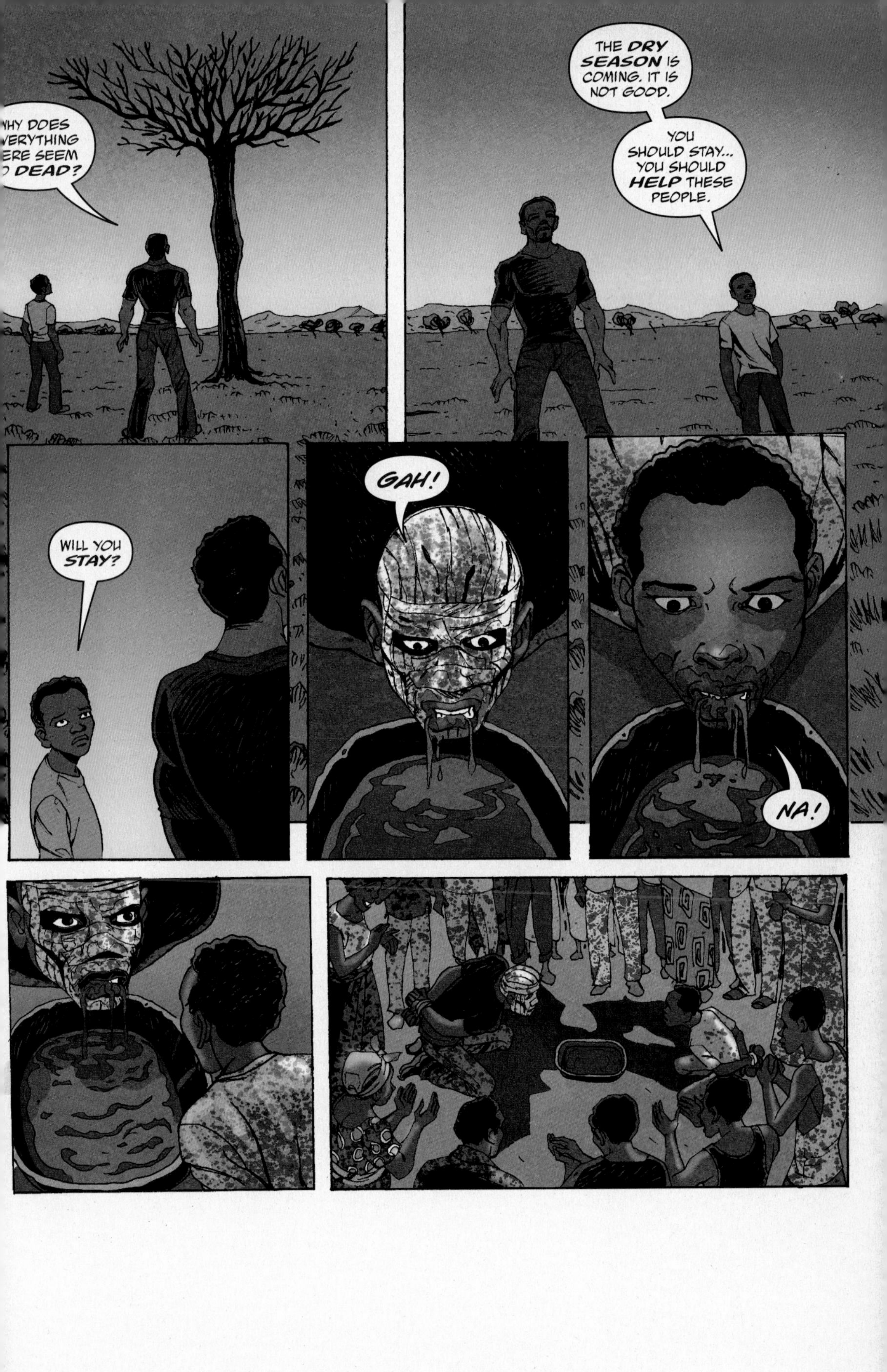

HY DOES
ERYTHING
ERE SEEM
 DEAD?
THE DRY SEASON IS COMING. IT IS NOT GOOD.
YOU SHOULD STAY... YOU SHOULD HELP THESE PEOPLE.
WILL YOU STAY?
GAH!
NA!

AFTERWORD

It was early in the life of this series when we started kicking around the idea for finding an artist from approximately the same region as the book takes place to fill in for Alberto when the time would finally come for the Italian stallion to have a much-needed break. But locating the perfect person for the job was no easy task. A lack of exposure to artists from that region of the world and the extremely jarring, culturally specific art styles of those we did find made the search difficult to say the least. But eventually we did discover our man — Pat Masioni, from the Democratic Republic of Congo (DRC). He's from a little further west than where our book occurs, but once you hear Pat's story, in his own words, you'll understand why he was the best choice for this mini-arc.

Let me say in advance that Pat wasn't entirely comfortable talking about the harder aspects of his life, and it took some coaxing to get as much from him as we have. Also, a very special thanks to Antonia Neyrins, a personal friend of Pat's and, now, ours, for assisting with all of our translation needs.

— Joshua Dysart

* * *

My name is Patrice Masioni Makamba. I am Congolese, born in Mikusi, Bandundu province in the early 1960s, to the Mbala tribe, and I do not exactly know when I first started drawing — from the moment I could hold a pen, I imagine.

I published my first drawing at 14, supported and recognized by two Spanish priests who helped my family financially support my studies.

Through their grace I learned painting, ceramics and sculpture in Kinshasa and eventually created a ceramic bas-relief for the cathedral in anticipation of the first visit by Pope Jean Paul II there. These priests, they gave me the tools I needed to live, and I am deeply in their debt for this.

It was not long before I was a professional illustrator and doing quite well for myself. My books were big sellers, and my name was not unknown. Mostly I worked on religious books, but I also published political cartoons in newspapers.

Art had set me free from poverty and obscurity, but it wasn't long before it also brought me trouble. Over the course of my life as an artist in Kinshasa, DRC I was arrested on multiple occasions, sometimes by child soldiers. I have been beaten for my drawings. And yet, still, others suffered worse. People disappeared. People died. I have seen things no one should see, things I'll never forget. In 2002, after receiving death threats from people with the will and power to back them, I — literally overnight — fled for France and began the hard path of the political refugee. There was no time to consider this decision.

It was extremely difficult to start over in another country. My past, my family, my friends, my home and money, they were all gone. Over time I rebuilt a reputation as an illustrator in France, found an apartment and had my family join me, but it wasn't easy. The culture here is very different from my own (the French sense of humor is a mystery to me), the struggle to assimilate is constant, and it reminds me of how much I miss my home. I very much look forward to becoming a French Citizen so that I may return to DRC to visit, safe and free.

I have been very happy to be working on UNKNOWN SOLDIER. I can feel from inside the story. Sometimes, it reminds me of my past, and true situations I've seen with my own eyes. Joshua Dysart's script depicts a notable reality, and I feel free and expressive in drawing them, all while adding a touch of African style to the endeavor. I can only hope that American audiences come to care for the truths these stories speak to.

I can define myself as a politically engaged illustrator and a world citizen. I am proud that you have elected Barack Obama as your president, and I hope to visit and discover your country one day.

* * *

Pat Masioni started as a professional illustrator in the Democratic Republic of Congo, where his books sold more than 250,000 copies. Since arriving in France, he has published graphic novels on the war in Rwanda and has been illustrating "Samba Diallo," a well-known comic published in the French-speaking African magazine Planète jeunes.

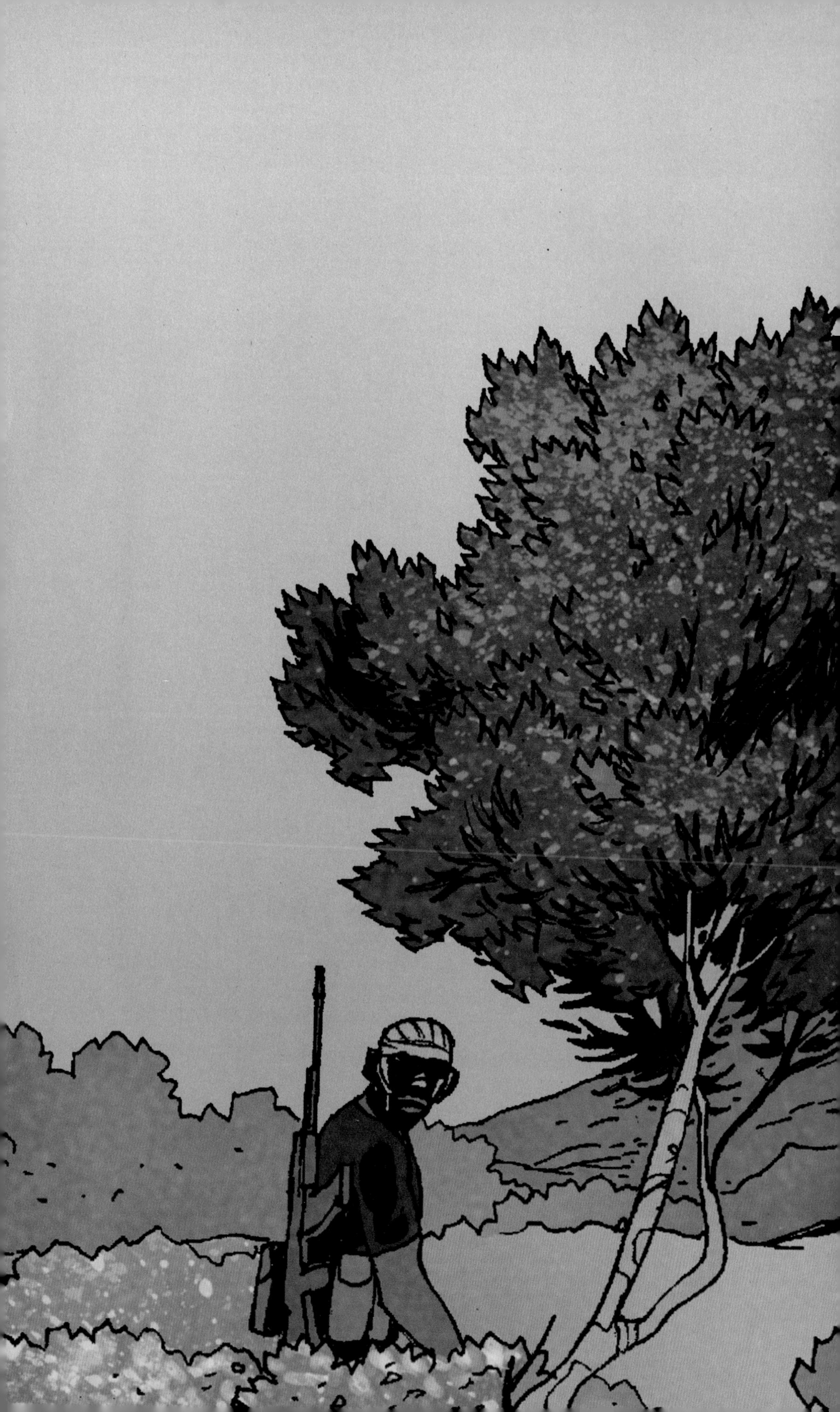

A CHRONOLOGICAL HISTORY OF THE WAR BETWEEN THE LRA AND THE UPDF

Sketches by Alberto Ponticelli

How did the war begin?

It's not an easy thing to answer. Like most conflicts, this war is part of a long cycle of violence and retaliation. What follows here is a reductive explanation of how northern Uganda became a war zone for over two decades, resulting in millions of displaced human beings, tens of thousands of kidnapped children forced into combat and "sex-slave" roles, and leaving virtually an entire population with Post Traumatic Stress Disorder.

To fully understand, we'll have to start back during the infancy of colonization. British explorers, searching for the source of the Nile, arrived in the aggregate kingdoms now known as Uganda in the 1860s – long after the coasts of the continent had been exposed to white men. True to Western form, the British proceeded to conquer, but not with the gun; that would come later. First they conquered with the Bible. Protestant missionaries arrived in 1877, Catholics in 1879, beginning the complex interweaving of Christianity and traditional faith that is such a huge feature of the LRA mindset. (As a side note: the presence of Islamic faith in the region is a holdover from the arrival of Swahili slave traders in the 1830s.)

In 1893, through political maneuvering and military force, the **Kingdom of Buganda** in the south was placed under British protectorateship. Inside of a year, British military expansionism swallowed the kingdoms of **Banyoro**, **Lango** and **Acholi**. The "Uganda Protectorate" included four separate kingdoms and a myriad of clan cultures. The British deposed kings and leaders and installed their own governors from **Buganda**. The British encouraged political/economic development in the south, while the Acholi and other northern groups had their development virtually stopped. So it was that the northern ethnic groups quickly became the manual labor and military force of the new collage nation, creating a military ethnocracy and installing a systemic tendency for militant aggression in the north. By 1900 the British had created "Uganda" – a country divided against itself – and set the stage for constant struggle between northern ethnic groups and the dominant kingdom of Buganda to the south.

Some 70 years later, in October of 1962 Uganda claimed its independence. Its haphazard inception had finally caused the nation to fragment along religious and ethnic lines to the point of chaos, and the British had retreated. What followed was a series of power and identity battles for the nation's soul. Among the first leaders was a man named **Apolo Milton Obote**, a Lango, from the north, and a Protestant. **Idi Amin Dada** in 1971, also a northerner, but a Muslim, deposed him. Then, in 1979 a group of exiled Ugandans with the help of **Tanzanian** forces, overthrew Amin in the **Uganda-Tanzania War** and Obote came back to power in what many viewed as a rigged election.

The perception of unfair electoral behavior led to ethnic civil war. From this tumult arose several guerrilla rebellions. One led by a man named **Yoweri Kaguta Museveni** in 1981 (the current President of Uganda). Approximately 100,000 people died as a result of fighting between Obote's Army and the guerrilla factions during **"The War in the Bush."**

In 1986, Museveni, a born-again Christian from the southwest, took the capital. By March his forces had occupied Acholiland in the north, the region where our story takes place. Now, former government soldiers from Acholiland who had sought sanctuary in southern Sudan moved to get Museveni's troops out of the north, their homeland, and began fighting for Acholi rights in the essentially Buganda-governed nation. This resistance to the southern leader Museveni spread, and several rebel groups appeared.

Among these groups came **Alice Auma's HOLY SPIRIT MOVEMENT** (HSM). Alice was an Acholi spirit-medium who claimed to channel a dead Italian army officer called "Lakwena" (messenger) which the Acholi believed to be a manifestation of the Christian Holy Spirit. This started a trend of Mystic-Christian military leaders in Acholiland, which would culminate, just one year later, in the emergence of Christian extremist **Joseph Kony**.

In 1987 Alice Auma's group disbanded after an unsuccessful attempt to march on the Ugandan capital. The remnants of the HSM fell into banditry as members drifted away or were defeated by government forces and other rebels. But from the ashes of the HSM came Kony, a 26-year-old Acholi who claimed he was the spokesperson for God and a medium of the Christian Holy Spirit. Superstition was at the heart of his rhetoric and, among other things, he had his followers use tree oil to ward off bullets and evil.

His group, the **Lord's Resistance Army** (LRA), operated as a guerrilla organization attempting to establish a theocratic government based on the Christian Bible and the Ten Commandments in Uganda. The LRA reached an astounding level of brutality under Kony's command, participating in sadistic murder, abduction, mutilation, sexual enslavement, and forcing children to operate as soldiers. As of 2006 they had abducted an estimated 60,000 people.

HISTORY OF THE LRA (THE FIRST DECADE)

After an unsuccessful push south towards the capital, Kony and his LRA began raiding Acholi villages (their own people) in an effort to show that Museveni was unable, or unwilling, to protect the populace. It is not certain when Kony began abducting children for indoctrination into military service, but it's most likely after he started to lose support among the Acholi themselves.

Between 1987 and 1991 the LRA remained active, but President Museveni seemed barely interested. The most cynical say that the war was to his political advantage. It destabilized the north where he had little support to begin with, so the Acholi were less and less able to participate in the political process. There was also some speculation that Museveni was

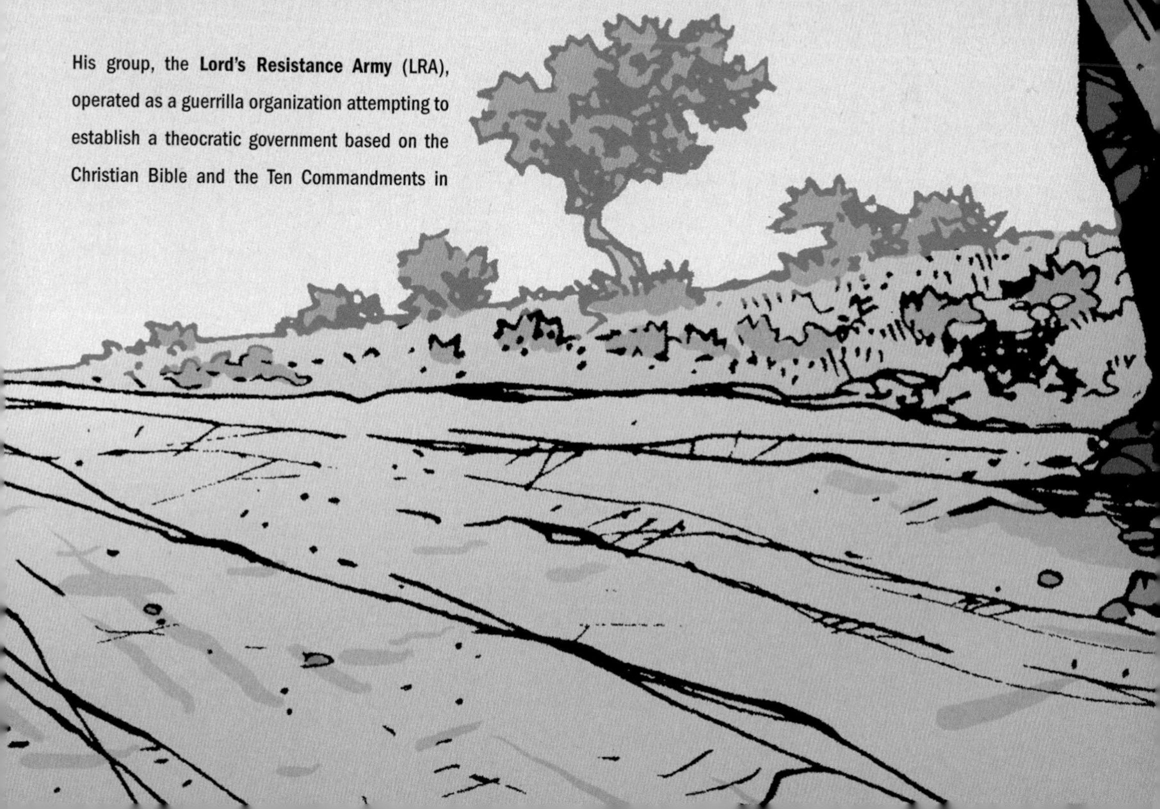

receiving aid to fight the rebels from the **African Union** and other nations - aid that he was funneling into development of the south and even, possibly, into his own pockets.

In the '90s the United States began the **Front Line States Initiative**, in which **Uganda**, **Ethiopia** and **Eritrea** were identified as linchpins in containing **Sudan**. Uganda was suddenly provided "defensive, non-lethal military assistance" against Sudan-backed insurgencies. In March of 1991 President Museveni, ever subservient to Western powers, launched "Operation North" in the hopes of stabilizing the LRA activity along the Sudan border. "**Operation North**" armed local Acholi villages, whose opinion had now turned firmly against the LRA (but not in favor of Museveni). This flooded even more weapons into the region. In retaliation Kony began to systematically massacre and mutilate. He, descending into paranoia like Amin before him, suspected everyone around him of secretly being a government supporter. The suffering of the Acholi population was taken to the next level.

From 1991 to '94 the LRA became more and more violent. Kony himself vacillated between mad religious ravings and making actual, reasonable demands on behalf of the Acholi people. But his organization reflected his true nature: cruel, ambitious and unreasonable. By 1994 the Acholi had begun to flee their villages, moving en masse into Sudan or central Uganda. There began to be talk among the conspiratorial-minded that Museveni was selling off the abandoned land.

In 1993 a member of Uganda's parliament, an Acholi woman named **Betty Bigombe**, did the extraordinary. She went out into the bush and initiated peace talks with Kony on her own. For this she was named Uganda's "Woman of the Year."

In February 1994, however, Bigombe's peace talks failed. Many reported that Museveni or his army sabotaged the talks. This prompted further the belief among the Acholi that Museveni was profiting both politically and financially from their misery. After the peace-talk failure, Kony began to establish bases in southern Sudan. In April, Uganda broke off diplomatic ties with Sudan for aiding the LRA.

October 1996, ten years into the conflict, 200 LRA rebels raided St. Mary's College in the Aboke area, abducting 139 girls. Many were given to LRA commanders as "wives." Others died in captivity. This single incident was the first from the conflict to be reported in the global media. The Ugandan government began forcibly moving virtually the entire Acholi population onto IDP camps "for their protection." But the camps were overcrowded, disease infested and totally susceptible to LRA attacks. Suspicion that this was really about further Acholi disenfranchisement as well as a land grab by Museveni ran rampant.

The situation at this point was not designed for an easy solution.

HISTORY OF THE LRA (THE SECOND DECADE)

By 1997 the Acholi had been forced off their land and onto some 200 Internally Displaced Persons camps across the north of Uganda. Despite the need for troops to stabilize this region, most of the Ugandan army was then sent to **Zaire** to take part in a conflict that would change the name of that country to the **Democratic Republic of Congo**. Uganda was interested in deposing the CIA/Belgium propped up leader **Mobutu** who had proved immensely unstable.

A year later Ugandan troops again intervened in the newly named DRC, but this time on the side of rebels seeking to overthrow the new leader that they helped install. Why would

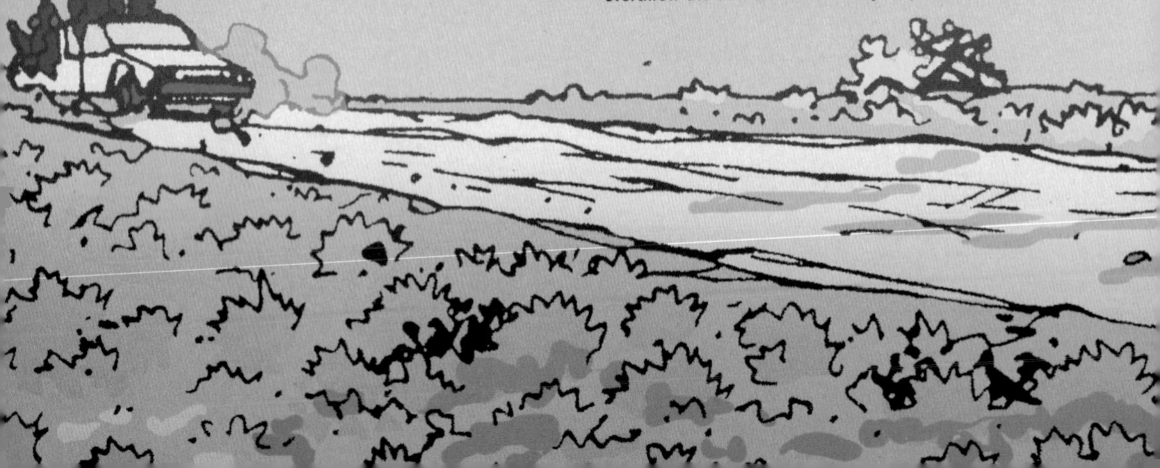

they do this? Well, in 2005 The **Hague Criminal Court** charged Uganda's President Museveni with stealing natural resources from DRC during this war. So it seems that Museveni was sending valuable troops on a military adventure to plunder resources from his neighboring country instead of fighting the LRA at home.

By 1999 oil in Sudan began to change the game. China suddenly moved into southern Sudan with Petrochina's oil pipeline. There were rumors, which still persist to this day, of massive amounts of Chinese troops sent in to protect China's interest (I have been told personally, by reliable sources, that this is not true). Now the Sudan/Uganda border, a border the LRA rebels freely moved across, needed to be stabilized more so than ever. Thirteen years after the start of the war Museveni stepped up and offered amnesty to the LRA's estimated 4,000 fighters.

By 2000 the amnesty offer had caused the LRA to split into two factions: one willing to negotiate with the government, and one determined to fight on. New cooperation between Uganda and Sudan began to put even greater strain on the LRA. And it seemed the end of the war was finally near.

Hoping he would be facing a weakened and split rebel force, Museveni initiated "**Operation Iron Fist**" in March of 2002.

This was a massive military offensive that swept across northern Uganda and into southern Sudan. But it did not end the LRA. In fact, the rebels launched a bloody counteroffensive. Areas untouched by the conflict were now absorbed in war, and further displacement of human beings occurred. The fight was now at its absolute bloodiest. This is when our tale takes place.

November 2003. Despite global interest in the months-old Iraq War, the UN's top humanitarian official said, "*I cannot find any other part of the world that is having an emergency on the scale of Uganda.*" Museveni asked the **International Criminal Court** (ICC) to investigate Kony and other LRA leaders for war crimes. In May, Uganda pulled the last of its troops from eastern DRC, and they were immediately stationed in Acholiland. Regular attacks against IDP camps ending in unfathomable amounts of civilian bloodshed began to occur more and more frequently. Northern Uganda became hell on earth.

In October of 2005 the ICC issued arrest warrants – the first since its 2002 founding. Kony and four of his top lieutenants were cited for murder, rape, mutilation, sexual slavery and enlistment of children as combatants. With the Iraq war becoming old news, global reportage slowly began to turn towards Acholiland.

In July 2006, peace talks began between the recognized Ugandan government and the LRA in Juba, Southern Sudan. The LRA was weakened by endless war. Kony, who had been in the bush for 20 years now, was tired and at talks he appeared saner than ever. By August both sides agreed to a temporary ceasefire. The Ugandan government established "satellite camps" – smaller IDP camps with access to farmland – as it was difficult to send the Acholi back to their villages and farms now that the entire region was heavily land-mined. Despite all of this, peace talks continued to be marred by regular walkouts.

In October of 2007, with the peace process moving forward in fits and starts, it was revealed that Kony had murdered his own deputy-leader (one of the five wanted by the ICC). The man's name was **Vincent Otti**, and Kony claimed that Otti was given money to assassinate him by international interests. Kony was showing his old signs of paranoia, and his obstruction of the peace process was becoming a sore spot for the Ugandan government.

For the next year the peace talks were static, then, on December 13, 2008, two months after we began publishing our humble book, a massive military attack was made against Kony by armies of the Ugandan, DRC and Southern Sudanese governments.

THE LRA IN 2009
(AFTER THE FAILURE OF THE SECOND PEACE PROCESS)

"Ssemusota guli mu ntamu. Bw'ogutta tolya, bw'oguleka tolya." (A snake in the cooking pot is a dilemma. Hit it and you break the pot. Leave it and you starve.) – Ugandan saying

After two years of convoluted peace talks with no definitive plan materializing, **"Operation Lightning Thunder"** was carried out by Ugandan air force and artillery, backed by the Congolese and Sudan Peoples Liberation forces. AFRICOM provided satellite phones, intelligence and fuel. US advisors – authorized by George W. Bush – lent expertise. They attacked LRA camps in Garamba National Park, DRC, with helicopter gun-ships and MiG-23 jets. A ground force then moved in. And that should've been the end of it. But due to poor planning and basic botchy-ness, Kony and survivors escaped deeper into DRC and towards the Central African Republic (CAR), away from the Ugandan border...and they've been acting like monsters ever since.

Following the attack, in January of 2009 alone, LRA soldiers were fingered for the deaths in DRC and Southern Sudan of more than 900 people, the displacement of 130,000 refugees and the kidnapping of hundreds of children. Take a moment. Think about those figures. That's one month. Northern Uganda, the source from which all this hardship had sprung, remained essentially untouched (and still does as of this writing) but Kony, reactivated, had cut a swath of death across DRC.

It was a tough political move. President Museveni attacks a currently peaceful Kony, and everything suddenly goes bat-shit crazy again. Complaints in the Ugandan government ranged from concerns regarding the moral complications of a war fought against children (the perennial argument), to the impatience of the Ugandan government with the peace process, to the idea that a successful peace negotiation had more of a chance of healing social wounds than a combat victory did. Supporters of the strike, however, believed this was Uganda's opportunity to ensure Kony's utter destruction and achieve permanent peace.

The LRA, on the other hand, claimed that this was a power play by President Museveni. That he hoped to push into Congo and steal resources as he had before. That it was Museveni's troops who were responsible for the atrocities. They were using the 2005 International Court of Justice ruling which found Uganda liable for war crimes during the **Congo War** as evidence of what Museveni was capable of.

Now, undeniably Museveni had marginalized this conflict and stalled its peace processes repeatedly. He's compromised his ability to protect the Acholi and acted in a questionable

manner towards his neighboring nations. But the LRA simply couldn't be trusted. They had made a modus operandi out of kidnapping children, slaughtering innocents and terrorizing populations. And now they were bogged down in a jungle swamp.

At that time the Ugandan Peoples Defence Force released this statement:

"Soon Kony will have no fighters. He will die of hunger, be captured or get killed." – UPDF Operation Commander, Brig. Patrick Kankiriho. 24th February 2009.

But that just didn't happen. The Ugandan Peoples Defence Force, Forces Armées de la République Démocratique du Congo (the Congolese Army) and the Sudanese Peoples Liberation Forces, three whole armies, failed to neutralize Kony despite overwhelming firepower and tactical knowledge.

With the failure of the three armies to bring in their man, the UN, long criticized for under-policing DRC, decided to step up. By March, Ugandan and Sudanese soldiers were pulled back out of DRC and supposedly replaced with a new United Nations military company. The UN Security Council had authorized the deployment of an additional 3,000 troops, an attack helicopter, two transport helicopters, 1,500 Egyptian police, Special Forces and soldiers, all to work in conjunction with the DRC military to stabilize the area and smoke out Kony (as of this writing I can neither confirm nor deny the successful deployment of these forces).

On top of that, the locals had their own ideas. Western Equatoria's Arrow Boys, a Sudanese self-defense group that use traditional weapons (bows, arrows, spears and clubs) treated with poisonous powder, said they were ready to fight the Ugandan Kony to the death and were urging Kony to surrender before they begin their march. Since that statement they have killed several LRA soldiers.

But neither the UN nor regional forces have helped in the long haul. As of October 2009, the UN reported that 400,000 people in this remote region of northern DRC had fled their homes due to renewed rebel attacks. There have been hundreds of kidnappings as Kony has begun to replenish his once dwindling forces with child soldiers and "wives." The full, horrible mechanism that is the LRA is now completely back in business. They are participating in serial murder/machete

disfigurations, forcing children to kill their parents and burning people alive inside their homes. Reportedly, roads in northern DRC are now so insecure that only aircraft can bring in supplies and staff. Towns such as Gangala and Banda are absorbing displaced people by the tens of thousands as surrounding fields and villages are being abandoned. And the LRA combatants aren't just in DRC, there's another force of more

than one thousand in the Central African Republic, led by Kony himself is actually on the move northwards. Whether this is a retreat or a more aggressive tactical move, there's no way of knowing. Ugandan Special Forces are using helicopters to attack Kony's personal group from Yambio in southern Sudan. It's possible Kony is trying to meet up with Jinjaweed gunmen in western Sudan.

Something else that's interesting now is that the Lord's Resistance Army is no longer a Ugandan, Acholi-speaking rebel group. They have gone multinational. Eyewitnesses are reporting that Arabic and other languages can now be heard in their ranks as Kony and underlings forcibly draft people from Central African Republic, Democratic Republic of Congo and Southern Sudan. And that brings up an interesting new question. What exactly is Kony's objective now? His struggle against the "tyrant" Museveni and the liberation of his people was invalidated last year. He is now a leader of a pan-African terrorist organization with no ideological direction. There's no "legitimate" political reason for the actions of his organization any longer. He is a thug on the run. A man hunted. Out of spite

and fear he continues to operate in the only way he knows how. A pattern abuser. A tiny Hitler. He will spend the rest of his life, however long that is, gnashing and fighting and gnawing and dragging every community he and his acolytes stroll through into his own personal hell.

And as for Acholiland? Well, the aura of suffering that Kony and his LRA emit, while not over, has been exported, and while we should cry for the DRC, CAR and Sudan, all of whom have inherited yet another madman, the people that our comic book is about, the Acholi, are busy rebuilding and reimagining their world. There's much to learn as banks and hotels and tourists flood into their post-war patch. What the new Acholi will look like, what of their culture will survive, no one can tell. But if they can hold on to the bucking bastard of modernity, then maybe...someday soon...there will be a whole generation living free and apart from the horrors of war.

— Joshua Dysart
November 27, 2009
Venice Beach, California

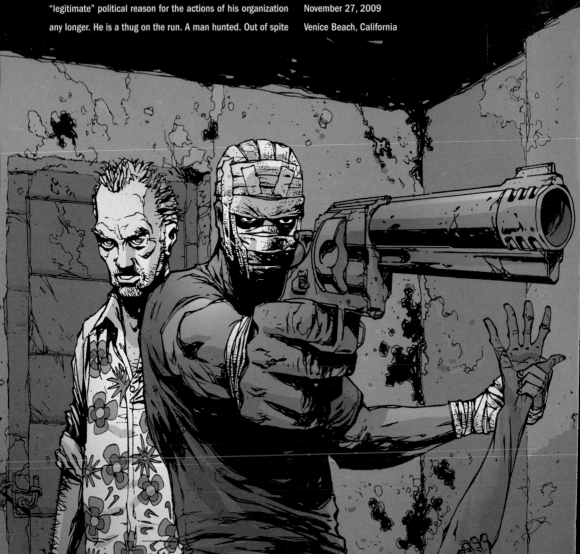